"This treasury of daily readings on the Holy Eucharist is a spiritual gold-mine! Drawing from the Church fathers, doctors, martyrs, saints, and mystics, this remarkable collection is certain to fulfill the prayerful call of Pope St. John Paul, to 'cultivate Eucharistic Amazement' among all the faithful—clergy and laity alike—every day! I know of no better resource for deepening our personal devotion to Our Lord in the Blessed Sacrament. This book is truly one of a kind!"

Scott Hahn
Author of *Hope to Die* and Founder of the St. Paul Center

"This substantial anthology shows by encompassing testimonies from every age and culture and language that there is no spiritual loneliness or hunger that cannot be cured by accompanying the Eucharistic Lord and feeding upon Him in faith and hope. The 'Desire of Nations' (Hag 2:7) desires in turn that those who seek Him should find Him on every holy altar."

Fr. George William Rutler
EWTN Host and Author of *Our Peculiar Times*

"I highly recommend this brilliant collection of historical reflections on the Eucharist. It's truly exciting to see this work finally in print, because I've long known Dr. Howell and the sincerity of his integrity, convictions, and devotion to the Eucharist. This is not merely a year-long apologetic for the real presence of Christ, body and blood, soul and divinity in the Eucharist—though in some sense it is. Nor is this an endorsement of a Newman-like development of this doctrine, for it is not. Rather, *Mystery of the Altar* is, in essence, a *lectio divina* of how Christ's faithful from the very beginning have accepted His words as life-giving truth: 'This is my body. . . . This is my blood . . .' (Mk 14:22, 24) and 'he who eats my flesh and drinks my blood has eternal life, and I will raise him up at the last day' (Jn 6:54)."

Marcus Grodi
Founder of the Coming Home Network and
Host of EWTN's *The Journey Home*

"The epicenter of our spirituality is the encounter with Jesus in the Eucharist. Because of poor catechesis and impoverished liturgical formation, our hearts are often not aligned to the magnitude of this encounter and how we can respond to God's invitation to enter ever more deeply into His heart. This book will heal and lift the hearts of all who read it and live it such that the Eucharist will become all that God desires it to be in us."

DAN BURKE
Founder of the Avila Institute for Spiritual Formation
and the Apostoli Viae Community

Mystery
of the Altar

Mystery
of the Altar

DAILY MEDITATIONS ON
THE EUCHARIST

Kenneth J. Howell &
Joseph Crownwood

EMMAUS
ROAD
PUBLISHING

Steubenville, Ohio
www.EmmausRoad.org

Emmaus Road Publishing
1468 Parkview Circle
Steubenville, Ohio 43952

Library of Congress Control Number: 2020944572
ISBN 978-1-949013-70-2 (Leather) 978-1-949013-71-9 (ebook)

Cover design and layout by Emily Demary

Nihil obstat:
Msgr. Philip D. Halfacre, V.G.
Censor Librorum

Imprimatur:
Most Rev. Daniel R. Jenky, C.S.C.
Bishop of Peoria

The *nihil obstat* and *imprimatur* are declarations that a book or pamphlet is free of doctrinal or moral error. There is no implication that those who have granted the *nihil obstat* or *imprimatur* agree with the contents, opinions, or statements expressed therein.

This book is dedicated to the Eucharistic Heart of Jesus
and to all those priests, religious, and laity
who have as their heart the Holy Host.

TABLE OF CONTENTS

PREFACE

You fed your people with the food of angels, and gave them bread from heaven prepared without labor; having in it all that is delicious, and the sweetness of every taste. (Wis 16:20)

The Church has ever extolled the Eucharist as that central Mystery of Faith whereby man is sanctified and redeemed. It is the Memorial of Christ's Passion and the pledge of future glory; the Bread of Angels and the lifeblood of men; the living presence of God made man, who came to make man God. The following pages seek to manifest the Eucharistic faith of the Church as it has been expressed by the saints of every generation. Their timeless witness has been arranged in accordance with the liturgical calendar so that the Blessed Sacrament might be contemplated in relation to the feasts and seasons of the Church. In this way, this collection may serve as a devotional for the laity, a homiletic resource for priests, or as a catalogue of Eucharistic texts for contemplation.

Every age of the Church reveals its own emphasis and key insights into the Eucharist. The earliest documents of the Church express a clear understanding of the sacrificial dimensions of the Mass. The Medieval Period saw the rise of the philosophical doctrine of transubstantiation, public exposition of the Blessed Sacrament, and the establishment of the Feast of Corpus Christi. Contemplating the union between God and man in Holy Communion, modern writers have focused more nearly on the relational dimensions of the Eucharist. Together, these historical accounts offer a rich theology of the Eucharist, grounded in Sacred Scripture, Tradition, and Magisterial Teaching.

For Catholics of the Latin Rite, it is important to acknowledge terminology used by the Eastern Fathers of the Church as they appear throughout this book. In the East, the normative expression for "altar" is "table," "sacraments" are called "mysteries," and the "Mass" is referred to as the "Divine Liturgy." In a minority of passages, parts of the Mass are referenced according to their Eastern names: "Anaphora" corresponds with the Western "canon" and the "Trisagion" is analogous to the "Sanctus." Each term is defined where it first appears.

Introductions are affixed to each passage to provide necessary background information and to highlight the prevailing Eucharistic theme. Many of the quoted texts have been newly translated, while others represent fitting English editions. In most cases, familiar poems and hymns have been retranslated with an eye toward the literal, avoiding poetic renderings that distort the original meaning.

As the Church begins the third millennium of Eucharistic faith, the voices of the past provide faithful witness to the truth of Christ's Real Presence. In these pages, one finds endless apologetics, exegetical insights, and miraculous works in confirmation of the faith. It is the hope of the authors that this volume may stir hearts to an ever more profound devotion to that love of loves, Jesus Christ in the Most Blessed Sacrament.

Kenneth J. Howell and Joseph Crownwood

JANUARY

Solemnity of Mary, Mother of God

On the Octave of the Nativity of Our Lord, the Church honors Mary with the exalted title, Mother of God, or Theotokos in Greek. Settling all possible debate, the Council of Ephesus declared that it is right and proper to acclaim Mary as the God-Bearer; for she is not merely the mother of Christ's human nature, but the mother of the Son of God Himself. In this excerpt from the *Canon on Pentecost*, St. Andrew of Crete (c. 660–740) compares Mary to the holy altar whereupon Christ is made present. Here, the normative Eastern expression for "altar" appears as "table."

> Your womb, O God-bearer, became a Holy Table holding the bread from heaven. No one who eats of this bread will die, for the One who feeds all has thus said. Therefore, we laud you who are virgin and mother after giving birth. As a virgin, you became a pure bride of God; for, it was from you that God was made flesh.
>
> *St. Andrew of Crete (c. 660–740)*

The Word made flesh in Nazareth is no less present on the altar at Holy Mass. St. John Chrysostom (349–407) reflects on the gravity of approaching this burning table of sacrifice, cautioning Christians to prepare for the coming of so great a King.

Do you not know that this table is full of spiritual fire? As springs naturally gush forth water, so this table has an ineffable flame. So do not come with straw, wood, or grass, hoping to bring about a greater conflagration, yet burning the soul instead. Rather, come with precious stones, gold, and silver that you may have a more pure kindling, and depart with great profit.

If there is anything evil, banish it from your soul. Does anyone have an enemy? Has he been wronged in a great way? Let him banish the enmity; let him check any disorder of mind so that no one might be distracted nor disturbed. For under your roof, you are about to receive the King in communion. And as the King enters your soul, you should be found in tranquility, profound silence, and deep peace of mind.

St. John Chrysostom (349–407)

JANUARY 2

Memorials of St. Basil the Great, Bishop and Doctor and St. Gregory of Nazianzus, Bishop and Doctor

St. Gregory of Nazianzus (c. 329–390) and St. Basil the Great (330–379) were among the most influential theologians of the fourth century. They ardently defended the doctrine of the Trinity as defined by the Council of Nicaea, developing a rich philosophical view of God's triune nature. In the following oration, St. Gregory praises the virtues of his sister, Gorgonia, who obtained miraculous healing through her Eucharistic faith. St. Gregory likens her persistence in prayer to those women of the Gospels who were cured by the touch of Jesus.

What did this great soul do who was worthy of such exalted things, and what was the medicine for her suffering? Here, we encounter the ineffable. Giving up on all other aid, she fled to the Physician of all. During the night, her sickness had some-

2

what advanced and she fell down before the altar in faith. She called upon the One who is honored thereon with a loud cry and all manner of petitions, recounting His powerful works, both ancient and new. Thus, she expressed a certain good and pious importunity in imitation of the woman whose flow of blood was healed by the hem of Christ's garment. She laid her head on the altar with a similar cry, admixed with tears, like the woman who had anointed the feet of Christ. And so she refused to be sent away before obtaining healing. In her tears, she applied her medicine to her body; that is, the reserved portion of the Precious Body and Blood she had treasured in her hands, and O what a marvelous thing! She left feeling sensible of her salvation; light in body, soul, and reason. She received the reward of her hope, gaining strength of body and soul. These great things are not a lie! All may believe, both the healthy and infirm, so that you might keep or regain your health.

St. Gregory of Nazianzus, Bishop and Doctor (c. 330–390)

JANUARY 3

Memorial of St. Fulgentius of Ruspe

Inspired by St. Augustine's writings, St. Fulgentius of Ruspe (467–532) renounced his role as the procurator of Byzacene and entered a monastic community. He subsequently became one of the foremost theologians of his day, writing treatises, sermons, and letters in the spirit of St. Augustine. In the following epistle, Fulgentius poignantly reflects on the dual meaning of the phrase, "the Body of Christ." Quoting St. Augustine at length, he notes that the Eucharist is the Body of Christ, even as the members of the Church make up the Mystical Body of Christ. Here, the Eastern term, "mystery," appears, which is synonymous with the Western term, "sacrament."

If you are the body of Christ and its very members, then the Mystery of your identity is upon the Lord's table. You receive the Mystery of the Lord, responding "amen" to what you are, and by responding, assent. As you hear, "the body of Christ," you respond, "amen." Be then a member of Christ's body that your "amen" may be true.

Why is it in bread? We claim nothing by ourselves; rather, let us hear the Apostle himself. When he speaks about that Sacrament, he says, "[Because there is] one bread, we who are many are one body" [1 Cor 10:17]. Hear and rejoice! Unity, devotion, truth, charity, one bread: we who are many are one body. Consider that bread is not made from one grain, but from many. When you were exorcised, it was as if you were softened. When you were baptized, it was as if you were sprinkled. And when you received the fire of the Holy Spirit, it was as if you were ignited. Be then what you see and receive what you are. The Apostle said this about the bread, yet we may clearly understand the cup as well. For in order to bring about the visible form of bread, many grains are gathered into one, even as Holy Scripture says of the faithful: "they had one soul and heart in God" [Acts 4:32]. Consider also, brothers, the manner in which wine becomes one. Many grains hang on a cluster of grapes, but the juice of those grains is brought together in unity. Thus, the Lord Jesus Christ shows that He wanted us to understand it in reference to Him. He consecrated the mystery of our peace and unity upon His table. And whoever receives the Mystery of unity, but does not preserve the bond of peace, does not receive it as a Mystery for his own benefit, but as a testimony against himself.

St. Fulgentius of Ruspe (467–532)

JANUARY 4

Memorial of St. Elizabeth Ann Seton

St. Elizabeth Ann Seton (1774–1821) was born and raised in an Anglican household, but converted to the Catholic faith after the untimely death of her husband. Elizabeth dedicated the remainder of her life to the Church, founding the first parochial school and the first women's religious congregation in America. In the following passage, she reflects on the hidden potential of the Eucharist to raise man up and to produce much fruit. Just as an ear of corn grows by a hidden power, so does the Eucharist invisibly work in souls, bringing them to maturity.

Consider *one ear of corn* as a figure. Behold the work of our Heavenly Father—what was its first beginning? Look at its separate grain. Recall the time it was first planted in the earth, covered with the frost and snows of winter and trampled over in mire and mud. And then, behold the fields covered with green, gradually adorned with these beautiful plants. They rise to the height of eight or ten feet. . . . On the very summit of the plant, the towering plume appears, containing within it the fruitful ear, wrapped in silken folds, producing the multiplied grains, pressed close together on every side. From whence did they proceed? From one single grain. And by what power? Our Heavenly Father.

What, then, must be His seed of faith, of His word, of His blood, of His cross, of His flesh in the Eucharist, deposited in our hearts through the winter of life? What must be the fruit in harvest of eternity, whose echoing vaults and ever verdant fields shall resound with praise and love forever! Oh, exulting—oh, delightful prospect! Joyful anticipations. How endearingly should we cherish this precious *faith*, this ineffable hope, this first seed of love now shooting in our hearts during the trial of patience and winter of life which will so soon pass away and bring us to the harvest of delights in eternity!!!

O, food of Heaven, how my soul longs for you with desire! Seed of Heaven, pledge of immortality and that eternity it pants for. Come, come, my Jesus, bury yourself within this heart. It shall do its best to preserve that warmth which will bring forth the fruits of eternity. Oh, amen. Our Jesus.

St. Elizabeth Ann Seton (1774–1821)

JANUARY 5

St. Charles of Sezze (1613–1670) was a Franciscan mystic whose writings enjoyed great popularity in seventeenth-century Italy. In his renowned work, *Interior Way of the Soul*, St. Charles treats various topics for devout contemplation, granting insight into his own inner life of prayer. Here, he illustrates the purifying nature of divine love found in the Blessed Sacrament. Employing the language of mystics, he lifts the veil between heaven and earth, describing the wonders that take place during the Holy Sacrifice of the Mass.

When receiving the Most Holy Sacrament of the Eucharist, the third desire and longing the soul feels is a fire of ardent charity. There, the devout soul is submerged in these flames, burns, and is completely melted by divine love. This holy fire spreads to the interior of the soul, and consumes it, making it pure, beautiful, and all divine. The infinite charity in the most Holy Sacrament is thus revealed to the soul, wherein the Son of God offered Himself as the immaculate and innocent lamb upon the altar of the Holy Cross.

The soul then contemplates the holy tabernacle surrounded by a multitude of angels, giving gracious audience to all, and succor to those in travail. For He is truly present in the Holy Sacrifice of the Mass, descending from heaven to earth by virtue of the holy words of consecration, appearing under the species of bread—though it is not bread, but truly the Body of the Lord. So too with the wine: the chalice does not contain wine, but rather the Blood of the same Christ our Lord under the appearance of wine.

St. Charles of Sezze (1613–1670)
[Memorial, January 6]

JANUARY 6

The Feast of Epiphany of the Lord

St. John Chrysostom (349–407), the great Patriarch of Constantinople, gained the posthumous title of "Chrysostom," or "Golden Mouth," for his eloquence of speech. Here, St. John likens the adoration of the Magi to the Divine Liturgy itself. For the Magi's worship of the Christ Child does not differ in essence from the daily approach to the altar. St. John thus exhorts his listeners to discern the gifts of gold, frankincense, and myrrh, instructing them to offer prayer, humility, and holy confidence.

For the Master's body shall also lie here, not wrapped in swaddling clothes as before, but wrapped on every side with the Holy Spirit. Those initiated into the Mysteries will understand these things. Now, the Magi only worshipped Him, but if you approach with a pure conscience and receive [the Sacrament], you will thus be united and can then depart for home.

Come then and bring your gifts, not like those of the Magi, but rather more solemn ones. They brought gold. But you, you bring discretion and virtue. They offered frankincense, but you are to bring pure prayers and spiritual sacrifices. They offered myrrh, but you should offer humble hearts and alms. If you approach with these gifts, you will enjoy this holy table with great confidence. For this reason I now exhort you, because many will approach on that day and stumble over the spiritual sacrifice. Therefore, let us do this in order that we do not come upon evil or judgment of our soul, but rather salvation. I am giving witness in advance and enjoin you who have cleansed yourselves in every way to come to the Holy Mysteries.

St. John Chrysostom, Bishop and Doctor (349–407)

JANUARY 7

Memorial of St. Angela of Foligno

St. Angela of Foligno (c. 1248–1309) spent the greater part of her life pursuing worldly pleasures until a vision of St. Francis of Assisi convicted her of the seriousness of sin. From that day forward, she dedicated herself to a life of prayer and penance, establishing a community of Third Order Franciscans. In the following passage, St. Angela speaks of God's union with man in Holy Communion. Touching upon the heart of Christian spirituality, she alludes to the doctrine of divinization as it relates to the Eucharist. As St. Athanasius had taught before her: the Son of God became man to make man God.

This Sacrament was ordained by the most Holy Trinity so that it might bind unto itself that which it most greatly loved; that it might draw the soul unto itself—unto God—and away from all created things, joining it together with the uncreated God. Thus did God bestow spiritual and divine love upon the soul, mortifying and purifying it from its sins. It was ordained by the most Holy Trinity in order that He might unite and incorporate Himself with us, and us with Him. He desires that we should receive the Sacrament so that He may receive us. And He desires that we should bear it so that He may bear us, fortify us, and comfort us.

If one considers the matter well, what soul is so wretched that it will refuse to be drawn nigh unto such a Lord, seeing how such clarity of vision has been given it from heaven in order to draw souls away from earthly things?

St. Angela of Foligno (c. 1248–1309)

JANUARY 8

The *Didache* (c. 100) is one of the oldest Christian documents, known to the Fathers of the Church, but lost for more than twelve centuries. Rediscovered in 1875, it was immediately recognized as an ancient text with detailed descriptions of early Church liturgy. While some had imagined first-century Christian worship to be spontaneous and free-flowing, the Eucharistic prayers recorded in the *Didache* exhibit a striking similarity with contemporary liturgical texts.

Regarding the Eucharist, hold the thanksgiving in this way:

First, concerning the cup: We give You thanks, our Father, for the holy vine of David, Your servant, which You made known to us through Jesus, Your servant. To You be the glory forever.

And concerning the broken bread: We give You thanks, our Father, for the life and knowledge which You have made known to us through Jesus, Your servant. To You be the glory forever.

As this broken bread was once scattered on the mountains and was gathered together as one, so let Your Church be gathered from the ends of the earth into Your kingdom. For, Yours is the glory and the power through Jesus Christ forever.

Let no one eat or drink of your Eucharist except those who are baptized in the name of the Lord. For, the Lord said: "Give not what is holy to dogs" [Matt 7:6].

The Didache (c. 100)

JANUARY 9

St. Justin Martyr (c. 100–165) was an early apologist who defended Catholic practice against second-century pagans and Jews. In his *First Apology*, St. Justin describes the liturgy of the early Church, referencing the liturgy of the word, the homily, the kiss of peace, the Eucharist, and so forth. Notably, each of these are found in modern-day celebrations of the Mass, evidencing the great continuity of Sacred Tradition.

> On the day called Sunday, all who live in the towns or country gather at the meeting wherein the memoirs of the apostles and writings of the prophets are read, as time permits. When the reader has finished, the presider gives a verbal admonition, exhorting us to imitate these beautiful things. Afterward, we rise together and offer up prayers. As said before, once we have finished our prayers, then the bread, wine, and water are brought forward and the presider offers prayers and thanksgivings as he is able. Then the people respond in assent, saying, "Amen." Following this is the distribution and reception of the elements made into the Eucharist. And then the deacons take it to those not present.

> Among the prosperous, each gives from his own goods as he sees fit, and what is collected is deposited with the presider. He then distributes it to the orphans and widows, giving it also to the sick or those who have some other need. Then it is given to prisoners and to strangers living with us—in short, to anyone in need.

> Now, on this day we all gather in an assembly since it is the first day, the day on which God made the universe by transforming darkness and matter. This is also the day on which our Savior, Jesus Christ, rose from the dead. They crucified Him on the day before Saturday, and on the day after Saturday, which is Sunday, He appeared to His apostles and dis-

ciples and taught them. It is these things we have offered for your investigation.

St. Justin Martyr (c. 100–165)

JANUARY 10

Memorial of St. Gregory of Nyssa

St. Gregory of Nyssa (c. 335–395) was born into a devout Christian family, blessed to produce four sibling saints: Basil the Great, Peter of Sebaste, Macrina, and Gregory. Though Gregory proved to be a poor administrator, his contemplative gifts enabled him to compose profound works of theology on the Trinity, creation, and celibacy. In the following selection from his *Catechetical Oration*, Gregory reflects on God's twofold approach to man in the Eucharist.

Since man is a twofold creature, composed of body and soul, it is necessary that the elect receive the Author of salvation by both these component parts. The soul has the means and opportunity for salvation by its union with him through faith; for, union with life implies fellowship and communion in life. On the other hand, the body uses a different means in partaking and mingling with the Savior. . . .

. . . Nothing else except the Body of Christ has been shown to be superior to death and has thus become the first-fruits of our life. For, in the manner that—as the Apostle says—a little leaven assimilates itself into the whole lump, so in like manner that Body that has received immortality by God, when it is in our own body, translates and transmutes the whole into itself.

St. Gregory of Nyssa (c. 335–395)

JANUARY 11

Memorial of St. Paulinus II of Aquileia

St. Paulinus II (c. 726–802) was an influential figure of the Caro-lingian Renaissance and famously opposed the Spanish Adoptionists. Though the Spanish Adoptionists rightly professed Christ to be the Eternal Son of God, they erroneously taught that He was the "adopted son of God" in His human nature. Because this implies two different persons in Christ, the teachings of the Adoptionists were condemned. In truth, the Son of God is one divine Person with two natures, and is in no way adopted. Here, St. Paulinus argues for the eternal sonship of Christ by pointing to the Eucharist.

And if He is the son by adoption, how can it be explained that without eating the flesh of the Son of man and drinking His blood, you do not have eternal life? Christ says: *Whoever eats my flesh and drinks my blood has eternal life, and I will raise him up on the last day. For my flesh is true food, and my blood is true drink* [John 6:54–55]. No one has the power to raise on the last day unless He is truly the ever-living God. For indeed, flesh and blood pertain to humanity, and by them He is Son of man; wherefore, these cannot refer to the divine nature. And yet, if he is the Son of man, to whom this flesh and blood is, He is one and the same both Son of God and Son of Man. For if He were not truly God, His flesh and blood that we eat and drink could not grant us eternal life. In this way, John the evangelist says: *the blood of Jesus His Son cleanses us from all sin* [1 John 1:7].

Whose flesh and blood can give life to those who eat and drink it except the Son of man, on whom God the Father has set his seal, who is the true and almighty Son of God? For, the Bread of Life came down from heaven for our sake to give life to the world, and whoever eats of Him shall never die. For this reason, He says: *I am the living bread that came down from heaven* [John 6:51].

St. Paulinus II of Aquileia (c. 726–802)

JANUARY 12

Memorial of St. Aelred of Rievaulx

St. Aelred of Rievaulx (1110–1167) was a Cistercian abbot, renowned for his eloquence of speech. While modern exegetes often focus on the literal interpretation of Scripture, St. Aelred sounds the depths of its mystical meaning. In the following excerpt from his Christmas homily, St. Aelred links the Nativity to the liturgical actions of Holy Mass. In both, God condescends to come among man—in the manger at Bethlehem and upon the altar at Mass.

Bethlehem, the *house of bread*, is the Holy Church wherein the Body of Christ, the true bread, is given. The manger of Bethlehem is the altar in the church. There, the animals are pastured and fed by Christ, as it is written: *In it shall your animals dwell* [Ps 67:11]. And of the altar, it is written: *You have prepared a table before me* [Ps 22:5]. In Bethlehem's manger, Jesus was wrapped and covered in swaddling clothes. These wrappings are the veil of the Sacraments; indeed, the species of bread and wine are truly the Body and Blood of Christ. Just as Christ was present in Bethlehem, though covered by swaddling clothes, He is invisibly present in these Sacraments. We have no greater or clearer of a sign of the Nativity of Christ than the holy altar whereupon we daily receive the Body and Blood of Christ, because He who was once born of the Virgin, we daily recognize upon the altar, immolated for our sake.

St. Aelred of Rievaulx (1110–1167)

JANUARY 13

Memorial of St. Hilary of Poitiers, Bishop and Doctor

St. Hilary (c. 310–367) was the fourth-century bishop of Poitiers known for his defense of the Trinity against the Arian heresy. In the following passage from *On the Trinity*, St. Hilary affirms the consubstantial union of the Father and Son as well as the Real Presence of Christ in the Eucharist. Emphasizing the profound union between God and man in Holy Communion, St. Hilary explains that the Eucharist allows man to participate in the divine life of the Trinity (2 Pet 1:4). This true union, brought about by grace, echoes that most profound of unions between the Father, Son, and Holy Spirit.

> But these things are thus commemorated by us, since the heretics fabricate the idea that the unity between the Father and the Son is only one of the will. They use the example of our union with God, as if our union with the Son, and through the Son with the Father, were only one of submission and a pious act of the will. No property of a natural communion through the Sacrament of the body and blood is conceded. Since we also are united bodily and inseparably in Him, through the honor of the Son given to us, and through the Son abiding in us physically, a mystery of true and natural unity ought to be affirmed.

> *St. Hilary of Poitiers, Bishop and Doctor (c. 310–367)*

JANUARY 14

St. Ignatius of Antioch (c. 35–107) was believed to have succeeded St. Peter the Apostle himself as the Antiochene bishop. On his way to martyrdom, St. Ignatius penned seven letters to the churches in Asia Minor (c. 100–117), which provide valuable insight into the life of the early Church. In these letters, he testifies to the hierarchical, sacramental, and catholic constitution of the Church, illustrating the visible and invisible nature of the Church. In the following excerpt from his *Letter to the Smyrnaeans*, St. Ignatius emphasizes the intrinsic unity that exists between the bishop, the Eucharist, and the laity. He thus cautions his hearers from breaking from this communion.

> All of you follow your bishop, as Jesus Christ does the Father. Follow also the presbytery as apostles, and honor the deacons

as the ordinance of God. Let no one practice anything having to do with the Church apart from the bishop. That Eucharist is to be considered valid which is under the authority of a bishop or under one he has appointed. Where the bishop appears, let the fullness of the people be, as wherever Jesus Christ is, there is the Catholic Church. It is not permitted to baptize or to hold an *agape* feast apart from the bishop. Rather, whatever he approves is acceptable to God so that everything you do may be safe and valid.

St. Ignatius of Antioch (c. 35–107)

JANUARY 15

Walter Hilton (c. 1340–1396) was an English Augustinian canon whose mystical writings enjoyed great popularity during the Middle Ages. His works describe the purification of the soul, the necessity of contemplation, and the infused knowledge granted to those dedicated to prayer. In this passage from *The Scale of Perfection*, Hilton offers advice for gaining victory over spiritual temptations; namely, against doubts concerning the Blessed Sacrament. According to his teachings, temptations against the faith are to be dismissed without distress, freeing the soul from empty debate.

> The devil maliciously tempts others to spiritual sins so as to doubt the Articles of Faith or the Sacrament of our Lord's Blessed Body. Also to despair, or to blaspheme God or the Saints, or to a wearisomeness of their life. . . . [One] remedy is for them to fear not, nor esteem these malicious stirrings to sin, nor lay to heart such despair, blasphemy, doubts against the Sacrament, or any such other, though never so ugly to hear.

> For the feeling of these *temptations* defiles the soul no more than if it heard a hound bark, or felt the biting of a flea. They vex the soul indeed, but do not harm it if a man despises them,

and sets them at naught. For it is not good to strive with them, as if you would cast them out by mastery and violence, because the more one strives with them, the more one cleaves to them. And therefore, such persons shall do well to divert their thoughts from them as much as they can, and set them upon some business.

Walter Hilton (c. 1340–1396)

JANUARY 16

Martin of León (1130–1203) was an Augustinian priest who produced several scriptural commentaries, composed in a contemplative style. In his commentary on the Book of Revelation, Martin considers the reward of those in heaven who are given to eat from the tree of life. Relating the tree of life to the Eucharist, St. Martin beautifully teaches that the fruits of Holy Communion will be fully realized in the age to come. Though Martin has not yet been canonized, he is celebrated as a saint by those of his own religious house on January 12.

> He says: *To him who has ears, let him hear what the Spirit says to the churches. To him who conquers I will grant to eat of the tree of life, which is in the paradise of God* [Rev 2:7]. It is as if He says: What I say to one, I say to all. I not only forbid avarice in the church of the Ephesians, but in all the other churches as well. Thus, the Father seems to say: *He who has ears*—that is, spiritual understanding—*listen to the Spirit*, namely the Holy Trinity. For *God is Spirit* who says to the Church: I hate their selfishness, not only in their lack of giving, but in their lack of counsel and preaching. It is as though he had said: All men must despise avarice and all other vices, and to him who perseveres, *I will give to eat of the tree of life*.
>
> Why listen to what the Spirit says to the Churches? Because Christ is the tree, the strength, and the sheltering bough of

fruit for him who conquers. And the fruit of this tree is the Body and Blood of Christ given now and wholly fulfilled in the age to come. It is as if he had said: Persevere in the love of God and neighbor, and *I will give you to eat from the tree of life*, and this is my Body, *which is in paradise*, the garden of delights, which is in the Church of *my God* on earth. The tree of life is the wisdom of God the Father, of whom is said: "She is a tree of life to those who lay hold of her; those who hold her fast are called happy" [Prov 3:18].

Martin of León (1130–1203)

JANUARY 17

Memorial of St. Anthony of Egypt, Abbot

St. Anthony of Egypt (c. 251–356) was a desert monk whose eremitic life inspired thousands of Christians to retire into the desert. He was memorialized by St. Athanasius of Alexandria who here recalls St. Anthony's prophecy of the Arian heresy. In this passage, the faith itself is signified by the Lord's Supper and its corruption is symbolically shown therein. Despite its disturbing quality, St. Anthony provides a lasting word of hope for the Church: in all its trials, betrayals, and persecutions, the Mystical Body of Christ will ever retain its beauty.

> "Wrath will seize the Church, and it will be betrayed by men who are like brute beasts. For I saw the Lord's Table surrounded by mules standing about it, kicking the things therein. You then saw how I sighed: for I heard a voice saying, 'My Altar shall be defiled.'"

This was the holy man's vision. And about two years later, there was an incursion of the Arians, and the plundering of churches, in which they took the holy vessels by force. And the vessels were thus carried by heathens who had been taken from prisons and made to join in the services. And they did upon the Table as they would. Then, we all understood that the kicking of the mules prefigured what the Arians are now doing.

But as soon as Anthony had said this, he added, "My children, do not be downcast. For as the Lord was angry, so again will He heal, and the Church will quickly recover its beauty."

St. Athanasius of Alexandria, Bishop and Doctor (c. 296–373)

JANUARY 18

The Beginning of the Octave of Christian Unity

St. Cyprian (c. 210–258) was the bishop of Carthage during Emperor Decius' persecution of the Church. His writings show a zealous concern for Church unity and emphasize its organization under St. Peter. Here, Cyprian notes that as many grains and fruit are gathered together as bread and wine, so too are the many members of the Church gathered in the Eucharist. While a mere symbol could not unite the people of God, the body and blood of Christ incorporates them as one (1 Cor 10:16–17).

But the Church cannot be outside itself, nor torn, nor divided against itself. Rather, it maintains the unity of an indivisible house as the divine faith in Scripture makes clear. For it is written of the sign [*sacramentum*] of the Passover and of the Lamb who represents Christ: "It shall be eaten in one house; you shall not throw the flesh outside the house" [Exod 12:46].

Finally, the sacrifices of the Lord manifest a Christian unanimity, joined to a firm and inseparable love. For when the Lord calls the bread his body, brought together by the joining of many grains, he is indicating our united people whom he receives. And when he calls the wine his blood, squeezed out of many grapes and berries and meshed into one, he signifies our flock, joined together by a mixture of a united multitude.

St. Cyprian of Carthage (c. 210–258)

JANUARY 19

Ven. Louis of Granada (1504–1588) was a Spanish Dominican, known for his outstanding intellectual gifts and captivating preaching. His most famous book, *Guide for Sinners*, remains one of the choice expressions of Spanish asceticism. In this passage, Ven. Louis rejoices in the measureless gift of the Blessed Sacrament and touches upon its many benefits; namely, its enduring presence, its expiatory value, and its eschatological significance.

I cannot pass over in silence that grace of graces, that sacrament of sacraments, whereby God is pleased to dwell with us on earth. And He does so in order to give Himself as our food and sovereign remedy each day. Though He was sacrificed on the cross once only, He is daily offered to His Father upon the altar as a propitiation for sin. *This is my body, which is given for you,* He says, *do this in remembrance of me* [Luke 22:19]. O precious pledge of our salvation! O divine sacrifice! O most acceptable victim! Bread of life! Most delicious nourishment! Food of kings! O Sweet manna, which contains all that is pleasing and delightful! Who can praise you as you deserve? Who can worthily receive You? Who can honor You with due respect and reverence? My soul quite loses itself when it thinks of You. My tongue fails me and I am unable to express the least part of Your wonders as I desire.

Ven. Louis of Granada (1504–1588)

JANUARY 20

Thomas á Kempis (1380–1471) was the subprior of a small religious community and the author of the classic work, *The Imitation of Christ.*

Second only to the Bible in its publication, *The Imitation* penetrates the heart of Christian living and offers uncompromising spiritual direction. Thomas' writings emphasize pious devotion over philosophical pursuits, placing love of God above all things. In this excerpt, Thomas writes in the voice of the Savior who dictates the sacrifice He desires at Holy Mass.

As I willingly offered myself to the Father for your sins, with hands outstretched upon the cross and body stripped bare so that nothing remained in me that was not made a sacrifice of divine propitiation, even so should you willingly offer yourself to me daily in the Mass as a pure and holy oblation, with all your powers, affections, and all inward devotion possible. What more do I ask than that you strive to wholly abandon yourself to me? Whatever else you might give is nothing commanded you: for it is not your gift that I seek, but you yourself. As it would not suffice if you had all things besides me, so neither could it please me if you give anything whatsoever without offering yourself. Offer yourself to me, give yourself wholly to God, and your offering will be accepted. Behold: I offered myself wholly to the Father for you, and have given my Body and Blood entirely as food so that I might be totally yours, and you might be forever mine. If, however, you remain in your own self, and will not freely offer yourself to me: your offering will not be complete, nor will the union between us be entire. Therefore, before all of your works, willingly offer yourself as an oblation into the hands of God, if you desire freedom and grace.

Thomas á Kempis (1380–1471)

JANUARY 21

St. Augustine of Hippo (354–430), that most illustrious of converts and Church Fathers, here contemplates Nicodemus' dialogue with Christ. In order to highlight his spiritual pilgrimage toward the sacraments, Augustine draws upon an allegorical interpretation of the crossing of the Red Sea. St. Augustine thus explains that as the Jews were baptized in the Red Sea, leading them to the manna, Nicodemus is told he must be baptized in Christ, leading him to the Eucharist.

> Since Nicodemus was of that number, he came to the Lord, but he came at night; and this detail is relevant to the matter at hand. He came to the Lord, and he came at night: he came to the light and he came in darkness. What do those reborn of the water and of the Spirit hear from the Apostle? "Once you were darkness, but now you are light in the Lord. Walk as children of light" [Eph 5:8, and again, "but we who are of the day, we are sober" [1 Thes 5:8]. So those reborn were of the night and now are of the day: they were darkness and are now light. Jesus now entrusts Himself to them, and they do not come to Jesus at night like Nicodemus. They do not seek the day in darkness. Such people now profess that Jesus came to them and granted salvation unto them because He Himself said, "Unless someone eats my flesh and drinks my blood, he has no life in himself" [John 6:53]. And because the catechumens now have the sign of the cross on their foreheads, they are part of a great house. Those who were servants have now been made sons and are not to be accounted as nothing.

> But when did the people of Israel eat the manna? When they crossed the Red Sea. Hear the Apostle on what the Red Sea signifies: "Do not be ignorant, brothers, that all our fathers were under the cloud, and all passed through the sea" [1 Cor 10:1]. And as if you sought to know the meaning of their crossing, he continues, "and all were baptized through Moses in the cloud and in the sea" [1 Cor 10:2]. So if the figure of the sea had so much force, how much efficacy will the reality of baptism have? And if what happened in a figure led those

in exodus to the manna, what will Christ impart in the reality of his baptism after leading his people out? Through baptism he led believers out, having destroyed all sins, as if enemies clinging to them like the Egyptians who perished in the sea. Where did he lead them out, brothers? Where did Jesus lead them out through baptism, which figure Moses accomplished at that time as he led them through the sea? Where did he lead them? To the manna.

St. Augustine of Hippo, Bishop and Doctor (354–430)

JANUARY 22

Early in life, St. Ildefonsus (607–667) entered a monastery near Toledo where he was eventually named abbot and bishop. In this excerpt from his work on baptism, Ildefonsus addresses those who have recently entered the Church. As with so many texts of Christian antiquity, the following description of the liturgy illustrates the unchanging nature of the Catholic faith. After enumerating the Sacraments of Initiation, he provides a gloss on the "Our Father," identifying the Eucharist as that "daily bread" of man's sanctification.

> After the Baptismal regeneration of the spirit,
> after the grace of heavenly Anointing,
> after the teaching of the Lord's prayer,
> and after the invocation of the Holy Fathers,
> they assemble, approach,
> and take part in the Celestial Refreshment.

They who say, "*Our Father, who art in heaven,*" are those who are now of the Father, reborn through water and spirit. Thus, they call upon Him in confidence, saying, "*give us this day our daily bread.*" This bread is Christ Himself, the Bread of Life, who descended from heaven to give life to the world [John 6:51]. And we rightly ask in the Lord's Prayer that

Christ Himself be given to us daily, so that we who live and abide in Christ do not fall away from His sanctification and from His Body.

St. Ildefonsus of Toledo (607–667)
[Memorial, January 23]

JANUARY 23

Memorial of Bl. Henry Suso

Bl. Henry Suso (1299–1366) was one of the Rhineland Mystics whose writings enjoyed great popularity during the Middle Ages. His ardent pursuit of union with God is reflected in his works, which range from the practical to the contemplative. In the following passage, Bl. Henry echoes St. Thomas Aquinas, calling the Eucharist a "Sacrament of Love" and praising it as Love Incarnate.

Lord, what is there else in all this world that could gladden my heart more? Or what more could it desire when You graciously give Yourself to me to enjoy and love? Truly is it called a SACRAMENT OF LOVE. When was there anything lovelier seen or heard of than to embrace love itself? To be changed by grace into love itself? Lord, I see no difference except that Simeon received You visibly, and I receive You invisibly. But as little as my bodily eyes can see Your real humanity, just as little could his bodily eyes contemplate Your divinity, except through faith, as I now do. Lord, what new power is lodged in this bodily sight? He whose spiritual eyes are opened has not much to see with his bodily eyes, for the eyes of the spirit see far more really and truly. Lord, I know by faith, so far as one can know it, that I have You here. What more could I wish? Lord, it is a thousand times better for me that I am unable to see You; for, how could I ever have the heart thus visibly to partake of You!

Bl. Henry Suso (1299–1366)

JANUARY 24

Memorial of St. Francis de Sales, Bishop and Doctor

St. Francis de Sales (1567–1622) was the renowned bishop of Geneva whose writings on the spiritual life masterfully balance mystical contemplation with practical instruction. In his *Introduction to the Devout Life*, St. Francis treats the basic mechanics of the spiritual life with a gentle and discerning spirit. In this excerpt, Francis argues that frequent reception of Holy Communion is appropriate at all stages of the spiritual life, for Christians must learn to rely on God and not their own strength.

If those of the world ask why you receive communion so often, tell them that it is to learn to love God, to purify yourself from imperfections, to be delivered from your miseries, to be comforted in your afflictions, and to be supported in your weakness. Tell them that two sorts of persons ought to communicate frequently; the perfect, because being well-disposed, they would be greatly to blame for not approaching to the source and fountain of perfection; and the imperfect, that they may be able to aspire to perfection; the strong, lest they should become weak; and the weak, that they may become strong; the sick, that they may be healed; and the healthy, lest they fall into sickness. Tell them that for your part, being imperfect, weak, and sick, you have need of frequent communion with Him who is your perfection, your strength, and your medicine. Tell them that those who do not have many worldly affairs to attend ought to communicate often, because they have the time for it; and that those who have much business on their hands should also communicate often, because they have need of it; that he who labors much and is burdened with cares ought to eat solid meats, and that frequently. Tell them that you frequently receive the Holy Sacrament to learn to receive it well, because one hardly performs an action well that he does not often practice.

Communicate frequently then, Philothea, and as often as you can with the advice of your spiritual Father. And believe me, as hares in our mountains become white in winter, because they neither see nor eat anything but snow; so too, by approaching and eating beauty, purity, and goodness itself in this divine sacrament, you will become fair, pure, and good.

St. Francis de Sales, Bishop and Doctor (1567–1622)

JANUARY 25

Memorial of St. Apollo, Desert Father

St. Apollo (d. 395) was one of the Desert Fathers whose words and deeds are recorded in the ancient tome of sayings, variously titled *The Sayings of the Desert Fathers* or *The Book of Paradise*. These sayings are expressed in a rustic and uncompromising way and together canvass the whole of the spiritual life. Here, St. Apollo counsels his fellow monks to frequently participate in the Eucharist as the sure means of union with God.

And if it is possible, it is fitting that the monks should partake of the Mysteries of Christ each day. Whoever makes himself distant from them shall remove himself from God, but whoever does this, shall receive our Redeemer always. For our Life-Giver says, "He who eats My Body and drinks My Blood remains in Me and I in him" [John 6:56]. And it is helpful for monks to remember the Passion of our Redeemer at all times, because by its remembrance, we make ourselves worthy of the forgiveness of our sins. Therefore, it is right that we should always make ourselves worthy to receive the Holy Mysteries of our Redeemer.

St. Apollo, Desert Father (d. 395)

JANUARY 26

St. Irenaeus (c. 130–202) was the bishop of Lyons and a fierce opponent of Gnosticism, a heresy that denied the value of the human body. The Incarnation of Our Lord, however, affirms the goodness of God's creation and promises the redemption of man's body. For Christ truly assumed a human nature, was crucified, rose, and bodily ascended into heaven. This glorified flesh of the Redeemer is received at Holy Communion, preparing man's body for eternal life.

> Entirely vain are those who deny the universal dispensation of God and the salvation of the flesh, spurning its regeneration and claiming that it is not capable of incorruption. For if these things cannot be saved, then the Lord did not redeem us by His blood, nor is the cup of the Eucharist a participation in His blood, nor is the bread that we break a sharing in His body. For blood is only from veins, flesh, and the rest of human substance, and it was this that the Word of God truly became. He redeemed us by His blood as the Apostle says, "in whom we have redemption through his blood and remission of sins" [Eph 1:7].
>
> Since we are members of Him, and are nourished by creation—and He Himself holds the creation, causing the sun to rise and rain to fall as he wishes—so He professed that the cup from creation was His very own blood. He affirmed the bread from creation to be His very body from which our bodies grow.
>
> *St. Irenaeus of Lyons (c. 130–202)*

JANUARY 27

Memorial of St. Angela Merici

St. Angela Merici (1474–1540) lost her parents and sister in childhood, leading her to seek refuge in Christ. In her maturity, she founded the Ursulines, a religious community dedicated to the education of young girls. In this passage from the order's constitutions, St. Angela details the duties of its members, assuring them that the ordinary means of sanctification are found in the sacraments. Her counsel is a timeless reminder that spiritual progress is not found in seeking after the extraordinary (1 Kgs 19:12), but in the quiet means given by God.

Let everyone go to Mass daily, hearing at least one with all modesty and devotion. In the most wonderful way, all the merits of the Passion of our dear Lord are contained in this adorable Sacrifice. The greater the attention, the faith, and the contrition of those assisting at Mass, the greater share they have in these blessed merits; and the deeper consolation they derive from it. Thus, you may communicate spiritually.

. . . You are exhorted to frequent Confession in order to receive the necessary remedy for the wounds of the soul. Let each present herself to the priest as she would to God, our Eternal Judge, and there, let her confess her sins and ask for pardon, grieving with heartfelt sorrow and a firm purpose of renouncing all sin. Let her kneel before her confessor with the reverence expected of persons of deep piety.

Furthermore, you must not forget that a particular place or church must be designated in which all meet on the first Friday of each month and receive communion from the spiritual father. Moreover, we exhort each of you to confess and receive communion in her own parish church on the great feasts of the year.

St. Angela Merici (1474–1540)

JANUARY 28

Memorial of St. Thomas Aquinas, Doctor of the Church

St. Thomas Aquinas (1225–1274) surprised and disappointed his noble family by refusing to pursue the abbacy at Monte Cassino, instead choosing to become a mendicant Dominican. Studying under St. Albert the Great, Thomas became the greatest scholastic and the most recommended theologian by the Church. He remains unrivaled in Christian history for his systematic account of the faith. Here, St. Thomas provides a philosophical explanation of transubstantiation.

> Yet this change is not like natural changes, but is entirely supernatural, and effected by God's power alone. Hence Ambrose says, "See how Christ's word changes nature's laws, as He wills: a man is not born save of man and woman; see therefore that against the established law and order a man is born of a Virgin," and, "it is clear that a Virgin conceived beyond the order of nature, and what we make is the body from the Virgin. Why, then, do you look for nature's order in Christ's body, since the Lord Jesus was Himself brought forth of a Virgin beyond nature?" Chrysostom likewise commenting on John 6:64 ("The words which I have spoken to you," namely, of this sacrament, "are spirit and life"), says: i.e. "spiritual, having nothing carnal, nor natural consequence; but they are rent from all such necessity which exists upon earth, and from the laws here established."

> For it is evident that every agent acts according as it is in act. But every created agent is limited in its act, as being of a determinate genus and species, and consequently the action of every created agent bears upon some determinate act. Now the determination of everything in actual existence comes from its form. Consequently, no natural or created agent can act except by changing the form in something; and on this account every change made according to nature's laws is a formal change. But God is infinite act . . . hence His action extends to the whole nature of being. Therefore He can work not only formal conversion, so that diverse forms succeed each other in the same subject, but also the change of all being,

so that, to wit, the whole substance of one thing be changed into the whole substance of another. And this is done by Divine power in this sacrament: for, the whole substance of the bread is changed into the whole substance of Christ's body, and the whole substance of the wine into the whole substance of Christ's blood. Hence this is not a formal, but a substantial conversion; nor is it a kind of natural movement, but, with a name of its own, it can be called "transubstantiation."

St. Thomas Aquinas, Doctor of the Church (1225–1274)

JANUARY 29

St. John Damascene (c. 675–749) is considered the last of the Eastern Fathers and is remembered for his staunch opposition of Iconoclasm—a heresy that denied the value and use of icons. In his treatise, *On the Orthodox Faith*, St. John argues that it is fitting to employ earthly images in service of worship, because God the Son truly became man. Material images may, therefore, serve as windows into heaven. In this excerpt below, St. John speaks of this integrated view of creation in light of the Eucharist, wherein God approaches man in both body and soul.

Since this Adam [Christ] is spiritual, there had to be a spiritual birth as well as spiritual food. Since we have a twofold and composite nature, the birth had to be twofold and the food composite. The birth given us was through water and Spirit—I speak about holy baptism—and the food itself is the bread of life, our Lord Jesus Christ who came down from heaven. On the night He was betrayed, when He was about to willingly go to His death, He established the New Covenant with His holy disciples, apostles, and all who believe in Him through them. So in that upper room of holy and glorious Zion, while eating the old Passover with His disciples in fulfillment of the Old Covenant, He washed His disciples' feet, providing a symbol of baptism. Then, breaking bread, He gave it to them saying, "Take, eat, this is my body which is broken for you for the forgiveness of sins." Likewise, taking the cup of water and wine, he gave it to them saying, "All of you, drink of it. This is my blood of the new covenant which is poured out for you for the forgiveness of sins. Do this in remembrance of me." For as often as you eat this bread, and drink this cup, you proclaim the Lord's death and confess his resurrection until he comes [see 1 Cor 11:26].

St. John Damascene, Doctor of the Church (c. 675–749)

JANUARY 30

William of St. Thierry (c. 1080–1148) was a Benedictine abbot and reformer who eventually joined the Cistercian order, seeking a more contemplative life. His rich theological writings rival the sublime works of his friend and fellow Cistercian, St. Bernard of Clairvaux. In the passage below, William reflects on the Paschal Mystery as the source of the sacraments. For it was from the wounded side of Christ that blood and water flowed out, signifying the sacraments of Baptism and the Eucharist. From this source, all sacraments draw their salvific power.

Unsearchable are the riches of your glory, Lord, that laid hidden secret with you in heaven, until the soldier's lance opened the side of Your Son and our Redeemer upon the cross, and the Sacraments of our redemption poured forth. We cannot now place a finger or hand into His side, like Thomas; yet, through this open door, all may enter into Your heart, Jesus, the sure seat of mercy, and into Your holy soul, filled with all the fullness of God, and filled with grace and truth, our salvation and consolation. Open Lord, the side of your Ark, wherein all who enter may be granted salvation from the flood that inundates the earth. Open unto us the side of Your body so that those who desire to perceive the secrets of the Son may enter and receive the Sacraments that flow from Him, the price of their redemption.

William of St. Thierry (c. 1080–1148)

JANUARY 31

Memorial of St. John Bosco

St. John Bosco (1815–1888) was an Italian priest who worked to improve the education of impoverished youth of the industrial age. Rather than mete out punishments, St. John gained the trust of his young followers by emphasizing kindness and fraternal duty. In the following passage, St. John addresses the necessity of fostering a regular sacramental life. For the work of evangelization is not merely the proposal of knowledge, but the cultivation of grace through contact with the divine. The sacraments are thus the surest means of intimacy with God.

The confirmed experience of those who have served in the education and formation of the youth is this: the Sacraments of Confession and Holy Communion are the best safeguards and the strongest supports for that critical period of their lives. If you can show me a boy who frequently receives the Holy Sacraments, it will be enough to convince me that he will pass through his years of youth, reach maturity, and (if God so disposes) arrive at a venerable old age, having always lived as an example for others. This should be impressed upon the young so that they may form this excellent habit. This should also be seriously considered by all those who form them so that they may assist them in cultivating this practice.

St. John Bosco (1815–1888)

FEBRUARY

FEBRUARY I

Pope St. John Paul II (1920–2005) was a charismatic evangelist, philosopher, and theologian who led the Church into the third millennium. He provided a much-needed interpretation of the Second Vatican Council, emphasizing its continuity with Sacred Tradition. In the following passage from his encyclical on the Eucharist, *Ecclesia de Eucharistia*, John Paul II affirms the centrality of the Eucharist in the life of the Church and its essential connection to the Paschal Mystery.

> The Church draws her life from the Eucharist. This truth does not simply express a daily experience of faith, but recapitulates *the heart of the mystery of the Church*. In a variety of ways she joyfully experiences the constant fulfilment of the promise: "Lo, I am with you always, to the close of the age" [Matt 28:20], but in the Holy Eucharist, through the changing of bread and wine into the body and blood of the Lord, she rejoices in this presence with unique intensity. Ever since Pentecost, when the Church, the People of the New Covenant, began her pilgrim journey towards her heavenly homeland, the Divine Sacrament has continued to mark the passing of her days, filling them with confident hope. . . . The Church was born of the paschal mystery. For this very reason the Eucharist, which is in an outstanding way the sacrament of the paschal mystery, *stands at the center of the Church's life*. . . . At

every celebration of the Eucharist, we are spiritually brought back to the paschal Triduum: to the events of the evening of Holy Thursday, to the Last Supper and to what followed it.

Pope St. John Paul II (1920–2005)

FEBRUARY 2

The Feast of the Presentation of the Lord, Memorial of Ven. Francis Libermann

Born the son of a rabbi, Ven. Francis Libermann (1802–1852) pursued Talmudic studies before converting to the Catholic faith. Much to his father's dismay, Francis was ordained a priest and founded the Order of the Immaculate Heart of Mary. In the following passage, Libermann recounts his grace-filled conversion and entry into the Church. Like Simeon, the privileged witness of the Presentation of the Lord, Ven. Francis was blessed to gaze upon the promise of Israel, the long-awaited Messiah.

Remembering the God of my fathers, I threw myself on my knees and entreated Him to enlighten me in my search for the true religion. I asked Him to make known if the Christian faith was the true one, but if it were false, to remove the reach of its influence from me. The Lord, ever near to those who invoke Him from the inmost depths of their hearts, heard my prayer. I was immediately enlightened. I saw the truth. Faith penetrated my mind and my heart. Having commenced the reading of Lhomond, I easily and firmly adhered to all that is related therein about the life and death of Jesus Christ. Even the mystery of the Eucharist, which was rather imprudently presented for my meditation, in no way disheartened me. I believed all without difficulty. From that moment, my most ardent desire was to be regenerated in the sacred waters of Baptism. That happiness was soon to be granted to me. I was immediately prepared for this august sacrament, which I received on Christmas Eve, 1826. On this festival, I was likewise admitted to partake of the Blessed Eucharist.

In the following letter, Francis writes to his niece on the occasion of her first Holy Communion. He counsels her to dismiss her fears of unworthiness and to be at peace.

Do not fear, dear child. Jesus, the most sweet and amiable Jesus will come with great complacency to embrace you in the ineffable tenderness of His love. He will not come to you as a judge: all the sins of your life will be forgotten. In the excess of His love, He will only think of pressing you to His Sacred Heart. Do you think, dear child, that St. Stanislaus Kostka was afraid when, in a vision, Mary deigned to place the holy and amiable Infant Jesus in his arms?

Ven. Francis Libermann (1802–1852)

FEBRUARY 3

Bl. Rabanus Maurus (c. 780–856) studied theology under the esteemed priest and scholar, Alcuin, and rose to become one of the great educators of his day. In the following passage, Rabanus illustrates the necessity of receiving the Eucharist, emphasizing man's dependence on Christ for salvation. Because human flesh has no ability to raise itself, it must be joined to that heavenly body that descended from heaven. And as the body naturally lives on bread, so must the soul subsist on this Bread from Heaven, which alone communicates everlasting life.

Just as material food nourishes the body and enlivens the exterior of man, so too does the word of God nourish and strengthen man's interior soul: for *not by bread alone does man live, but by every word that proceeds forth from the mouth of God* [Deut 8:3]. Also, *the Word became flesh, and dwelt among us* [John 1:14]. Therefore, Truth itself declared to man: *My flesh is true food, and my blood is true drink* [John 6:55].

The flesh of Christ is the true food that He feeds us, which nourishes man unto everlasting life, and His Blood is the true drink, which eternally satisfies those who hunger and thirst in their souls for justice. While it is possible to have earthly life without this food or drink, eternal life is absolutely not possible. For this food and drink signify the Head and Source of the members of the eternal communion. He says: *He who eats my flesh and drinks my blood remains in me and I in him* [John 6:56]. Wherefore, it is necessary for us to receive His Body and Blood, and remain in Him as members of His body since *no one has ascended to heaven except He who descended from heaven, the Son of Man, who is in heaven* [John 3:13].

Bl. Rabanus Maurus (c. 780–856)
[Memorial, February 4]

FEBRUARY 4

Memorial of St. Isidore of Pelusium

St. Isidore of Pelusium (d. c. 450) was an Egyptian monk who worked for reform within the Church. In the following passage, St. Isidore reflects on the Divine Liturgy and explains that the priest's actions symbolize the events of the Passion. In this way, he likens the corporal used on the altar to the burial cloth of Christ and compares the actions of the priest with those of Joseph of Arimathea. St. Isidore thus teaches that the death, burial, and Resurrection of Christ are symbolized in the liturgical gestures of the celebrant.

During the ministry of the divine gifts, the spreading of the pure linen cloth is as the same service performed by Joseph of Arimathea. When Joseph wrapped the Lord's body in the linen cloth, he brought it to the tomb from which our entire human race enjoyed the fruit of the resurrection. So too, when we consecrate the bread of presentation on the linen cloth, we undoubtedly find the body of Christ, and from that body there gushes forth the incorruption that Jesus the Savior graciously grants; this same Jesus who was buried in Joseph's tomb and rose from the dead.

St. Isidore of Pelusium (d. c. 450)

FEBRUARY 5

St. Catherine of Ricci (1522–1590) was a Dominican mystic, known for her intense devotion to the Passion of Christ. For more than a decade, she went into ecstasy during the hours of the Passion, until humbly praying this gift be removed. In the following letter, St. Catherine instructs her sisters to live in a spirit of obedience and to frequent Holy Communion. For she understood that reception of Holy Communion is the great means of gaining knowledge of Christ, and of oneself.

My daughters, be reverent and obedient to your superiors like [St. Catherine of Alexandria] who out of reverence and obedience for her mother went to speak to that holy Romito, whom she believed and obeyed in simplicity. For St. Catherine did not say: *"You are speaking childishness! saying that I should pray, and thus see the Bridegroom."* And because of her obedience, she merited to see Jesus. You, my daughters, must give yourself to holy obedience, and frequent confession and Holy Communion if you want to see Jesus. One can neither see nor love Jesus better than by being united to Him in Holy Communion. For there we come to know His goodness and mercy—as well as our own cowardice and misery—just as this saint was illumined with truth through prayer. After Catherine realized her error, she repented and began to fervently follow her spouse, Jesus.

St. Catherine of Ricci (1522–1590)
[Memorial, February 4]

FEBRUARY 6

The Memorial of the Martyrs of Nagasaki

Bl. Charles Spinola (1564–1622) was a Spanish Jesuit and a missionary to Japan. He arrived in Nagasaki during the height of Christian persecution and was captured, imprisoned, and martyred at the stake. His letters describe the grave conditions of imprisoned Catholics, but refer to his prison as a "paradise," since he still could celebrate Mass. In these extracts, Bl. Charles expresses the joy of a life wholly centered upon the Eucharist. Like so many martyrs before him, his sufferings only worked to increase his Christian charity.

> The Divine Sacrifice constitutes our sole consolation, and by a signal favor of Divine Providence, we have all that is required for the service of the altar. The Bread of Life sustains both body and soul, and the heavenly wine raises us above all our troubles, making us desirous to sacrifice our lives a thousand times for Him who with such great love gave Himself up for our sake.

> . . . It appears to me that for a year God has prepared us for [martyrdom] with the attention of a novice master—above all during the last two months. He permitted the guards to be more severe and the food worse. We no longer have the consolation of receiving letters. Nevertheless, the greatest of all consolations has not been wanting: by a special protection of Heaven we always have hosts and wine for the Holy Sacrifice.

> . . . In any case, my strength is so exhausted that in all probability I shall be unable to write to you again. Farewell, then, very reverend Father, till we meet in heaven! I beg you, in all humility, not to forget this poor prisoner for Christ at the altar and to recommend him to all our Fathers and brothers. I, in turn, pray every day at the holy sacrifice for them all—and particularly for your paternity.

> *Bl. Charles Spinola (1564–1622)*

FEBRUARY 7

Memorial of Bl. Pope Pius IX

As the longest-reigning pope, Bl. Pope Pius IX (1792–1878) coura-geously defended the Church against the growing threats of relativism, socialism, and theological modernism. In his landmark bull, *Ineffabilis Deus*, he declared the Immaculate Conception a dogma of the faith, af-firming the Church's belief in the sinlessness of Mary (see Luke 1:28). In this excerpt from *Amantissimi Redemptoris*, Bl. Pius IX speaks on the gratuitous gift of the Eucharist, emphasizing the expiatory value of Holy Mass.

Christ's love towards men was so great that not only was He willing to endure most cruel sufferings for our salvation and an atrocious death on the cross, but also He wished to nourish us eternally in the sacrament of His body and blood. In this way, He might strengthen us by the presence of His divinity and be the safest bulwark of our spiritual life. And not content to have loved us with such an outstanding and truly divine love, He heaped benefits on benefits, poured out the riches of His love upon us, and, as you know so well, having loved His own He loved them to the end. For, declaring Himself to be an eternal Priest according to the order of Melchizedek, He in-stituted permanently His priesthood in the Catholic Church. He decreed that [this] same sacrifice which He performed is to redeem the whole human race from the yoke of sin to rec-oncile all things in heaven and earth, and to remain until the consummation of the world. He decreed that it be renewed and take place daily by the ministry of the priesthood. Only the reason for the offering is diverse, namely, that the salvific and most abundant fruits of His passion might forever be dis-persed upon mankind. . . .

No unworthiness or wickedness on the part of those offering it can ever defile this oblation. The Lord predicted through

Malachi that it would be great and would be cleanly offered from sunrise to sunset in all places to His name. This oblation abounding with an unspeakable richness of fruit embraces the present and future life. For by this oblation God is pleased and, granting the grace and gift of repentance, remits even great crimes and sins. Although grievously offended by our sins, He is moved from anger to mercy, from the severity of just chastisement to clemency; by it the title and obligation of temporal punishment is dissolved; by it the souls of the departed in Christ who have not yet been fully purged are aided.

Bl. Pope Pius IX (1792–1878)

FEBRUARY 8

St. Caesarius (c. 468–542) served as Bishop of Arles for forty years, where he gained notoriety for his charismatic preaching. In the following sermon, St. Caesarius counsels his congregation not to leave the Eucharistic celebration too soon and laments that the Sacred Host is paid less respect than earthly dignitaries. In this way, he illustrates the dichotomy between those who revere God above all things and those who honor the world.

Now, if a king or another powerful person invited such people to dine, I want to know if they would presume to leave before the whole meal was finished. Even if the host did not detain them, appetite would do so. Why, then, do we not depart from the meal of a man and fear offending mortals, unless it is because we want to fill our stomachs more than it is fitting?

Why, then, do we quickly depart from the spiritual and divine banquet? I am afraid to say it lest some become angry, but I will say it because of the danger that affects us both. We do this because we do not care about the food of the soul. We neither fear God, nor revere man [see Luke 18:2].

St. Caesarius, Bishop of Arles (c. 468–542)

FEBRUARY 9

Memorial of Bl. Anne Catherine Emmerich

Bl. Anne Catherine Emmerich (1774–1824) lived as an Augustinian nun until her order was shuttered by Jerome Bonaparte, brother of Napoleon. She was a mystic and stigmatist whose visions of the Passion were recorded by Clemens Brentano in *The Dolorous Passion of Our Lord Jesus Christ*. In the following excerpt, Bl. Anne recounts Christ's Agony in the Garden, recognizing Jesus' assailants as those who disrespect Him in the Eucharist. These words surely carry prophetic significance for the modern age.

It was made known to me that these apparitions were all those persons who in varying ways insult and outrage Jesus, really and truly present in the Holy Sacrament. Among them, I recognized all those who in any way profane the Blessed Eucharist. I beheld with horror all the outrages thus offered to our Lord, whether by neglect, irreverence, and omission of what was due to Him; by open contempt, abuse, and the most awful sacrileges. . . .

I beheld with terror that many priests, some of whom even fancied themselves full of faith and piety also outraged Jesus in the Adorable Sacrament. I saw many who believed and taught the doctrine of the Real Presence, but did not sufficiently take it to heart, for they forgot and neglected the palace, throne, and seat of the Living God; that is to say, the church, the altar, the tabernacle, the chalice, the monstrance, the vases and ornaments; in a word—all that is used in His worship or to adorn His House. . . .

I saw neglect of this kind in churches, the pastors and congregations of which were rich, or at least tolerably well off. I saw many others in which worldly, tasteless, unsuitable ornaments had replaced the magnificent adornments of a more pious age. I saw that often the poorest of men were better lodged in their cottages than the Master of heaven and earth in His churches. Ah, how deeply did the inhospitality of men grieve Jesus, who had given Himself to be their Food!

Bl. Anne Catherine Emmerich (1774–1824)

FEBRUARY 10

Johannes Tauler (c. 1300–1361) was a Rhineland Mystic whose writings treat the ascetic journey toward God. His sermons overflow with warmth and understanding, even as they challenge listeners to follow the difficult path of the cross. In this excerpt, Tauler speaks of the power of the Blessed Sacrament to purify those who receive it, making them to live unto God.

Again, our Lord says, "he who eats My flesh and drinks My blood has eternal life" [John 6:54]. If you would gain the life of Jesus, you must receive the Blessed Sacrament often; for the old Adam within you shall thereby be wholly destroyed. As the forces of nature fill our veins with the strength from food, making it one with ourselves, so shall the Divine food entirely change you into Itself. You will know if this has been done if, after receiving this Sacrament, you feel your heart wholly detached from whatever is not God. And this new life within you will work outwardly and be manifest in your conduct, actions, and conversation. This adorable Sacrament separates all that is bad, profitless and superfluous, casting it all out of the soul. And then God enters into all one's life, love, thought, and intention; renewing it, cleansing it, and making it more divine.

This Sacrament cures a man's inner blindness, helps him to know himself, and teaches him how to turn away from self and all created things. Thus, the wise man says: "With the bread of life and understanding, she [Wisdom] shall feed him" (Ecc 15:3). This divine food changes a man into Itself so that his whole life is regulated by God. Through this food, he is led by God and changed by God. Therefore, if a man goes to Communion and remains empty of heart, vain and arrogant, and his demeanor frivolous; if he is attached to fine clothes and given to amusements, then his going to Communion is a perilous thing if he wilfully remains attached to these defects.

Johannes Tauler (c. 1300–1361)

FEBRUARY 11

The Feast of Our Lady of Lourdes

Little is known about the life of Gelasius of Cyzicus (c. 475), except that he faithfully opposed Monophysitism, the false teaching that Christ possessed one nature only. In the following passage, Gelasius gives witness to his vibrant faith in the Eucharist, affirming its intrinsic unity with the sacrifice of Christ on Calvary. Notably, when Gelasius speaks of "symbols of the resurrection," he does not employ the term "symbol" in the modern sense of a sign devoid of reality. Rather, the Greek Fathers used the word "symbolon" to indicate a visible sign that possessed what it signified.

Concerning the mystery of the Body and Blood of Christ that lies upon the divine table: let us humbly abstain from fixating upon the [visible] bread and cup presented upon it. Rather, lifting up our minds in faith, let us fix them upon the Lamb of God who takes away the sins of the world, lying upon the altar; the Lamb sacrificed by the priests in an unbloody manner. Let us also understand that we truly receive the precious body and blood, believing that these things are our symbols of the resurrection. For this reason, we do not receive a great portion, but a little, that we may know that they are not for satiation, but for sanctification.

Gelasius of Cyzicus (c. 475)

FEBRUARY 12

The Catholic Faith flourished in Celtic lands, producing a vibrant local church, inspired by the spirit of St. Patrick. The Celtic liturgical practices are recorded in *The Stowe Missal*, a ninth-century book of prayers and rituals stemming from the monastery of Tallaght in County Dublin. While each culture expresses the faith with its own particular accent, the selection below evidences the universality of Christian faith in the Eucharist.

I anoint thee with the sanctified oil, that thou recover thy health: in the Name of the Father and of the Son and of the Holy Spirit, unto ages of ages.
R. Amen.

O Lord, look upon us as Thy servants, that praying with confidence, we may be worthy to say: [*Our Father, etc.*] Deliver us O Lord from every evil and preserve us in all good, O Jesus Christ, the Author of all that is good, Who reigneth unto ages of ages.
R. Amen.

We pray Thee, O Lord, for our brother (sister)—N—who is weighed down by his (her) infirmity. Let him (her) participate in the Act of Communion, that whenever the blots of this era attack him (her), or worldliness may taint him (her), he (she) may be forgiven and cleansed by the Gift of Your Faith, through our Lord Jesus Christ, Who reigneth with the Father and the Holy Spirit, unto ages of ages.
R. Amen.

O Lord, Holy Father, we faithfully beseech Thee, that by the reception of this Sacrosanct Eucharist of the Body and Blood of Our Lord Jesus Christ, that as much as possible of the flesh and as much as possible of the soul may be made well, through our Lord Jesus Christ Who reigneth with Thee and the Holy Spirit, unto ages of ages.

R. Amen.

The Stowe Missal (9th century)

FEBRUARY 13

Born in Thessalonica after the Great Schism, Nicholas Cabasilas (c. 1322–1392) was a layman who composed influential works of Byzantine theology. Though he is counted among the Orthodox communion, the Catholic Church includes passages of his works in the Office of Readings. In the following selection, Cabasilas identifies the sacrifice of the altar with that of Calvary, meditating upon the unity of the two events. Here, the words of St. Paul find a particular place: "I want to know him and the power of his resurrection, and share in his sufferings, being conformed to his death that somehow I may attain to the resurrection of the dead" (Phil 3:10–11).

Once the words of consecration are spoken, the entirety of the Divine Liturgy is accomplished, complete, and the gifts sanctified. The sacrifice is complete, and the great and divine Sacrificial Victim, slain for the world, is seen lying upon the holy table. The bread of the Lord's body is no longer a type or simple gift, as if it merely bore an image of the true gift. Nor does it merely bear in itself an inscription of the saving sufferings as upon a tablet. Rather, it is the true gift, the all-holy body of the Master who truly endured all those insults, arrogant mistreatment, and bruises. After truthfully testifying before Pontius Pilate, His body was crucified and slain: this body was beaten, tortured, endured spittings, and tasted gall.

Likewise, the wine is the blood that gushed forth from that slain body. This is the body and the blood that was conceived from the Holy Spirit, born of the blessed Virgin, buried, rose on the third day, taken up into heaven, and sits at the right hand of the Father.

Nicholas Cabasilas (c. 1322–1392)

FEBRUARY 14

St. Gregory the Great (540–604) was a man of extraordinary spiritual depth and administrative skill. He served as an ambassador under Pope Pelagius II, but desired the monastic life he knew at the Monastery of St. Andrew—a religious house that he himself had established. Once elected to the papacy, he employed his active and contemplative gifts in service of the Church. In the following passage, St. Gregory reflects on the Good Shepherd in Eucharistic terms. For Christ lays down His life to feed His flock with His own body and blood.

In the Gospel reading, dear brothers, you heard your instructions and also our danger. For behold: He who is good, not by an occasional gift, but in essence, says, "I am the good shepherd" [John 10:11], and we imitate a kind of His goodness. He added, "The good shepherd lays down His life for His sheep" [John 10:11]. He accomplished what He counseled and demonstrated what he commanded. The Good Shepherd gave His life for the sheep that He may turn His body and blood into our Sacrament and that He may fill those sheep whom He had redeemed with the nourishment of His flesh.

Pope St. Gregory the Great, Doctor of the Church (540–604)

FEBRUARY 15

Memorial of St. Claude de la Colombiére

St. Claude de la Colombiére (1641–1682) was the spiritual director of St. Margaret Mary Alacoque and a zealous promoter of the Sacred Heart of Jesus. He vowed himself to a life of perfection, promising to follow the Jesuit rule with exactitude; yet, no trace of rigorism can be found in his spiritual counsels. In the following letter, St. Claude advises a penitent to pray for—and to accept—God's merciful embrace in the Eucharist. Instead of remaining self-enclosed in fear, St. Claude instructs this man to allow the Lord to touch him, and enter into him, so that he might be healed.

> Again, go to the Blessed Sacrament, and pray to Jesus Christ that He may have mercy on you. Present yourself to Him as a poor and unhappy soul, full of leprosy and bound by a million chains so that He will see the state that you are in. Then, allow Him to touch you. Above all, however, I recommend that you receive Communion. Afterward, pray in astonishment, remembering the life you have led, and present the thoughts of your heart to Jesus Christ, allowing Him to repose therein.
>
> St. Claude de la Colombiére (1641–1682)

FEBRUARY 16

As the seventh Minister General of the Order of Friars Minor, St. Bonaventure (1221–1274) strenuously worked to reconcile opposing factions within the order. His writings address a vast range of theological topics, from mystical theology to practical spirituality. In the following passage, St. Bonaventure applies the words of Psalm 107 to the Eucharist, showing the manner in which God sustains man. The Body of Christ is thus shown to nourish, console, and illuminate those faithful souls who partake of it.

> Let them confess to the Lord his mercies, and his wonders to the children of men. For he has satisfied the empty soul and filled the hungry soul with good things; those who sat in darkness and in the shadow of death, those bound in poverty and iron. (Ps 107:8–10)

"Let them confess to the Lord . . ." because Christ filled the empty soul, satisfied the hungry, illumined those sitting in darkness, reconciled those lying in the shadow of death, enriched the poor and softened the iron heart. Men were empty, and He gave Himself to dwell in them. Men were hungry, and He gave Himself to them for refreshment. They sat in darkness, and He gave Himself to illumine their hearts. They were lying in the shadow of death, and He gave Himself to them as a sacrifice of reconciliation. Men were bound in poverty as beggars, and He gave Himself to them as a power for working; they were obstinate of heart, and He gave Himself to soften their hearts. For the Lord Himself is sustenance to the hungry, refreshment to the hungry, the light of those sitting in darkness, the reconciliation of those lying in the shadow of death, the wealth of beggars, and the softening of those with an iron-hard heart.

St. Bonaventure, Bishop and Doctor (1221–1274)

FEBRUARY 17

Ven. Fulton J. Sheen (1895–1979) was born in a farming town in Illinois, but rose to great prominence as a scholar, media evangelist, and eventually the archbishop of Rochester and titular archbishop of Newport, Wales. His profound interior life and oratorical skills helped him to reach countless souls. In this newly published letter, Sheen writes to a friend on the value of intercessory prayer. He speaks of the unitive dimensions of the Mass, noting how the faithful are gathered together in the Body of Christ.

Your generous response to my plea for prayers has touched me deeply. Anything else you might have given would have been from what you <u>have</u>; but prayers come from that deeper treasure of what you <u>are</u>. Nor can they be given except by the soul that lives by faith and is in intimate communion with

God. In this way do I know the depth of your friendship.

That my gratitude may not be verbal, I shall offer the Holy Sacrifice of the Mass for your intentions on Thursday, April 15, that the redemption purchased on the Cross may be personalized in your heart, and that God's Divine Love may be the Architect of your every thought, word, and deed. Thus in our mutual prayer to God for one another we prove that the only true bond between friends, peoples and nations is God. One cannot tie together two roses except by something outside the roses, nor can one bind hearts except by something outside the hearts themselves. It takes three, not two, to make friends: two human hearts and the Sacred Heart of the Savior.

During the past radio season it was often said that as no greater misery could come to a mind than to live only by itself, for itself and within itself, so no greater happiness can come to the soul than to live by God's grace, for God and within God. Since Our Lord did not disdain either a stable or a tomb, we may be sure He will not shrink, if we so desire, from making us the Temple of His Presence.

Ven. Fulton J. Sheen, Archbishop (1895–1979)

FEBRUARY 18

In the following selection, St. Augustine (354–430) lends both a historical and allegorical reading to the night-visit of Nicodemus. Augustine's treatment remains faithful to the rhetorical style of the Gospel of John, which characteristically moves from the literal to the spiritual. Here, Nicodemus is challenged to move beyond his earthly conceptions and to perceive the true nature of the Sacraments of Baptism and the Eucharist. Their sacramental mystery is, in part, illumined through an allegorical reading of Old Testament events.

What is the manna? Christ says, "I am the living bread that descended from heaven" [John 6:51]. The faithful receive the manna having now been brought through the Red Sea. Why the Red Sea? Why also "red"? The Red Sea signified the baptism of Christ. For where does the baptism of Christ get its redness if not from being consecrated by Christ's blood? Where, then, does He lead the faithful who have been baptized? To the manna. Behold, I say manna. We know well what the Jews, those people of Israel, received; what God rained down from heaven. And yet catechumens do not know what Christians receive. Let them blush because of their ignorance. Let them go through the Red Sea; let them eat manna so that as they believe in Jesus' name, Jesus may entrust Himself to them.

My brothers, pay attention to the response of Nicodemus who came to Jesus at night. Though he came to Jesus, since he came at night, he still speaks from the darkness of his own flesh. He does not understand what he hears from the Lord. He does not understand what he hears from the Light that illumines every man come into this world. The Lord said to him, "unless a man is born again, he will not see the kingdom of God" [John 3:3]. Nicodemus says to Him, "how can a man be born when he is old?" [John 3:4] The Spirit speaks to him, yet he understands according to the flesh. He understands his own flesh because he does not yet understand the flesh of Christ.

St. Augustine of Hippo, Bishop and Doctor (354–430)

FEBRUARY 19

Memorial of St. Beatus

St. Beatus (d. 798) was a Spanish monk and the theological opponent of Elipandus of Toledo, a bishop who held the heretical position of Adoptionism. St. Beatus and his religious brother, Heterius, composed an epistle directed toward the archbishop and successfully repelled his error. In the following passage, St. Beatus explains the authority on which the Holy Mass stands: it was instituted by Christ in fulfillment of the Old Covenant. The New Covenant is, therefore, the Eucharist itself, which makes present the once-for-all sacrifice of Christ.

As previously stated, Christ our Lord first instituted the Sacrifice that Christians offer to God. For, He entrusted the Apostles with His Body and Blood before being handed over as it is written in the Gospel. There it records, *Jesus took bread and the chalice, blessed and gave to them.* Melchizedek, the King of Salem, was the first to offer a type of this Sacrament, which is the Body and Blood of Christ, and the first to distantly express the mystery of so great a sacrifice, thereby forming a likeness of our Lord and Savior Jesus Christ the Eternal Priest, of whom it is written: *You are a priest forever, according to the line of Melchizedek.* The sacrifice celebrated by Christians is indeed a precept, fulfilling and relinquishing the Jewish sacrifices that men of old were commanded to offer. It makes present to us what our Lord Himself fashioned, the fruit of His offering at the evening Supper.

St. Beatus (d. 798)

FEBRUARY 20

Memorial of Ss. Francisco and Jacinta Marto

St. Francisco (1908–1919) and St. Jacinta Marto (1910–1920) were two of the young shepherd children who witnessed the apparitions of the Blessed Virgin Mary at Fatima. Their older cousin, Lúcia, faithfully served as the custodian of their memory as she was the only visionary to reach adulthood. Here, Lúcia recounts her conversations with St. Francisco regarding Our Lord's presence in the Most Blessed Sacrament. Despite his young age, Francisco's words reveal piety and wisdom beyond his years. He remains a profound example for all those who have abandoned visits to the Most Blessed Sacrament and all those who have refused to "become as little children" (Matt 18:3).

> Sometimes on our way to school, as soon as we reached Fatima, he would say to me: "Listen! You go to school, and I'll stay here in the church, close to the Hidden Jesus. It's not worth my while learning to read, as I'll be going to Heaven very soon. On your way home, come here and call me."

> The Blessed Sacrament was kept at that time near the entrance of the church, on the left side, as the church was undergoing repairs. Francisco went over there, between the baptismal font and the altar, and that was where I found him on my return.

> Later, when he fell ill, he often told me, when I called in to see him on my way to school: "Look! Go to the church and give my love to the Hidden Jesus. What hurts me most is that I cannot go there myself and stay awhile with the Hidden Jesus."

> When I arrived at his house one day, I said goodbye to a group of school children who had come with me, and I went in to pay a visit to him and his sister. As he had heard all the noise, he asked me:

> "Did you come with all that crowd?"

> "Yes, I did."

> "Don't go with them, because you might learn to commit sins. When you come out of school, go and stay for a little while near the Hidden Jesus, and afterwards come home by yourself."

> *Lúcia of Fatima (1907–2005)*

FEBRUARY 21

Memorial of St. Peter Damian, Bishop and Doctor

Despite his great intellectual abilities and the esteem of others, St. Peter Damian (1007–1072) renounced positions of honor and chose to retire to a hermitage. He understood well the value of the eremitic life and that its religious solitude was directed toward communion with Christ and His Church. Here, St. Peter speaks of the profound communion of all Christians who are united in the Body of Christ.

This is the unity of the Church that St. Paul speaks of when he says: "Because there is one bread, we who are many are one body" [1 Cor 10:17]. So great is the unity of the Church in Christ that all those throughout the entire world are one in the bread of Christ's body and one in the chalice of Christ's blood. For, just as the divinity of the Word of God is one and fills the entire world, so it is possible that the body of Christ is consecrated in many places and on many different days; yet, there are not many bodies, but one body of Christ. And as the bread truly changes into the body of Christ, so those who are in the Church rightly perceive that, without any doubt, all are made one in the body of Christ as He Himself testified when He said: "He who eats my flesh, and drinks my blood, abides in me, and I in him" [John 6:56].

St. Peter Damian (1007–1072)

FEBRUARY 22

Memorial of St. Margaret of Cortona

St. Margaret of Cortona (1247–1297) spent over ten years in a sinful relationship before experiencing a radical conversion to Christ. After discovering her companion murdered in the woods, Margaret realized the gravity of her sins and began a life of heroic penance. Her many mystical experiences were recorded by her spiritual director, Fra Giunta Bevegnati, who here relates the words spoken to her by Christ. In this excerpt, Jesus speaks to St. Margaret on unworthy reception of Holy Communion.

> My daughter, I am dead in most men of this age as far as their interior lives are concerned; for, few are those in whom I dwell by grace. Their offenses are so great that if sorrow could enter me, their God, I would cry out, bursting into tears at the sight of their horrible vices when they communicate. They crucify me again by receiving me unworthily, giving me a drink more bitter than that given me by [My persecutors] . . . as a rule, I am grievously offended in communion by persons in the world and by their lives. Woe to the souls that sin unceasingly and dare to receive me without correcting their faults. There will be a strict account for them at a future day.
>
> *St. Margaret of Cortona (1247–1297)*

FEBRUARY 23

The *Liturgy of St. Mark* is an ancient Alexandrine liturgy no longer in use, but related to contemporary Byzantine liturgies. In the following prayer, called the "prayer of the bread of presentation," the Eucharistic faith of the ancient Church is expressed in familiar terms. When the prayer speaks of the "Word," it is the divine and eternal Logos of John's Gospel that is referenced (John 1:1). The phrase "rational and bloodless sacrifice" refers to the spiritual worship of St. Paul (see Rom 12:1), even as it alludes to the sacramental nature of the Eucharistic sacrifice. Lastly, the phrase "lover of men," is a favorite term among the Greek Fathers for God, which here evokes the tremendous love and grace that flows from Christ in the Blessed Sacrament.

> The priest says the prayer of oblation: O Sovereign Lord, Christ Jesus the Word, who are equal in power with the Father and the Holy Spirit; the great high priest, the bread that

came down from heaven and saved our souls from ruin, who gave Yourself, a spotless Lamb, for the life of the world. . . . We pray and beseech You, O Lord, in Your mercy, to let Your presence rest upon this bread and these chalices on the all-holy table, while angels, archangels, and Your holy priests stand around and minister for Your glory, and the renewal of souls, through grace, mercy, and love of Your only-begotten Son, through whom and with whom be glory and power to You.

We offer this rational and bloodless sacrifice, which all nations, from the rising to the setting of the sun, from the north and the south, present to You, O Lord; for great is Your name among all people, and in all places are incense, sacrifice, and oblation offered to Your holy name.

We pray and beseech You, O Lover of Men, O good Lord, remember in Your good mercy the Holy and only Catholic and Apostolic Church throughout the whole world, and all Your people, and all the sheep of this fold. Safeguard the hearts of all the peace of heaven, but grant us also the peace of this life.

Liturgy of St. Mark (Alexandria)

FEBRUARY 24

In the following passage, St. Gregory of Nyssa (c. 335–395) comments on a verse from the Song of Songs: "Eat, my friends, and drink, and become inebriated, my brothers" (Song 5:1). Characteristic of the Church Fathers, St. Gregory interprets this Old Testament text in relation to Christ and His mysteries, here discerning the Eucharistic overtones of the passage. In this way, St. Paul's admonition, "Do not be drunk with wine, wherein is luxury, but be filled with the Holy Spirit" (Eph 5:18), is not without relevance. For the reception of the Eucharist produces a kind of ecstasy (literally, "outside oneself") for the communicant.

When the Word said these things to the bride, He placed the mysteries of the Gospel before the neighbors with these words, "Eat, my friends, and drink, and be inebriated, my brothers" [Song 5:1]. For the one who understands the mystical meaning of the Gospel, there is no difference between the expression used here and that of the initiation of the Mysteries for the disciples. For the Word says the same thing in both places: "Take and eat" [see Song 5:1; Mt 26:26]. The invitation to inebriation, which the Word made to His brothers, appears to many to contain more than the Gospel does. But if anyone diligently searches this out, these words will be found to agree with those of the Gospel. What He first commended to His friends in words is what He later accomplished through actions. For inebriation customarily produces an ecstasy of the mind once it has been induced by wine. Therefore, what is first advocated by the Word later came about by the divine food and drink. This inebriation always takes place as a transformation from worse to better and introduces an ecstasy that enters through food and drink.

St. Gregory of Nyssa (c. 335–395)

FEBRUARY 25

Memorial of St. Serapion of Egypt

St. Serapion (c. 300–362) was the fourth-century bishop of Thmuis who compiled of a book of prayers for liturgical use. The following prayer is taken from the anaphora, the Eucharistic prayer in which the elements are changed into the body and blood of Christ. Composed in a high liturgical style, it richly expresses the praise and thanksgiving that lies at the heart of the Mass. Its words reveal a rich Trinitarian theology wherein man praises God the Father, through the Son, by virtue of the indwelling of the Holy Spirit.

It is worthy and right to praise, laud, and glorify You, un-begotten Father of the only begotten Son, Jesus Christ. We praise you, O uncreated God, beyond words, indescribable, uncomprehended in every created being. We praise You who are known by Your only begotten Son. You are announced, ex-plained, and known by Him in created nature. We praise You who knows the Son and reveals His glories to the saints. You are known by the begotten Word and are seen and explained to the saints. We praise You, invisible Father, liberal giver of immortality.

You are the fount of life and the fount of light, the fount of all grace and truth, O lover of man and of the poor. It is You who are reconciled to all as You draw all to Yourself through the sojourner of Your beloved Son. We beg You to make us living men. Give us the Spirit of light that we may know you, the True One, and Jesus Christ whom You sent [see John 17:3]. Grant us the Holy Spirit, that we may be able to tell and pro-claim Your unutterable mysteries. Let the Lord Jesus speak in us and the Holy Spirit laud You through us.

St. Serapion of Egypt (c. 300–362)

FEBRUARY 26

St. John Chrysostom (349–407), that golden-mouthed preacher of the fifth century, speaks of the awesome power of the Eucharistic litur-gy, comparing it to the dramatic descent of fire upon Mt. Carmel (1 Kgs 18:38). The following passage highlights the wonders of the Old Covenant and their still more wonderful fulfillment in the New. Here, imagery of fire serves as a metaphor for the power and holiness of God, which either wounds the soul set against God or inflames the faithful soul with love.

Picture with me Elijah, a great throng standing about the

sacrifice laid upon the stones, and the rest of the people in profound silence; only the prophet praying. Then, suddenly a flame descends from heaven upon the sacrificial animal; these amazing wonders being full of dread. Now, move from the past and to the present sacrifice. Not only is it marvelous to behold, but it surpasses awe. For the priest stands, not to bring down fire, but the Holy Spirit. And the priest makes lengthy supplication, not so that a torch may descend from above and consume the gifts laid out, but so that the grace coming upon the sacrifice may illuminate all souls, making them to shine forth more brightly than silver refined by fire. Who could despise this awe-inspiring mystery, except by madness or lunacy? Or do you not know that a human soul would not even be able to bear the fire of that sacrifice, but all would be utterly destroyed, if it were not for the great help from the grace of God?

St. John Chrysostom, Bishop and Doctor (349–407)

FEBRUARY 27

Memorial of St. Gregory of Narek, Doctor of the Church

St. Gregory of Narek (c. 951–1010) was the son of a well-known commentator on liturgical prayer, Bishop Chosrov of Andzevatsentz. He composed many poems, elegies, and homilies, which hold a central place in the Armenian Christian culture. In the following prayer, St. Gregory asks to be made worthy to receive the most holy body and blood of Christ. This prayer was eventually embedded into the prothesis of the Armenian liturgy wherein the Eucharistic elements are prepared.

As one Person of the Trinity is being offered and another accepts the offering, being well-pleased in us through the reconciling blood of His firstborn Son, receive our supplications and make us an honored place of dwelling, with every preparation for partaking of the Heavenly Lamb. And prepare us to receive this manna of life and new salvation, which grants immortality, without the punishment of damnation. Let all of our offenses be consumed by this fire as the prophet's were so consumed by the burning coal brought by tongs. Thus in all Your mercy, You may be proclaimed as the Father's loving-kindness, manifest through the Son who brought the prodigal son into the inheritance of his father and directed harlots into the heavenly kingdom, the bliss of the righteous. O yes, yes: I too am one of them. Receive me along with them as one in need of great mercy. And save me by Your grace as one purchased by the Blood of Christ.

St. Gregory of Narek, Doctor of the Church
(c. 951–1010)

FEBRUARY 28

At the request of Pope Urban IV, St. Thomas Aquinas (1225–1274) composed the liturgical sequence *Lauda Sion* for the Feast of Corpus Christi. Thomas combines a wealth of scriptural themes in praise of the Eucharist, variously intimating its heavenly, sacrificial, and sustaining nature. Below, a shortened form of this sequence is given, commonly titled *Ecce panem angelorum*. In only a few verses, Thomas references the sacrifice of Isaac, the Good Shepherd, and the Syrophoenician woman, offering a kaleidoscopic view of the Eucharist.

Behold, the Bread of Angels!
Food for earthly pilgrims.
Truly, the bread of sons,
to dogs, forbidden.

Prefigured by Isaac
in his willing immolation.
The Paschal lamb, consecrated;
the manna of the Fathers, given.

Good Shepherd and True Bread,
Jesus, our very Mercy:
You feed us, You defend us,
and You tenderly pasture us
in the land of the living.

You who are all-knowing and all-powerful,
You who nourish and sustain us,
grant that we may be seated
as inheritors, made holy.
Amen. Alleluia.

St. Thomas Aquinas, Doctor of the Church
(1225–1274)

FEBRUARY 29

St. Clement of Alexandria (c. 150–215) was an early theologian who headed the catechetical school at Alexandria, an emerging center of Christianity in Egypt. He applied the fruits of philosophy to the faith, but lacked the precision and organization of later theologians. Several passages of his writings clearly affirm the Real Presence of Christ in the Eucharist, and in the selection below, St. Clement suggests that as Christ's human body was sustained by the Word, so too is man sustained by the Eucharist.

The blood of the Lord is twofold. There is His blood of flesh by which we are redeemed from corruption, and there is the spiritual body with which we have been anointed. And to drink the blood of Jesus is to partake of the Lord's incorruption. The Spirit is the power of the Word, just as blood is of the flesh. Just as wine is mingled with water, so the Spirit is with men. The one mixture nourishes faith, while the other, the Spirit, leads to incorruption. The mixture of both, the drink and the Word, is called the Eucharist. It is lauded as grace and beauty, and those who partake by faith are sanctified in body and soul. By the Father's will, the divine mixture mystically mingles men with the Spirit and the Word. Indeed, as the Spirit truly dwelt in the soul sustained by Him, so also the flesh is sustained by the Word, for which reason the Word became flesh.

St. Clement of Alexandria (c. 150–215)

MARCH

MARCH I

Fr. Lorenzo Scupoli (1530–1610) was a Theatine priest and the author of the classic text, *The Spiritual Combat*. He was unjustly accused of breaking the rule of his order—an accusation he was not cleared of until late in life. Using this humiliation in service of his sanctification, Lorenzo accepted this trial and bore it with patient suffering. In this excerpt from his writings, Lorenzo meditates on the tremendous power of the Eucharist to drive away evil. For there is no greater weapon against the enemy than the sacramental presence of Christ Himself.

> Thus far, I have endeavored to furnish you with four types of spiritual weapons and to teach you how to employ them. It now remains to lay before you the great assistance you may draw from the Most Holy Eucharist to subdue the enemies of your perfection and salvation. As this august Sacrament surpasses all the rest in dignity and efficacy, it is also the most terrible of all weapons to the infernal powers. The four we have already treated have no force but through the merits of Jesus Christ and the grace He has acquired for us with His Precious Blood, but this contains Jesus Christ Himself: His Body, Blood, Soul, and Divinity. The former are bestowed upon us by God so that with them we can subdue our enemies through Jesus Christ, but this is given us that we may

fight against them with Him; because, by eating His Body and drinking His Blood, we may dwell with Him, and He in us.

. . . After communion, we should remain in profound recollection, adoring our Lord with great humility and saying in our hearts: You see, O God of my soul, my wretched propensity to sin. You see how this passion domineers over me, and that of myself I cannot resist it. It is You who must fight my battles, and if I have any share in the combat, it is from You alone that I must hope for victory. Then addressing ourselves to the Eternal Father, let us offer Him this Beloved Son, now bestowed upon and dwelling within us. Let us offer Him in thanksgiving for so many benefits received and in order to obtain complete victory over ourselves through His assistance. Let us form a resolution of fighting courageously against that particular enemy from whom we suffer most. And we may expect to conquer, since God will sooner or later crown our endeavors with success, if we are not lacking on our part.

Lorenzo Scupoli (1530–1610)

MARCH 2

St. Justin Martyr (c. 100–165), the illustrious second-century apologist, here describes a catechumen's entry into the Church. He explains that after being cleansed by the Sacrament of Baptism, the new Christian is admitted to the Sacred Banquet. St. Justin's description of the Eucharistic liturgy notably recounts the same parts of Mass celebrated today: the prayers of the faithful precede the Eucharistic rite, wherein the kiss of peace is exchanged, the bread and wine are consecrated, and the congregation responds with the great "Amen."

After the adherent and believer has washed [i.e., baptism], we lead him to those called brothers [Christians]. Once they have all gathered in common, they fervently pray for themselves, the now-enlightened one, and for everyone in every place. We do this so as to be found worthy of being thought good citizens through our works and as guardians of the commandments, having learned the truth. And this is so that we can be saved with an everlasting salvation. After we finish our prayers, we greet one another with a kiss. Then, bread and a cup of water and mixed wine are brought to the presider over the brethren. After receiving these, he offers up praise and glory to the Father of all through the name of the Son and the Holy Spirit. And he renders thanks [Eucharist] on behalf of those who have been counted worthy by him. When he has completed the prayers and thanksgiving, all the people present respond by saying, "Amen," which in Hebrew means, "let it be so." When the leader has finished the Eucharist, and the people have responded, those who are called deacons give part of the Eucharistic bread and wine mixed with water to each one present. They also carry it to those not present.

St. Justin Martyr (c. 100–165)

MARCH 3

Jacopo da Todi (c. 1230–1306) was a Franciscan Friar whose eccentric behavior as a "fool for Christ" earned him the derisive nickname, Jacopone. He is credited with composing the "Stabat Mater Dolorosa," and is popularly called "blessed" in the Order of Friars Minor, though he has not yet received recognition from the Universal Church. Echoing St. Thomas Aquinas, Jacopone here describes the senses' failure to perceive Christ in the Eucharist and the power of faith to illumine the intellect.

With these my bodily eyes,
the Sacrament, I see, divine.
Manifest by the priest, and seen
as Bread from of our altar shrine.
But by the mystic light of faith,
other vision that is mine,
The eye of the mind beholds it
shine,
My mind, whose power is reasoning.

And if you ask, "How can this be?"
Would, by reason, you see and show?
And would you force the Power divine
in reason's narrow gate to go?
He, for His pleasure, made the heavens
unquestioned, yet your questions flow,
the secret of this Act to know,
though quick be its transforming.

Four of my senses thus speak to me:
"This that you see is simple bread."
Yes, all but hearing are deceived,
deprived of their sensibility.
For behold! beneath these visible
forms
stands Christ, hid deep in humility.
And to the soul, O mystery dread!
He gives Himself for nourishing.

Come, with the staff of faith, approach
the mystery senses fail to see;
Come to this Holy Sacrament.
In confidence and certainty;
For Christ, who hides Himself therein,
His sweet goodwill bestows on thee,
and binds you to this mystery,
this grace that He is offering.

Jacopone da Todi (c. 1230–1306)

MARCH 4

St. Paulinus of Nola (c. 354–431) was the bishop of Nola who learned
the poetic craft from the famous author, Ausonius. In the following
letter, Paulinus expresses the unity of the martyrs' sacrifice with that
of Christ. It is for this reason that the Church has ever honored Christian martyrs by placing their relics beneath the altar of sacrifice (see
Rev 6:9). The death of Christ on the cross is the pattern and reason for
the martyr's reciprocal act of love: the former provides the life-giving
power for the latter, and the latter conforms himself to the former.

Venerated altars cover the Divine Covenant

Martyrs placed with the holy cross
Every witness united to the saving Christ.
God Himself, the body and blood of the martyr's cross.
For God ever preserves His gifts for you;
And where Christ is, there also the Spirit and Father
Indeed, where the cross is, there too the martyr, since it is
    the cross of that martyr too.
For the saints of martyrdom, it is their devoted cause.
It is the food of life for mortals; it is the crown
that made them the servants for the Lord.

Flesh is fixed on the cross where I am fed, O blood of the
    cross
It flowed, giving life which I drink, hearts I wash.
O Christ, let these things unite your gifts to your Severus at
    once.
May he be carrier and witness to your cross.
Let him live from Your flesh, let Your blood provide a chalice
    for him.
Let him live and act in Your word.
And where your Martin ascends to his companion, Clerus
He sees, and let him be conveyed by Your gift.

St. Paulinus of Nola, Bishop (c. 354–431)

MARCH 5

Born in Bohemia, St. John Neumann (1811–1860) immigrated to the United States and became the fourth bishop of Philadelphia. He is responsible for initiating the first diocesan school system in America and for proposing perpetual "Forty Hours" devotions in Philadelphia. In the following passage from his journal, St. John writes exultantly of his ordination to the priesthood.

At last my dearest Jesus, I have attained that which my soul has for so long sighed! Ah, behold Your own work! O God, I am amazed at the grandeur of this grace, at my own high dignity and its responsibility! O Jesus, You have conferred upon me the power of offering You, my God, to Yourself—my God to my God! O far too high a privilege for me! Angels of God and you saints of heaven, descend upon earth and adore my Jesus, for the stammerings of my poor heart are only imperfect echoes of what our Holy Church bids me say! O grace of the Holy Spirit, how I glory in exalting You today! How I glory in being able to thank You, my Creator, my Redeemer, for Your three great gifts: Creation, Redemption, and our Holy Church! O joy above all earthly joys, I am a member, a servant of that same Holy Church! I pray You, grant me and all the living and dead the forgiveness of sanctification. Now I can efficaciously pray for myself, my parents and relations, my dear friend N., and for all in Bohemia who have recommended themselves to my prayers.

In a letter to Fr. Dichtl, St. John recounts the 1853 synod in Philadelphia and his proposal to institute a form of perpetual adoration.

Last month, I assembled all the priests of my diocese and gave them the spiritual exercises. Then followed a synod.... These synods are especially needed in the United States in order to secure uniformity in the performance of clerical functions. ... Besides several statutes enacted upon various points of discipline, it was also proposed to introduce into the larger churches of the diocese the devotion of the Forty Hours so that there might be no week in the year in which the Blessed Sacrament would not be exposed for the adoration of the faithful.

St. John Neumann (1811–1860)
[Memorial, January 5; Bohemian feast, March 5]

MARCH 6

Memorial of St. Colette of Corbie

Born in Corbie, France, St. Colette (1381–1447) entered several religious houses before ultimately joining the Franciscan order. After her entry, St. Colette set about a reform of the order, emphasizing strict poverty and ascetic practice. In this excerpt from a letter to her religious daughters, St. Colette prescribes a host of spiritual weapons for fighting daily temptations. Far from introducing novel practices, she guides her sisters on the sure path of the sacraments, prayer, and ordinary means of sanctification.

As for the perilous temptations of your household enemy: you are to oppose them with chastity, continual prayer, fasting, vigilance, cold and bare feet, mortification of the senses, silence, the chapter, correction, tears, sighs, religious discipline, the Divine Office, Holy Scripture, the Holy Sacrifice of the Mass, reception of the Precious Body of our Lord Jesus Christ, the word of God, remembrance of death, the noble guard of your good angel, thought of the reward of the elect, and the punishments of the damned. So, cast far from you your own will, and the inclinations of your corrupt nature, which would lead to your eternal loss. But let yourself be guided by the impulse of right reason, which will lead you to all that is advantageous for your eternal salvation.

St. Colette of Corbie (1381–1447)

MARCH 7

Memorial of St. Siméon-François Berneux, Martyr

St. Siméon-François Berneux (1814–1866) was a French missionary to Asia who was arrested and sentenced to death in Vietnam. His Vietnamese captors, nevertheless, released him, allowing for St. Siméon to spread the gospel in South Korea. After years of evangelization, he was ultimately captured again and executed in Seoul. In this excerpt from one of his letters, St. Siméon recommends regular Eucharistic devotion, praising its benefits. His personal witness demonstrates the intimate friendship born of devotion to the Blessed Sacrament.

> Do not omit a single day to make a visit to the Blessed Sacrament, if only for five minutes. Acquire the habit at any cost. In time, you will discover the benefit of it. Frequent Communion seems to frighten you. Why? It is true that if we considered only our own miserable sins and weaknesses, we should never dare approach the holy table. But after we have made the best preparation we can, we must throw ourselves on the goodness and mercy of God and believe that He will supply what is wanting in us. I only wish I could tell you, dear child, all the consolation that I find in Holy Communion, especially during this last month when a time of greater quiet has enabled me to receive it several times a week.

> *St. Siméon-François Berneux, Martyr (1814–1866)*

MARCH 8

Memorial of St. Julian of Toledo

St. Julian (642–690) was the archbishop of Toledo who here poses a series of questions and answers about difficult passages in Scripture. He addresses a seeming contradiction in John 6, which contains several different senses of the word "flesh." While this word is sometimes used to describe an earthly mind frame (i.e., in an analogous sense: "thinking as flesh"), at other times it is used to reference the true Body of Christ; namely, the Eucharist. Though St. Julian does not address the interpretative difficulties in full, he rightly underscores the central issue: Christ does not retract the Bread of Life discourse in John 6:63; rather, He invokes an idiom indicative of the analogous use of the word "flesh." For St. Julian, Christ's words in John 6:63 caution men from the pride of an earthly mind frame.

Why did Christ say, *"The flesh profits nothing"* [John 6:63], contrary to His saying, *"He who does not eat my flesh or drink my blood does not have life in him"* [John 6:53]?

The flesh surely profits nothing without the life-giving spirit, just as knowledge without charity puffs up, rather than builds up. It is likely of this that the Apostle says, *"flesh and blood will not inherit the Kingdom of God"* [1 Cor 15:50].

Now, surely, what Christ had already said, *"He who does not eat my flesh and drink my blood does not have life in him,"* is preferably understood as the eating of the Sacrament of His flesh, and the drinking of His blood. For, it is the means whereby we abide in Him, and He in us.

St. Julian of Toledo (642–690)

MARCH 9

Memorial of St. Catherine of Bologna

In her early religious life, St. Catherine of Bologna (1413–1463) was beset by temptations against the faith. Her perseverance in this trial was met with supernatural assistance from God, who enlightened her and set her at peace. In this passage from her treatise, *The Seven Spiritual Weapons*, she offers comfort to those who struggle with doubts concerning the Blessed Sacrament. Writing in the third person, St. Catherine recounts her own triumph over doubts and counsels those similarly tormented to receive the Eucharist.

Hence, one morning when she was spending time in this present church standing in prayer, God visited her mind and spoke to her intellectually. He gave her clear knowledge that the entire divinity and humanity of him who is our God is truly in the host which the priest consecrates. He went on to show how in what manner it was possible that under these small appearances of bread were present God and man in their entirety. And in brief, he gave her knowledge of everything that bothered her regarding faith in this sacrament and put an end to the struggle and doubt that she had undergone and could have undergone in the future, convincing her completely with beautiful and natural examples. And beyond this, he showed her how a person who receives communion without a taste of devotion is not deprived of receiving the grace of this sacrament, although she has a strict conscience, even if her spirit is tempted in faith or about some other contradiction, but she does not consent. He showed her also that the merit of the soul who receives communion in the midst of such a battle, bearing with patience the spiritual storm, is greater than is the merit of one who receives communion with much sweetness and gentleness.

St. Catherine of Bologna (1413–1463)

MARCH 10

Memorial of St. John Ogilvie, Martyr

St. John Ogilvie (1579–1615) was raised Calvinist at a time when the Catholic faith was illegal in Scotland. Despite this prohibition, he entered the Catholic Church and joined the Society of Jesus. After he was ordained to the priesthood, St. John returned to Scotland to offer the sacraments, but was captured, imprisoned, and tortured. The following exchange, transcribed by John himself, is a reminder of the grave duties of conscience that supersede all unjust laws and conventions that oppose God's command.

They say: Are you unwilling to obey the king?

R. All things that are due the king, I will render him.

They say: The king forbids Mass and yet you will celebrate them.

R. Whether Christ or the king is "rather to be obeyed, you judge." The king forbids them, but Christ has ordained it in Luke 22, and commands Mass to be celebrated, as I will prove, if you wish. And if the king condemns that which Christ has instituted, how will he escape being called a persecutor?

St. John also remarks on the nature of ordination as it relates to the Apostolic faith.

Andrew Knox, the Bishop of the Isles, said that he could celebrate Mass as well as I. I asked if he was a priest, and he replied in the negative. Then, I replied, you are not a bishop, nor can you say Mass. He says, if you will forsake human inventions and follow the religion preached by the Apostles and professed by them, you will be well taken care of. . . .

I said: Your religion is not yet ten years old. For when I was a boy, you held as an article of faith that there was no head of the Church, and that no one ought to be called so, except Christ alone. And now, all swear and believe that the king is the head of the Church in his lands. And you yourself formerly swore and believed the contrary. This is not Apostolic doctrine.

St. John Ogilvie (1579–1615)

MARCH 11

In this passage from *The Imitation of Christ*, Thomas á Kempis (1380–1471) offers practical advice for those who are troubled by doubts. He distinguishes faithful inquiry into the truth from skeptical analysis, approving the former and condemning the latter. Thomas recommends dismissing all doubts from one's mind and tacitly echoes the famous maxim of the Fathers: Credo ut intelligam—I believe so that I might understand.

You must guard against curious and useless scrutiny of this most profound Sacrament if you do not seek to be plunged into profound doubt. He who searches too closely into its majesty shall be overcome by its glory. God can work more than man can fathom. Pious and humble inquiry into the truth is allowable, ever maintaining a docile spirit, and ever seeking to walk in the security of the fathers' judgments. O Blessed Simplicity that abandons the way of difficult investigations, and proceeds on the plain and secure path of God's commandments! Many have destroyed devotion while they would scrutinize things above them. It is faith that is required of you and sincerity of life, not the heights of understanding nor the depths of the mysteries of God. If you do not understand nor comprehend those things that are below you, how will you understand those things that are above you? Submit to God, and humble your understanding to your faith, and the light of knowledge will be given to you inasmuch as it is profitable and necessary.

Some are gravely tempted in regards to faith in this Sacrament, but this is not to be imputed to them, but rather to the enemy. Do not attend to, nor dispute with, these thoughts. Neither should you answer doubts suggested by the devil. Rather, believe the words of God, believe the saints and prophets, and the enemy will flee from you.

Thomas á Kempis (1380–1471)

MARCH 12

Memorial of St. Symeon the New Theologian

Born into a wealthy family, St. Symeon (949–1022) received an exemplary education before entering the monastic life. The title "theologian" is only applied to three individuals in the East: John the Apostle, Gregory Nanzianzus, and Symeon. In this context, the appellation indicates a man who speaks from personal intimacy with God, not academic scholarship. Here, Symeon teaches that the Body of Christ received in Holy Communion is the same that was born of the Virgin Mary, highlighting the intrinsic connection between the Incarnation and the Eucharist.

On the one hand, the grace of the Spirit, or rather, the fire of Divinity, is from the nature and being of our Savior and God but his body is not from that. Rather, it comes from the all-pure and holy flesh of the God-Bearer [Theotokos] and from her completely immaculate blood which by assuming he made his own, as the holy saying asserts, "The Word [Logos] was made flesh" [John 1:14]. In this way, the Son of God and the Immaculate Virgin shares grace with the saints out of the nature and being of his co-eternal Father, as was said, of the Spirit. That is his Divinity as said by the prophet, "It will come to pass in the last days that I will pour out from my Spirit on all flesh" (Joel 2:28). This clearly means the flesh believed which he assumed from the nature and being of her who truly and really gave him birth. And as we have all received from his fullness [John 1:16], so we all receive what He assumed from the spotless flesh of his all-holy Mother.

The ineffable eternal things said to Paul in Paradise are the good things that "eye has not seen, nor ear heard, nor which have entered into the human heart" (1 Cor 2:9). These things are not up in the lofty heights, not limited by place, nor hidden in the depths, nor held in the far corners of the earth or sea. No, they are right in front of you, right in front of your eyes in fact. What sort of things are these things that are stored away with the good things of heaven? The very body and blood of our Lord Jesus Christ, things which we see and eat and drink every day. These things are surely those good things. You will not be able to find one thing apart from the things mentioned, even if you scan all creation.

St. Symeon the New Theologian (949–1022)

MARCH 13

St. Gaudentius' (d. 410) holiness of life was of such renown that the citizens of Brescia insisted he be appointed bishop. Agreeing with the sentiments of the laity, the surrounding bishops recalled Gaudentius from his pilgrimage to the Holy Land and ordained him to the episcopacy. In the following excerpt from his commentary on Exodus, St. Gaudentius beautifully describes the renewal of Christ's Passion at Holy Mass, touching on the themes of sacrifice, sanctification, and unity. His kaleidoscopic view of the liturgy offers a glimpse into its spiritual riches, encouraging the laity to "taste and see that the Lord is good" (Ps 34:8).

He wanted His benefits to remain with us and for souls redeemed by His precious blood to ever be sanctified through the image of His own Passion. And so He commanded those faithful disciples whom He had appointed as the first priests of His Church to unceasingly conduct these Mysteries of Eternal Life. All priests throughout the whole world should celebrate them in every church until Christ returns from heaven. For, this is where the priests and the faithful have a daily exemplar of Christ's Passion before their very eyes, holding it in their hands and receiving it with their mouths and hearts. Let us hold this indelible memorial of our redemption and pursue this sweet medicine of eternal protection against the poison of the devil, as the Holy Spirit encourages us, "Taste and see that the Lord is sweet" (Psalm 34:8).

There is a twofold reason why He chose to offer the Sacrament of His body and blood in the form of bread and wine. First, that the spotless lamb of God might be delivered over as a pure offering, celebrated on behalf of a purified people, without roasting and without blood . . . so that it might be readily and easily offered for all. Also, since bread is taken from many grains of wheat and is made by water and fire, so it is quite reasonably taken as a figure of Christ's body. We know that this body was taken from the multitude of the human race to be made one body, made complete by the fire of the Holy Spirit.

St. Gaudentius of Brescia (d. 410)

MARCH 14

The ancient document of the Church known as the *Didache* (c. 100) contains instructions on the Eucharistic celebration. Its Eucharistic prayers are astonishingly similar to contemporary liturgical prayers, both in its content and cadence. In the following excerpt from this text, the Church offers thanksgiving for salvation and prays for unity, echoing the High Priestly Prayer of Jesus (John 17). Finally, the prayer asks the Lord to come (maranatha), recalling the voices of St. Paul (1 Cor 16:22) and St. John (Rev 22:20).

Celebrate the Eucharist in this way: We thank You, Holy Father, for Your holy name which You have made to dwell in our hearts and for the knowledge, faith, and immortality which You made known to us through Jesus, Your child. To You be glory forever.

You, Lord Almighty, have created all things for your name's sake. You have given food and drink to men for enjoyment that they may thank You. But You have graciously given us spiritual food and drink and eternal life through Your child. Above all, we thank You that You are mighty. To You be glory forever.

Remember, Lord, Your Church. Rescue it from every evil, make it perfect in Your love, and from the four winds gather it completely sanctified into Your kingdom, which You have prepared. Let grace come and this world pass away. Hosanna to the God of David! If anyone is holy, let him come. If anyone is not, let him repent. Maranatha! Amen.

The Didache (c. 100)

MARCH 15

Memorial of Bl. William Hart, Martyr

Bl. William Hart (1558–1583) was ordained to the priesthood during the persecution of the Catholic Church in England. He personally witnessed the capture of Bl. William Lacy and was himself martyred at twenty-five years of age. Here, William boldly writes to the Dean of York, questioning his rejection of the Catholic faith. William's questions highlight the authority upon which the doctrine of the Real Presence stands: the unanimous witness of the ancient Church in obedience to Christ.

> Sir: Since our religion is suppressed as false and accounted as erroneous, I beseech you for the love of Jesus to deign to answer this one question, either privately or publicly. If Purgatory, the invocation of Saints, prayers for the dead, the Real Presence, the Sacrifice of the Mass, justification by works, and the like, are errors, show when, in what way, and by what means they crept into the Church. Bring forth one Father or one historical or authentic testimony that informs us as to their origin. If they are errors, who wrote against them, or what really pious or erudite doctor contradicted them? If no one can be produced, what is there against all these things that belong to the approved truth, and not to any condemned error? This is the question, Reverend Sir, in which I so greatly desire to be satisfied, in order that the truth, which now lies hidden, may be made clear.
>
> *Bl. William Hart, Martyr (1558–1583)*

MARCH 16

St. John Chrysostom (349–407) here reflects on Christ's bodily sufferings and identifies His Sacred Humanity with the Eucharist. Alternating between the various meanings of "the body of Christ," St. John Chrysostom reminds his hearers that they receive nothing less than the same body that endured the Passion, was buried, and resurrected on the third day. Ending on a moral tone, he exhorts his congregation to benefit from this exalted means of sanctification and turn from the illusions of the world.

Since we are speaking of the Lord's body, let us recall it as it was crucified, nailed, and sacrificed. If you are the body of Christ, bear the cross, since He Himself bore it. Bear the spitting, bear the slaps, bear the nails. Such was His body. That body was without sin; for Scripture says, "he committed no sin, nor was guile found in his mouth" [1 Pet 2:22]. His hands were only for the benefit of others; they would do anything for those who asked. Nothing unfitting came out of His mouth: "You have a demon," He heard and answered nothing back.

Now, this discourse has to do with the body given for us. Ponder then in Communion, that as many of us as share the body and taste this blood, we share in that which is no different, nor divided, from that body. For, we taste of Him who is seated above, next to the incorruptible Power, where He is worshipped by the angels.

Alas! How many paths there are for our salvation! He made us His own body! He shared His own body with us; yet, none of these turn us away from evil. O the darkness! O the profound lack of feeling! He says, "Set your mind on the things above, where Christ is seated at the right hand of God" [Col 3:1]. Still, some are anxious for money; others are trapped by their passions.

St. John Chrysostom, Bishop and Doctor (349–407)

MARCH 17

Memorial of St. Patrick

St. Patrick (385–461), the much-beloved Patron Saint of Ireland, is celebrated for his conversion of the Celtic lands to Christianity. The following passage is drawn from an Irish saint of the following century, St. Columbanus (543–615), who founded numerous monasteries in Italy. Having inherited the faith of St. Patrick, St. Columbanus here speaks on the soul's unending hunger for Christ in the Eucharist. Even as the Eucharist is received, it can never be exhausted, for it is the glorified body of Christ, risen from the dead.

> Consider the source of the fountain; bread comes down to us from the same place, since the same one is the bread and the fountain, the only-begotten son, our God, Christ the Lord, for whom we should always hunger. We may even eat him out of love for him, and devour him out of desire, longing for him eagerly. Let us drink from him, as from a fountain, with an abundance of love. May we drink him with the fullness of desire, and may we take pleasure in his sweetness and savor.
>
> For the Lord is sweet and agreeable; rightly then let us eat and drink of him yet remain ever hungry and thirsty, since he is our food and drink, but can never be wholly eaten and consumed. Though he may be eaten, he is never consumed; one can drink of him and he is not diminished because our bread is eternal and our fountain is sweet and everlasting. Hence the prophet says: *You who thirst, go to the fountain.* He is the fountain for those who are thirsty but are never fully satisfied. Therefore he calls to himself the hungry whom he raised to a blessed condition elsewhere. They were never satisfied in drinking; the more they drank, the greater their thirst.
>
> *St. Columbanus (543–615)*

MARCH 18

Memorial of St. Cyril of Jerusalem, Bishop and Doctor

St. Cyril of Jerusalem (c. 313–386) delivered his *Catecheses*, an exalted series of catechetical lectures, prior to his elevation to the episcopal see of Jerusalem. In the following passage, St. Cyril differentiates the appearances of bread and wine from the reality of Christ's body and blood—a fundamental distinction operative in the doctrine of transubstantiation. That the Fathers of the Church understood well the dynamics of this mystery of faith is thus clear. Accordingly, St. Cyril cautions Christians to purify their hearts before receiving the living God.

> Do not consider the bread and wine as bare elements; for, according to the Lord's declaration, they are the Body and Blood of Christ. Even though your senses may suggest otherwise, let instead your faith establish you. Do not judge the matter from taste, but be fully assured by faith, without doubt, that the Body and Blood of Christ have been presented to you.
>
> Having learned these things, and been fully assured that the seeming bread is not bread—though it may seem so by taste—but the Body of Christ; and that the seeming wine is not wine—though it may seem so by taste—but the Blood of Christ; and of this David sang: And bread strengthens man's heart to make his face shine with oil [Ps 104:15]. Then, strengthen your heart by spiritually partaking, and make the face of your soul to shine. And so having [this Mystery] unveiled with a pure conscience, may you reflect as a mirror the glory of the Lord [2 Cor 3:18] and proceed from glory to glory in Christ Jesus our Lord, to whom be honor, might, and glory, forever and ever. Amen.
>
> *St. Cyril of Jerusalem, Bishop and Doctor (c. 313–386)*

MARCH 19

Solemnity of St. Joseph, Spouse of the Blessed Virgin Mary

On the Solemnity of St. Joseph, the Church honors that most august spouse of the Blessed Virgin Mary and foster father of Jesus, St. Joseph. As Mary and Joseph were wholly dedicated to Jesus while He was on earth, St. Peter Eymard (1811–1868) teaches that Christians must likewise be devoted to Christ in the Eucharist. In this meditation on the Holy Family, St. Peter urges his hearers to find happiness, as St. Joseph did, in a life centered on Christ.

> Let us meditate upon the life of the Holy Family, the life of Mary and Joseph in Jesus. Jesus was the center of Mary and Joseph's love. Where the body is, there shall the eagles be. Where the treasure is, there is the heart. To possess Jesus was the sole joy of those happy parents. They held neither to Bethlehem, nor to Nazareth, nor to Egypt. To possess Jesus was their all. He was the home of their heart. After a forced absence, how quickly did St. Joseph return, with what eagerness and joy, to the house in which was the Divine Child! He lost no time far from Him, for he knew that Jesus was Divine Love incarnate.
>
> My house, my family, my center is the Eucharist, the tabernacle near which I dwell. Like Mary and Joseph, I ought to be happy only there.
>
> Jesus was the end of Mary's and Joseph's life. They lived only for Him; they labored only for Him. O how gladly did St. Joseph labor to gain for Him and His divine mother their daily bread! With what satisfaction he brought home the small returns of his work! And when it had cost him a little more fatigue, how sweet that fatigue was to Him, since it was all for Jesus!
>
> And so should Jesus in the Eucharist be the object of my life,

the joy of my life, the joy and happiness of my labor. And what life more beautiful than that passed in the companionship of Jesus in the Most Blessed Sacrament?

St. Peter Julian Eymard (1811–1868)

MARCH 20

Josefa Menendez (1890–1923) was a Spanish mystic whose writings overflow with tender expressions of Jesus' merciful love. In this excerpt, Christ speaks to Josefa on the sentiments of His heart during the Institution of the Eucharist, providing insight into the personal nature of His gift. Because Christ's divine knowledge permitted Him to gaze upon all things at once, it allowed Him to be mindful of all persons during the consecration of the Host.

The hour of Redemption was at hand. My Heart could no longer restrain its love for mankind nor bear the thought of leaving them orphans. So to prove My tender love for them, and in order to remain always with them till time has ceased to be, I resolved to become their food, their support, their life, their all. Could I but make known to all souls the loving sentiments with which My Heart overflowed at my Last Supper when I instituted the Sacrament of the Holy Eucharist. . . . My glance ranged across the ages and I saw the multitudes who would receive My Body and Blood and all the good It would effect. . . . how many hearts I saw that from Its contact would bud forth virginity! . . . and how many others that It would awaken to deeds of charity and zeal! . . . How many martyrs of love did I see. . . . How many souls who had been enfeebled by sin and the violence of passion would come back to their allegiance and recover their spiritual energy by partaking of this Bread of the strong! . . . Who can describe the overwhelming emotions that filled My soul? Joy, love, tenderness . . . but alas, bitter sorrow also. . . .

Servant of God Josefa Menendez (1890–1923)

MARCH 21

In the following reading, St. Augustine (354–430) explains the manner in which the great feasts of the Church are said to be real. The commemoration of historical realities, like Christ's Resurrection from the dead, forms a likeness with the event itself. Therefore, the grace of past events may be applied in the present. In a surpassing way, the sacraments convey the reality they signify; for the Eucharist makes present the same sacrifice that was offered upon the cross of Calvary.

> As Easter approaches, we often say that the Passion of the Lord will be tomorrow or the day after, even though he suffered many years before, and once only. On the Lord's Day, we say that "the Lord is risen today," though many years have passed since the Resurrection. Who is so ridiculous to argue that we are lying by speaking this way? For we proclaim a similitude between the day that these events happened and this present day as the former gave rise to the annual celebration of the sacrament. It is real, even though the event took place not on this day, but a long time ago. Was not Christ sacrificed a long time ago and once only? Yet in the sacrament, not only is he sacrificed by the people during the solemnities of Easter, but every day. No one is lying at all if he responds by saying that Christ is sacrificed.

> *St. Augustine of Hippo, Bishop and Doctor (354–430)*

MARCH 22

Echoing the teachings of St. Paul (1 Cor 10:17), St. Ignatius of Antioch (c. 35–107) here explains the intrinsic link between Church unity and the Eucharist; the latter being the sign of the former. To ensure that they are a part of the Mystical Body of Christ, St. Ignatius teaches that all must partake of the Eucharist confected by the bishop. In this way, the faithful are gathered into the one body of Christ. To them who fracture this unity, following after schismatics, St. Ignatius warns of condemnation.

> Abstain from those evil vines that Jesus Christ does not cultivate, because they are not of the Father's planting. Not that I have found division among you, but rather discretion. As many as belong to God and to Jesus Christ, these are with the bishop. Let those who have repented come to the unity of the Church. These persons belong to God that they may live in accord with Jesus Christ. Do not be deceived, my brothers! If someone follows a schismatic, he will not inherit the kingdom of God. If someone walks in a strange mindset, he has no part in the Passion. So be diligent to have but one Eucharist, for there is only one flesh of our Lord Jesus Christ and one cup for unity in His blood. There is one altar as there is one bishop together with his presbyters and deacons, my fellow servants. This is so that whatever you do, you may do in accordance with God.
>
> *St. Ignatius of Antioch (c. 35–107)*

MARCH 23

St. Thomas Aquinas (1225–1274) composed the hymn *Sacris solemniis* for the Feast of Corpus Christi, of which the final two stanzas form *Panis angelicus*. These exclamatory verses highlight the marvelous condescension of God who gives what is heavenly to those on earth. Like so many great hymns, *Panis angelicus* ends with a Trinitarian doxology, beseeching God's provident guidance.

Panis Angelicus	Lo! The Bread of Angels
fit panis hominum;	becomes the bread of men;
Dat panis coelicus	the Bread of Heaven given,
Figuris terminum:	ending all figures:
O res mirabilis!	O marvelous gift!
Manducat Dominum	That the poor, servile, and
Pauper, servus, et humilis	humble
	now feast upon the Lord.

Te trina Deitas	To You, Triune God
unaque poscimus,	we beseech You
Sic nos tu visita	to visit us thereby
sicut te colimus.	as we worship You.
Per tuas semitas	On Your narrow way,
duc nos quo tendimus,	guide us who proceed
Ad lucem, quam inhabitas.	to that light where You dwell
Amen.	therein.
	Amen.

St. Thomas Aquinas, Doctor of the Church (1225–1274)

MARCH 24

Memorial of St. Óscar Romero

St. Óscar Romero (1917–1980) served as the archbishop of San Salvador until his death in 1980, when he was fatally shot while celebrating Holy Mass. While many priests first viewed Óscar as a bookish man who would not make waves in the civil strife plaguing the country, his devotion to the Eucharist impelled him to seek peace on behalf of warring factions. Such efforts won him the hatred of both camps, resulting in his death. His words remain a sublime reminder that the Eucharist allows man to look back to Calvary, while gazing forward to the eschatological hope of its fulfillment in heaven.

The eucharist makes us look back to Calvary twenty centuries ago and beyond that to Moses and the old covenant, an incomparable horizon of history. But it also looks ahead to the future, to the eternal, eschatological, and definitive horizon that presents itself as a demanding ideal to all political systems, to all social struggles, to all those concerned for the earth. The church does not ignore the earth, but in the eucharist it says to all who work on earth: look beyond. Each time the Victim is lifted up at Mass, Christ's call is heard: "Until we drink it anew in my Father's kingdom." And the people reply: "Come, Lord Jesus." There is a hope. They are a people that march to encounter the Lord. Death is not the end. Death is the opening of eternity's portal. That is why I say: all the blood, all the dead, all the mysteries of iniquity and sin, all the tortures, all those dungeons of our security forces, where unfortunately many persons slowly die, do not mean they are lost forever.

St. Óscar Romero (1917–1980)

MARCH 25

Solemnity of the Annunciation

St. Maria Faustina Kowalska (1905–1938) was a religious sister in the Congregation of the Sisters of Our Lady of Mercy in Poland where she received the message of Divine Mercy. In the following passage, St. Faustina reflects on the reception of Holy Communion as it relates to the Incarnation. Just as Jesus dwelt bodily within the Blessed Virgin Mary, so too does He enter the sanctuary of the heart in Holy Communion. To prepare for this sublime favor, St. Faustina invokes the assistance of the Immaculate Virgin so that her soul might be made worthy to receive so great a King.

Today, I felt the nearness of my mother, my heavenly mother, although before every Communion I earnestly ask the Mother of God to help me prepare my soul for the coming of her Son, and I clearly feel her protection over me. I entreat her to be so gracious as to enkindle in me the fire of God's love, such as burned in her own pure heart at the time of the Incarnation of the Word.

O Sacred Host, fountain of divine sweetness,
You give strength to my soul;
O You are the Omnipotent One, who took flesh of
the Virgin,
You come to my heart in secret,
Beyond reach of the groping senses.

St. Maria Faustina Kowalska (1905–1938)

MARCH 26

During the High Medieval Period, England was home to many anchoresses who led solitary lives in cells adjoined to churches. There, these religious souls were able to pray and counsel those seeking spiritual direction. The *Ancrene Riwle* (c. 1225) was written by one such anchoress to provide instructions on the eremitic way of life. In this passage, the author stresses the power of the Eucharist to overcome all evil.

Wherefore, my dear sisters, hold yourselves invariably and always upright in true faith. Firmly believe that all the devil's power melts away through the grace of the Holy Sacrament, which you see elevated above all, as often as the priest says Mass and consecrates that Virgin's child, Jesus, the Son of God. There, Jesus sometimes descends bodily to your inn, and humbly takes His lodging within you. God knows that she who does not fight bravely with the aid of such a guest is overly-weak and evil-hearted. You ought truly believe all that the holy Church reads and sings, and that all her sacraments give spiritual strength, but none so much as this. For the Holy

Sacrament brings to naught all the wiles of the devil; not only his forceful and violent assaults, but his powerful stratagems, his cunning sorceries, and all his deceits. . . . In temptations of this kind, there is none so wise and guarded who is not sometimes deceived, unless God defends him. But this sublime Sacrament, with steadfast faith, more than anything else, unmasks his artifices and breaks his strongholds. Truly, dear sisters, when you perceive the devil near you, while you have steadfast faith, you will only laugh him to scorn, because he is such an old fool, who comes to increase his own punishment, and plait a crown for you.

Ancrene Riwle (c. 1225)

MARCH 27

Pope Leo XIII (1810–1903) is remembered for his widespread renewal of Thomistic thought as well as his engagement with the modern world. While grave political circumstances caused his predecessor to shrink from dialogue, Leo XIII attempted to address contemporary concerns, applying the teachings of the faith to new cultural situations. In this excerpt from *Mirae Caritatis*, his encyclical on the Eucharist, Pope Leo XIII teaches that the divisions plaguing society cannot be remedied by human effort alone. Rather, the divine gift of the Eucharist stands as the supernatural means of unifying all of mankind.

Furthermore, if anyone will diligently examine the causes of the evils of our day, he will find that they arise from this: that as charity towards God has grown cold, the mutual charity of men among themselves has likewise cooled. Men have forgotten that they are children of God and brethren in Jesus Christ; they care for nothing except their own individual interests; the interests and the rights of others they not only make light of but often attack and invade. Hence frequent disturbances and strifes between class and class: arrogance, oppression, fraud on the part of the more powerful: misery, envy, and turbulence among the poor. These are evils for which it is in vain to seek a remedy in legislation, in threats of penalties to be incurred, or in any other device of merely human prudence. Our chief care and endeavor ought to be, according to the admonitions which we have more than once given at considerable length, to secure the union of classes in a mutual interchange of dutiful services, a union which, having its origin in God, shall issue in deeds that reflect the true spirit of Jesus Christ and a genuine charity.

This charity Christ brought into the world; with it He would have all hearts on fire. For it alone is capable of affording to soul and body alike, even in this life, a foretaste of blessedness, since it restrains man's inordinate self-love, and puts a check on avarice, which "is the root of all evil" (1 Tim. 6:10). And whereas it is right to uphold all the claims of justice as between the various classes of society, nevertheless it is only with the efficacious aid of charity, which tempers justice, that the "equality" which St. Paul commended (2 Cor. 8:14), and which is so salutary for human society, can be established and maintained. This then is what Christ intended when he instituted this Venerable Sacrament, namely, by awakening charity towards God to promote mutual charity among men.

Pope Leo XIII (1810–1903)

MARCH 28

Cassiodorus (c. 490–583) was a Roman statesman who served as both governor and councilor to the king. After completing his political career, Cassiodorus founded a monastery on his estate, modeled after the newly established Monte Cassino. In his *Commentary on the Psalter*, he reflects on the allegorical meaning of the Exodus as it is recounted in

Psalm 78. Here, Cassiodorus considers the miraculous manna and its Eucharistic meaning.

"He commanded the clouds above, and opened the doors of heaven" [Ps 78:23]. At the beginning, the Psalmist testified that these words are said in "parables" and "dark sayings" [Ps 78:1–2]. So, although these sayings are historical facts, they should nevertheless be referred to the Lord and Savior. Thus, the preceding saying suits us well, which says, "he commanded the clouds," which is to say, preachers, in order that the glorious proclamation may announce the arrival of the Lord's salvation "through the doors of heaven"—in other words—through the Sacred Scriptures. And this manna is truly consumed when it is tasted through worshipful Communion.

"And he rained down upon them manna to eat, and gave them bread from heaven" [Ps 78:24]. The meaning of this verse depends on what preceded. For he had first said, "he opened the doors of heaven" [Ps 78:23] and then, "he rained down manna for them to eat" [Ps 78:24]. He uses the words "it rained" to show an excess of food, which fell from heaven like rain. And so as not to doubt what rain it was, it specifies, "manna to eat." How should "manna" be interpreted? We fittingly understand it as Holy Communion; for inasmuch as that food is desired with reverence, the gifts of the Lord's body are revealed. He adds, "he gave them the bread of heaven." What other bread of heaven is this than Christ the Lord?

Cassiodorus (c. 490–583)

MARCH 29

St. Andrew of Crete (c. 660–740) was a bishop and theologian remembered for his vast contributions to Greek hymnody. In the following extract from his work, St. Andrew contemplates the Passover events of Holy Thursday and the Institution of the Eucharist. Highlighting an unusual theme, he likens the preparation of the Upper Room to the preparation of the heart for Holy Communion. St. Andrew further teaches that Christ Himself prepares His own heart as an "upper room of devotion."

An upper room received You, O Creator, and Your intimate friends, and there You fulfilled the Passover. There, You brought forth Your Mysteries into being. For there, two disciples had arranged things and prepared the Passover for You.

Jesus, who knew all things, told the apostles in advance, "go to a certain man." Blessed is he who faithfully welcomes the Lord into his house. You have indeed prepared Your heart as an upper room of devotion for supper.

As You ate with Your disciples, Master, You mystically showed Your holy death, through which we who honor Your solemn sufferings were ransomed from corruption. You who wrote the law on tablets of stone at Sinai, fulfilled the command of the law.

The children of Israel ate the shadowy Passover of old, but now the true Passover and living sacrifice has come.

St. Andrew of Crete (c. 660–740)

MARCH 30

St. Irenaeus of Lyons (c. 130–202) remains a valuable witness to the faith of the early Church as he personally heard the preaching of St. Polycarp, who had sat at the feet of St. John the Apostle. This living tradition is expressed in the following passage, wherein St. Irenaeus affirms the doctrine of the Eucharist. Here, he repels the error of dualism by appealing to the Eucharist, noting that the goodness of the human body is evidenced by the goodness of the Eucharist itself.

Again, how can they say that flesh corrupts and is incapable of receiving life when it is flesh nourished by the body and blood of the Lord? Let them either change their view or abstain from offering the things commanded. Our view is consistent with the Eucharist and the Eucharist again confirms our view. For we offer to Him the things that are His, consistently teaching the communion and unity of flesh and spirit and professing a resurrection of flesh and spirit. For once the bread that comes from the earth receives the invocation of God, it is no longer ordinary bread, but the Eucharist. Thus, it consists of two things: one earthly and another heavenly. So also your bodies: once they receive the Eucharist, they are now incorruptible because they possess the hope of the resurrection.

St. Irenaeus of Lyons (c. 130–202)

MARCH 31

Theodore of Mopsuestia (350–428) was ordained to the priesthood in Antioch before his appointment to the episcopacy in Asia Minor. Though he was considered orthodox during his lifetime, he was later condemned for his Christological views, which were similar to those of Nestorius. In his *Catechetical Homilies*, Theodore marvels at the awesome nature of the Divine Liturgy, which is nothing less than the union of heaven and earth. It is, therefore, only right that those in attendance approach with humility, wonder, and profound devotion.

We all stand in reverential fear, bowing our heads as if unable to look upon the magnificence of this service. And echoing the words of the invisible hosts of heaven, we manifest the greatness of the grace that has been so unexpectedly poured out upon us. Because of the dignity of that which is taking place, we do not cast this awe from our minds, but preserve it throughout the service. And we bow our heads before and after reciting the *Sanctus* in full voice, rightly expressing such fear.

In all this, the priest associates himself with the invisible hosts, praying and glorifying the Godhead. He rightly remains in fear like all the others, and more so than the others, since it is he who performs this awesome service.

Theodore of Mopsuestia (350–428)

APRIL

APRIL I

St. Cyprian (c. 210–258), the third-century bishop of Carthage, here explains how Christ fulfills the figure of Melchizedek, the priest and king to whom Abraham paid tithes. He further shows how Christ fulfills the figure of the bread and wine offered by Melchizedek. Together, these two types communicate Christ's dual role as both priest and victim. And the sacrificial priesthood of Christ continues to be exercised through the priests of the Catholic Church, who offer the Eucharist in the very person of Christ.

In Melchizedek the priest, we see the mystery of our Lord's sacrifice prefigured, as Holy Scripture testifies, saying *"And Melchizedek, king of Salem, brought out bread and wine"* [Gen 14:18]. He was *"the priest of the most High God,"* and *"blessed Abraham"* [Gen 14:19]. And the Holy Spirit declares in the Psalms that Melchizedek bore a type of Christ as the Father says to the Son, *"Before the daystar I have begotten you. You are priest forever after the order of Melchizedek"* [Ps 110:4]. From the sacrifice of Melchizedek, the priest of the Most High God who offered bread and wine and blessed Abraham, this priestly order descends and is here present. For who is more a priest of the Most High than our Lord Jesus Christ? For he offered to God the Father the same that Melchizedek had; bread and wine, namely, his body and blood. . . . In Genesis, that the blessing of Abraham by Melchizedek might be fittingly celebrated, the type of Christ's sacrifice—namely, bread and wine—precedes its fulfillment, which the Lord accomplished. For, He who is the truth offered bread and the cup mixed with wine, fulfilling the truth of the prefigured image.

St. Cyprian of Carthage (c. 210–258)

APRIL 2

Richard Rolle (1305–1349) was an English mystic who abandoned an academic career in favor of the eremitic life. Although Richard's works achieved great popularity during the Middle Ages, his cause for canonization was never completed. The following excerpt is from one of his most popular works, *The Prick of Conscience*, which sings of the Church's teachings on the sacraments. In a felicitous rhyming scheme, Richard explains that the sacraments remain efficacious apart from the personal sanctity of the priest.

Also a priest, although he be
sinful and out-of-charity,
He is God's minister and Holy Church's,
that the sacrament of the altar works.
He is nevertheless of might,
although the priest's life not right.
For if a priest that sings mass
be ever so full of wickedness,
the Sacrament that is so holy,
may not impaired be through his folly.
Then may mass souls from pain bring,
although a sinful priest it sing.
For in God's name he sings the mass,
under whom in order he is.
But special prayers with good intent,
that is made beside the sacrament.
Of a good priest are well better

than of ill, and to God sweeter;
But the offering of God's body
helps the souls principally;
wherefore it seems that mass singing
may most quick the soul out of pain bring.

Richard Rolle of Hampole (1305–1349)

APRIL 3

In the following passage from *On the Orthodox Faith*, St. John Dam-ascene (c. 675–749) reflects upon Christ's recapitulation of mankind and relates this truth to the Blessed Sacrament. While the sons of Adam inherit his curse and corruption, the sons of God inherit the blessing and incorruption of Christ, the New Adam. As newborns require nour-ishment to grow, those born anew through baptism need "new food" to mature. The Eucharist is this spiritual food that nourishes the soul and brings man in union with Christ, the new head of mankind.

Not only should the first fruits of our nature partake in a higher good, but every man who so desires. And such will undergo a second birth and be fed with a new food so as to become fit to attain the measure of perfection. Through His birth, that is, the Incarnation, Baptism, Passion, Death and Resurrection, Christ delivered our mortal nature from the sin of our first parent. So too did He deliver us from death and corruption. He became the first-fruit of the resurrection and set Himself as the way, the model, and the example so that fol-lowing in his steps, we may become by adoption what He is by nature: sons and heirs of God and coheirs with Him. As it was said, He gave us a second birth so that we who were born of Adam, and became like him inheriting the curse and corrup-tion, may now share in Christ when born of Him, becoming heirs to His incorruptibility, blessing, and glory.

St. John Damascene, Doctor of the Church (c. 675–749)

APRIL 4

St. Isidore of Seville (560–636) was among the most learned scholars of his age whose writings establish an early synthesis of Western thought. In his encyclopedic work, *Etymologies*, St. Isidore treats the Holy Sacrifice of the Mass, discussing the various names given to the Eucharist. This brief excerpt underscores the exalted nature of these names and the reality they indicate.

> The sacrifice is named after the manner of a sacred deed; for by a mysterious prayer it is consecrated for our sake in memorial of the Passion of the Lord, whence, by His command, we affirm it to be the Body and Blood of Christ. The sacrifice is of the fruits of the earth until it is sanctified by the invisible Spirit of God and made the Sacrament. And the Greeks call the bread and chalice of this Sacrament the *Eucharist*, which is translated in Latin, *bona gratia* [good grace, or favor]. And what greater good is there than the Body and Blood of Christ?
>
> *St. Isidore of Seville, Bishop and Doctor (560–636)*

APRIL 5

Memorial of St. Vincent Ferrer

St. Vincent Ferrer (1350–1419) was a Dominican priest and renowned preacher who lived during a period of Eucharistic controversy. At that time, it was customary for the priest alone to consume the Precious Blood in order to avoid profanation. This caused dissent from those who believed they were not receiving the fullness of Christ in the Eucharist. St. Vincent Ferrer dispels this notion by showing that it is a simple logical error. In a living body, one cannot possibly have the body without the blood, or the blood without the body. Thus, Christ is present whole, entire, and living in each species.

Among the simple-minded, there are some who say: "O, these priests are deceiving us! giving us the Body of Christ in Communion, but not giving the Blood," even as they consume the whole Christ! Let it be said that this question comes from ignorance. For in the consecrated Host is the fullness of the Blood, just as in the Chalice is the living Body of Christ. The Body lives not without the Blood, so the Blood resides truly therein. Therefore, he who consumes the Body also consumes the Blood, and thus the consecrated Host is both food and drink. Otherwise, eating would be ruin and destruction; but Christ says, "Amen, Amen I say to you: If you do not eat the flesh of the Son of Man and drink His blood you do not have life in you. He who eats my flesh and drinks my blood has everlasting life" [John 6:54–55].

St. Vincent Ferrer (1350–1419)

APRIL 6

Memorial of St. Juliana of Liège

Following the tragic loss of both her parents, St. Juliana of Liège (c. 1192–1258) was placed in a Norbertine house at the age of five. Upon maturity, she professed religious vows in a Norbertine canonry and was later elected prioress. In the following excerpt from a letter, St. Juliana describes the vision that inspired the Feast of Corpus Christi—a feast she successfully promoted in the city of Liège. When her vision was related to Pope Urban IV in 1264, the feast was made universal.

For a long time I have been oppressed with a very heavy burden, and though for years I have made great efforts to shake it off, it has not been possible for me to do so. I have never yet made this public, but as it is now necessary to do so, I have taken the opportunity of confiding it first to you.

Twenty years ago, the globe of the moon, shining with great luster, was presented to my gaze. This spectacle struck me with awe. I then noticed that there was one dark spot that took away from the perfection of its beauty. At first I was troubled by this vision because I feared some deception on the part of the malignant spirit, and so I endeavored to banish it from my mind altogether. Yet, whatever efforts I made, the vision was continually presented to my view and followed me everywhere. I consulted enlightened persons and they counseled me to banish it from my mind. This, however, was impossible, and so I prayed to be enlightened upon the subject. At length, God graciously heard me and made me understand that the globe of the moon represented the Church of Jesus Christ, and the one dark spot that hindered the perfection of its beauty signified that one feast was wanting. And this Feast was one in honor of the Sacrament of the Altar, which God had determined should be instituted, and had chosen me to solicit its institution: I who am only a vile slave and incapable of succeeding in so important an affair.

St. Juliana of Liège (c. 1192–1258)

APRIL 7

Memorial of St. Jean-Baptiste de La Salle

St. Jean-Baptiste de La Salle (1651–1719) was a priest who worked to reform Catholic education, founding the first "normal school"—a college specifically for the formation of teachers. His instructions for teachers include daily works of piety, such as the recitation of the Rosary and adoration of the Blessed Sacrament. In the following prayer, St. Jean-Baptiste reflects on the abundant benefits of visiting the Blessed Sacrament.

I have only to approach you, Divine Jesus, present in the Most Holy Sacrament of the Altar, who are ever here as on a throne to receive our praise and adoration, for you to fill me with every kind of grace. In any state I find myself— whether in dryness, sorrow, or temptation—I have only to come before you to find relief from my troubles and help in my difficulties so that I may overcome all obstacles and do what is right. You are always ready to come to my aid. You give me refuge when I am distressed. When I am weak, it is you who animates me to do what is right. And when I find myself lukewarm, I have only to call upon you who are a God of love, and who has a tender love toward us in your Divine Sacrament, and you are able to pierce me through, filling me with what is lovable and loving in you, and inspiring me with ardent Charity for you and others. Here, I may become united with you, O My Jesus, present in the Blessed Sacrament to be a victim for my sins, since in this Sacrament you continually offer the merits of your Passion and death to the Eternal Father as a satisfaction for my transgressions.

St. Jean-Baptiste de La Salle (1651–1719)

APRIL 8

Pope Innocent III (1160–1216) reigned at the height of papal power, uniting all of Christendom under his spiritual leadership. In the following excerpt from *On the Holy Mystery of the Altar*, he reflects on the words of St. Paul: "He has no need, like those high priests, to offer sacrifices daily . . . he did this once for all when he offered up himself" (Heb 7:27). Innocent III thus affirms the surpassing dignity of the New Covenant and its once-for-all character, contrasting it with the sacrificial laws of the Old Covenant.

He took the bread: It is written that Melchizedek was the first to celebrate the sacrificial ritual *offering bread and wine; for he was a priest of the Most High God* [Gen 14:18]. Accordingly, David said of Christ: *You are a priest forever, accord-*

ing to the order of Melchizedek [Ps 110:4]. The sacrifice of
the Gospel, therefore, surpasses the law not only in dignity, but also in its once-for-all character, which the Apostle
clearly describes in his Epistle to the Hebrews [Heb 7:27].
Christ thus instituted bread and wine for a sacrifice of His
body and blood. In the same way that bread strengthens the
human heart above that of other food and drink, and wine
gladdens the heart, so too the body and blood of Christ restores and satiates the interior man above all other spiritual
food and drink. Therefore the Psalmist says, "Your cup overflows" [Psalm 23:5]. Full and complete refreshment consists
in these two as Christ testifies, "My flesh is true food and my
blood is true drink" [John 6:55].

But bread should possess the nature of a grain, and wine
should contain the essence of the vine. Christ compared Himself to such grain when He said: "Unless a grain of wheat falls
to the earth and dies, it remains alone" [John 12:24]. And of
the vine, He says: "I am the true vine" [John 15:1]. Yet, it is
not a cluster of grapes, nor the grain of wheat that is properly offered; rather, it is wine that is pressed, and bread that
is ground. For although Christ compares Himself to grain,
He gives Himself as Bread. When Christ took the bread and
chalice in His holy and venerable hands, and the priest, after the pattern of Christ, takes the bread and chalice in his
hands, both are blessed by the sign of the cross. And though
the priest blesses a multiplicity of offerings, he receives in his
hands the once-for-all sacrifice, because all such offerings are
converted into the one Body of Christ.

Pope Innocent III (1160–1216)

APRIL 9

Meister Eckhart (c. 1260–1328) was a Dominican theologian and mystic who fell under suspicions of heresy, partially due to his less-than-systematic use of language. Pope John XXII condemned seventeen of his propositions as heretical and censured still others as rash. Modern Dominicans have attempted to rehabilitate Meister Eckhart as he was never personally condemned. In this brief excerpt, Meister offers invaluable practical advice. When experiencing dryness of spirit, one should not refrain from the Eucharist out of fear, but should hasten to receive it as the remedy.

> The more frequently you receive the Holy Eucharist, the better and more salutary it is for you. . . . Now you would object, saying that you are devoid of all feeling, indolent, and dare not thus approach your Lord. The greater need you have to receive your God. For He will sanctify you and unite Himself to you. For this Sacrament is the very source and font of grace.
>
> *Meister Eckhart (c. 1260–1328)*

APRIL 10

Local Memorial of St. Fulbert of Chartres

Though some have attempted to associate St. Fulbert of Chartres (c. 960–1029) with the heretical teachings of his student, Berengarius of Tours, it is clear that St. Fulbert strenuously professed and defended the orthodox faith. In this letter, St. Fulbert expresses a rich theology of the Eucharist and condemns excessive rationalism, for which he had a personal disdain. Rather than limiting God to the finite reasoning of man, he places his trust in the certainty of faith, which flows from the highest principle, God. The local memorial for St. Fulbert is celebrated in Chartres and Poitiers on April 10.

> Because our Savior was soon to take His Body from our sight in order to ascend to Heaven—the very Body He had once of-

fered as a ransom for us—He left us a saving pledge of His Body and Blood so that we might not be deprived of its protecting presence. And this was not the symbol of an empty mystery, but rather the true Body of Christ, formed by the Holy Spirit, and produced by a hidden power during the sacred solemnities under visible forms for the daily veneration of people.

Of this mystery, Christ said to those gathered close to Him on the eve of His Passion, "this is my body," and a little later, "this is my blood of the New Testament, which shall be shed for you," and elsewhere, "he who eats my flesh and drinks my blood abides in me and I in him." Animated by the authority of our truth-speaking Master, let us boldly confess while we communicate of His Body and Blood that we are, as it were, transfused into His Body and that He abides in us.

... If you believe that God can do all things, it follows that you believe this as well. And you will not curiously search with human reasoning, stopping to discuss whether God can take the very creation He has been powerful enough to make out of nothing and convert it into a substance of much nobler nature—into the substance of His own Body.

St. Fulbert of Chartres (c. 960–1029)

APRIL II

Memorial of St. Gemma Galgani

St. Gemma Galgani (1878–1903) was a laywoman and mystic who twice refused marriage, dedicating herself instead to a life of prayer and penance. Though her frail health prevented her entry into the Passionist order, she was blessed with extraordinary graces and received visions, locutions, and the stigmata. In the following letter, Gemma writes of a powerful experience during exposition of the Blessed Sacrament. While some might grow accustomed to the familiarity of the sacraments, Gemma keenly perceives the presence of God in the Holy Host and is overwhelmed by His loving gaze.

Jesus continues to make me taste much sweetness in prayer. Yes, Father, Jesus is Sweetness Itself and is poured out whole and entire in the Most Holy Sacrament. But how is it possible that so great a Majesty suffers to be in the presence of a most vile creature? How can this be? Does not the Divine Master see the ingratitude of my soul or my heart without devotion? Nevertheless, He supports and loves me. And if Jesus loves me as I am, how could I not love Him who is rich? Father, help me! If things go on in this way, I feel that I shall die! May I have the happiness of truly going to Paradise! May I at least hope for it! But all my sins! My God, my God, have mercy! Yesterday, when I approached Jesus exposed in the most Holy Sacrament of the altar, I felt I was burning with such force that I had to withdraw. I was burning everywhere; ardor rising toward my face. *Vive Jesus!* I am astounded, my Father, that so many stand before Jesus without being reduced to ashes.

St. Gemma Galgani (1878–1903)

APRIL 12

Adam of St. Victor (d. 1146) entered monastic life in his youth and became an outstanding author of hymns and sequences. Though these poetic texts flourished in the High Medieval Period, the Council of Trent removed nearly all such sequences from the Mass. In the following Easter sequence, Adam praises Christ's victory over death and prays for entrance into the wedding feast of the lamb. In this brief text, Adam movingly describes how participation in Christ's body and blood allows man to share in His Resurrection.

Mors et vita conflixere,	Death and life's long strife is ended!
Resurrexit Christus vere,	Christ hath risen indeed, attended
Et cum Christo surrexere	By a witness crowd, ascended
Multi testes glorise.	With Him, who His glory show.
Mane novum, mane Isetum	Morning new, morn joy now reaping!
Vespertinum tergat fletum:	Wipe away our eve of weeping
Quia vita vicit letum,	Life o'er death is triumph keeping,
Tempus est laetitiae.	This the time for gladness now!
Jesu victor, Jesu vita,	Jesu Victor, life bestowing!
Jesu vitse via trita,	Jesu, Way to true life going!
Cujus morte mors sopita,	Through Thy death, death now
Ad Paschalem nos invita	overthrowing!
Mensam cum fiducia.	At Thy Paschal feast o'erflowing
Vive panis, vivax unda,	Grant us in full trust a place!
Vera vitis et fecunda,	Bread of life and Water living!
Tu nos pasce, tu nos munda,	Plenteously the true Vine giving!
Ut a morte nos secunda	Feed us, cleanse us from sin's striving,
Tua salvet gratia. Amen.	That, at second death arriving,
	We escape it through Thy grace!
	Amen.

Adam of St. Victor (d. 1146)

APRIL 13

Ven. Mother Marie-Thérèse of the Heart of Jesus (Théodelinde Dubouché) (1809–1863) was the foundress of the Congregation of the Restorative Adoration in Paris, an order dedicated to adoration of the Blessed Sacrament for the reparation of sins. At a time when frequent reception of Communion was relatively uncommon, Mother Marie-Thérèse boldly taught the importance of Eucharistic living and emphasized the primacy of divine action in the spiritual life. Instead of relying on her own strength, she embraces Jesus' teaching: "Apart from me, you can do nothing" (John 15:5).

Frequent communion is the nourishment for your soul *par excellence*. Consume the Bread of Life as frequently as you are able, and may the fear of your frailty never stop you. When you are sluggish, you must be fortified. The blood of your Savior flowing through your veins will give you the required energy to endure the interior and exterior battles you have to endure. In Jesus alone is the living and pure water. Knowledge, reason, even virtue itself are only avenues which lead to the Source. But you must be plunged into the life of Jesus itself to be purified, and for your thirst to be quenched. This is why Jesus placed His life completely within our reach. He does not just figuratively say, "If anyone thirsts, let him come to me and drink" [John 7:38]; rather, one can truly approach and drink all His blood. And if my soul is filled with faith, it becomes inebriated with this divine drink. It itself becomes a river in which living water and grace flows. Jesus says, "Those who believe in me will have in their hearts rivers of living water" [John 7:38].

Ven. Mother Marie-Thérèse of the Heart of Jesus
(Théodelinde Dubouché) (1809–1863)

APRIL 14

St. Gregory of Nyssa's (c. 335–395) *Catechetical Oration* is one of the finest compositions of the Church Fathers for its clarity of expression and depth of thought. Here, Gregory explains the power of the Eucharistic Lord to transform man into Himself. Gregory speaks of the Eucharist as a medicinal remedy, seeing it as the answer to man's fallen condition. Through Baptism and the Eucharist, man is gathered under the headship of Christ, the New Adam, and may participate in the life of grace. As St. Gregory explains, this restoration from sin leads even unto deification.

As those who have taken poison through some treachery quell its destructive power with an antidote—and it is necessary for the remedy to be distributed throughout the organs of the entire body, just as the poison is—in the same way, we who have tasted of Adam's fall necessarily need to taste of the antidote in order to drive away the harmful presence of the poison. What then is this remedy? It is nothing other than that Body shown to be greater than death, and which makes a beginning of life for us.

For as the Apostle says, "a little leaven leavens the whole" [Gal 5:9], so too the body that has been made incorruptible by God. By coming wholly into our body, He transforms ours into His and gives us a share in it. For just as the admixture of a wholesome liquid with a poisonous one robs the entire drink of its deadly effect, so too does the immortal body of Christ transform everything into its own nature by coming into the one who receives. And nothing may enter the body except by being absorbed through eating and drinking, so stir yourself up to admit this life-producing power in the one way possible.

St. Gregory of Nyssa (c. 335–395)

APRIL 15

Inspired by the example of their founder, St. Francis of Assisi, the Franciscans have ever fostered devotion to both the Incarnation and the Passion of Christ. In this meditation, St. Bonaventure (1221–1274) teaches that the Eucharistic body of Christ is the same that was born of the Virgin Mary and underwent the torments of the Passion. In this way, St. Bonaventure urges his hearers to discern the gift of the Eucharist, recognizing that it is nothing other than Christ Himself.

"Do this in remembrance of me" [Luke 22:19]. This is that sweet and precious memorial which renders the soul most grateful and pleasing to God as often as it is worthily received.

The consideration of this most excellent gift should inflame our souls with love and wholly transform us into the Giver. For, what could He have given us more dear, more sweet, or more precious than Himself? He whom we receive in the sacrament is the Son of God, Christ Jesus, who took flesh and blood, was born of the Virgin Mary, suffered death upon the cross, rose on the third day, and ascended into heaven where He sits at the right hand of the Father. On the last day, He will come again to judge the living and the dead. For, He holds the power of death and life, and can punish or reward. He who is both God and Man is contained in the tiny host in the form of bread, which is daily offered to God the Father. He is our Lord Jesus Christ, the Son of the ever-living God.

St. Bonaventure, Bishop and Doctor (1221–1274)

APRIL 16

Memorial of St. Bernadette Soubirous

St. Bernadette Soubirous (1844–1879) was born to an impoverished family in the remote village of Lourdes, France, where she witnessed a series of apparitions of the Blessed Virgin Mary. These visitations gave heavenly affirmation of the dogma of the Immaculate Conception and opened up a font for pilgrims to cleanse themselves in devotion. Here, St. Bernadette writes to her younger cousins on the occasion of their first Holy Communion. She instructs them on how best to prepare, noting the connection between the reception of the Eucharist and union with God in eternity.

My dear little friends, this sweet day, the object of your desires, so rich in the happiness and holy joy you have heard spoken of so often, will soon arrive. This day will be beautiful, great and solemn. It will fill your young hearts with consolations. It will be a precious memory, since, for the first time, you will be given a place at the heavenly banquet, where you will be nourished with the Body of God. You will be washed and your thirst quenched in his Blood, intimately united with his divinity and blessed with the grace of his love.

Ask Jesus, our Savior, to come prepare a place for himself in your young hearts so there will be nothing to grieve him when he arrives. Think only of Jesus, since he is choosing to rest in your souls. Make his dwelling place like a sanctuary of innocence and peace.

O my dear children, we would have to have the hearts of angels to receive Our Lord as he deserves, so try to receive him with as much faith, humility, and love as you can. And when Our Lord is in your heart, trust Him completely and dwell in the delights of his presence. Love, worship, listen, praise. Oh, the happy moment! Eternity alone holds greater joys for us.

Take advantage of Our Lord's presence to ask for all kinds of graces, for yourselves, your parents, for all those who prepared you for this important act, for the Church, for our Holy Father the Pope, for the dear souls in Purgatory, for poor sinners.

St. Bernadette Soubirous (1844–1879)

APRIL 17

One of the dominant heresies of the second century was Gnostic Dualism, which set the body and soul against one another. According to Gnostic teaching, the body was an irredeemable evil, while the soul could be saved through secret knowledge (gnosis). In the following passage, St. Irenaeus (c. 130–202) responds to these errors by teaching that man is saved by Jesus Christ come in the flesh. Not only does Christ's assumption of a human body affirm its essential goodness, but Irenaeus argues that it is the means whereby man may participate in the resurrected life. By receiving Holy Communion, man may share in Christ's victory of death in both body and soul.

110

When the mingled cup and the bread receive the word of God and become the Eucharist, it is the body of Christ, upon which the substance of our flesh grows and subsists. How, then, can they say that the flesh cannot receive the gift of God, which is eternal life? For, this flesh is fed by the body and blood of the Lord and becomes His member. As blessed Paul says in his letter to the Ephesians, "we are members of his body, of his flesh and of his bones" [Eph 5:30]. He was not saying these things about some spiritual and invisible man, because a spirit has neither flesh nor bones. Rather, he spoke about the constitution of a true man, which consists of flesh, nerves, and bones. This constitution is nourished by the cup of His blood and likewise grows from the bread that is His body.

Just as the arched wood of the vine bears its fruit in due time, and the grain of the wheat falls into the ground, dissolves, and emerges by the Spirit of God who holds everything, and by the Wisdom of God is then used by men to make the Eucharist when it receives the Word of God; so too our bodies. The Eucharist is the body and blood of Christ, and when our bodies have been nourished by it, and have been buried in the ground and dissolved, they shall rise in their own time; the word of God giving them resurrection to the glory of our God and Father.

St. Irenaeus of Lyons (c. 130–202)

APRIL 18

After his conversion to the faith, St. Hilary of Poitiers (c. 310–367) lent all of his intellectual powers to the theological controversies of the fourth century. In the following passage, he warns Christians against rash interpretations of sacred doctrine and exhorts them to discern the true meaning of Scripture. Applying this nuanced view to the Bread of Life discourse, St. Hilary underscores its unmistakable meaning: Christ gives Himself to man so that man might be wholly united to Him.

When we speak of the things of God, our words should not be used in a merely human or worldly sense, nor should we employ impetuous or imprudent speech. One should expunge the perversity of foreign and impious interpretations from pure and heavenly sayings. Let us read what is written and understand what we read, and then fulfill the duties of a perfect faith.

Now, we would be speaking foolishly and impiously by claiming that Christ's nature dwells within us, unless we had learned it from Him. For He Himself said, "My flesh is truly food and my blood is truly drink. Whoever eats my flesh, and drinks my blood remains in me and I in him" [John 6:56]. He leaves no room for ambiguity regarding the truth of the flesh and blood. And once these things are accepted and received, they prove that we are in Christ, and that Christ is in us. And is this not the truth?

St. Hilary of Poitiers, Bishop and Doctor (c. 310–367)

APRIL 19

In the following sermon, St. Caesarius (c. 468–542) warns his flock against the sins of sloth and impiety. He admonishes the laity to remain present throughout the entirety of the Mass, shunning any worldly cares that might tear them from it. To those who do remain throughout the entirety of the liturgy, he warns to worship in spirit and truth, not harboring divided hearts and minds. In this way, he counsels Christians to diligently attend Mass with all due reverence.

When the greater part of the people—or rather the worse part, that is—leave the church after the readings, to whom will the priest say: "Lift up your hearts?" Or how can they respond to lift up their hearts when they descend into the streets with both body and soul? Or rather, it is just like their cry with trembling and joy, "Holy, Holy, Holy. Blessed is he who comes in the name of the Lord." Or when the Lord's Prayer is said, who humbly and truthfully prays, "forgive us our debts, as we forgive our debtors?" For even those who do remain in church pronounce the Lord's Prayer to their judgment, rather than for healing, if they do not forgive debtors their debts. For such persons do not fulfill it with their actions. And if they do not cease returning evil for evil, it is without justification that they say, "deliver us from evil."

If those within the church are exposed to danger, because they do not intend to fulfill what they promised, what do they think of themselves who are so immersed in insatiable desires and love of the world that they cannot stand in church for even one second?

St. Caesarius of Arles (c. 468–542)

APRIL 20

St. Augustine (354–430) was a successful rhetorician in Carthage and Milan before he came to embrace the Christian faith. His penetrating insights into the meaning of words is here applied to the term "sacrament." He explains that a sacrament is a sign, but not an empty symbol devoid of reality. Rather, a sacrament is a sign that contains the invisible reality it signifies. In this way, the sacrament of the "body of Christ" is indeed the Lord's true body.

For if the sacraments did not have a certain similitude to the things of which they are sacraments, they would not be sacraments at all. And the sacraments generally acquire their names from the realities they signify. Thus, in a certain manner, as the sacrament of the body of Christ is the body of Christ, and the sacrament of the blood of Christ is the blood of Christ, so the sacrament of faith is faith. Now, to believe is nothing else than having faith. When a child is said to believe who does not yet have capacity to exercise belief, he may rightly be said to have faith because of the sacrament of faith, and he is turned to God because it is the sacrament of conversion. Thus the Apostle says about baptism, "We are buried with Christ through baptism into his death" [Rom 6:4]. He does not say, "we signify a burial," but rather, "we are buried." Accordingly, he names the sacrament of such a great reality by a term of the same reality itself.

St. Augustine of Hippo, Bishop and Doctor (354–430)

APRIL 21

Memorial of St. Anselm of Canterbury
Doctor of the Church

Maintaining a high view of human reason, Catholic theologians of the Middle Ages sought to systematically treat the knowledge of mankind, recovering that which was lost by Adam's sin. St. Anselm (1033–1109) is considered the first of the scholastics and is noted for his integration of philosophical reasoning in his theological treatises. In the following meditation on Christ's life, St. Anselm summarizes the events of Holy Week, providing moral interpretations of each scene. Treating the Last Supper, he emphasizes Christ's sublime humility so that man might similarly approach the Sacrament of the Altar.

Jesus woke Lazarus from sleep while in Bethany—and Bethany may be translated as *"house of obedience"*—thereby showing that those who rest in the bosom of obedience with a good will, and a right desire to die to the world, shall be awakened by Him to everlasting life. Entrusting His Body and Blood to His disciples in the mystic supper, Jesus humbly washed their feet, teaching us that the dread ministries of the altar must be celebrated with purity of deed and pious humility of mind.

And before He was exalted in His glorious Resurrection, He endured the taunts and abuse of perfidious men, the shame of the Cross, the bitterness of gall, and at last death. In all this, Jesus admonished His own, teaching that those who desire everlasting glory should not only endure the toil and distress of the present life with equanimity, but also the oppressions of the wicked, loving all difficulties that this world can give for the sake of eternal rewards: Christians should, therefore, love them, court them, and thankfully embrace them.

St. Anselm of Canterbury (1033–1109)

APRIL 22

Hugh of St. Victor (1096–1141) rose to become one of the great scholars and lecturers as a Canon Regular of St. Augustine at the monastery school of St. Victor. This monastery was one of the institutions responsible for the establishment of the University of Paris, the second-oldest university in Europe. Like many medieval theologians, Hugh clearly saw theology as a preparation for contemplation and final beatitude, giving order and meaning to academic studies. In this passage from *On the Sacraments*, Hugh explains why the body and blood of Christ is veiled under the appearances of bread and wine.

The wisdom of God, which manifests itself through visible things, wanted to show that the nourishment of souls is food and he put forth his assumed flesh as edible food that he might invite us to taste Divinity through the food of that flesh. But since human weakness might shudder at the thought of touching and tasting flesh, he veiled it under the appearance of normal and basic food. He set it forth to be received that our senses might be strengthened in the appearances and faith be built up in the reality. Now we don't say that in the bread the body of Christ is consecrated such that the body of Christ receives from the bread its existence or that a new body has suddenly been made from a changed essence. Rather, we say that the essence has been changed into the true body itself. The substance of the bread and wine has not been reduced to nothing because it ceased to be what it was, but rather that it was changed because it began to be something which it was not.

Hugh of St. Victor (1096–1141)

APRIL 23

Peter Lombard (1096–1160) was the author of the preeminent medieval summary of theology, *The Four Books of Sentences*, which provided the groundwork for St. Thomas Aquinas' own *Summa Theologiae*. In the following passage, Peter makes note of the traditional ordering of the sacraments, explaining that Baptism and Confirmation lead to Holy Communion. He then provides an allegorical reading of the Exodus in the spirit of the Church Fathers, yet with the exactitude of the scholastics. In this way, Peter Lombard represents a unique link between the first and second millennium of Christianity.

After the sacraments of Baptism and Confirmation follows the sacrament of the Eucharist. Through Baptism we are cleansed, through the Eucharist we are made complete in what is good. Baptism extinguishes the fires of sin, the Eucharist restores us spiritually. Wherefore it is well called the Eucharist, that is, good grace, because in this sacrament there is not only an increase of virtue and grace, but He who is the fount and source of all grace is received entire.

There was a previous type of [the Eucharist], when God rained manna on the Fathers in the wilderness, and fed them with heavenly food; wherefore, "Man has eaten the bread of angels" (Ps 78:25). But those who ate that bread then died. But this is the living bread, which "came down from heaven"

[John 6:51] and gave life to the world. That manna was from heaven, this *above* heaven; that when reserved for another day became full of worms; this is free from all corruption; whoever has tasted it religiously shall not see corruption. That was given to the ancients after the crossing of the Red Sea, where the Hebrews were freed by the drowning of the Egyptians; so this heavenly manna ought only be given to those reborn. That bread for the body led the ancient people through the desert to the land of promise; this heavenly food sustains the faithful going through the desert of this world to heaven. Wherefore, it is rightly called the *viaticum* because it restores us on the way, and leads us into the fatherland.

Peter Lombard (1096–1160)

APRIL 24

Memorial of St. Mary Euphrasia Pelletier

St. Mary Euphrasia Pelletier (1796–1868) was the foundress of the Congregation of Our Lady of Charity of the Good Shepherd, a religious institute dedicated to the care of orphaned and impoverished girls. In her instructions to fellow religious sisters, St. Mary reveals a zeal for souls, grounded in a Eucharistic spirit of sacrifice. In this passage, she underscores the necessity of uniting oneself to Christ in the Blessed Sacrament in order to assist souls.

What are we doing in the world, and for what purpose are we here, if not to work for the salvation of our fellow men? Let us unite ourselves to our Lord in the Blessed Sacrament. There, He continually annihilates Himself, presenting Himself to the Eternal Father as a sacrifice in reparation for the insults offered to His Divine Majesty. He does this for the transgressions of those who wander from the right path and for those who shut their eyes to the wrath they are heaping up by their own iniquities. But Jesus loves these erring souls and continually shows His wounds to the Father; the wounds whereby He suffered Himself to be pierced for their salvation. These souls belong to him, and He has acquired the right to them by so many titles. He desires that all should be saved and should be united to Him for all eternity. Was it not to rescue and ransom them that He came down from Heaven? Behold and see how infinite is the Divine charity!

St. Mary Euphrasia Pelletier (1796–1868)

APRIL 25

Bl. Pauline von Mallinckrodt (1817–1881) was born in Prussia, where she founded the Congregation of the Sisters of Christian Charity. Vocations to the new order were so prolific that Bl. Pauline soon established houses in Brussels, the United States, and Chile. That the love of Christ motivated her prolific works is clear in her personal writings. Here, Bl. Pauline describes the Mass of her first religious vows. She expresses the profound exchange that occurred between Jesus and herself; namely, through holy vows and the reception of the Eucharist.

During the Litany, we lay prostrate before the altar, with face resting on the lowest step. What took place in my soul! I asked God to pour upon us the fullness of all that the bishop and priests sought in prayer. Tears of emotion and holy confidence came into my eyes—I do not remember exactly what I prayed, it came from the depth of my heart. . . .

Holy Mass continued up to Communion. O blessed hour! In the vows I had given myself to the Lord, to the Beloved of my soul, and in Holy Communion He gave Himself to me. Here, our covenant was sealed. O fullness of God's grace!—Lord, I thank You for all the graces which You have imparted to me during my whole life through the Most Blessed Sacrament. O Holy Mother of God, accept the spouse of your beloved Son as your daughter. On the day of my first Holy Communion, Mary was given to me as my protectress—Oh! She has cared well for me, but may she be my mother now more than ever. How happy did I consider myself in being espoused to Jesus—the happiest one of our family!

Bl. Pauline von Mallinckrodt (1817–1881)

[Memorial, April 30]

APRIL 26

Memorial of St. Paschasius Radbertus

St. Paschasius Radbertus (785–865) was the abbot of the Monastery of Corbie and the author of the first treatise exclusively dedicated to the Eucharist, *On the Body and Blood of the Lord*. In this work, he argues that the Eucharistic Body of Christ is the same that was born of the Virgin Mary, nailed upon the cross, and rose from the dead. Here, St. Paschasius stresses the incomprehensibility of this mystery, which surpasses the finite reason of man.

Tell me, what could be more lovable than this mystery of the Lord's body and blood? What could be more pleasing when grasped or sweeter when worthily received? When seen in all its splendor, what surpasses it in grace? My dear son, to glimpse the dignity of so great a mystery, let the few things in this present work be enough. The only thing necessary to know with certainty is that these things cannot be sufficiently explained by us. And this should not surprise us when the angelic powers, in their ethereal nature, are scarcely strong enough to penetrate the mysteries and can only admire and tremble in contemplation. If the nature of the blessed spirits, lacking the weight of their bodies, are hardly capable of examining these realities, how can man adequately or worthily speak of God?

Here we see: The Mortal from the Immortal, The Visible
from the Invisible,
The Mutable from the Immutable, The Craft from the
Craftsman,
The Creature from the Creator, The Product from its Maker,
The Miniscule from the Immense, The Temporal from the
Eternal,
The Lowly from the Most High, The Fashioned from the Dust
Created from Nothing.

His omnipotence is beyond all telling: by this He saved us
with His all-powerful mercy. In His omnipotence, He freely
created and filled the work of saving grace with all power. In
creation, Jesus Christ our Lord, the Only Begotten One, has
the power of creating and ruling His creature. In salvation, He
has the power of laying down and taking up His life for us.
It is He who with God the Father and the Holy Spirit lives,
is glorified, and reigns in perfect Trinity and Unity, the God-
Man for all ages. Amen.

St. Paschasius Radbertus (785–865)

APRIL 27

St. Marie of the Incarnation (1599–1672) was a French mystic who
was married and widowed by nineteen years of age. Her intimate en-
counters with Christ led her to join the Ursuline Order and to travel
to New France as a missionary. Her son also became a religious, with
whom she corresponded by letter. In the following excerpt from their
exchange, St. Marie contrasts the self-sacrifice of Jesus in the Eucharist with man's selfishness and infidelity. She further highlights a foun-
dational principle of metaphysics: God is existence itself, and man is
nothing apart from Him.

It is still an excess of our misery to have the Holy of Holies within us and to not have become holy the first time we touched or received Him. O my beloved son! that there is distance between Him and us, though He is in us, and united to us, after receiving the Most Blessed Sacrament! If in good faith we desired to follow our exemplary way of life, we would have become holy at our first communion. But what! Although we have moments of good dispositions that the Heavenly Spouse accepts, which the Church prescribes in order to worthily receive, and which yield the effects of sanctification; yet, we are so feeble and weak that we take back what we have already given Him. Our miserable self-love does not want to suffer annihilation as completely as the One who desires only those souls that resemble Him. Note this well: our self-love makes us slaves and reduces us to nothing. For, is it to be anything at all, to turn from the all and back to ourselves, who are pure nothingness? Do not search, therefore, for any other reason why we do not have holiness from our first communion.

St. Marie of the Incarnation (1599–1672)
[Memorial, April 30]

APRIL 28

Memorial of St. Louis-Marie Grignion de Montfort

Few have contributed to the field of Mariology, the study of the Blessed Virgin Mary, as St. Louis de Montfort (1673–1716). With a zealous love, St. Louis propagated devotion to Jesus through Mary, proposing a program for total consecration. His veneration for Mary was ever directed toward his adoration of Christ and he here provides instructions for a post-Communion thanksgiving. Emphasizing Mary's role as Mediatrix, he recommends praying to Jesus through Mary for the coming of the kingdom of God on earth.

After Holy Communion, while you are inwardly recollected and keeping your eyes closed, introduce Jesus into the heart of Mary. Give Him to His Mother, who will receive Him lovingly, will place Him honorably, will adore Him profoundly, will love Him perfectly, will embrace Him closely, and will render to Him, in spirit and truth, many homages which are unknown to us in our dense darkness. Or else, keep yourself profoundly humbled in heart, in the presence of Jesus residing in Mary. Or sit like a slave at the gate of a king's palace, where he is speaking with the queen; and while they talk one to the other without need of you, you will go in spirit to heaven and over all the earth, praying all creatures to thank, adore, and love Jesus and Mary in your place: *Venite, adoremus, venite.* Or else you shall ask of Jesus, in union with Mary, the coming of His kingdom on earth, through His holy Mother.

St. Louis-Marie Grignion de Montfort (1673–1716)

APRIL 29

Memorial of St. Catherine of Siena, Virgin and Doctor

St. Catherine of Siena (1347–1380) was a laywoman and mystic who held extensive conversations with Our Lord, recorded in *The Dialogue.* In this excerpt, St. Catherine is instructed by God on the nature of the Eucharist and the impossibility of separating the body, blood, soul, and divinity from one another. Here, Catherine is taught to believe that Christ is present, whole and entire, in each piece of the Eucharist. This teaching is central to a mature understanding of the Eucharist; for the host is not some fragment of the crucified Christ, but rather the living, resurrected, and glorified Christ, present in His entirety.

With whom have I entrusted the administration [of the Eucharist]? My ministers in the mystical body of the Holy Church so that you may have life, receiving His Body as food and His Blood as drink. I have said to you that this Body is, as it were, a Sun. And thus you cannot receive the Body without the Blood, or the Body and Blood without the Soul of the Incarnate Word, nor can you receive the Body and Soul without the Divinity of Me, the Eternal God. This is because none of these can be separated from each other. As I said to you earlier, the Divine Nature never left the human nature—neither in death, nor from any other cause. Consequently, you receive the whole Divine Nature in that most Sweet Sacrament, concealed under the whiteness of the bread. For as the sun cannot be divided into light, heat, and color, the whole of God and the whole of man cannot be separated under the white mantle of the host. Even if the host should be divided into a million particles (if it were possible), in each particle should I be present, whole God and whole Man. When you break a mirror, the reflection seen in it is not broken. In like manner, when the host is divided, God and man are not divided, but remain in each particle.

St. Catherine of Siena, Virgin and Doctor (1347–1380)

APRIL 30

Memorial of Pope St. Pius V

Pope St. Pius V (1504–1572) was a zealous defender of the faith, credited with enacting categorical reforms within the Vatican and Church. As the executor of the Council of Trent, Pius V commissioned a universal catechism in order to communicate the teachings of the faith to the laity. In this passage, the sacrificial nature of the Mass is emphasized against the novel teachings of Zwingli, Cranmer, and those who had rejected the faith.

We, therefore, confess that the sacrifice of the Mass is one and the same as the sacrifice of the cross. The victim is the one and the same, Christ Jesus, who once only offered himself in bloody sacrifice on the altar of the cross. The bloody and unbloody victim is still one and the same, and oblation of the cross is daily renewed in the Eucharistic sacrifice in obedience to our Lord's command: "Do this in remembrance of me." The Priest is also the same, Christ our Lord. The ministers who offer this sacrifice, consecrate the holy mysteries not on their own but in the person of Christ. The words of consecration show that the priest does not say: "This is the body of Christ," but rather, "This is my body." Thus invested with the character of Christ, he changes the substance of the bread and wine into the substance of his real body and blood. That the holy sacrifice of the Mass is, therefore, not only a sacrifice of praise and thanksgiving, or a commemoration of the sacrifice of the cross, but also a sacrifice of propitiation by which God is appeased and rendered propitious, the pastor will teach as a dogma defined by the unerring authority of a General Council of the Church. If, therefore, with pure hearts and a lively faith, and with a sincere sorrow for past transgressions, we immolate and offer in sacrifice this most holy victim, we shall doubtlessly receive from the Lord "mercy and grace in seasonable aid." So acceptable to God is the sweet odor of this sacrifice, that through its oblation he pardons our sins, bestowing on us the gifts of grace and of repentance. This is the solemn prayer of the Church. As often as the commemoration of this victim is celebrated, so often is the work of our salvation promoted. And through this unbloody sacrifice, plenteous fruits of that bloody victim flow in upon us.

The Catechism of the Council of Trent

MAY

MAY 1

Born Antonius, St. Antoninus (1389–1459) reigned as the Archbishop of Florence during a time of great tribulation on the Italian peninsula. His faithful care over his flock earned him the diminutive form of his name, Antoninus. The following prayer of unknown authorship has historically been paired with his work because of its Tuscan origin. Here, the many benefits of Holy Communion are emphasized, particularly its life-giving effects.

> I pray, Lord, that by this holy and living mystery of Your Body and Blood, which we in the Church Militant continually feed upon and are nourished, and by which we are cleansed and sanctified, and through which we have been made to participate of Your One and highest Deity, that You grant unto me Your holy virtues, so that with a right conscience I may receive this great Sacrament, which is indeed my very life and well-being.
>
> You, my Lord, said, "I am the living bread which came down from heaven; if anyone eats of this bread, he will live forever" [John 6:51]. O Holy Bread! Living Bread! Come into my heart, enter into my soul, and heal and sanctify me through and through. Thus fortified by You, I might arrive at Your triumphant Kingdom where I will see You not in mystery! Not

veiled like now, but face to face. Then You will be wholly in us, and will fulfill me with wonderful abundance so that I shall never hunger, nor thirst, throughout all eternity.

St. Antoninus of Florence (1389–1459)
[Memorial, May 2]

MAY 2

Memorial of St. Athanasius of Alexandria, Bishop and Doctor

St. Athanasius (c. 296–373) courageously defended the orthodox faith against Arianism, a widespread heresy that denied the divinity of Christ. For his faithful witness to the truth, Athanasius spent nearly twenty years in exile and became associated with the phrase, "Athanasius contra mundum;" that is, "Athanasius against the world." In the following letter, Athanasius illustrates Christ's fulfillment of the Passover Feast in the Holy Eucharist. Whereas the former was typological in nature, the latter is offered in deed and in truth. For this reason, he cautions his readers against returning to the Mosaic rites, thereby exchanging the resplendent reality at hand for a mere figure.

Israel of old fought for victory and came to the feast as in a figure; and these things were shadows and types. But for us, my beloved, the shadow has received its fulfilment and the types have been fulfilled. Therefore, we should no longer consider this feast normative, neither should we go to the Jerusalem below to sacrifice the Passover according to the unseasonable observance of the Jews; lest, while the season passes, we be regarded as acting unseasonably. Rather, in accordance with the command of the Apostles, let us go beyond the types and sing the new song of praise.

Perceiving this, and being assembled together with the Truth, the Apostles drew near and asked our Savior, "Where will You have us prepare the Passover?" [Matt 26:17] For these things that had belonged to the earthly Jerusalem were no longer to be done and neither was the feast to be celebrated there alone, but wherever God willed it to be. Now He wills it to be in every place so that "in every place incense and a sacrifice might be offered to Him" [cf. Mal 1:11]. For although, as in the historical account, the Feast of the Passover could only be observed in Jerusalem; yet when the things of that age were fulfilled, and those things that belonged to shadows had passed away, and the preaching of the Gospel was about to extend everywhere, when indeed the disciples were spreading the feast in all places, they asked the Savior, "Where will You have us prepare?" [Matt 26:17]. The Savior also, since He was exchanging the typical for the spiritual, promised them that they should no longer eat the flesh of a lamb, but His own, saying, "Take, eat and drink; this is My body, and My blood" [Matt 26:26, 28]. When we are thus nourished by these, my beloved, we also shall truly keep the feast of the Passover.

St. Athanasius of Alexandria, Bishop and Doctor
(c. 296–373)

MAY 3

The following prayer is taken from the Divine Liturgy of St. James, an ancient Eastern liturgy traditionally ascribed to the Apostle James. In preparation for the Eucharistic sacrifice, the priest quietly recites this prayer, acknowledging the enormity of the privilege entrusted to him. Making free use of Psalm 51, the priest confesses his own unworthiness and begs to be made fit for the sacrifice. This beautiful prayer serves as a reminder of God's condescension in calling fallen men to embrace the most precious body and blood of Jesus Christ.

O Master and Lord who has watched over us in mercy and

compassion, You have graciously given confidence to us who are humble sinners and Your unworthy servants to stand before Your holy altar and to offer this awesome and bloodless sacrifice for our sins and for the hidden errors of your people. Look on me, Your unprofitable servant, and in Your mercy, wipe away my transgressions. Cleanse my lips and heart from every defilement of flesh and spirit. Remove from me every base and useless thought and make me worthy for this liturgy by the power of your All-Holy Spirit. Receive me who approaches this holy altar because of Your goodness. Be pleased, O Lord, that these gifts which are brought to You through our hands be acceptable. Coming down to aid my weakness, do not turn Your face from me. Do not consider my unworthiness an abomination, but have mercy on me, O God, according to Your great mercy. In the abundance of Your mercies, turn aside from my transgressions, that coming before Your glory without condemnation I may be counted worthy of the protection of Your only-begotten Son, and of the illumination of your all-holy Spirit, and that I may not be counted a servant of sin. Rather, as Your servant, may I find grace, mercy, and forgiveness of sins in this life and in the age to come. Yes, Master, Almighty, All-powerful Lord: hear my prayer and graciously grant me amnesty from my evils. For you are the One who works out all things in all. On behalf of all, we seek help and assistance from You, Your only-begotten Son, and from Your good and life-giving and consubstantial Spirit, both now and forever and unto all ages. Amen.

The Divine Liturgy of St. James

MAY 4

Memorial of the Forty English Martyrs

St. Robert Southwell (1561–1595) was a Jesuit priest and poet, martyred under Queen Elizabeth I. Counted among the "Forty English Martyrs," St. Robert is memorialized with St. Edmund Campion and St. Margaret Clitherow. In the following excerpt of his poem, *On the Blessed Sacrament of the Altar*, St. Robert reflects on God's omnipotence in transforming bread and wine into the body and blood of Christ.

The God of hosts in slender host doth dwell,
Yea, God and man with all to either due,
That God that rules the heavens and rifled hell,
That man whose death did us to life renew:
That God and man that is the angels' bliss,
In form of bread and wine our nurture is.

Whole may His body be in smallest bread,
Whole in the whole, yea whole in every crumb;
With which be one or be ten thousand fed,
All to each one, to all but one doth come;
And though each one as much as all receive,
Not one too much, nor all too little have.

One soul in man is all in every part;
One face at once in many mirrors shines;
One fearful noise doth make a thousand start;
One eye at once of countless things defines;
If proofs of one in many, Nature frame,
God may in stranger sort perform the same.

God present is at once in every place
Yet God in every place is ever one;
So may there be by gifts of ghostly grace,
One man in many rooms, yet filling none;
Since angels may effects of bodies show,
God angels' gifts on bodies may bestow.

What God as author made He alter may;
No change so hard as making all of naught;
If Adam framéd were of slimy clay,
Bread may to Christ's most sacred flesh be wrought:
He may do this that made with mighty hand
Of water wine, a snake of Moses' wand.

St. Robert Southwell, Martyr (1561–1595)

MAY 5

Born in Gaza, Procopius (c. 465–528) there established a career teaching theology, rhetoric, and logic. His scriptural commentaries employ the catena form, in which the author adduces quotations from distinguished predecessors interspersed with his own remarks. Procopius here comments on the prophecy of Isaiah as it relates to the sacraments. For the sake of clarity, the passage from Isaiah is first given in full.

For behold the sovereign the Lord of hosts shall take away from Jerusalem, and from Judah the valiant and the strong, the whole strength of bread, and the whole strength of water. (Isa 3:1).

"Strength of bread," he says, and "strength of water." He does not simply say bread or water, but *strength of.* Another prophet interpreted it this way: "Behold, the days are coming, says the Lord, when I will send a famine on the land: not a famine of bread, or of thirst for water, but a famine of hearing the word of the Lord" [Amos 8:11]. They imagine that they share in this hunger by searching the divine Scriptures and their zeal for a thorough knowledge of them; yet, they do not have the strength of those nourishing words and of the life-giving fount.

This is the bread which David spoke of, "He gave them bread from heaven" [Ps 78:24]. And these are the waters which the prophet spoke of, "You shall draw water with joy from the springs of salvation" [Isa 12:2]. The Savior said, "whoever drinks from the water that I will give to him, it will become a fount of water springing up to eternal life" [John 4:14], and again, "My flesh is true food, and my blood is true drink" [John 6:55]. If men do not have these, they do not have the strength of bread and water. Those who eat corruptible food are languoring.

It is necessary to open one's eyes to be filled with such bread and water; for he says, "Open your eyes and be filled with bread" [Prov 20:13]. And, he says, "God opened her eyes, and she saw a well of water" [Gen 21:19]. Otherwise, the life-giving bread has been taken away from the Jews; that bread which gives life to the world, as well as the water of holy baptism.

Procopius of Gaza (c. 465–528)

MAY 6

Memorial of St. Dominic Savio

St. Dominic Savio (1842–1857) was one of the many youths to be catechized and formed by the gifted priest and mentor, St. John Bosco (1815–1888). Upon Dominic's death at fourteen years of age, St. John published a memoir of his extraordinary life of holiness. In the following passage, Dominic's devotion to the Blessed Sacrament is recalled and shown to be marked by ecstatic states. His spiritual maturity in youth provides a timeless witness to Christ's words that men must "be converted, and become as little children" (Matt 18:3).

Very often when Dominic went into the church, principally on the days he received Communion or when the Blessed Sacrament was exposed, he fell into what was clearly a sort of rapture or ecstasy and would thus remain for a very long time if he were not called away to fulfill his ordinary tasks.

It happened one day that he was absent from breakfast, from class, from the mid-day meal, and no one knew where he was: he was not in the study, nor in the dormitory. The director was informed, who suspected that he knew where Dominic might be found, namely in the church as had happened before. He went into the church and in the choir, near the sanctuary, there stood the boy like a statue; one foot was in front of the other, one hand was on a book stand, and the other was on his breast. His face was turned towards the sanctuary and his gaze was fixed on the tabernacle. His lips were not moving. The director called him. No reply. He shook him gently. Dominic then turned and said: "Oh, is the Mass over!" "See," said the priest, showing him his watch, "it is two o'clock." The boy said he was sorry for his transgression of the rule, and the director sent him off to dinner, saying: "If anyone asks you where you have been, say that you have been carrying out an order of mine."

St. John Bosco (1815–1888)

MAY 7

Counted among the Desert Fathers, Abba Parnaya (c. 400) was the disciple of the much-respected father Arsenius the Great (c. 350–445). In this story of Eucharistic faith, two wise monks correct a third in error, demonstrating true Christian love and mercy. In this way, the wise monks assume the goodwill of their fellow brother while speaking the fullness of truth. Ultimately, their unwavering faith in the Eucharist is shown to be grounded in the authority of the Catholic Church.

Abba Daniel Parnaya, the disciple of Abba Arsenius, used to speak of a man of Scete who was great in his labors, but simple in the faith. In this man's ignorance, he professed and believed that the bread which we receive is not in very truth the body of Christ, but a likeness of His body. And two of the fathers heard what he had said, yet knowing of his sublime works and labors, imagined that he had spoken it in his innocence and simple-mindedness. So they came to him and said, "Father, we have heard a thing from a man which we do not believe. For, he said that the bread we receive is not in very truth the body of Christ, but merely a likeness." And he replied to them, "It is I who have said this thing." So they entreated him, saying, "You must not say thus, father, but according to what the Holy Catholic Church has handed down to us, even so do we believe: this bread is the body of Christ in very truth, and not merely a likeness. For, just as God directly took dust from the earth, and fashioned man in His image, so also was it truly the case with the bread of which He said, 'This is My body.' For, it is not to be regarded as merely a commemorative object. We believe that it is indeed the Body of Christ."

Abba Parnaya, Desert Father (c. 400)

MAY 8

Ven. Marie-Thérèse of the Heart of Jesus (1809–1863) was blessed with a vision of Christ on the Feast of the Sacred Heart of Jesus, requesting that a new congregation dedicated to adoration of the Blessed Sacrament be established. Her writings reveal a sincere love of Jesus in the Eucharist and here speak of the unifying effects of such love. Marie-Thérèse not only experiences union with Jesus in the Host, but is touched and transformed by each of His mysteries. She thus allows herself to be shaped and moved by the graces from each mystery of Christ.

Without destroying me, he [Christ] imprints his existence in me; not in image but a real, living one. Some chains of fire and light visibly leave from the point that sums up and contains my faith, my life, my eternity. Flung down by the hand of God, they lead into my heart like an anchor tossed out in the port.

And sweetly, but forcefully, the distance that separates me disappears. The Host and my heart are one. And I know things that only the blessed in heaven understand. I can accomplish on earth what the Saints have been able to do. And without losing sight of the monstrance on earth which contains this Host invented by mercy, I sense beatitude within me, as well as the glory and the power of humanity of my Divine Savior; I admire his virtue and understand its effectiveness. I adore the means and the end of his Incarnation and his Redemption. I identify with these mysteries. Feeling that they will happen in me, I abandon myself to all the workings that the Word made flesh produces in humanity. I let myself be united to God. I let myself be sacrificed to God. I accept Tabor and Calvary. I give myself over to purification of the annihilation of obedience even to the point of the Cross. I aspire to and desire the glories, the joys of the Resurrection.

Ven. Mother Marie-Thérèse of the Heart of Jesus
(Théodelinde Dubouché) (1809–1863)

MAY 9

Memorial of St. Louise de Marillac

After the death of her husband, St. Louise de Marillac (1591–1660) worked alongside St. Vincent de Paul to found a new religious order, the Daughters of Charity. In her personal notes, Louise reveals her scruples regarding Holy Communion and the alleviation of those fears. Crucially, she realizes that she belongs to Jesus and, therefore, has no right to refuse Him visitation. In this way, she exchanges her desires for His.

In response to my fears, it seemed that my soul was made to understand that my God willed to come and abide in it; not as a place wherein to take delight, but as His property and possession. So, in that sense, I had no right to deny Him entrance. Therefore, I was to receive Him as its sovereign owner and implore Him to make my heart the seat of His divine Majesty.

Among her notes is the following brief, but profound, exclamation.

The Holy Communion of the Body of Jesus Christ causes us to enter into possession of the Communion of Saints and the joys of Paradise.

St. Louise de Marillac (1591–1660)

MAY 10

Memorial of St. John of Ávila, Doctor of the Church

St. John of Ávila (1499–1569) was a beloved preacher and theologian whose reform-minded sermons earned him the reproach of the elite. After criticizing the excesses of wealth, he was reported to the Inquisition, only to be lauded by them. In the following excerpt from a letter, St. John meditates on the tremendous majesty of the Holy Sacrifice of the Mass, poetically noting that Christians need only be mindful of its dignity to worthily prepare.

Let such a one reflect upon this mystery and say to himself: "It is God Almighty Who will come down upon the altar at the words of consecration. I shall hold Him in my hands, converse with Him, and receive Him into my heart." If only we remember this, and if by the help of God's Holy Spirit, it penetrates our soul, it will suffice (and more than suffice) to enable us frail mortals to perform this sacred duty as we ought.

Who can help being inflamed by love when reflecting that he is about to receive the Infinite Goodness within his bosom? Who would not tremble with reverential fear in that Presence, before which the powers of heaven are awed? Who would not resolve to never offend Him, but to praise and serve Him evermore? Is it possible for anyone not to be confounded and overwhelmed with grief at having sinned against that great Lord whom he bears in his hands? Can the Christian fail to trust such a pledge, or can he want for strength to walk the way of penance through the desert of this world when nourished by such food?

St. John of Ávila, Doctor of the Church (1499–1569)

MAY II

The following poem hails from a fourth-century Byzantine author, likely a layman. It illustrates the pious devotion of one who recognizes that the same Lord Jesus who walked on earth is present in the Eucharist. In these expressions of the faith, the laity evidence the "consensus fidelium" (the consent of the faithful), which manifests the unchanging truths of the faith.

Here is the blood of Him who was made flesh from the holy
    Virgin, that is, of Jesus Christ
Here is the blood of Him born of the holy Theotokos, that
    is, of Jesus Christ.
Here is the blood of Him who was baptized in the Jordan by
    John His forerunner, that is, of Jesus Christ.
Here is the blood of Him who offered Himself as a sacrifice
    for our sins, that is, of Jesus Christ.

The prayer of the Holy Church when the priest shares with
    the people:

Let us pray to the Lord.
Here is the holy body of Christ, the Lamb of God.
Here is the holy body of Him who was delivered up and
    given for our salvation.
Here is the holy body of Him who lavished the mysteries of
    grace of the New Covenant on His disciples.

Here is the holy body by which we received the bloodless
    sacrifice.

Here is the holy body of Him who washed the feet [of His
    disciples] in water and purified the souls of His apostles
    by the Holy Spirit.

Here is the holy body of Him who justified the prostitute
    with tears and purified us with His own blood.

Here is the holy body of Him who was betrayed treacher-
    ously with a kiss and who loved the world for which He
    suffered.

Here is the holy body of Him who consented to betrayal
    to Pilate and who presented the church to Himself as
    blameless.

All this because His name is blessed and glorified.

Byzantine-Greek Poetry (4th Century)

MAY 12

Memorial of St. Germanus of Constantinople

St. Germanus (634–733), Patriarch of Constantinople, composed one
of the most outstanding commentaries on the Divine Liturgy. Here,
he contemplates the mystery of the Church as that privileged house
of worship wherein Christ's sacrifice is renewed. The Paschal Mystery
is thus shown to be the central worship of the Church. Drawing upon
dread images of the Old Covenant, St. Germanus assures his reader
that the liturgical reality at hand exceeds all former wonders.

The Church is the assembly of people, Christ's body, and His
Name. It is Christ's Bride, purified by the water of His holy
Baptism, sprinkled with His Blood, arrayed in bridal array,
sealed with the ointment of the Holy Spirit, and on which are
the pearls of the divine dogmas of the Lord to His Disciples.
She was prefigured in the Patriarchs, foretold in the Prophets,
founded in the Apostles, adorned in the Hierarchs, perfected
in Martyrs, and whose Head is Christ.

The Church is God's temple, a holy precinct, a house of prayer, heaven on earth, wherein the God of heaven dwells and walks. Yet, it is also the mark [*antitypos*] of what He has accomplished through the Crucifixion, burial, and the Resurrection of Christ; glorified beyond Moses' Tabernacle of Witness. For within is the Mercy Seat and the Holy of Holies, the mystic living Sacrifice and the table that nourishes and gives life, which is enthroned upon the relics of the holy martyrs, summoning the people to repentance and prayer.

St. Germanus of Constantinople (634–733)

MAY 13

Feast of Our Lady of Fatima

Sr. Lúcia of Fatima (1907–2005) was the privileged witness of the apparitions of Our Lady of Fatima who was tasked with promoting its message. In the year prior to the apparitions, the three shepherd children were visited by the Angel of Peace, who taught them a prayer of adoration and reparation. This angelic visitation gives modern witness to the truth that the Eucharist is the Bread of Angels given to men.

As soon as we arrived there, we knelt down, with our foreheads touching the ground, and began to repeat the prayer of the Angel: "My God, I believe, I adore, I hope and I love You . . ." I don't know how many times we had repeated this prayer, when an extraordinary light shone upon us. We sprang up to see what was happening, and beheld the Angel. He was holding a chalice in his left hand, with the Host suspended above it, from which some drops of blood fell into the chalice. Leaving the chalice suspended in the air, the Angel knelt down beside us and made us repeat three times:

"Most Holy Trinity, Father, Son and Holy Spirit, I adore You profoundly, and I offer You the most precious Body, Blood, Soul and Divinity of Jesus Christ, present in all the tabernacles of the world, in reparation for the outrages, sacrileges and indifference with which He Himself is offended. And, through the infinite merits of His most Sacred Heart, and the Immaculate Heart of Mary, I beg of You the conversion of poor sinners."

Then, rising, he took the chalice and the Host in his hands. He gave the Sacred Host to me, and shared the Blood from the chalice between Jacinta and Francisco, saying as he did so: "Take and drink the Body and Blood of Jesus Christ, horribly outraged by ungrateful men! Make reparation for their crimes and console your God."

Lúcia of Fatima (1907–2005)

MAY 14

Theodoret of Cyrrhus (393–457) opposed St. Cyril of Alexandria during the Christological debates of the fifth century, siding instead with the Antiochene bishops. Nevertheless, his belief in the Real Presence is evidenced in the passage below, where he offers insight into Hebrews 10:19–20: "Having therefore, brothers, confidence in entering into the holies by the blood of Christ; a new and living way which he has dedicated for us through the veil, that is to say, his flesh." Here, the temple veil separating the holy of holies is interpreted by St. Paul to be the flesh of Christ, and Theodoret extends this notion to the Eucharist. In this way, the reception of Holy Communion grants the faithful unparalleled access to the holy of holies, which is the body of the Lord.

Therefore, brethren, since we have confidence to enter the sanctuary by the blood of Jesus, by the new and living way which he opened for us through the curtain, that is, through his flesh, and since we have a great priest over the house of God, let us draw near with a true heart in full assurance of faith. (Heb 10:19–22)

The author of Hebrews called the Lord's flesh "a veil," because through it, we enjoy entrance to the holy of holies. Just as in the law, the high priest entered the holy of holies through the veil—and it was impossible for another to enter—so those who believe in the Lord enjoy citizenship in heaven through the reception of the all-holy body. He calls the faithful the "house of God," and he necessarily adds, "in full conviction of faith." And this is because everything invisible is seen only through faith, including the forbidden places of the tabernacle, the sacrifice, and the high priest. This is, then, the sense of the things already said. Since he has shown, he says, that the things of grace are greater than those of the law, heaven has been opened for us—the way is beautiful. The Master, Christ himself, first traveled this way; let us approach with a sincere disposition believing these things to be true, banishing all double-mindedness of the soul. This is what he called "full conviction."

Theodoret of Cyrrhus (393–457)

MAY 15

In his celebrated treatise *On the Orthodox Faith*, St. John Damascene (c. 675–749) teaches that Christ's humanity is the tangible means whereby His divinity is communicated to man. For this reason, participation in the body and blood of Christ at Holy Communion allows Christians to partake in His divinity (see 2 Pet 1:4). Ever eager to defend the integrity of God's creation of body and soul, the material and the immaterial, St. John Damascene here teaches that the Eucharist is for the maintenance of both.

The body and blood of Christ is for the support of our own body and soul, without being consumed, corrupted, or expelled (may it never be). Rather, it is for our being and preservation. It is a protection against all kinds of injury and a purification from uncleanness. For as gold is purified through fire, so too are we, lest we be condemned with the world in the future age. It purifies from diseases and all kinds of calamities as the divine Apostle says, "If we judged ourselves, we would not be condemned. But when we are judged, we are chastened by the Lord that we may not be condemned with the world" [1 Cor 11:31–32]. And he further says, "So then the one who shares in the body and blood of the Lord unworthily eats and drinks judgment to himself" [1 Cor 11:29].

As we are cleansed by Him, we are united to the body of the Lord and to His Spirit, and become the body of Christ. This bread is the first fruit of the bread that is to come, which is *epiousios*. The word "daily" shows either the bread of Him to come, that is, of the coming age, or the bread of Him received for sustaining our being. So whether it is the former or latter, the body of the Lord shall fittingly be spoken, for the Lord's flesh is a life-giving spirit since he was conceived by the life-giving Spirit. For that which is born of the Spirit is spirit. I do not say this to take away from his bodily nature, but because I want to show its life-giving and divine character.

St. John Damascene, Doctor of the Church (c. 675–749)

MAY 16

The Council of Nicaea (325) was the earliest Ecumenical Council outside of the New Testament, which was called to affirm the divinity of Christ against the Arian heresy. The following canon offers insight into the disciplines of the early Church. Not only does it give witness to the hierarchy and order intrinsic to their Eucharistic worship, but it manifests the gravity with which they approached liturgy. Far from blurring ministerial roles, they celebrated Holy Mass in humility and obedience to St. Paul's liturgical admonition: "all things should be done decently and in order" (1 Cor 14:40).

It has come to the knowledge of the holy and great synod that in some districts and cities, the deacons administer the Eucharist to the presbyters, whereas neither canon nor custom permits that they, who have no right to offer, should give the body of Christ to them that do offer. And it has also been made known that certain deacons now touch the Eucharist, even before the bishops. Let all such practices be utterly done away, and let the deacons remain within their own bounds, knowing that they are the ministers of the bishop and the inferiors of the presbyters. Let them receive the Eucharist according to their order, after the presbyters, and let either the bishop or the presbyter administer to them. Furthermore, let not the deacons sit among the presbyters, for that is contrary to canon and order. And if, after this decree, any one shall refuse to obey, let him be deposed from the diaconate.

Council of Nicaea (325)

MAY 17

In his famous letter to Januarius, St. Augustine (354–430) considers when it is proper to withdraw from receiving Holy Communion. Instead of simply stating his view, St. Augustine presents a mock debate: the first person argues that one should only receive Communion on days of outstanding virtue, while the second argues it should be frequently received. The following selection voices the third opinion, which summarizes St. Augustine's own view.

Perhaps a third party intervenes with a more just judgment on the question and reminds them that the primary issue is that each remain united in the peace of Christ and free to do what he conscientiously believes is his duty, according to his belief.

For, neither of them lightly esteems the body and blood of the Lord; on the contrary, both are debating who shall more highly honor the sacrament of blessing. There was no controversy between those two mentioned in the Gospel, Zacchaeus and the Centurion; nor did either of them think he was better than other. Whereas the former received the Lord joyfully into his house, the latter said, "I am not worthy that You should come under my roof," both honoring the Savior, though in different ways; even mutually opposing ways. Both were miserable with sin and both received the mercy they needed. We may borrow another illustration from the fact that the manna given to the ancient people of God tasted as he desired it might. It is the same with this world-subduing sacrament in the heart of each Christian. For, he that dares not take it every day, and he who dares not omit it any day, are both similarly moved by a desire to do it honor.

St. Augustine of Hippo, Bishop and Doctor (354–430)

MAY 18

Among the many texts St. Thomas Aquinas (1225–1274) composed for the Feast of Corpus Christi is a sermon that recognizes the Eucharist as an ever-renewing sign of Christ's love. An excerpt of this text is here presented alongside the famous hymn, *O sacrum convivium*. In only a few verses, Thomas explains how the Eucharist embraces the past, present, and future. The Passion of Christ is thus remembered, grace is imparted, and man is prepared for communion with God in heaven.

In the end, no one can fully express the sweetness of this sacrament in which spiritual delight is tasted at its very source, and in which we renew the memory of that surpassing love for us which Christ revealed in his passion. It was to impress the vastness of his love more firmly upon the hearts of the faithful that our Lord instituted this sacrament at the Last Supper.

O sacrum convivium!	O sacred banquet!
in quo Christus sumitur	in which Christ is received
recolitur memoria passionis eius	the memory of His Passion is recalled
mens impletur gratia:	the mind is filled with grace
et futurae gloriae nobis pignus	and the pledge of future glory is
datur.	given to us.
Alleluia.	Alleluia.

St. Thomas Aquinas, Doctor of the Church (1225–1274)

MAY 19

St. John Baptist de Rossi (1698–1764) was an Italian priest known for his pastoral care for the poor of Rome. He dedicated himself to the Sacrament of Confession, bringing grace and spiritual liberation to the imprisoned, uneducated, and forgotten. Here, St. John reflects on the connection between faith and works, noting that Jesus revealed Himself to the world through works. According to St. John, Christian works must include acts of piety. Holy Mass and the Divine Office must be prayed with devotion, evidencing one's faith and love.

In the Gospel this Sunday, we read that while John the Baptist was in prison, he sent two of his disciples to the Savior, asking if He was the One to come or if they should look for another. Notice that our Lord did not reply, "I am the Messiah." He only told them to look at the fruits He had brought forth and to thereby find out. "Go and relate to John what you have heard and seen; the blind see, the lame walk, the lepers are cleansed, the deaf hear, the dead rise again, the poor have the Gospel preached to them" [Matt 11:4–5]. What a lesson this is, my brothers! We are clerics and priests, but can we answer as our Savior did by pointing to our works? We say Holy Mass daily, but do we celebrate these tremendous mysteries with all the devotion they demand? We say our Office, but how? as a wearisome task which must be completed, or with earnest attention and love? God does not will that these great actions should be done lightly or negligently, yet even good and spiritual persons are often sadly wanting in these respects. Let us watch, then, over our daily actions. Remember that our lives, our work, should be filled with supernatural fervor so that nothing should hinder us from doing all that we can to save souls. If we are idle or indifferent to the things pertaining to God's service, we shall fall into a thousand imperfections.

St. John Baptist de Rossi (1698–1764)
[Memorial, May 23]

MAY 20

Memorial of St. Bernardine of Siena

St. Bernardine of Siena (1380–1444) was a Franciscan priest, famed for his popular sermons preached in the streets of Italy. Though something of a firebrand, he is credited with helping cleanse medieval culture of materialism and immorality. In this excerpt, St. Bernardine points to a common abuse among the laity, irreverence during the liturgy. Instead of falling in dread silence before the majesty of God, the laity distract one another with empty speech. For St. Bernardine, the key to reclaiming this reverence is the remembrance of Who it is that is upon the altar.

Oh . . . how much fault you are in the morning when I am saying Mass. You make so great a noise that, in truth, I seem to hear a whole mountain of bones, so do you cry out! Oh, is this great devotion that you show when hearing Holy Mass? For me, it seems to be a great confusion without devotion or reverence. Do you not recognize that here is celebrated the glorious Body of Christ, the Son of God, for your salvation? that you should carry yourselves in such a manner that no one should utter even "*shh!*"

St. Bernardine of Siena (1380–1444)

MAY 21

Memorial of St. Eugène de Mazenod

St. Eugène de Mazenod (1782–1861) was exiled from his home city of Aix-en-Provence during the French Revolution, which forced his family to take refuge in the Italian peninsula. He nevertheless returned to France as a seminarian and priest and founded the Oblates of Mary Immaculate. The new order sent missionaries to serve those devastated by the French Revolution and, by extension, the poor. In his instructions for missionaries, St. Eugène places the Eucharist at the very center of their lives. Neither locked churches, nor public travel, are to interrupt their devotion to the Blessed Sacrament.

When travelling, they will endeavor to find an opportunity to say Mass each day. If all cannot have this happiness, at least one should say Mass at which the others should communicate. Still, the Fathers should make all possible effort to avoid being deprived of the fruits of offering the Holy Sacrifice even one day.

If they are travelling on foot through a town or village, they will go to the local Church to visit the Blessed Sacrament. Should the Church be closed, they will kneel at the gate for a short time in adoration. If they are travelling by public transportation, they will, in spirit, direct their thoughts to our Lord in the Holy Eucharist and recite the *Tantum ergo*; to which they will add prayers to the Blessed Virgin, Guardian Angel, the Patron Saints of the place, and also prayers for the souls of those buried in the local cemetery.

St. Eugène de Mazenod (1782–1861)

MAY 22

St. Madeleine Sophie Barat (1779–1865) received an outstanding education from her older brother, a professor awaiting ordination. She suffered cruelly under the Reign of Terror, but subsequently founded the

Society of the Sacred Heart for the intellectual and spiritual formation of girls. In the following passage, St. Madeleine recounts an exhortation she delivered to the novices on the Institution of the Eucharist. Emphasizing Christ's exceeding love for each person in the sacrament, St. Madeleine encourages each to generously return love for love.

I spoke to them of the infinite love of our Blessed Lord in instituting this Divine Eucharist and on the tender and loving words He spoke to His Apostles during the Last Supper. How, I asked, can we help loving Him who has given us such unheard of marks of love? It was to us, as well as to His Apostles, that He said: *"With desire I have desired to eat this Pasch with you"* [Luke 22:15]; that is, to give Myself to you as your food. Yes, the Jews are about to put Me to death. I must leave you, but My love cannot abide the separation. I shall institute this Divine Sacrament and thus always remain with you—and with those who will come after you until the end of time. Oh, Sisters, shall we still be unmoved? Shall we still refuse Him anything? Can we keep anything back? It would be monstrous ingratitude!

Time passed quickly while speaking on so engrossing a subject. It was ten o'clock, and I told them it was time to go; though they were ready to stay all night. Nevertheless, duty prevailed. And before separating we gave one other the kiss of peace.

St. Madeleine Sophie Barat (1779–1865)
[Memorial, May 25]

MAY 23

St. Mary Magdalene de Pazzi (1566–1607) was a Carmelite mystic whose extraordinary life of grace was marked by ecstasies, raptures, and the ability to read hearts. Her intense devotion to the Blessed

Sacrament is evidenced in her letter to Cardinal Alessandro de Medici. Here, St. Mary counsels the cardinal to profit from the Light of the World, Christ present in the Most Blessed Sacrament.

> So much did the Eternal Father love, and still loves, this His creature that He was not satisfied to give His Only-Begotten for our redemption, but continues to give Him as a help, relief, and consolation. Furthermore, He gives Him to us so that He may ever enkindle and enflame our hearts with His divine love, giving us His divine light. And this is so that we may know ourselves and His goodness. But many, I repeat, love darkness rather than light. So immense, O Lord, is Your greatness and Your love that it extends over all the earth; among the blessed spirits above, men here below, and all other creatures! I tell you then, although we are in darkness due to our fallen natures, if we wish to dispose ourselves well and profit, the light is in the world, because the loving Word, who is the True Light, dwells in our midst by our reception of His body and blood.

> St. Mary Magdalene de Pazzi (1566–1607)
> [Memorial, May 25]

MAY 24

St. Bede the Venerable (673–735) was an English monk who rose to become one of the greatest historians and scholars of his day. His "Letter to Egbert" is notable for his counsel on the reception of Holy Communion. While St. Bede lauds frequent reception of Holy Communion, he attests to its rarity in England and recommends it adopt the custom of other lands. In this way, the laity may be sanctified, and God may be more fully honored.

> How advantageous it is for Christians of every kind to receive the Body and Blood of the Lord daily, as the Church

of Christ in Italy, Gaul, Africa, Greece, and the whole of the East practices, which you well know. What sort of religious observance is it to the God of devotion and sanctification that so many—practically all—of the laity of our province abstain, finding this practice foreign through carelessness of teaching. And those who are more pious still do not presume to receive the Most Holy Sacraments unless it is Christmas, Epiphany, or Easter. Yet, there are innumerable boys and girls who are of innocent and chaste conduct, young men and virgins, and older men and women, who can, without any scruple, receive the heavenly Sacraments every Sunday, or even on the feast days of the Holy Apostles or martyrs. And this is the way you have seen it practiced within the Holy Roman and Apostolic Church.

St. Bede the Venerable, Doctor of the Church (673–735)
[Memorial, May 25]

MAY 25

Memorial of Pope St. Gregory VII

Pope St. Gregory VII (1015–1085) was loved and despised for enacting much-needed reforms throughout the Church. He reinforced existing disciplines on priestly celibacy, prohibited the incontinent from ministry, and forbade simony. His epistles overflow with the tenderness of his devotion, and in the following passage, he exhorts a woman to deeper faith in the Real Presence.

We should, O daughter, take refuge in this singular Sacrament, desiring this incomparable medicine. For this reason, beloved daughter of Peter, I send this letter in order that your faith and confidence may increase in the Body of the Lord. Indeed, so excellent is this treasure, so distinguished is this gift! For it is not gold, nor precious stones, but the love of your Father, the clear Sovereign of heaven, which seeks your soul from my priestly hand; and you may also receive it from other priests as well who are more worthy than myself.

Pope St. Gregory VII (1015–1085)

MAY 26

Memorial of St. Philip Neri

Known as the "Third Apostle of Rome," St. Philip Neri (1515–1595) declined missionary travels in order to devote himself to the reconversion of Rome. In the following series of maxims, St. Philip offers a variety of perspectives on Eucharistic devotion. Some of his exclamatory sayings marvel at the gratuitous gift of the Eucharist, while others provide instruction. Like his contemporary, St. Teresa of Ávila, St. Philip appears to view works of charity as an indicator of spiritual health and requires that communicants grow in virtue.

Before communion, we ought to exercise ourselves in many acts of virtue.

Prayer and communion are not to be made or desired for the sake of the devotion we feel in them, for that is seeking self and not God. And we must be frequent in both the one and the other in order to become humble, obedient, gentle, and patient.

When we see these virtues in a man, then we know that he has really gathered the fruit of prayer and of communion.

Our sweet Jesus, through the excess of His love and liberality, has left Himself to us in the Most Holy Sacrament.

Let all go to the Eucharistic Table with a great desire for that Sacred Food. *Sitientes! Sitientes!*

St. Philip Neri (1515–1595)

MAY 27

St. Peter (c. 380–450) was the faithful bishop of Ravenna whose eloquence of speech merited him the title, "Chrysologus," or "Golden Worded." In the following passage, St. Peter speaks of Christ's radical gift of self in the Eucharist. He praises the faith of the Pharisee who asked Jesus to dine with him and contemplates the mystical meaning of this request. For Jesus offers man more than a simple meal. Rather, He promises to give Himself away in Holy Communion, now and at the everlasting banquet in heaven.

> [The Gospel] says that "a certain Pharisee asked the Lord to eat with him." Brothers, a Pharisee was a Catholic among the Jews, for he believed in the resurrection, disagreeing with the Sadducees who denied it. And so he asks Christ, the author of the resurrection, to eat with Him. For whoever lives with Christ does not know death; indeed, he lives forever.
>
> "He asked the Lord to eat with him." You may ask, O Pharisee, to eat with Him. Believe, be a Christian and you may eat of Him. He says, "I am the bread which came down from heaven" [John 6:51]. God always gives more than He is asked. For He who was asked [to dine], gave Himself to be consumed. And this was so that He could bestow with Himself the faith linked to eating. And yet He gave this so as not to deny what was requested. Did He not willingly promise this to His disciples? "You are those who have persevered with me, and you will eat and drink at my table in my kingdom" [Luke 22:28-30].

St. Peter Chrysologus, Bishop and Doctor
(c. 380–450)

MAY 28

Optional Memorial of Bl. Lanfranc

Bl. Lanfranc (c. 1005–1089) was the famed archbishop of Canterbury, known for his philosophical defense of Christ's Real Presence in the Eucharist. Navigating a path between the extreme views of the ultra-realist school and the erroneous views of Berengarius of Tours, Lanfranc affirmed Christ's substantial presence in the Eucharist while acknowledging its veiled nature. Lanfranc's teachings lay as a backdrop for the doctrine of transubstantiation, which would be fully developed in the following centuries.

> We believe that the earthly substances on the altar of the Lord, placed there for divine consecration by the priestly ministry, are ineffably, incomprehensibly, and wonderfully overturned by a heavenly power, and converted into the essence of the Body of the Lord, preserving the appearance and qualities of the species so as not to be perceived in a crude or bloody manner, which might terrify. One, rather, recognizes an increase in the reward of faith for him who believes: This is the very Body of the Lord who resides in heaven at the right hand of the Father, immortal, inviolate, entire, impeccable, and impassible. Thus, it may truly be said that we receive the very same Body, born of the Virgin, and yet it is not the same: It is indeed the same in essence, nature, and virtue. It is not in the sense that one sees the species of bread and wine while recognizing the higher gift [the Body and Blood]. This is the faith that was held in ancient times and is now held by the Church, and has spread throughout the entire world by those of the Catholic name.

Bl. Lanfranc (c. 1005–1089)

MAY 29

In this passage from his landmark treatise, *On the Trinity*, St. Augustine (354–430) teaches that the priest's power to effect the sacraments comes from Christ Himself. When the priest speaks the mystical prayer of consecration, the bread and wine are transformed into the body and blood of Christ because he acts in the person of Christ. In this way, the personal holiness of the minister is irrelevant to the efficacy of the sacrament, since it is Christ who acts.

> Although the Apostle Paul carried the burden of the body, which is subject to corruption and disturbs the soul, and although he could see only in part and dimly, and wanted to die so as to be with Christ as he groaned within himself awaiting the adoption—the redemption of his body—nevertheless, he could preach the Lord Jesus Christ with his tongue, through letters, and by the sacrament of Christ's body and blood. For, it is not Paul's language, nor paper, nor ink, nor sounds, nor letters written on parchments that are important; rather it is, we say, Christ's body and blood. This great thing we receive is taken from the fruit of the earth and consecrated by the mystical prayer for our spiritual salvation in memory of the Lord's Passion. While the visible species is brought forward by man, it is only sanctified as so great a sacrament by the invisible work of God's Spirit; since God works everything that happens through those physical actions of this work by setting into motion those invisible actions of the ministers.

> St. Augustine of Hippo, Bishop and Doctor (354–430)

MAY 30

Memorial of St. Joan of Arc

St. Joan of Arc (1412–1431) remains an icon of God's providence over human affairs. By her obedience to divine inspiration, this humble maiden shaped the political and military landscape of Medieval Europe, driving the English from Orléans. Her courageous actions ultimately preserved the Catholic faith in France inasmuch as the English outlawed Catholicism in the following century. Here, St. Joan's personal chaplain, Fr. Jean Pasquerel, recounts her personal devotion to the Most Blessed Sacrament.

> She went to confession nearly every day, and took the Sacrament often. When near any community of mendicant friars, she asked me to remind her of the days on which the beggar children received the Eucharist so that she might receive it along with them. It was her delight to receive the Sacrament with the poor mendicant children. She often shed tears at confession.

> *Fr. Jean Pasquerel*

Transcripts of St. Joan's trial have been preserved, giving witness to her arresting simplicity of spirit. Here, Joan makes her final requests, revealing that which she most valued.

> I render you my best thanks for what you have said concerning the salvation of my soul. And it seems to me, seeing the illness I am now suffering, that I am in danger of dying. If this is to happen, God's will be done. I only ask that you allow me to go to confession and to partake of the Blessed Sacrament, and that my body may be laid in holy ground.

> *St. Joan of Arc (1412–1431)*

MAY 31

Memorial of St. Camilla Battista da Varano

St. Camilla Battista da Varano (1458–1524) was born into Italian royalty, but renounced her worldly status to join the Poor Clares. In this passage from her autobiography, written under obedience to her confessor, she expresses her great hunger for the Eucharist. Because St. Camilla lived at a time when frequent Communion was almost unknown, she was often unable to receive Him whom she so desired. Here, St. Camilla gives voice to the suffering this caused her, while noting the peace afforded her by God.

The Sacrament of the Eucharist is truly the Bread of Angels. I say this because after the angelic visitation, I was left with so great a hunger and desire for the Sacrament that I could not be satisfied. For nearly two years, I continued to communicate every Sunday, but my desire was to receive daily. And the thought of waiting for more than an octave seemed to cause me anguish, so great was the pain. Thus it was during those three years before my tribulations began. I celebrated and sanctified the Sabbath in solemnity of my angelic peace. Then, all the ways of Zion—that is, of holy paradise—were freely and peacefully given to me. And I sped forward without any impediment, proceeding with holy desire and devoted prayer. Truly then, my Father, it was the case, or so it seemed, that my heart was more angelic than human; more heavenly than earthly.

St. Camilla Battista da Varano (1458–1524)

JUNE

JUNE I

Memorial of St. Justin Martyr

Born in Flavia Neapolis in Syria, St. Justin (c. 100–165) studied Greek philosophy before converting to the Catholic faith. This most excellent of apologists ultimately gave his life for the faith, suffering martyrdom under Junius Rusticus. In his *First Apology*, Justin provides one of the earliest accounts of the Church's liturgy and reverently describes the Eucharist. In the following excerpt, he gives early witness to the Real Presence of Christ, noting that this sacrament is solely reserved for the baptized. Because Holy Communion is the sign of unity with Christ, it is thus restricted to those who are joined to Him in charity.

> And this food is called the Eucharist among us. No one is allowed to partake of it other than him who believes the things taught by us to be true, and by him whose sins are washed away in the washing unto regeneration. In this way, one lives as Christ has commanded. For we do not receive these as common bread or common food. Rather, in the manner that Jesus Christ our Savior, who was made flesh through the word of God, taking on flesh and blood for our salvation, so we are taught that the food that is made the Eucharist by the prayer of His word is, in fact, the flesh and blood of that Jesus who was made flesh. This food nourishes our blood and flesh by way of a transformation. The apostles, in those memoirs called gospels, handed on the

things they were commanded; namely, that Jesus took bread, gave thanks [Eucharist] and said, "Do this in remembrance of me. This is my body." And taking the cup similarly, He gave thanks and said, "This is my blood," giving it to them alone.

St. Justin Martyr (c. 100–165)

JUNE 2

Adam of St. Victor (d. 1146) composed the following sequence for the Feast of Pentecost, which speaks of the descent of the Holy Spirit using Eucharistic themes. Noting the division found in the Old Covenant, Adam highlights the unity found in Christ's Body, the Church. And as the Church is one, so must the Christian heart be undivided in charity, lest it be found unworthy of the Sacrament of Unity.

O how happy, how festive the Day
Wherein the Church first received
Three thousand souls, the first-fruits
of the newborn Church, now believed.

Loaves of the Old Law gave way to two people
Adopted children under one faith at last.
The Cornerstone, the Head, Himself inserted
Making the two, one people fast.

New skins, not old, can hold the new wine.
The widow prepares the jar, but Elijah gives the oil anew.
To us, God gives to renew.
Hearts aligned to His Holy Dew.

Of this wine or oil, we may not be
Worthy of the dew if lives disagree.
The Paraclete cannot dwell in hearts
If darkened and divided they be.

Adam of St. Victor (d. 1146)

JUNE 3

Pope Urban IV (c. 1195–1264) was the son of a French cobbler who was trained in law and theology before his rise to the Petrine ministry. He instituted the Feast of Corpus Christi at the behest of St. Juliana of Liège, publishing the bull, *Transiturus*. In this excerpt, Pope Urban IV expresses heartfelt thanksgiving for the Eucharist, stressing its power to restore man to everlasting life. Though the forbidden fruit of Adam brought death, the bread of angels brings eternal life.

O most worthy and ever venerable memorial, which reminds us that death has no sting, that we are no longer lost, since the vivifying Body of the Lord, which was nailed to the tree of the Cross, has restored us to life! This is that glorious memorial which fills the faithful with a salutary joy, and which causes them to shed tears of love and gratitude. At the remembrance of our Redemption we triumph; and in calling to our minds the death of Jesus Christ who has redeemed us, we cannot refrain from weeping. This sacred memorial of the death of Christ, therefore, procures us both joy and tears; we rejoice in weeping, and we weep in rejoicing; because our hearts being overwhelmed with delights, by the memory of so great a gift, we cannot refrain from shedding tears of gratitude. . . .

O eminent and admirable liberality, where the Giver passes into the Gift, where the thing given is the same as Him Who gives it! O prodigality unparalleled, where the Giver gives Himself! Our God has therefore given Himself to be our food, because man, condemned to death, can only return to life by this means. He died in eating of the forbidden fruit, and he lives by tasting of the Tree of Life. The eating of the former gave a wound, the tasting of the latter restored to health; the former taste has wounded, and the latter has healed. For He said of the former: "In the day you eat of it you shall die" (Gen 2:17), but of the latter, He said: "Whoever eats of this bread shall live forever" [John 6:51].

Pope Urban IV (c. 1195–1264)

JUNE 4

Bl. Mary of the Divine Heart (1863–1899) was a German religious whose private revelations led Pope Leo XIII to consecrate the world to the Sacred Heart of Jesus. Her writings overflow with love of the Blessed Sacrament and recount her mystical exchanges with Christ. In the following letter, Bl. Mary recounts a series of extraordinary graces given her the day before Ash Wednesday.

On Shrove Tuesday, after Holy Communion, Our Lord said to me: "Until now Holy Communion has been your life; strive that this may continue." Then He promised that He would grant whatever I asked of Him in the Blessed Eucharist, provided it were for the greater glory of God and the salvation of souls, and therefore, I ought to have profound devotion and unbounded confidence towards the Blessed Sacrament, accompanied by an ardent love. He added, "The Blessed Sacrament is the life of your life. I give Myself to you every day with My Body and My Blood, while awaiting the hour of death to give Myself to you with the fullness of My love for all eternity." . . .

On Shrove Tuesday, I spent two hours before the Blessed Sacrament in the most intimate union with my Divine Spouse. I prayed for the conversion of sinners and offered myself, with my whole heart to the Divine Heart of Jesus, in expiation and reparation for the crimes committed on that day. I felt myself quite on fire with Divine love and holy desires! Our Lord, in His infinite mercy, united Himself to me more and more closely, and overlooking my wretchedness and ingratitude, He said to me in the excess of His love: "If I had not instituted the Holy Eucharist, I would do so now for you, so great is my desire to dwell in your heart, and there find My consolation in the midst of so many offenses committed in the world." I cannot express what passed within me. . . . When the time came for the deposition of the Blessed Sacrament, I told Our Lord how grieved I was that He did not stay longer with us. He consoled me and said, "I will remain with you by the efficacy of My Passion, to inflame your love, sustain your weakness, dilate your heart, and to strengthen you in your sufferings."

Bl. Mary of the Divine Heart (1863–1899)
[Memorial, June 8]

JUNE 5

St. Marcellin Joseph Champagnat (1789–1840) grew up in poverty, lacking even a basic education. Despite his disadvantage, he went on to found the Marist Brothers to serve the educational and spiritual needs of children. After St. Marcellin's death, his instructions and maxims were set down for remembrance. Here, St. Marcellin draws a distinction between the spiritual joys that proceed from prayer and those pleasures that come from the world.

A good religious experiences more consolation and happiness in a solitary exercise of piety—such as prayer, assistance at Holy Mass, or a quarter-hour visit to the Most Holy Sacrament of the Altar—than the men of the world with all the greatest benefits and advantages of fortune, who cannot taste [such happiness] in all the pleasures that they could procure throughout a long life.

Why are the worldly so noisy in their pleasures and profane enjoyments? Because they cannot entirely suppress the remorse that pursues them. It is because their happiness is only apparent, and their heart full of misery, finding only bitterness in sensual satisfactions.

St. Marcellin Joseph Champagnat (1789–1840)
[Memorial, June 6]

JUNE 6

Memorial of St. Norbert of Xanten

St. Norbert of Xanten (1080–1134) lived a life of decadence until a lightning strike caused him to be thrown from his horse, inspiring deep conversion. Thereafter, he entered the priesthood and founded the Order of the Premonstratensians, commonly called the Norbertines. In this exclamatory exhortation, St. Norbert marvels at the high dignity of the priesthood, noting that mere men stand in the place of Christ Himself.

O Priest! You are not yourself, because you are God. You are not of yourself, because you are the servant and minister of Christ. You are not your own, because you are the spouse of the Church. You are not for yourself, because you are the mediator between God and man. You are not from yourself, because you are nothing. What then are you, O Priest? Nothing and everything. O Priest! take care lest what was said to Christ on the Cross be said to you: He saved others, but himself he cannot save.

St. Norbert of Xanten (1080–1134)

JUNE 7

Memorial of Bl. Anne of St. Bartholomew

Bl. Anne of St. Bartholomew (1550–1626) was a Discalced Carmelite who cared for St. Teresa of Ávila during her final years. After St. Teresa's death, Bl. Anne went on to found her own reformed convents, spreading the spirit of renewal in France. Her autobiography details her growth in the spiritual life and is composed in a style not unlike that of St. Teresa's own. Here, Bl. Anne records a vision of Christ upon receiving Holy Communion, an event that would strengthen her resolve to walk in the way of virtue.

> But the Divine Master, who showed me so much love at that time, suddenly hid Himself from me for several days. It was as if my soul was alone in a desert and in deepest darkness. Moreover, I feared that all the favors I had received until that time were only illusions. I resigned myself to the will of God in all things, but felt a contraction of the heart as if it were held in a press. All this was during the Christmas season, which I passed in a very different state than in other years.

> On Epiphany, I was approaching the Holy Table with fear, due to my want of fervor, when our Lord appeared to me most lovingly. Before being united in communion, I was filled with an impetuous attraction of love and deep recollection. While receiving the Sacred Host, the Adorable Master said to me, "I will be your companion, until I take you with me to heaven." My soul seemed to be burning with love and penetrated with reverence and gratitude toward His divine Majesty who had granted me so great a grace, and one which I had not merited. This vision and experience passed very quickly; but for several days I enjoyed the presence of God in a remarkable degree, which was accompanied by habitual peace and consolation, and an ardent desire to begin to walk in the path of virtue, which I had never done until then.

Bl. Anne of St. Bartholomew (1550–1626)

JUNE 8

Born in Nisibus, St. Ephraem (c. 306–373) was an Eastern deacon and prolific author of sacred hymns, poems, and exegetical works. The following sermon voices a prayer, beseeching the grace to benefit from Holy Communion. Mindful of the inconstancy of man, St. Ephraem prays that Christians might be made worthy to possess the joys of heaven, which he sees foreshadowed in the Holy Eucharist.

> In your sacrament we daily embrace you and receive you into our bodies; make us worthy to experience the resurrection for which we hope. We have had your treasure hidden within us ever since we received baptismal grace; it grows ever richer at your sacramental table. Teach us to find our joy in your favor! Lord, we have within us your memorial, received at your spiritual table; let us possess it in its full reality when all things shall be made new. We glimpse the beauty that is laid up for us when we gaze upon the spiritual beauty your immortal will now creates within our mortal selves.
>
> *St. Ephraem, Doctor of the Church (c. 306–373)*
> *[Memorial, June 9]*

JUNE 9

Memorial of St. Columba

Born in Ireland, St. Columba (521–597) established several monasteries in his native land before departing to Scotland, where he evangelized the Picts. Here, St. Columba's younger relative, St. Adomnán (624–704), recounts a miraculous event that occurred during St. Columba's celebration of the Mass. This story is as much of a commentary on the Mass as it is on St. Columba; for the heavenly appearance of light occurs during the holy sacrifice, signifying its heavenly character.

> Another time, four holy founders of monasteries came from Ireland to visit St. Columba in the island of Hinba. These distinguished men were [St.] Comgall McAridhe, [St.] Cainnech MacDalanu, St. Brendan MacAlti, and Cormac ua Leathain.

They all selected St. Columba to consecrate in their presence the Holy Mysteries of the Eucharist. The saint complied with their wishes and entered the church with them on Sunday, as usual, after the reading of the gospel. During the celebration of the holy sacrifice of the Mass, St. Brendan MacAlti saw, as he told Comgall and Cainnech afterwards, a ball of fire like a comet burning very brightly on the head of Columba the whole time he stood before the altar, offering the holy sacrifice and engaged in the most sacred mysteries.

St. Adomnán of Iona (624–704)

JUNE 10

St. John Chrysostom (349–407) delivered no less than eighty-eight homilies on the Gospel of John, dedicating six of them to the Eucharistic-themed chapter six. In the following homily, Chrysostom treats those mysterious words of Christ: "As the living Father sent me, and I live because of the Father, so he who eats me will live because of me" (John 6:57). He rightly perceives that the life offered by Christ is not unending mortality, but a radical participation in Him who is life itself. For this reason, Christ said, "this is eternal life, that they may know you the only true God, and Jesus Christ whom you have sent" (John 17:3). This transcendent life is communicated to man in the Eucharist (see John 6:53).

What is meant by the phrase, "because of the Father" [John 6:57]? He only hints at the meaning, saying, "As the living Father sent me, and I live because of the Father, so he who eats me will live because of me" [John 6:57]. Here, He speaks of life, but of that most abundant life; for it is clear that He spoke not of life simply, but of that glorious and ineffable life. For, both unbelievers and the profane "live," though they do not eat from that flesh. Thus, you see that the statement is not about this life, but about that other [eternal life]. What He says is this: "He who eats my flesh is not lost or punished, though he has come to the end of his life" [see John 6:50, 11:25]. And He is not speaking about the general resurrection, as all will rise again; rather, He speaks about the choice and glorious resurrection, which holds a reward.

"This is the bread that has come down from heaven, not as your fathers ate and died. He who eats this bread will live forever" [John 6:50]. He continually returns to the same theme so that it might be impressed in their minds (for the teaching on these matters was a kind of final teaching) and to confirm the dogma of the resurrection and eternal life. Therefore, He mentions the resurrection, since He spoke of eternal life, showing that it is not that life now, but after the resurrection. And where are these things clearly manifest? He answers, from the Scriptures.

St. John Chrysostom, Bishop and Doctor (349–407)

JUNE 11

St. Thomas Aquinas (1225–1274) composed the Eucharistic hymn, *Pange lingua*, for the feast of Corpus Christi, building upon a sixth-century hymn of the same name. Thomas' own composition contains a wealth of Biblical themes that reference the Incarnation, Last Supper, and Passion. In this most famous of hymns, St. Thomas summons the whole strength of his poetic gifts, encouraging all to adore the most holy body and blood of Christ.

Sing, my tongue, the glory
of the Mystery of His Body
and Precious Blood
that for the price of the
    world
this Fruit of Nobility,
this King of Nations,
was poured forth.

The Word-Made-Flesh
    becomes true Bread,
by a word, becomes true
    Flesh;
from wine, His Precious
    Blood.
And if the senses lack,
then the heart finds
    strength in faith, which
    alone suffices.

For us given, for us born
of the Ever-Virgin
to dwell among men;
the Word, to sow seed.
His dwelling ending
with most wondrous deed.

Therefore, so great a Sacra-
    ment,
let us adore in prostration,
and the old rites
give way to the new.
Let faith give strength
where the senses fail.

On that sacred night at
    supper,
reclining among brothers,
He fulfilled the law
with foods prescribed,
and gave Himself to many,
by His very hands.

To the Begetter and the
    Begotten
be praise and jubilation,
reverence, honor, and might,
and blessing.
And to the One who pro-
    ceeds from both,
may equal praise be.
Amen.

St. Thomas Aquinas, Doctor of the Church (1225–1274)

JUNE 12

The Council of Trent was called to reaffirm the Apostolic faith against the theological errors of sixteenth-century Protestant Reformers. One of the major issues the council addressed was the sacrificial nature of the Mass, which had been denied by Luther, Zwingli, and even Cranmer. In the *Tridentine Creed*, Pope Pius IV (1499–1565) reiterated this unchanging belief of the Church, along with the doctrines of transubstantiation, the Real Presence, and the validity of Communion under one species.

> I profess likewise that at Mass is offered to God a true, proper, and propitiatory sacrifice for the living and the dead. And that in the most Holy Sacrament of the Eucharist, there is truly, really, and substantially the body, blood, soul, and divinity of our Lord Jesus Christ. And also that there takes place a conversion of the entire substance of the bread into the body; and of the entire substance of the wine into the blood, which conversion the Catholic Church calls transubstantiation. I also confess that under one kind alone, Christ is sacramentally taken whole and entire.
>
> *Pope Pius IV (1499–1565)*

JUNE 13

Memorial of St. Anthony of Padua, Doctor of the Church

St. Anthony of Padua (1195–1231) was a well-educated Augustinian Friar who joined the Order of Friars Minor, seeking radical discipleship of Christ. In this excerpt from his homily, St. Anthony echoes the counsel of St. Augustine on the reception of Holy Communion. Employing the figures of Zacchaeus and the Centurion, St. Anthony illustrates two ways of honoring the Eucharistic Lord: one through reverent reception and the other through reverent abstinence.

Whereas the Centurion said, "Lord, I am not worthy that you should enter under my roof, but only [say the word]," Zacchaeus, by contrast, received the Lord with joy. These two illustrate diverse approaches to the Lord. Some, out of reverence for the Body of Christ, say, "Lord I am not worthy," and they frequently abstain from receiving the Eucharist. Others honor the Body of Christ by gratefully receiving Him. Thus, Augustine says: I neither praise nor condemn daily reception of the Eucharist. Some honor the Body of Christ by not daring to receive daily, while others honor Him by not daring to allow a day pass without.

St. Anthony of Padua, Doctor of the Church (1195–1231)

JUNE 14

St. Gaudentius (d. 410) composed many homilies on the Exodus and here illustrates its preparation for the Eucharist. Recalling the Lord's instructions for the Passover Meal (see Exod 12), Gaudentius applies their dictates to the present Eucharistic Feast. Thus, he interprets the command to "eat in haste" (Exod 12:11) as a moral imperative to approach the Eucharist with a fervent heart. In all things, he stresses the spiritual fulfillment of the earthly types of old.

Earlier, we were taught by God's command to put to death the desires of the flesh and thus to receive the body of Christ, which was sacrificed for us who are slaves in the Egypt of this world. For this reason, the Apostle says, "let a man test himself before eating of the bread and drinking from the cup" [1 Cor 11:28]. He commanded that it should be eaten in haste lest we partake of the sacrament of the Lord's body and blood with a sluggish heart and a lifeless countenance. We should partake of it with all the passion the soul can muster as if truly hungering and thirsting for justice. For the Lord Jesus Himself said, "Blessed are they who hunger and thirst for justice for they will be satisfied" [Matt 5:6]. So this reading concludes with a worthy end: "This is the Passover of the Lord" [Exod 12:11]. O the depths of the riches of knowledge of God! [see Rom 11:33] It is the Lord's Passover, the passing over of the Lord, so you would not think of what happened as earthly, but as heavenly. Through Him who passed over into it, He made it His body and His blood.

St. Gaudentius of Brescia (d. 410)

JUNE 15

Luis de León (1527–1591) was a Spanish Augustinian canon, known for the beauty of his religious poetry. His setting of the Song of Songs earned him the ire of the Inquisition, who cautioned his rash speech. In this excerpt from *The Names of Christ*, Luis offers a rich theology of marriage and the Eucharist. Drawing upon the teachings of St. Paul, Luis describes Holy Communion as the sacramental consummation of the Bridegroom and bride; that is, of Christ and the Church. The passage begins with a reference to the hypostatic union before treating the sacramental union between God and man.

And besides the union that He made with our flesh—having made it His own and showing Himself so vested before the eyes of all men so as to be embraced—so also this same flesh of His body, taken from our own, unites Him with the body of His Church and Spouse, and all those members of it that properly receive the Sacrament of the altar, taking His flesh to their own and identifying with it as much as possible. And He says, *the two shall become one flesh. This is a great sacrament, but I speak of Christ and His Church* [see Eph 5:31–32]. St. Paul does not deny the spousal meaning of Adam and Eve; both will be one flesh as it was said in the beginning [see Gen 2:24]. But, he says that this truth was a likeness of another hidden truth. And I say that in this the reason was manifest and discovered, but here it also says that it is a secret mystery. And this real and true body of His and ours clearly understands those words of Christ, "If you do not eat my flesh and drink my blood you do not have life in you" [John 6:53]. And later in the same place, "He who eats my flesh and drinks my blood remains in me and I in him" [John 6:56]. And this is neither more nor less than what St. Paul says, "We are one body that participate in the same Body" [see 1 Cor 10:17].

Luis de León (1527–1591)

JUNE 16

St. Jerome (c. 347–420) was one of the greatest biblical scholars of antiquity who was commissioned by Pope Damasus I to newly translate the Scriptures into Latin. In his *Commentary on St. Matthew*, St. Jerome demonstrates his expert knowledge of Hebrew, Latin, and Greek, whereby he explains the meaning of the phrase, "give us this day our daily bread" (Matt 6:11). For the Greek word "epiousios" ("daily") was a neologism that escaped even those fluent in Greek. Here, Jerome defines the term as "extraordinary," noting that it consequently cannot mean mere bread, but rather Christ Himself, the Bread of Life.

"Give us this day our supersubstantial bread" [Matt 6:11]. . . . But we have explicitly said that "supersubstantial" is *epiousiov* [επιουσιον] in Greek. This word is very frequently translated as *periousion* by the interpreters of the Septuagint. We have investigated various texts in Hebrew, and wherever they choose *periousion*, we have discovered *segola* in Hebrew, which Symmachus translated *exaireton*, that is, special or distinguished and extraordinary, although in certain texts it is interpreted as peculiar. So when we ask God to give us that peculiar or special bread, we are asking Him who said, "I am the living bread who came down from heaven" [John 6:51].

St. Jerome, Doctor of the Church (c. 347–420)

JUNE 17

St. Gregory of Nyssa (c. 335–395) delivered fifteen homilies on the Song of Songs and here comments on the verse: "Eat, my friends, and drink, and become inebriated, my brothers" (Song 5:1). Gregory identifies this inebriation with "ecstasy," for the latter is a transliteration of the Greek word, "ekstasis," which literally means "to stand outside oneself." This is no subjective experience of disembodied joy; rather, in a Christian context, it bespeaks true union. For the soul is removed from itself, so to speak, and passes into God. According to St. Gregory, this union is the result of friendship with Christ, which demands a life of virtue. It is those holy companions of Christ, then, that receive the invitation to this feast, and not those ill prepared.

> But such a proclamation was made for three reasons: that we may learn by one statement that God the Father purifies, that God the only-begotten Son purifies, and that God, who purifies every unclean thing, is the Holy Spirit. So then, as such inebriation happens from wine that the Lord sets before his fellow drinkers, an ecstasy with regard to more divine realities takes place in the soul. With these words, the Lord rightly urged those who, through the exercise of virtue, became His close companions, "Eat my friends, and drink, and become inebriated" [Song 5:1]; and not those who remained at bay. "For the one who eats and drinks unworthily eats and drinks condemnation for himself" [1 Cor 11:29]. Well does the Lord call those His brothers who are worthy of such food. For, the one who does His will is called his brother, and sister, and mother by the Lord [see Matt 12:50].

> *St. Gregory of Nyssa (c. 335–395)*

JUNE 18

Memorial of St. Elisabeth of Schönau

St. Elisabeth of Schönau (c. 1129–1164) was a Benedictine nun whose mystical writings echo those of St. Hildegard von Bingen in their bold prophetical style. In this excerpt from *The Ways of God*, those priests and religious lacking conversion and sincerity of heart are chastised by God. Their dishonorable lives culminate with unworthy celebration of the Eucharist—the very sacrament that should signify their holiness.

This exhortation of God is addressed to you who have chosen to serve God in the clerical or monastic state. You have chosen the best part, but take heed lest it slip from you. Carefully avoid the sinfulness of those who outwardly bear the semblance of religion, but shame its worth by their actions. With their lips they honor God, but by their ways they blaspheme Him. Some of them strive for knowledge of the law, but they do not know how to apply it. They turn their back on the truth, and yet boast of moving in the path of contemplation. They make the law of God, and their propagation of it, to serve their pride, avarice, and desires. And they boldly seize wealth and honors from those who dwell in Jesus Christ, cherishing their own foulness. They visit the sanctuary of God, and places to be hallowed by angels, with pride and pollution. And there they raise the adorable treasures of Christ's Sacrament in irreverent ministration with impure hearts.

St. Elisabeth of Schönau (c. 1129–1164)

JUNE 19

In the East, the Sacraments of Initiation—Baptism, Confirmation, and Holy Communion—are administered together, even to infants. Here, Nicholas Cabasilas (c. 1322–1392) speaks of their significance in the life of grace. Just as fleshly existence progresses from one stage to the next, so too do the sacraments mature the spiritual growth of souls. Because man is powerless to raise himself to God, Nicholas emphasizes that God condescends to man through the sacraments.

Baptism gives us existence and establishes us with Christ. This mystery takes the dead and corrupt and leads us into life. The chrism of oil perfects the one born, imparting a power fitting for such a life. The divine Eucharist then guards and preserves this saving life. For the bread of life grants preservation for what was acquired, and perfects those who were given life. Because of these things, we have our life by this bread; are moved by the oil; after having received our existence from the washing.

Through the sacraments, we live in God, transferring from the life of this visible world to the world unseen. This does not happen by exchanging places, but by exchanging this life with another kind. For we are not pulled toward God nor ascend to Him; rather He came down to us. We did not seek Him, but were sought out, since the sheep did not seek the shepherd, nor the coin its owner. He stooped down to earth, found the image, and came into places where the sheep had been misled. He destroyed the deception and established those remaining on earth; not by removing them, but by making them heavenly. He inaugurated heavenly life in them, not by leading them up to heaven but by bending heaven and coming down. Thus, the prophet says, "God bent the heavens and came down" [Ps 18:9].

Nicholas Cabasilas (c. 1322–1392)

JUNE 20

St. Paulinus (c. 354–431), bishop of Nola, was deeply devoted to Sacred Scripture and left behind numerous letters and poems imbued with its language. Here, Paulinus reflects on the unity of the Christian body, gathered together in the "one bread" of Holy Communion. By participating in this heavenly body, man may transcend the bonds of this world, escaping its corruption and death.

It is not strange if we are present while being absent, and if we know while being ignorant. This is because we are members of one body, have one head, and are flooded with one grace. We live by one bread, advance along one way, and live in the same house. Finally, in everything we exist in complete hope and faith. In this, we stand in the present and press on into the future. We are one with the Lord in both spirit and body, lest we become nothing, falling away from the one.

Here, St. Paulinus offers further insights into the Eucharist, distinguishing it from those earthly foods made to satisfy the appetite. Holy Communion, by contrast, only increases the soul's desire for unending communion with Christ.

"And he gave food to all flesh" [Ps 135:25]. This is not the food that perishes, but that food made into eternal nourishment, which the diligent soul, or the Catholic Church, makes. It is the body of the true bread that came down from heaven, and which grants life-giving food to "those who hunger for righteousness" [see Matt 5:6]. It does not satiate the flesh; rather, it strengthens the heart of man. This is the bread and font that the more one eats, the more one hungers. And the more one drinks, the thirstier one becomes. So as to eternally eat of this bread, let us produce good wheat in the mill of this world: for such is faithful work of obedience, a heart of pure love, and sincere faith.

St. Paulinus of Nola (c. 354–431)
[Memorial, June 22]

JUNE 21

St. John Fisher (1469–1535) was an English bishop and martyr whose imprisonment and execution was concurrent with that of St. Thomas More. In his trial, St. John refused King Henry VIII's self-proclaimed title as "Supreme Head of the Church," for which he was beheaded. In the following commentary on Psalm 51, St. John explains how the animal sacrifices of the Old Law prefigured the salvific blood of Christ. He thus applies the words of Psalm 51 "sprinkle me, O Lord with hyssop" (Ps 51:7)—a petition referring to the Passover ritual of placing blood on the doorpost with hyssop—to the Eucharist.

No one may doubt that the blood of animals, sprinkled before the time of the Incarnation, signified and represented the effusion of Christ's blood for our redemption. And this blood is of incomparable strength to eradicate sin than that of beasts. As often as the Holy Sacraments are repeated according to the commandment of Christ's Church, so often is the blood of our Lord sprinkled abroad to cleanse and put away sin. Then with the prophet [psalmist], let us say: *Thou wilt sprinkle me, O Lord, with hyssop, and I shall be cleansed* [Ps 51:7]. It is as if we say: Lord, our faith is so clear and without doubt by the perfect merit of Your Son, our Lord Jesus Christ, which by the effusion of His holy blood has given great efficacy and strength to the Holy Sacraments of His Church, that when we receive any of them, we shall be sprinkled and made clean by the virtue of His Precious Blood.

St. John Fisher (1469–1535)
[Memorial, June 22]

JUNE 22

Memorial of St. Thomas More, Martyr

St. Thomas More (1478–1535) was the chancellor of England who was martyred for refusing King Henry VIII's claim to religious authority. His fidelity in persecution earned him universal acclaim as he is even honored in the Anglican calendar of saints. In the following meditation, St. Thomas contemplates the Passion of Christ as the model for all Christian suffering. The Paschal Mystery is the source of the sacraments, which conform all Christians to their exemplar, the Crucified and Risen Christ.

So I now say for a painful death: If we would with due compassion conceive in our minds a remembrance of Christ's bitter and painful Passion—of the many sore bloody strokes that the cruel tormentors gave Him with rods and whips upon every part of His holy tender body; of the scornful crown of sharp thorns beaten down upon His holy head, so straight and so deep that on every part his blessed blood issued out and streamed down; of His lovely limbs drawn and stretched out upon the cross, to the intolerable pain of His sore-beaten veins and sinews, feeling anew, with the cruel stretching and straining, pain far surpassing any cramp in every part of His blessed body at once; of the great long nails then cruelly driven with the hammer through His holy hands and feet; of His body, in this horrible pain, lifted up and let hang, with all its weight bearing down upon the painful wounded places so grievously pierced with nails; and in such torment, without pity, but not without many despites, suffered to be pinned and pained the space of more than three long hours, till He himself willingly gave up unto his Father His holy soul; after which yet, to show the mightiness of their malice, after His holy soul departed, they pierced his holy heart with a sharp spear, at which issued out the holy blood and water whereof His holy sacraments have inestimable secret strength—if we could, I say, remember these things, in such a way as would God that we would, I verily suppose that the consideration of his incomparable kindness could not fail so to inflame our key-cold hearts, and set them on fire with His love, that we should find ourselves not only content but also glad and desirous to suffer death for his sake, who so marvelously and lovingly consented to sustain so far passing painful death for ours.

St. Thomas More, Martyr (1478–1535)

JUNE 23

Memorial of St. Joseph Cafasso

St. Joseph Cafasso (1811–1860) was an Italian priest who dedicated himself to serving the outcast and imprisoned. In this passage, St. Joseph movingly writes of the renovation of cultures due to the cult of the Blessed Sacrament. By making daily visits to the Blessed Sacrament, Christians express its centrality in their lives. St. Joseph singles out priests as exemplars for this practice as they are uniquely positioned to establish religious norms.

> I know of certain countries where churches were always empty on workdays, but after priests began to practice visits to the Most Blessed Sacrament and recommend it to others, it was a marvel to see the gathering of people in the church; artists, peasants, old men, youths, all walking to the church at evening to thank the Lord. They were not only called by their faith, but by the example of the good priest. So, I cannot recommend a more holy, excellent, and exemplary practice for the people than to visit our good God.

> *St. Joseph Cafasso (1811–1860)*

JUNE 24

Solemnity of the Nativity of St. John the Baptist

On the celebration of the Nativity of St. John the Baptist, the Church honors that zealous forerunner of the Messiah, greatest born of women in the Old Covenant. St. Caesarius of Arles (c. 468–542), the sixth-century bishop of southern France, here exhorts Christians to imitate St. John in his ascetical purity. For the tongue of him who receives Holy Communion must be worthily prepared for such a King. Caesarius accordingly warns Christians that they cannot be devoted to both God and the world.

Since we desire to celebrate the birth of St. John the Baptist with joy, as with other coming feasts, all should foster whole-hearted purity and honesty as the auspicious solemnity is near. And this is so that all may celebrate that feast with joy and be worthy to approach the altar of the Lord with a free and sincere conscience . . . Warn others, my brothers, not to bring forth from the mouth of your family base and decadent songs, inimical to purity and honesty. For it is not right that a decadent and suggestive song should proceed from the mouth into which the Eucharist of Christ enters.

St. Caesarius of Arles (c. 468–542)

JUNE 25

In the fourth century, Donatus Magnus contended that a holy priest could validly perform the sacraments and that a sinful priest invalidated their efficacy and power. St. Augustine (354–430), however, professed that it was not the moral character of the priest that effects the sacraments, but Christ Himself. He understood well that God would not leave Christians uncertain in so grave a matter as the sacraments. Accordingly, St. Augustine enunciates the orthodox view that the sacraments are valid so long as they are carried out by the proper minister. Whether it is a saint or sinner who works the sacraments, it is Christ Himself who operates as high priest.

Therefore, the Lord Himself sent those cleansed from leprosy to the same sacraments so that they might offer a sacrifice for themselves before the priests; for the sacrifice had not yet become efficacious for them. This is because He wanted it to be celebrated afterwards in the Church on behalf of all, since He had announced it among them all. If this is so, how much more ought we to attribute to them the sacraments of this New Testament when we find them among certain heretics or schismatics, and not reject them as something unrecognized. Rather, recognize the gifts of the true Husband, though in the possession of an adulteress, and correct with a truthful word the fornication which really belongs to the adulteress; not holding the gifts guilty, which belong entirely to the merciful Lord.

. . . Just as Judas, to whom the Lord gave a morsel, allowed the Devil to have first place within himself—not by receiving something evil, but by giving a place to evil in himself—so anyone receiving the Lord's sacrament unworthily does not make it evil because he is evil, or he would receive nothing if he did not worthily receive unto salvation; however, it is the body and blood of the Lord even for those to whom the Apostle says, "he who eats and drinks unworthily eats and drinks condemnation to himself" [1 Cor 11:29].

St. Augustine of Hippo, Bishop and Doctor (354–430)

JUNE 26

Memorial of St. Josemaría Escrivá

St. Josemaría Escrivá (1902–1975) was a Spanish priest and the founder of Opus Dei, an organization of priests and laity dedicated to the sanctification of work. In the following passages from *The Way*, St. Josemaría offers a series of pious thoughts meant to recollect the soul and enkindle it in prayer. Drawing upon his own vision of faith, he encourages Christians to a living awareness of Christ's personal presence in the Blessed Sacrament.

534 Going to Communion every day for so many years! Anybody else would be a saint by now, you told me, and I . . . I'm always the same!

Son, I replied, keep up your daily Communion, and think: What would I be if I had not gone?

537 When you approach the Tabernacle remember that he has been awaiting you for twenty centuries.

538 There he is: King of Kings, and Lord of Lords, hidden in the Bread.

To this extreme has he humbled himself through love of you.

539 He has stayed here for you. It is not reverence to omit Communion when well disposed. It's irreverence only when you receive him unworthily.

St. Josemaría Escrivá (1902–1975)

JUNE 27

Memorial of St. Cyril of Alexandria, Bishop and Doctor

St. Cyril (378–444) was the archbishop of Alexandria and the leading voice of orthodoxy against the errors of Nestorius. Whereas Nestorius separated Christ's two natures so as to posit two persons (prosopon) in Christ, Cyril articulated the Church's faith in the unity of Christ. Christ thus possesses two natures, divine and human, that are united in His one divine person. According to the orthodox view, the only subject of the humanity of Christ—and by extension the Eucharist— is the divine person of the Son. For this reason, the humanity of Christ and the Eucharist are worthy of adoration.

He clearly says, "this is my body" and "this is my blood" [Matt 26:26, 28] that you may not think the appearances are only a figure, but that the proffered gifts we partake in are, in fact, transformed into the body and blood of Christ in accordance with the truth of God who is ineffable and omnipotent. And by receiving them, we receive into ourselves the life-giving and sanctifying power of Christ. For through the Holy Spirit, He had to be mingled in a way fitting for God to be in us; dwelling within us bodily by His holy flesh and precious blood. We have these things as a life-giving blessing under bread and wine that we may not grow faint when beholding the flesh and blood being offered on the sacred tables of the churches. Because God wanted to assist us in our weaknesses, He imparted the power of life to the gifts, and transformed them to contain the effects of His life. Do not doubt that this is true, because He clearly said, "this is my body" and "this is my blood" [Matt 26:26, 28]. Rather, receive the Savior's saying by faith, because it is true and no lie.

St. Cyril of Alexandria, Bishop and Doctor (378–444)

JUNE 28

Memorial of St. Irenaeus of Lyons

St. Irenaeus of Lyons (c. 130–202) is known for his theological writings on the "recapitulation theory," which teaches that Christ is the New Adam, the new head of humanity. Here, St. Irenaeus explores Christ's establishment of the New Covenant in place of the sacrificial rites of the old. Citing the prophet Malachi, Irenaeus explains that the Hebraic cult of sacrifice was prophesied to cease and that a new universal cult would stand in its place. The Eucharist is thus revealed as the pure sacrifice to God, offered in every land and every place (see Mal 1:10–11).

Christ counseled His disciples to offer the first-fruits of creation to God—not as if God needed anything, but that they might not be unfruitful or ungrateful—and He took the bread from creation, and gave thanks saying, "this is my body" [Matt 26:26]. So too, He took the cup from creation and professed it to be His own blood, teaching them that it is the new offering of the New Covenant. It is this offering that the Church has received from the Apostles, and which it offers to God throughout the world. It is thus offered to God who gives us nourishment, which is to say, the first-fruits of His own gifts in the New Covenant. Of this, Malachi the prophet intimated in advance: "I am not pleased with you, says the Lord Almighty, and I will not accept a gift from your hands. For from the rising of the sun to its setting My name is glorified among the nations, and in every place incense is offered to My name as well as a pure sacrifice; for my name is great among the nations, says the Lord Almighty" [Mal 1:10–11]. This clearly shows that the first people [the Israelites] would cease to offer a sacrifice to God, but that in every place a sacrifice is offered to Him: one that is pure, and in which His name is glorified among the nations.

St. Irenaeus of Lyons (c. 130–202)

JUNE 29

The Solemnity of Ss. Peter and Paul

On the Solemnity of Ss. Peter and Paul, the Church honors the great founders of the Roman diocese—that twice-blessed Church that presides in love. St. Gregory the Great (c. 540–604), the sixth-century head of the Roman See, here writes of the universal dimensions of the Church, noting that the Church Militant is mystically united with the Church Triumphant. Both offer sacrifice, one of suffering and the other of glorious praise. Together, the two are united in the flesh of Christ, offered upon the altar of God.

For the Holy Church has two lives: one that it conducts in time, the other it receives in eternity. In the former, it labors on earth; in the latter, it is rewarded in heaven. In the one, it gathers rewards, but in the other, it rejoices in the rewards received. And in both it offers sacrifice. In the first, it is sacrifice of compunction, and in the second, there a sacrifice of praise. About this first sacrifice, it is said, "the sacrifice offered to God is a contrite spirit" [Ps 51:17]. But about the other, it is written, "then you will accept a sacrifice of righteousness and holocausts" [Ps 51:19]. But about this he says, "that my glory may sing to you, and that I may not be regretful" [Ps 30:12]. Yet in both sacrifices, flesh is offered, since here the offering of flesh is the torment of the body; there the offering of flesh is the glory of the resurrection in praise of God. Then, in that flesh would be offered as in a holocaust when it would have nothing of contradiction; nothing of mortality once it has been changed into eternal incorruption, because it will all abide forever in praise once it has been ignited by the fire of His love.

In this second reading, St. Gregory highlights the connection between Christian sacrifice and the thanksgiving—the Eucharist—of Christ.

But let Him instruct all those that believe in Him that when they are scourged, they may know how to bless God by the following words: "As it has pleased the Lord, so it is done, blessed be the name of the Lord" (Job 1:21). And likewise in the Gospel, when He is shown drawing near to His Passion, He is described taking bread and giving thanks. And so He who bears the stripes of the sins of others gives thanks.

St. Gregory the Great (c. 540–604)

JUNE 30

Memorial of Bl. Antonio Rosmini-Serbati

Bl. Antonio Rosmini-Serbati (1797–1855) was a noted Catholic philosopher who dedicated himself to reforming academic philosophy in accordance with Thomistic principles. His deep piety and intellectual gifts are evidenced in his letter to Giulio Padulli, a man whose ill health had kept him from visiting church. Just as the body hungers for bread, Bl. Antonio reasons that the faithful have spiritual senses that hunger and thirst for the Bread of Life. In this way, he commiserates with Padulli who was unable to quench his spiritual thirst.

You are quite right in desiring to be once more in church, in the presence of our Divine Love, and should anyone reprove this desire you might answer in the words of Job: "Does not the ear discern words and the palate taste food?" (Job 12:11). For one who has bodily senses, it is impossible not to have the corresponding sensations. In like manner, he who has a spiritual sense—something rarer and more sublime but which all Christians possess who love Jesus Christ—he, I say, cannot but feel pain at being separated from his Lord and deprived of Him. It is true that with our heart, at least, we may seek and find Jesus everywhere; but our Lord, who understood us because He had made us, condescended to make His presence not only real, but corporeal also. He was pleased to take unto Himself a body that should be like our own, so that our dead bodies may be restored to life by contact with His living body, which can never again be subject to death. And there is a sense peculiar to Christians which gives us a perception of this new happiness and makes us eagerly expect it. It is this spiritual sense which makes it impossible for you not to desire to be in the church before the Tabernacle, holding converse with our Lord.

Bl. Antonio Rosmini-Serbati (1797–1855)

JULY

Memorial of St. Junípero Serra

St. Junípero Serra (1713–1784) was an eighteenth-century Franciscan who established Catholic missions along the coast of California. In the following letter, St. Junípero describes the momentous occasion of arriving in Monterey, California, the spot Sebastian Vizcaino had abandoned 167 years earlier. Heralding the Gospel in new lands, this occasion was providentially marked by the celebration of the Feast of Pentecost. St. Junípero's account remains a precious testimony to the early years of missionary activity in America and the primacy of the Mass in the efforts of evangelization.

On the 31st of May, by the favor of God, after a month and half of a somewhat dangerous voyage, the vessel *San Antonio*, commanded by Captain D. Juan Perez, arrived and anchored in the beautiful port of Monterrey; the same in reality and detail as that of the expedition of D. Sebastian Vizcaino in 1603. That same night, I was much consoled when they told me that the land expedition had arrived eight days earlier with Fr. Juan Crespi, and that all were in good health. On the day of Pentecost, the third of June, all the officials of the land and sea expedition, and all the people in the ship, were united together. The fathers built an altar, suspended and rang the bells, sang the hymn *Veni Creator*, blessed the water, raised and blessed the large cross and the royal standards. The mass was sung, the first known to have been celebrated here since [Vizcaino]. Afterwards we sang the Salutation of Our Lady before the image which occupied the altar. We concluded the ceremony by singing the *Te Deum*.

St. Junípero Serra (1713–1784)

JULY 2

Memorial of St. Bernardino Realino

St. Bernardino Realino (1530–1616) was an Italian Jesuit, known for his compassion for the poor. Among his poems and prayers is *Jubilation after Holy Communion*, which gives voice to the soul who has received the Lord. In these few lines, St. Bernardino expresses the dispositions of a saint whose will is wholly fixed on the love of God. At the moment of communion, the soul is thus at rest, possessing the all in all.

> Other goods, other loves, other treasures:
> grant that I may never desire nor obtain them.
> He, the Lord whom I adore, dwells with me.
> What more could I want? when such cost the ancient curse!
>
> If from such heavenly joy, I do not die,
> It is because You, who are life, give it.
> To Mary, no great gift have I.
> She merited the Redeemer, but I am unworthy.
>
> You can obtain as much as you desire,
> Virgin Mother of the Son of God.
> I am not ungrateful for your gifts.
> Fulfill my great desires:
>
> Let the sinful world ever weary me
> And all its delights be forgotten.

Let heaven sigh, and my soul
Speak not, save *Jesus and Mary.*
Laus Deo!

St. Bernardino Realino (1530–1616)

JULY 3

Feast of St. Thomas, Apostle

On the feast of St. Thomas the Apostle, the Church remembers the confession of him who required sight to believe. In this reading, St. John Chrysostom (349–407) explains that Christians who make similar demands are met by Christ in the Eucharist. Not only does the Blessed Sacrament allow man to draw near to Christ as Thomas had, but it makes possible a union otherwise unattainable. The Eucharist is the door to heaven and the great means of intimate union between God and man.

> Let His word be stronger than our own reasonings and sight. And this we practice in regard to the Mysteries, not focusing on the things we see before us, but holding fast to His words. His word cannot deceive, but our senses can easily be deceived. God has never failed, yet our senses have been overturned many times. Since He says, "this is my body" [Matt 26:26], let us be persuaded, believe, and look on with spiritual vision. For, Christ has delivered nothing to us that can be seen with the senses, but rather metaphysical realities in observable things. So also in baptism: the gift comes through the sensible element of water, but what is produced is metaphysical, i.e., birth and regeneration. If you did not have a body, He would have given you the gifts in bare reality without physical form. But since the soul is bound up with the body, He gives you metaphysical realities in physical things. So many say, "I would like to see His form, His distinctive appearance, His clothes, His sandals." Look, you do see him, you touch him, you eat him. Yes, you desire to see His garments, but He gives

you Himself; not only to see, but to be touched, eaten, and received within. Let no one approach staggering nor dissolute; rather, all should be inflamed, full of zeal, and fully awake. If the Jews stood ready with their sandals and staff in hand, eating with haste, how much more should we be sober and disciplined. They were about to enter Israel and walked with a roadmap, but we are about to journey to heaven.

St. John Chrysostom, Bishop and Doctor (349–407)

JULY 4

Blind from the age of four, Didymus (c. 313–398) was called "the Seer" by St. Jerome, who recognized his profound spiritual vision. In the passage below, Didymus reflects on the enlightenment given to man in the sacraments. For him, it is not only baptism that floods the soul with supernatural light, but the sacrament of the Eucharist, which unites man to the source of all grace. Didymus begins by meditating on the seventh chapter of John wherein Jesus proclaims: "He who believes in me . . . 'Out of his heart shall flow rivers of living water'" (John 7:38).

Because the word "water" designates the Holy Spirit, he speaks of the Spirit in baptism, and John testifies of the Savior's words: "He who believes in me, as Scripture says, out of his heart will flow rivers of living water" [John 7:38]. And John immediately adds, "this he said of the Spirit, in whom those who believe were to receive" [John 7:39]. Because we are gratuitously made righteous on account of the surpassing goodness of the Trinity, though unworthy, Paul's saying to the Romans applies: "since all have sinned and fall short of the glory of God, they are justified by his grace as a gift through the redemption in Christ Jesus" [Rom 3:23–24]. Blessing those made worthy of this gift, the Lord says to his disciples in Luke, "Blessed are the eyes that have seen what you see. I say to you. Many prophets desired to see what you see and did not see it, to hear what you hear and did not hear it" [Luke 10:23–24]. We who are spiritual not only see and hear it, but we also are enlightened freely by the Holy Spirit as we partake of Christ's body and taste the immortal source.

Didymus the Blind (c. 313–398)

JULY 5

In the following treatise, St. Basil (330–379) asks whether it is dangerous to receive Holy Communion in the state of sin. In order to address this question, he engages the whole of divine revelation, employing the Old Testament in service of the New. In this way, St. Basil cites passages from Leviticus in order to warn Christians against unworthy reception of the Eucharist.

Question: Whether it is dangerous for one not free from every defilement of flesh and spirit to eat the body and to drink the blood of the Lord. Answer: God established a greater punishment for those who dare to touch the holy things in impurity. It was written by way of their example to admonish us: "The Lord said to Moses: Tell Aaron and his sons to keep away from the holy things of the people of Israel, which they dedicate to me, so that they may not profane my holy name: I am the Lord. Say to them, 'If any man of your generations approaches the holy things, which the children of Israel dedicate to the Lord, while he has an uncleanness, that person shall be cut off from my presence. I am the Lord'" [Lev 22:2–3]. If such a threat was given to anyone who simply came into His presence in the things made holy among men, what could be said about the one who dared to do something with such a great mystery as this? Inasmuch as the Lord said, "Something greater is here" [Matt 12:6], so much more terrible and fearful is the one who dares to touch the body of Christ in a state of defilement than to touch rams and bulls. The Apostle says,

"Whoever, therefore, eats the bread or drinks the cup of the Lord in an unworthy manner will be guilty of profaning the body and blood of the Lord" [1 Cor 11:27]. Even more vehemently and fearfully does he present the judgment by repetition when he says, "Let each one examine himself and so let him eat of the bread and drink of the cup. For the one who eats and drinks unworthily eats and drinks judgment to himself by not discerning the Lord's body" [1 Cor 11:29]. So let us cleanse ourselves from every defilement: the difference between a defilement and uncleanness is evident to all who consider it, so let us approach the holy gifts that we may flee the judgment of those who killed the Lord. Let us possess eternal life as the Lord and God Jesus Christ, who cannot lie, promised.

St. Basil the Great, Bishop and Doctor (330–379)

JULY 6

In his defense of Christ's Real Presence in the Eucharist, St. John Damascene (c. 675–749) recalls a wealth of scriptural passages that illustrate God's power over matter. Moving from the supernatural work of creation to the miracle of the Incarnation, St. John shows transubstantiation to be of the same cloth. Because God is not merely a competing power in the universe but wholly transcendent of it, St. John ends by noting the mysterious and exalted status of the Eucharistic gift.

If then, the word of God is living and effective [Heb 4:12], and the Lord made whatever He wanted; if He said, "let there be light, and it happened" [Gen 1:3], and "let there be a firmament and it came about" [Gen 1:7]; and if the heavens were established by the word of the Lord, and all their power by the breath of His mouth; if heaven and earth, water and fire, and air, and their whole order were perfected by the word of the Lord, afterwards the noble man was perfected by the word. If God the Word willed to become a man, and without generation took up for His own flesh the pure and spotless blood of the holy Ever-Virgin, is He not able to make bread His body, and the wine and water blood? He said in the beginning, "Let the earth bring forth green vegetation" [Gen 1:11], and even now as rain comes, it brings forth growth as it is supplied and strengthened by divine ordinance. God said, "This is my body" and "this is my blood," and "do this in remembrance of me" [Luke 22:19–20]. And it comes about by His all-powerful ordinance "until he comes" [1 Cor 11:26]. So he said, "until he comes," and the rain takes place in this new vineyard through the Epiclesis, that is, the power of the Holy Spirit overshadowing it. In the same way, whatever God made, He made through the power of the Holy Spirit, so also now the power of the Spirit effects things above nature, which faith alone can receive. "How can this be to me" says the holy Virgin, "since I don't know a man?" [Luke 1:34] The archangel Gabriel answers her, "The Holy Spirit will come over you and the power of the most High will overshadow you" [Luke 1:35]. And now you ask how the bread can become the body of Christ and the wine and water the blood of Christ? I tell you, the Holy Spirit visits with His presence and makes these things something beyond human intellect and understanding.

St. John Damascene, Doctor of the Church (c. 675–749)

JULY 7

In the following passage from *The Imitation of Christ*, Thomas á Kempis (1380–1471) speaks of spiritual warfare and the Eucharist. Because the devil well knows the power of this great sacrament, he works to draw men away from it through fear, anxiety, and shame. When the devil accuses the just man, Thomas recommends rejecting these thoughts and rushing forth to receive Holy Communion. So long as one is properly disposed, Christians should hasten to the source of their strength and sanctification.

Frequently return to the fountain of grace and divine mercy, to the fountain of goodness and all purity, that you may be healed of your passions and vices, obtaining strength and vigilance against all the temptations and deceit of the devil. The enemy knows the fruit and the great remedy that Holy Communion offers and thus strives by all means and occasions to hinder men, drawing the faithful and devout away from it. For when some are preparing for Holy Communion, they suffer all the worse assaults of the devil. This wicked spirit, as it is written in Job, comes among the sons of God to disturb them, or fill them with excessive fear. He does this to lessen their devotion, or attack and rob them of faith so that they might abandon Communion all together—or at least cool their fervor. But nothing is gained by averting to his cunning and illusions, however disgraceful and horrid they may be. Rather, all his suggestions are to be cast back against his own head. This wretch is to be scorned and derided: Holy Communion is not be omitted on account of his provocations and revilings.

Thomas á Kempis (1380–1471)

JULY 8

Julian of Norwich (c. 1342–1416) was an English anchoress who recorded her mystical visions in the renowned work, *Revelations of Divine Love*. Julian's writings emphasize God's providence over all things, a theme summarized by the famous phrase: "All shall be well, all shall be well, and all manner of thing shall be well." In the following passage, Julian contemplates the Precious Blood shed during Christ's Passion and its power over sin and death. Notably, Julian views the Precious Blood as a true drink, not a mere figure, which superabundantly flows from the side of Christ.

And then came to my mind that God has made waters plenteous on earth for our service, and for our bodily ease, because of the tender love that He has for us. Yet does He prefer that we take full homely His blessed blood to wash us from sin. For there is no drink that is made that He likes so well to give us. For it is most plenteous as it is most precious; and that by the virtue of His blessed Godhead. And it is of our kind, and all-blissfully belongs to us by the virtue of His precious love.

The dearworthy blood of our Lord Jesus Christ as verily as it is most precious, so verily it is most plenteous. Behold and see! The precious plenty of His dearworthy blood descended down into hell and burst her bands and delivered all that were there which belonged to the Court of Heaven. The precious plenty of His dearworthy blood overflows all Earth and is ready to wash all creatures of sin which be of goodwill, have been, and shall be. The precious plenty of His dearworthy blood ascended up into Heaven to the blessed Body of our Lord Jesus Christ and there is in Him, bleeding and praying for us to the Father—and is, and shall be as long as needed, and ever shall be as long as it is needed. And evermore it floweth in all Heavens, enjoying the salvation of all mankind that are there, and shall be, fulfilling the number [of the Blessed].

Julian of Norwich (c. 1342–1416)

JULY 9

Memorial of St. Veronica Giuliani

From her childhood, St. Veronica Giuliani (1660–1727) exhibited extraordinary mystical gifts that paved the way for her entry into the Poor Clare monastery at Citta di Castello. In the following extracts from her diary, St. Veronica reveals her supernal joy in receiving Holy Communion, evidencing a life of intimate encounter with God. Her movements of the heart are said to transcend all earthly delights, even as they press it into exalted praise.

When I went to Holy Communion, it seemed that the door of my heart was thrown wide open, as if to receive a friend, and as soon as He had entered, it was closed. Thus, it came to pass that my heart shut itself up alone with its God. It is beyond my power to describe all the effects, movements, and exultations that His presence produced. If I were to give an illustration of every pastime and pleasure which a dearest friend could provide for us, I should say that they are nothing in comparison. And if all the joys that the universe could offer were united, I should pronounce them to be nothing when compared with what my heart enjoys with her God; or rather, with what God works in my soul, for it is all His own operation.

. . . If I were to relate all the effects which are wrought in the heart by love at the time of Holy Communion and at other seasons, I should never finish. Suffice it to say that the Holy Eucharist is the very palace and sanctuary of love. The heart becomes more inflamed than ever when it sees itself the dwelling-place of the most holy Trinity, and when Jesus comes to me in the Blessed Sacrament and I hear the words, 'Hail thou temple of the whole Trinity!' Then, my heart becomes so enlarged and enkindled that sometimes I seem to hear sweet melodies and am ravished with heavenly music. When engaged in laborious duties, I find myself ready to do anything. Sometimes I am impelled by such mighty desires to praise and bless God that my heart would gladly be converted into tongues, wherewith to invoke and glorify its sole and highest good.

St. Veronica Giuliani (1660–1727)

JULY 10

The ancient Liturgy of St. James has its roots in Jerusalem and Antioch and is still in use among Eastern rite churches. The following prayer, known as the "Prayer of the Veil," is fashioned after St. Paul's words in the Letter to the Hebrews: "Having therefore, brothers, confidence in entering into the holies by the blood of Christ; a new and living way which he has dedicated for us through the veil, that is to say, his flesh" (Heb 10:19–20). This liturgical prayer underscores the truth that Christ's human flesh is the new temple veil whereby man has access to the holy of holies, God Himself.

> We thank You Lord, our God, for You have given us confidence to enter into Your holy place, which You have renewed for us as an undefiled and living way through the veil of the flesh of Your Christ. Having been made worthy to enter into the place of Your glorious dwelling, to come within the veil, and to look upon the holy of holies, we fall down before Your goodness. Master, be merciful to us. In fear and trembling, we prepare to stand before Your holy altar to offer this awesome and unbloody sacrifice for our sins and for the errors of humanity. O God, send Your good grace; sanctify our souls, bodies, and spirits. Turn our minds toward godliness so that in good conscience, we may offer You a sacrifice of praise. [Accomplish this] by the mercy and love of Your only begotten Son for mankind, with whom You and Your all-holy, good, and life-giving Spirit are now and forever.

> *The Divine Liturgy of St. James*

JULY 11

Memorial of St. Benedict of Nursia

St. Benedict of Nursia (d. 547), the father of Western monasticism, provided a balanced rule of life that inspired countless souls to seek the consecrated life. His efforts ultimately preserved the intellectual life of Europe as his monasteries served as stable centers of learning. In the following passage, Pope St. Gregory the Great (540–604) relates a story about St. Benedict that highlights the connection between holiness and communion with Christ. The Eucharist is shown to be the sign of true unity, and those who do not strive for sanctity are excluded from this Holy Communion.

Not far from his Abbey, there lived two nuns of noble birth in a place by themselves, served by a religious man for their external business. As nobility of family often breeds ignoble minds, making them consider their superiority over others and lack in humility of speech, so it was with these nuns. For, they had not learned to temper their tongues and to keep them trained under the bridle of their habit. Their indiscreet speech often provoked the religious man to anger, and after bearing this for a long time, he complained to the man of God [St. Benedict], relating their reproachful words. Thus, the man of God sent them this message:

"Amend your tongues, or I will excommunicate you." He did not pronounce this sentence against them, but only threatened to if they did not amend themselves. Yet for all of this, they did not change their conditions at all, and soon, both departed from this life. While the solemn Mass of burial was being celebrated inside the church, the deacon said with a loud voice, as is the custom, "If there is anyone who does not communicate, let them depart." The nurse who used to give an offering to the Lord for them beheld them rise out of their graves, and depart from the church.

Having seen them leave the church, unable to remain within it, the nurse remembered what the man of God had said to them while they were alive. For he told them that he would deprive them of communion unless they amended their tongues and conditions.

Pope St. Gregory the Great, Doctor of the Church (540–604)

JULY 12

Memorial of Ss. Louis and Zélie Martin

Ss. Louis and Zélie Martin (1823–1894; 1831–1877) led extraordinary lives of virtue and were the first married couple to be canonized together. In the following reflection from their daughter, St. Thérèse of Lisieux (1873–1897), their daily visits to the Blessed Sacrament are fondly recalled. Highlighting the centrality of Sunday Mass, St. Thérèse further describes their fidelity and devotion to the liturgy.

Every afternoon I went out for a walk with him, and we paid a visit to the Blessed Sacrament in one of the churches . . . each week brought [a feast] very dear to my heart, and that was Sunday. What a glorious day! The Feast of God! The day of rest! First of all the whole family went to High Mass, and I remember that before the sermon we had to come down from our places, which were some way from the pulpit. This was not always easy, but everyone offered a place to little Thérèse and her Father . . . I really did listen attentively, but I must admit I looked at Papa more than the preacher; for I read many things in his face. Sometimes his eyes were filled with tears, which he strove in vain to keep back. And as he listened to the eternal truths, he seemed no longer of this earth; his soul was absorbed in the thought of another world. Alas! Many long and sorrowful years had to pass before Heaven was to be opened to him, and Our Lord with His Own Divine Hand was to wipe away the bitter tears of His faithful servant.

Here, St. Thérèse recounts her entry into Carmel, describing her father's spirit of abandonment and his reflexive devotion to the Eucharist.

My Father came to meet me at the enclosure door, his eyes full of tears, and pressing me to his heart exclaimed: "Ah! Here is my little Queen!" Then, giving me his arm, we made our solemn entry into the public Chapel. This was his day of triumph, his last feast on earth; now his sacrifice was complete, and his children belonged to God. Céline had already confided to him that she also wished to leave the world for the Carmel later on. On hearing this he was beside himself with joy: "Let us go before the Blessed Sacrament," he said, "and thank God for all the graces He has granted us, and the honor He has paid me in choosing His Spouses from my household."

St. Thérèse of Lisieux, Virgin and Doctor (1873–1897)

JULY 13

In his commentary on Psalm 78, Cassiodorus (c. 490–583) follows the Western Fathers in exploring the "bread of angels" theme, found in the Old Testament. Earlier in his remarks, Cassiodorus identified the bread of angels with the Eucharist. Here, he ponders how angels could be said to eat this bread, being incorporeal. Explaining that the substance of the Eucharist is Christ Himself, Cassiodorus concludes that the angels feast upon this bread through their contemplation.

Men ate of the bread of the angels; he sent them provision of grain in abundance. (Ps 78:25)

Finally, it says that "men ate the bread of angels" [Ps 78:25]. The bread of angels is rightly said to be Christ, since they indeed feast on His praise. For angels cannot be believed to eat physical bread; rather, they nourish themselves on that contemplation of the Lord by which such sublime creatures are refreshed. But this bread fills the angels in heaven and feeds us on earth, delighting the angels by contemplation, and refreshing us with a holy visitation.

He continues by saying, "he sent them provision of grain in abundance" [Ps 78:25]. Thus, he further expresses that plenty, which was great enough to overcome the people's longing. Finally, it adds, "in abundance;" for that abounds which cannot be consumed by any longing.

Cassiodorus (c. 490–583)

JULY 14

In the wake of the French Revolution, Bl. Anne-Marie Javouhey (1779–1851) established the Institute of St. Joseph of Cluny for the education and formation of children in the Catholic faith. In this passage, Bl. Anne-Marie writes on the charism of her new congregation and its grounding in prayer and sacrifice. To this end, she recommends intercessory prayer in the form of offering one's Holy Communion for the intention of another. This practice is not only most efficacious, but constitutes a sublime act of charity.

> The special purpose of the Congregation is the formation of good Christians. For this, it is necessary to pray and receive communion for the intention of children often. Give them good examples and a love for their religion. Attach great importance to the study of religion and the catechism. Teach them to pray well, and commend all their deeds to God. And instruct them to offer their hearts to God upon waking, to prayerfully assist at Holy Mass, and to confess their sins. Teach them to make pious reflections from time to time, and explain to them the canticles they sing and the texts that they read.

Bl. Anne-Marie Javouhey (1779–1851)
[Memorial, July 15]

JULY 15

Memorial of St. Bonaventure, Bishop and Doctor

Among St. Bonaventure's (1221–1274) most famous works is his *Breviloquium*, a concise exposition of the Christian faith. The following passage speaks to the efficacious nature of the Eucharist, noting its power to accomplish the union of love it signifies. To this end, St. Bonaventure makes reference to Christ's headship over the mystical body, explaining that grace is only received by being gathered under the head. Holy Communion is, therefore, the sign of unity between Christ and His Mystical Body.

> Likewise, because the time of grace demands that the sacrament of union and love not only signify this union and love, but also be a means inflaming the heart toward them so as to bring about what it represents; and because what chiefly inflames toward mutual love, and chiefly unites the members, is the oneness of the Head from whom the stream of mutual affection flows into us through the all-pervading, uniting, and transforming power of love: therefore this sacrament contains the true body and immaculate flesh of Christ, in such a way that it penetrates our being, unites us to one another, and transforms us into Him through that burning love by which He gave Himself to us [in the incarnation], offered Himself up for us [in the passion], and now gives Himself back to us, to remain with us until the end of the world.

St. Bonaventure, Bishop and Doctor (1221–1274)

JULY 16

Feast of Our Lady of Mount Carmel

On the Feast of Our Lady of Mount Carmel, the Church remembers the Blessed Virgin Mary and the protection she affords those gathered under her mantle. Though Mt. Carmel was witness to the dramatic deeds of Elijah (1 Kgs 18), St. Ambrose (c. 340–397) teaches that all such events were merely shadows of the New Covenant. Here, Ambrose contemplates the manna of the Old Covenant, which prefigured Christ, the Bread of Life. Whereas the former was purely material, the latter is living, spiritual, and the source of salvation.

It has been proven that the sacraments of the Church are more ancient; now, recognize that they are also superior. It was truly a marvel that God rained down manna for the fathers, feeding them daily with the food of heaven. This is why it says, "man ate the bread of angels" [Ps 78:25]. But though they ate that bread, they nevertheless all died in the desert. Yet, the food that you receive is the living bread which came down from heaven. It furnishes the substance of eternal life, and whoever eats this bread will never die: for it is the body of Christ. Consider now whether the bread of angels, or the flesh of Christ, is more excellent. Certainly, His flesh is the substance of life. That former manna came from heaven; this one is beyond heaven. That first was of heaven; this one is from the Lord of heaven. That first one was liable to corruption if it stayed until the next day; this one is free of all corruption, because whoever devoutly tastes it cannot be touched by corruption. For them, water flowed from the rock; for you blood flows from Christ. Water satisfied them for a time; the blood washes you for eternity. A Jew drank and still had thirst; when you drink you cannot thirst. That one was in a shadow; this one is in truth.

If you marvel at that which is a shadow, how great is that which the shadow points to. Listen, a shadow took place among the fathers: The apostle Paul says, "They drank from the rock that followed them; that rock was Christ. But with most of them God was not pleased; for, they died in the desert" [1 Col 10:4–5]. But these things happened as figures for us. You have recognized more excellent things for the light is more powerful than the shadow, truth than the figure, the body of the creator than manna from heaven.

St. Ambrose of Milan, Bishop and Doctor (c. 340–397)

JULY 17

St. Germanus (634–733), Patriarch of Constantinople, here comments on the Divine Liturgy, highlighting the symbolic value of its
actions. Drawing upon a rich variety of scriptural passages, Germanus
shows the connection between the liturgy and the historical actions
of the Christ. Notably, his use of the term "imitation" is not like the
modern concept of a bare copy; rather, the ancient Christian usage of
"imitation" indicates a memorial (anamnesis) that makes present the
reality signified.

> The wine and water are the blood and water that flowed
> from His side, as the prophet says: "bread shall be given to
> him, and water to drink" [Isa 33:16]. The lance signifies that
> which pierced Christ on the cross, and the bread and cup
> really and truly imitate the mystical supper wherein Christ
> took bread and wine and said, "All of you, take, eat, and
> drink. This is my body and blood" [Matt 26:26]. By this,
> He showed that He made us partakers of His death, resur-
> rection, and glory. So when the priest takes the basket offer-
> ing from the deacon or subdeacon, he also takes the lance,
> cleanses it, and cuts into it the form of a cross. As he does
> this, he says, "like a sheep led to slaughter, and a lamb before
> its shearer is silent" [Isa 53:7]. Having done this, he places
> the offering on the paten, and points over it saying, "so he
> opened not his mouth; in his humiliation and judgment, he
> was taken away. Who will tell of his generation because his
> life is taken away from the earth?" [Isa 53:8] After he says
> this, the priest takes the holy cup, and while the deacon is
> pouring wine and water into it, he again says: "Blood and
> water flowed out of his side. The one who saw this has testi-
> fied and his testimony is true" [John 19:34–35]. After this,
> he places the holy cup on the divine table, and offering it,
> he points to the slain lamb through the bread and the blood
> poured out through the wine. Again he says, "there are three

that bear witness: the Spirit, the water, and the blood. And these three are one" [1 John 5:8].

St. Germanus of Constantinople (634–733)

JULY 18

St. Hilary (c. 310–367), bishop of Poitiers, ardently defended the Trinitarian dogma as formulated by the Council of Nicaea. His concern for Christ's divinity is evidenced in the following passage, which explains that Christ's body—and by extension the Eucharist—is a "heavenly body." Hilary's words are not meant to deny Christ's true human nature, nor that His humanity came from the flesh of the Blessed Virgin Mary; rather, St. Hilary seeks to explain that Christ's body arose by the power of the Holy Spirit, not from natural human conception. This sacred body had as its proper subject the divine Person of the Word. For this reason, the body of Christ affords man immediate access to the Son of God Himself.

But the Lord Himself discloses the mystery of His birth by saying, "I am the living bread which has come down from heaven. If anyone eats of my bread, he will live forever" [John 6:51]. He calls Himself the bread, for He Himself is the origin of His body. And lest it be thought that the power and nature of the Word were forsaken, Himself turned into flesh, He said that He was indeed His bread, so that from the substance of bread descending from heaven, the origin of His body may be thought not from human conception, as it is shown to be a heavenly body. However, since it is His bread, there is a declaration of His body assumed by the Word; for He added: "Unless you eat the flesh of the Son of Man, and drink his blood, you have no life in you" [John 6:53]. This was so that the assumption of flesh, conceived from the Holy Spirit and born of the Virgin, may be understood. Inasmuch as it is understood that the One who is the Son of Man descended as bread from

205

heaven by the phrase, "bread descending from heaven," so also by the phrase, "flesh and blood of the Son of Man," must be understood His assumption of flesh, conceived by the Holy Spirit, and born of the Virgin.

St. Hilary of Poitiers, Bishop and Doctor (c. 310–367)

JULY 19

In his commentary on the Gospel of John, St. Augustine (354–430) reflects on the virtue of faith as it relates to the Eucharist. He teaches that as man must receive his salvation from Christ, so must he receive his understanding from Him. In this way, Christians accept Christ's teachings not because of their own human insights, but because of their trust in Christ's divine authority.

For when the Lord Jesus said to them, "unless someone eats my flesh, and drinks my blood, he will not have life within himself" [John 6:53], some who had followed Him were scandalized. They said among themselves, "This is a hard saying; who can listen to it?" [John 6:60] For they imagined that Jesus meant that they could cook and eat him after being cut like a lamb, and horrified by His words, they turned back and followed Him no more. Then the evangelist says, "The Lord remained with the twelve, who said to him, 'See Lord, they have left you.' And He said, 'Do you also want to go away?'" [John 6:67–68]. For He wanted to show that he was necessary to them; not they necessary to Christ. Let no one imagine that He impresses Christ when He says He is Christian as if Christ would be more blessed if you were a Christian. It is good for you to be a Christian; however, if you were not, it would not be ill for Christ. Hear the voice of the Psalmist, "I said to the Lord, You are my God: for I have no good apart from you" [Ps 16:2]. Therefore, "you are my God because you lack none of my good things" [Ps 16:2].

If you were to be without God, you would be less but if you were with God, God would not be greater. He is not greater because of you, but you are less without Him. So, grow in Him, and do not withdraw.

St. Augustine of Hippo, Bishop and Doctor (354–430)

JULY 20

In the following commentary, St. Gregory of Agrigentum (c. 559–638) provides an allegorical interpretation of a verse from Ecclesiastes: "For laughter they make bread, and wine makes the living glad: and all things are subject to money" (Eccl 10:19). Gregory first explains that Sacred Scripture is imbued with mystical meanings, hidden beneath the bare letter of the text (see 2 Cor 3:5–6). He then sounds the depths of this particular passage, uncovering the Eucharistic overtones in the bread and wine of laughter and gladness.

Then, the wise Teacher says: "*For laughter they make bread, and wine makes the living glad: and all things are subject to money*" [Eccl 10:19]. Divine grace contains an unexpressed wealth of concern for man in that . . . He joins higher visions to the letter. By means of sensible concepts, as if behind mirrors and veils, He conceals a spiritual meaning. Thus, in this present expression of the Teacher, we find the meaning of the interpretation hidden in sensible attributions. For, when He says, "they make bread for laughter, and wine makes the living glad" [Eccl 10:19], He shows that ordinary bread comes from those who made it for joy, and He named joy "laughter," as was the case for Blessed Sarah in giving birth to Isaac: "The Lord has made me laugh and whoever hears of this will rejoice with me" [Gen 21:6]. He expresses how bread imparts joy for those who hunger and are in need of food, "and wine makes the living glad," as David says, "wine gladdens the heart of man" [Ps 104:15]. It is well that the Teacher speaks of "the living," for it is drunk by such people, and not by those who have passed on and died. And in the aforementioned words, you will discover the mystical bread "that came down from heaven and gave life to the world" [John 6:51]. The Lord spoke about this, saying: "Take, eat. This is my body which is broken for you for the forgiveness of sins" [Matt 26:26]. And again, of the mystical wine from the fruit of the vine, especially that which makes the living glad, the Lord spoke: "Drink of it, all of you. This is my blood which is poured out for you and for many, for the forgiveness of sins" [Matt 26:28]. And again, "I am the living bread which has come down out of heaven. If anyone eats of this bread, he will live forever" [John 6:51]. And again, "The one who eats my flesh and drinks my blood has eternal life" [John 6:58].

St. Gregory of Agrigentum (c. 559–638)

JULY 21

St. John Cassian (c. 360–435) was an early monastic whose life and teachings influenced St. Benedict of Nursia, the father of Western monasticism. In this passage, St. John reveals his keen understanding of human nature, noting that certain acts of humility may actually be rooted in pride. He explains that those who abstain from the Eucharist out of a desire to first become perfect fall into a hidden pride. For when such persons do approach Holy Communion, they imagine that they have made themselves worthy. In truth, however, no man is worthy to receive the Divine Guest.

Yet, we should not exclude ourselves from the Lord's Communion because we confess ourselves to be sinners, but should more eagerly hasten to it in order to heal our soul, purify our spirit, and to seek a remedy for our wounds with humility of mind and faith, considering ourselves unworthy to receive so great a grace. Otherwise, we cannot worthily receive Communion even once a year, as some do who live in monasteries and so regard the holiness and value of the heavenly sacraments as to think that none but saints and spotless persons should venture to receive them, rather than believing that the sacraments would purify us and make us saints by receiving them. And these, thereby, fall into greater presumption and arrogance than what they believe themselves to avoid; because, at the time when they do receive them, they consider that they are worthy to receive them. It is much better, however, to receive them every Sunday for the healing of our infirmities, with humility of heart, whereby we believe and confess that we can never touch those holy mysteries worthily, rather than to be puffed up by a foolish persuasion of heart and believe that, at the year's end, we are worthy to receive them.

St. John Cassian (c. 360–435)
[Memorial, July 23]

JULY 22

Memorial of Ven. Pauline Jaricot

Ven. Pauline Jaricot (1799–1862) was a consecrated virgin who founded the Society of the Propagation of the Faith, an international organization designed to aid missionaries around the world. In the following reflection, Pauline explains that the Eucharist is the source of all the other sacraments. She thus reasons that the sacraments flow from the side of Christ's crucified body, and that this holy body is nothing other than the Eucharist.

The Eucharist is truly the source of the other Sacraments since it is from there, as from a divine fountain, that the Blood of Jesus Christ flows in perpetuity down to the consummation of the ages; since it is there that the Infinite Victim is perpetually sacrificed for us.

From His tabernacle, Jesus Christ pours upon infants in Baptism the Precious Blood that flowed from His august forehead during the crowning of thorns, restoring to these sons of Adam the right to the eternal crown. Likewise, this Blood flows upon the heads of the successors to the Apostles, granting them the crown of the holy priesthood.

From His tabernacle, Jesus Christ pours upon spouses in the Sacrament of Matrimony the Precious Blood shed at His bitter scourging, by which He had merited for them the grace to live a holy life.

From His tabernacle, the Savior, at the tribunal of Penance, sheds upon poor sinners the Blood that had flowed from His hands and feet at the crucifixion, absolving iniquities committed by the hands and feet of sinners. And by the ministry of priests, He reopens the portals of heaven.

From His tabernacle, Jesus Christ, the sovereign consoler, pours upon the sick in Extreme Unction the blood that He shed in the Garden of Olives so that sinful hearts, by the mortal sadness of His adorable Heart, may be made pure.

Finally, from His tabernacle, Jesus Christ, the Son of God, clothes those who have the happiness of receiving the Holy Spirit in Confirmation with all the merits of His Resurrection and Glorious Ascension.

Ven. Pauline Jaricot (1799–1862)

JULY 23

Memorial of St. Bridget of Sweden

After the death of her husband, St. Bridget (1303–1373) established the Order of the Most Holy Savior and worked for reform within the Church. Among her most famous works is the *Fifteen Our Father and*

Hail Mary Prayers cycle, which was widely circulated in Medieval Europe. Though its authorship is contested, the work remains a choice expression of Medieval piety with its intense focus on the Passion of Christ. In this, the fifteenth prayer, St. Bridget contemplates the wound in Jesus' side, from which the precious blood poured forth, highlighting the price Christ paid for the Eucharist.

O Blessed Jesus, true and fruitful vine, remember Your Passion and the plenteous blood You shed, as from a cluster of ripened grapes. When they pressed Your blessed body upon the pressor of the cross, you gave us to drink both blood and water, which flowed from your body, pierced by a soldier's lance, leaving not a drop of blood or water left in Your body. There at last, You hung high upon the cross as a bundle of myrrh: Your tender flesh thus changed its color, and Your bones dried of their moisture. Remembering this bitter Passion, sweet Jesus, transpierce my heart, that my soul may be sweetly fed with the water of penance, and my tears continually flow for love of You. O Good Jesus, sanctify me, that my heart may ever be Your dwelling place, and my life may be made acceptable to You. At the end of my life, may I be found worthy to forever praise You in union with all the saints in heaven without end. Amen.

St. Bridget of Sweden (1303–1373)

JULY 24

In his treatise on perfection, St. Gregory of Nyssa (c. 335–395) contemplates St. Paul's words regarding the reception of Holy Communion, "Let each man test himself, and so eat the bread"(1 Cor 11:28). Because the Eucharist affords a real participation (*metousia*) in the body and blood of Christ, it requires self-examination and discernment. St. Gregory thus proposes Joseph of Arimathea as a model for Holy Communion (see John 19:38–40). As Joseph placed Christ's body in an unstained tomb, so must the communicant make fit his interior to receive the Body of Christ.

> Participation in such food and drink is not without examination and discrimination. The Apostle himself sets the guidelines: "Let a man examine himself, and so eat of the bread and drink of the cup. For any one who eats and drinks without discerning the body eats and drinks judgment upon himself" [1 Cor 11:28-29]. It seems to me that the evangelist understands this, assuredly indicated at that moment of mystical suffering when the noble member of the Council [Joseph of Arimathea] takes the body of the Lord with a spotless and pure cloth and places it in a new and clean tomb. This is so that the Apostle's command, and the evangelist's observation, may become a rule for us all to receive the holy body with a clean conscience.

> *St. Gregory of Nyssa (c. 335–395)*

JULY 25

In the following sermon, St. Caesarius of Arles (c. 468–542) cautions Christians against attending Mass in body, but not in spirit. He perceives such superficial worship as a sign of worldliness and attachment to temporal pleasures. St. Caesarius thus exhorts men to lead lives that flow from, and are consistent with, the pure worship of God in the Holy Mass. In this way, the Eucharist serves as the locus and means of an integrated life of sanctity.

> For such people as these, it is not enough that they are constantly occupied throughout the week with necessities, or more likely, desires. Over and above that, after the space of one or two hours in which they appear to come together (in body more than in heart), they return from the sacrifices and priests of God and revert to embracing the desires of this world with-

out delay. They follow darkness and desert the light. They embrace shadows and despise the truth. They lose the beauty of Christ and seek the bitterness of the world, loving vanity and seeking a lie. Truly, those who quickly leave the church do not know how great is the good done in celebrating the Mass.

St. Caesarius of Arles (c. 468–542)

JULY 26

In his famous work *On the Mysteries*, St. Ambrose (c. 340–397) interprets the Song of Songs through a Eucharistic lens. The Song of Songs has been traditionally understood as an allegory of the spousal relationship between God and His people, and the Holy Mysteries here take central place in this exchange of love. Christ is the bridegroom who announces a share of food and drink, intimating the union found in Holy Communion.

> So the Church, as it preserves the heights of the heavenly Mysteries, repels the fiercer windstorms and invites the sweetness of blossoming grace, because she knows that its garden cannot be displeasing to Christ as she invokes the Spouse Himself, saying, "Arise, O north wind and come south; blow upon my garden, and let the aroma of spices thereof flow. Let my brother come down into his garden and eat the fruit of his trees" [Song 4:16]. For, it has good and fruitful trees, which soak their roots in the water of the holy font and sprout the bud of a new fecundity, bearing good fruit. They are no longer cut down with the ax that the prophet had so spoken, but are fertilized with the productivity of the Gospel [see Matt 3:10]. So too the Lord, delighted with their fruitfulness, responds, "I entered my garden, my spouse, my sister, I have gathered my myrrh with my ointments; I ate my food with my honey; I have drunk my drink with my milk" (Song 5:1).

St. Ambrose of Milan, Bishop and Doctor (c. 340–397)

JULY 27

Origen of Alexandria (c. 184–253) was one of the most prolific writers of the early Church whose bold theological writings sometimes strayed from orthodox teaching. After his death, Origen was condemned for his teachings on Universalism, the errant belief that God would provide a universal restoration (apokatastasis) of all creatures, thereby eradicating hell. His works are, nevertheless, a source of great light, and in the following passage, he provides an allegorical reading of the multiplication of the loaves. Noting that Christ healed the sick before distributing the bread, Origen discerns a moral command for worthy reception of the Eucharist.

When it was evening, the disciples came to him and said, "This is a lonely place, and the day is now over; send the crowds away to go into the villages and buy food for themselves." (Matt 14:15)

First, notice that when He was about to give His disciples the loaves of blessing for the crowds, He healed the sick so that they could partake of the loaves in good health. For, those who are sick are not yet able to bear Jesus' loaves of blessing. Therefore, one must consider the warning, "let a man test himself and then eat of the bread" [1 Cor 11:28], and so forth. If someone does not obediently listen, and carelessly partakes of the bread and cup of the Lord, then he becomes weak and infirm. Or, to put it another way, he is confounded by the power of the bread and is put to sleep.

Origen of Alexandria (c. 184–253)

JULY 28

St. Peter Faber (1506–1546) was one of the founding members of the Society of Jesus and the only priest among the original group. The Society of Jesus provided a learned defense of the Catholic faith against the novel teachings of Martin Luther, John Calvin, and Ulrich Zwingli, manifesting a true spirit of reform. In his diary, St. Peter expresses grief over the loss of Eucharistic devotion due to lukewarmness and abandonment of the faith. His own pious practices, by contrast, reveal a tender and personal love for Jesus in the Blessed Sacrament.

> On the feast of St. Bernard, I experienced immeasurable devotion and many tears at Mass as I considered the loss of honor due the Most Holy Sacrament, which is the result of the tepidity of Christians and those who leave the Church. I considered also the loss [of assistance] that comes to souls in purgatory on account of false opinions and the irreverence done to prelates and to the things of God. Added to which are the prevailing faults of evil speech against our neighbors and contempt for those who do not share our individual way of doing things. That same day, I felt great devotion in offering myself to St. Bernard, praying that he would accept me for his disciple, since he was so entirely pleasing to the Blessed Virgin Mary.

> On the feast of St. Louis, bishop and confessor, I experienced much devotion, thinking that I would apply my Mass, among other things, for all my negligence in failing to examine and write down the benefits that are offered to me every day by means of the works of God, His words interior and exterior, and also by means of His own Body, which every day I have in my hands and before my eyes.

St. Peter Faber (1506–1546)
[Memorial, August 2]

JULY 29

St. Justin de Jacobis (1800–1860) was a missionary priest and bishop who helped establish the Church in Abyssinia, modern-day Ethiopia. The founding of the local Church was marked by persecution, imprisonment, and the martyrdom of St. Justin's companions. In this excerpt from a letter, St. Justin describes the profound atmosphere of devotion that surrounded the consecration of a church in Abyssinia. This scene captures the gravity and beauty of the liturgy, even in the most humble of circumstances.

> The entire assembly walked in procession three times around the church, repeating the consecration psalms. Then, I celebrated the Holy Sacrifice. Every man, woman, and child took part in the service with the greatest earnestness and devotion, and a very large number received Holy Communion from their bishop's hand. A solemn benediction closed the day's services; the remembrance of which will ever remain in my heart, and I am sure that it will in theirs. The result was not only an evanescent enthusiasm, but a solid conversion of a great many to the faith of Christ, the reality of which we had abundant proofs when the days of fiery trial came.

Elsewhere, St. Justin praises the Abyssinian faith while providing practical advice for missionary priests.

> . . . belief in the Real Presence is stronger in Abyssinia than in any other country in the world. A man will not spit for three days before and three days after taking the Holy Communion. And were it not for fear of offending you by the account of their habits, I could give you several other instances of their intense veneration for the Holy Eucharist. Therefore, it needs but the advent of a pure and holy priesthood to regenerate these people. Only, the missionary must be cautious not to offend their prejudices unnecessarily and to win his way by patience, charity, and forbearance.

> *St. Justin de Jacobis (1800–1860)*
> *[Memorial, July 31]*

JULY 30

Memorial of St. Peter Chrysologus, Bishop and Doctor

In his sermon on the Lord's Prayer, St. Peter Chrysologus (c. 380–450) offers a Eucharistic interpretation of the petition, "give us this day our daily bread" (Matt 6:11). Meditating on the figure of "bread," St. Peter illustrates the sacrificial nature of the Blessed Sacrament through the analogy of making dough. Each step of the process suggests an allegorical meaning tied to Christ's self-gift. In everything, St. Peter emphasizes how Christ loved man to the end, holding nothing back.

> "Give us this day our daily bread" [Matt 6:11]. After the kingdom of heaven, we are not told to ask for earthly bread. He forbids it when He says, "Take no thought what you shall eat or drink" [Matt 6:25]. But since He is the "Bread which came down from Heaven" [John 6:51], we seek and pray that the very Bread whereby we shall daily (*i.e.* continuously live in eternity) we may this day (*i.e.* in the present life), receive from the Feast of the Holy Altar for the strengthening of body and mind.

> But because He Himself is the bread that comes down from heaven, which through the millstone of the law and grace was formed into flour, kneaded by the Passion of the cross, leavened in the Sacrament of great goodness, which bore from the tomb the light dough to lighten our sorrows, that it might be baked in the heat of its Divinity, Itself burnt away the oven of hell, which is daily brought to the Table of the Church for heavenly food, broken for the forgiveness of sins, and which nourishes those who eat to life everlasting: this is the bread we daily ask be given us, until we enjoy it wholly in that endless day.

> *St. Peter Chrysologus, Bishop and Doctor (c. 380–450)*

JULY 31

Memorial of St. Ignatius of Loyola

St. Ignatius of Loyola (1491–1556) served as a soldier in the Spanish army before a grievous battle injury ended his career and prompted deep conversion of heart. He dedicated more than a decade of his life to theological studies before founding the Society of Jesus for the propagation of the faith. In the following letter, St. Ignatius describes the kind of payment that is given a soldier of Christ, which culminates with the Eucharist. His meditation is a veritable summary of God's gifts to man and a reminder of man's utter reliance on God.

His recompense is all that you are by nature, all that you possess by that same nature. For, He has given you yourselves, and He preserves your life and being, and all the parts and perfections of your body and soul, as well as all gifts from without. His pay is also the spiritual gift of His grace, which He has bestowed upon you with liberality and benevolence, and which He continues to bestow, even when you are recalcitrant and rebellious. His pay is the ineffable gift of His glory which, without any benefit to Himself, He keeps for you ready and prepared, imparting to you all the treasures of His blessings so that, by eminent participation of His divine perfection, you may be that which He is by essence and nature. His pay is, lastly, the whole universe and everything corporal or spiritual contained therein. For, He has not only placed within our hands everything beneath the heavens, but also the most sublime court of His own, without omitting any of the celestial hierarchies, *'qui omnes sunt administratorii spiritus propter eus qui hereditatem capturi sunt.'* And as if all these kinds of pay did not suffice, He has made Himself our pay, giving Himself as a brother in our flesh; as the price of our salvation on the Cross, and as the food and the companion of our wanderings in the Eucharist.

Oh, how worthless must a soldier be for whom such an accumulation of recompense does not suffice to make him toil for the honor of such a Prince!

St. Ignatius of Loyola (1491–1556)

AUGUST

AUGUST 1

Memorial of St. Alphonsus Liguori, Bishop and Doctor

St. Alphonsus Liguori (1696–1787) is counted among the greatest moral theologians of the Church. So trustworthy were his writings that the Holy Office uniquely granted them unreserved approval for use by professors and confessors, even if such persons did not themselves understand their theological reasoning. His writings reveal a fervent spirit of piety and a vast knowledge of Christian texts. In the following meditation, St. Alphonsus speaks to the mutual self-donation proper to receiving Holy Communion: Christ offers Himself wholly to man as man offers himself wholly to Christ.

> O Savior of the world, what do You desire from men that has led You to give Yourself to them in food? What can there be left for You to give after this Sacrament in order to oblige us to love You? Ah, my most loving God, enlighten me, that I may know what an excess of goodness this has been, to reduce Yourself to becoming my food in Holy Communion! If You have given Yourself entirely to me, it is only right that I should also give myself wholly to You. Yes, my Jesus, I give myself entirely to You. I love You above every good, and I desire to receive You in order to love You more. Come, therefore, and come often, into my soul and make it entirely Yours. Oh, that I could truly say to You, as the loving St. Philip Neri said to

You when he received You in the Viaticum, "Behold my love, behold my love; give me my love."

. . . Ah, my beloved Jesus, tell me, what more is there left for You to invent in order to make Yourself loved? And shall I then continue to live so ungrateful to You as I have? My Lord, permit it not. You have said that he who feeds on Your flesh in Communion shall live through the virtue of Your grace: *He that eateth Me, the same also shall live by Me.* Since, then, You do not disdain that I should receive You in Holy Communion, grant that my soul may always live the true life of Your grace.

St. Alphonsus Liguori, Bishop and Doctor (1696–1787)

AUGUST 2

Memorial of St. Peter Julian Eymard

Known as the Apostle of the Eucharist, St. Peter Julian Eymard (1811–1868) founded two congregations dedicated to this Most Holy Sacrament: the Congregation of the Blessed Sacrament for men and the Servants of the Blessed Sacrament for women. Throughout his priestly ministry, St. Peter composed reflections on this supreme gift in order to stir souls to frequent Communion. In the following excerpt, St. Peter emphasizes the importance of Eucharistic adoration for those who serve in active ministry.

Eucharistic adorers share Mary's life and mission of prayer at the foot of the Most Blessed Sacrament. It is the most beautiful of all missions, and it is without danger. It is also the most sacred, for it is the exercise of all the virtues. It is the most necessary for the Church, which has much more need of souls of prayer than of preachers, of men of penance than of men of eloquence. Today more than ever, we want men who disarm, by self-immolation, the anger of God against the ever-increasing crimes of nations. We must have souls who, by their importunity, reopen the treasures of grace, which general indifference has closed. We must have true adorers, that is to say, men of fervor and of sacrifice. When they have become numerous around their Divine Chief, God will be glorified, Jesus will be loved, and society will be Christian; conquered for Jesus Christ by the Apostolate of Eucharistic prayer.

St. Peter Julian Eymard (1811–1868)

AUGUST 3

The following fourth-century poem speaks of that great and terrible moment when blood and water poured forth from the side of Christ. The fruits of this event are manifest in the sacrificial liturgy, allowing for true communion with Christ and participation in His mystery of salvation. While the poem expresses the wonder of one who has received this gift, the prose that follows elaborates on the implications of this mystery.

Again, the Word Himself, and our Life, said:
This is the blood shed for you and spread abroad for the
    forgiveness of sins.
Beloved, we drank this holy and immortal blood.
Beloved, we drank from the font of the Lord's side, which
    heals every disease and frees every soul.
We drank the blood by which we were bought and redeemed,
    and which was shown to us and enlightened us.
Brethren, see what manner of body we ate!
See what promises we make to God!
All this that we may not be ashamed in that fearful day of
    retribution.

And who is able to praise the mystery of Your grace? We have been privileged to partake of the gift. Let us guard it till the end that we may be deemed worthy of hearing his bless-

ed, sweetest, and holy voice saying, "Come, you blessed by my
Father. Inherit the kingdom prepared for you" [Matt 25:34].
Then, let those who crucified the Lord stand in fear, and let
those who do not believe in the Father, the Son and the Holy
Spirit be ashamed. So also for those who deny and do not
confess the Holy Trinity in one Godhead. But as for us, beloved, we would do well to celebrate the feast of Christ's baptism and his holy and life-giving resurrection. Through this
salvation has come to the world. May we all obtain this by the
grace and love of Jesus Christ for humanity, for whom it is
fitting to give glory, honor, and worship.

Byzantine-Greek Poetry (4th Century)

AUGUST 4

Memorial of St. John Vianney

St. John Vianney (1786–1859) was the humble pastor of Ars whose
holiness of life sanctified the entire city, leaving it a permanent place
of pilgrimage. Though he was not known for intellectual gifts or academic writings, his counsels overflow with extraordinary piety and
insights into the spiritual life. Here, St. John meditates on the intimate exchange that takes place in Holy Communion. Alluding to the
wedding imagery found in the Gospel of St. Matthew and the Song of
Songs, he urges Christians to recognize Christ's show of love in the
Blessed Sacrament.

There is yet another Sacrament where Jesus Christ makes
Himself still more intimately known. Not content with having purified the unfaithful soul, He further desires to give the
greatest sign of His love: He calls the soul to His sacred banquet, He opens the door of the hall to the feast, and He offers the Bread of Angels [see Matt 22; Song 5]. It is His own
Body that He gives as food: O excess of the love of Jesus! that
His heart desires to unite Itself to us, and to inflame us with

the fire of His love. His delight is to be with us, to converse with us, to win us over, and to inseparably bind Himself to us. Having done all this, He still cries out:"*Sitio!* I thirst, and I desire to further reveal my tender love for you. As proof, you daily see Me descend upon the altars by the voice of My minister. Hence, I desire that all know that My happiness is to be with those whom I call My children and My brothers." O Christians, righteous or sinful, respond to the kindness of your Savior. Make yourselves worthy, and come to the Sacred Banquet, the Feast of the Lamb. You will learn to know and love Him by considering what He has done, and still does daily, for you.

St. John Vianney (1786–1859)

AUGUST 5

Didymus the Blind (c. 313–398), the famous lay teacher of Alexandria, here treats the fifty-fifth chapter of Isaiah, which promises an inheritance for those who serve the Lord. Characteristic of the Church Fathers, Didymus offers an allegorical interpretation of the water, wine, and fat, which symbolize the Holy Spirit and the Eucharist. Didymus thus shows the figures of the Old Law to be shadows of the reality to come.

Isaiah cries out to those who do not believe in the Holy Spirit, and consequently have no part in the future inheritance, saying: "This is the inheritance for the servants of the Lord, and their justice with me, says the Lord. Everyone who thirsts, come to the waters; and he who has no money, come, buy and eat wine without money . . . delight yourself in rich fat" [Isa 54:17–55:2]. The water is the Holy Spirit and the streams that flow from His pool. By the words, "wine and rich fat," he thus signified things on the Jewish preparation table, but now it refers to immortal communion in the Lord's body and blood.

We purchased these very things with our renewal [baptism], using not money, but faith, and we freely receive the gift.

Didymus the Blind (c. 313–398)

AUGUST 6

The Feast of the Transfiguration

The Feast of the Transfiguration celebrates the revelation of Christ's divinity on Mt. Tabor, manifest in the tabernacle of His body. Here, St. Anastasius of Sinai (c. 630–701) affirms both the divine and human natures of Christ against the errors of Timothy the Monophysite, who professed only one. On the basis of the liturgy, St. Anastasius demonstrates how Christ must be both fully God and fully man. The sacrificial nature of the Eucharistic liturgy depends on the humanity of Christ, even as its salvific nature depends on His divinity. Though St. Anastasius' sacramental theology lacks the refinement of later centuries, he nevertheless voices wholehearted faith in the reality at hand.

Is Timothy not being impious when he says, "The nature of Christ is only divinity with the taking on of flesh?" But if Christ is only divinity, and divinity is invisible, untouchable, without sacrifice, without parts, and inconsumable, then Timothy is clearly denying, like the Jews, that there is the sacrifice and communion in the Holy Mysteries. He neither believes, nor confesses, a true body and a visible, created, and earthly blood.

What we offer is shared with the people with these words: "The body and blood of our Lord and God, the Savior Jesus Christ." For if Timothy says that the nature of Christ is divinity alone, then something foreign to the divine nature is grasped, broken, divided, broken in small pieces, poured out and emptied, transformed, and chewed up with teeth. Timothy falls into one of these two pits: either divinity is capable of suffering and is changeable, or he denies the body and blood of Christ, which is precisely what he offers and eats in the mystical sacrifice when he shares it with the people, saying, "The body and blood of our Lord Jesus Christ." In that case, it would be necessary for him to say to the recipient, "this is only the divinity of our Lord Jesus Christ." Finally, in Timothy's case, the teaching about the Incarnation would be a myth.

St. Anastasius of Sinai (c. 630–701)

AUGUST 7

Memorial of St. Cajetan

St. Cajetan (1480–1547) was an Italian priest who founded the Oratory of Divine Love, a confraternity of priests dedicated to supporting clerics amid the confusion caused by sixteenth-century Protestantism. In the following letter, St. Cajetan writes of the folly of those who might possess the Lord of Heaven in the Eucharist, but remain cold and indifferent. He thus warns those who seldom receive that they will be powerless against the enemies of their salvation.

Oh, how much are those to be pitied who do not appreciate the inestimable gift bestowed upon us in the Blessed Eucharist! We could possess Jesus Christ Himself, and we will not! Woe to the soul who is indifferent to the reception of her Savior! The enemies of her salvation will quickly assault and tempt her, and they will triumph over her. Let us frequently receive Him who by giving Himself to us, is ready to bestow upon us all the graces that we stand so greatly in need.

St. Cajetan (1480–1547)

AUGUST 8

Bl. John of La Verna (1259–1322) was a Franciscan mystic who spent his youth in quiet contemplation before ultimately entering active ministry. Details of his life are recorded in the *Fioretti*, a fourteenth-century collection of Franciscan stories based on the chronicles of Thomas of Celano (1185–1265). The following passage relates Christ's miraculous appearance to Bl. John during the Mass, underscoring the fearful majesty of the liturgy. These events reveal Christ's majestic presence, hidden beneath the sacramental veil.

> Having come at length to the act of consecration, and having spoken half of the words over the Host, "*Hoc est*," he was in no way able to proceed further, but only repeated the same words, "*Hoc est enim.*" And the reason he could not proceed was that he felt and saw the presence of Christ with a great company of Angels whose majesty he was not able to endure. And he saw that Christ did not enter into the Host, or rather, that the Host was not changed into the body of Christ until he should utter the other half of the phrase, "*corpus meum.*" Thus, in his anxious state he could proceed no further. The guardian, brothers, and many laymen present in Church for Mass drew near to the altar, astonished to behold and see Brother John's actions, and many were weeping out of devotion. At last, after a long period, when it so pleased God, John uttered the words, "*enim corpus meum*" in a loud voice, and immediately the form of the bread vanished, and in the Host appeared Jesus Christ, the Blessed One, incarnate and glorified. And He thus showed forth the humility and love which incited Him to become incarnate of the Virgin Mary, and which makes Him daily descend into the hands of the priest when He consecrates the Host.

> *Bl. John of La Verna (1259–1322)*
> [*Memorial, August 9*]

AUGUST 9

Memorial of St. Teresa Benedicta of the Cross

Born Edith Stein, St. Teresa Benedicta of the Cross (1891–1942) was a Jewish philosopher and phenomenologist who converted to the Catholic faith. Inspired by St. Teresa of Ávila, Edith entered a Carmelite monastery where she and her sister were ultimately arrested by the Gestapo and martyred in Auschwitz. In the following poem, Edith speaks of the unitive love found in Holy Communion and its transformative effects. Because the Eucharist affords a share in the divine life, it illuminates the soul, enlightening man from within.

This Heart, it beats for us in a small tabernacle
Where it remains mysteriously hidden
In that still, white host.

That is your royal throne on earth, O Lord,
Which visibly you have erected for us,
And you are pleased when I approach it.

Full of love, you sink your gaze into mine
And bend your ear to my quiet words
And deeply fill my heart with peace.

Yet your love is not satisfied
With this exchange that could still lead to separation:
Your heart requires more.

You come to me as early morning's meal each daybreak.
Your flesh and blood become food and drink for me
And something wonderful happens.

Your body mysteriously permeates mine
And your soul unites with mine:
I am no longer what once I was.

You come and go, but the seed
That you sowed for future glory remains behind
Buried in this body of dust.

A luster of heaven remains in the soul,
A deep glow remains in the eyes,
A soaring in the tone of voice.

St. Teresa Benedicta of the Cross (1891–1942)

AUGUST 10

St. John Berchmans (1599–1621) acquired great holiness of life in his youth and died at the age of twenty-two, leaving behind a legacy of profound piety. In this excerpt from his writings, St. John details his Eucharistic devotions, explaining his practices at Holy Mass. These devotions reveal an integrated life in which all things are united in the sacrifice of the Mass: adoration, contrition, petition, and thanksgiving.

In going to the chapel, I will reflect on what I am about to do, namely, to receive the true Body and Blood of Him who is the Son of God and Son of the Blessed Virgin. I will invite my patrons to prepare my heart for Him. When there, I will beg grace and renew my morning intention. Then, reflecting a little upon my miseries, sins, and imperfections, I will grieve for all the sins which I have committed, and purpose sincere amendment.

From the Oblation to the *sanctus* I will say some vocal prayers, and go through the whole of the Passion of Christ. About the time of the Elevation, I will call to mind that the same Christ descends from heaven on to the altar in order that He may from then in a few minutes enter into my soul. I will adore Him, reciting with St. Thomas *Tu Rex gloriae Christe* to *Salvum fac*, out of the *Te Deum*. Then I will continue in acts of faith and love until the *Pater noster*. Here I will begin to make aspirations to Christ, saying, Who will give You to me, my Brother . . . As the hart longs for running streams . . . Let my Beloved come into His garden . . . etc. And I will offer Him these desires through the Blessed Virgin. . . .

As soon as I have received, I will make an act of faith that what I have received is truly the Son of God and the Son of the Blessed Virgin. Then, with all humility, I will ask Him, "How is it that my Lord should come to me?" By some short vocal prayer, I will give Him thanks, and beg of my patrons to do the same. Then, I will offer Him my body and soul, and some little gift in particular; for instance, of mortification.

St. John Berchmans (1599–1621)
[Memorial, August 13]

AUGUST II

Memorial of St. Clare of Assisi

Under the guidance of St. Francis of Assisi, St. Clare (1194–1253) founded the Second Order of Franciscans, commonly known as the Poor Clares. St. Clare's faith in the Eucharist is epitomized by her famed victory over the armies of Frederick II. Here, Thomas of Celano (1185–1265) recounts St. Clare's heroic actions that safeguarded the convent from destruction. Like Joshua before her (see Josh 6:1–27), St. Clare obtained military victory through faith and trust in Divine Providence.

The hearts of the sisters sank in fear, and their voices trembled with terror as they went in to the mother. Although she was ill, Clare stout-heartedly directed that she be led to the door, and thus she held a silver pyx, enclosed in ivory, in which was the Body of the Holy of Holies. Prostrate before the Lord in prayer, she tearfully prayed to Christ: "Can it please You, my Lord, to deliver Your defenseless handmaids, whom I have nourished with Your love, into the hands of pagans? Defend O Lord, I beseech You, these Your servants whom I am now unable to defend."

. . . Then the virgin, raising her tearful face, comforted the weeping, saying: "Rest assured, little daughters, that you shall suffer no harm. Only trust in Christ." Not an instant had passed before the boldness of these dogs was changed into fear, and they quickly descended the walls they had scaled, being overthrown by the power of her prayers.

In the Rule, St. Clare provides instruction for her religious sisters regarding the reception of Holy Communion. While not restricted to this number, its infrequency does bespeak the gravity with which the Eucharist was regarded.

> The Sisters, with permission of the Abbess, shall confess at least twelve times a year, and shall be careful not to introduce any words that do not pertain to Confession, and the salvation of souls. They shall communicate seven times; namely, on the Nativity of the Lord, Thursday of Holy Week, Easter Sunday, Pentecost, the Assumption of the Blessed Virgin, the Feast of St. Francis, and the Feast of All Saints. The chaplain may enter within the monastery to communicate either the Sisters who are in good health, or those who are ill.
>
> *St. Clare of Assisi (1194–1253)*

AUGUST 12

Memorial of St. Jane Frances de Chantal

With the help of St. Francis de Sales, St. Jane Frances de Chantal (1572–1641) founded the Congregation of the Visitation, a women's religious order for older vocations. Her personal letters reveal firsthand knowledge of St. Francis' character and describe his love of the Eucharist. In this excerpt, St. Jane speaks of St. Francis' devotion to the Mass, showing it to be the center of his life.

> Whoever observed his outward bearing was unfailingly impressed. Whether at prayer, reciting the office, or saying Mass, his countenance shone with angelic splendor; but, it was above

all at the consecration of the Mass that it seemed to radiate. This has been remarked to me a thousand times. He had a special devotion to this adorable Sacrament. It was his true life, his sole strength, and when carrying it in a Procession he looked like one on fire with love. Because his outpourings of love before the Divine Sacrament, and his wonderful devotion to our Lady are treated of elsewhere, I will not speak of them here.

In the following letter, St. Jane responds to a woman who had written of her newfound awareness of Christ's presence within her. While St. Jane Frances praises this gift, she checks it against the superior mode of Christ's presence in the Blessed Sacrament.

I tell you everything quite openly so that you may speak of me to the *Heart* of our divine Savior, whom I bless and thank for the graces that He continues to bestow upon you with the growth of that intimate realization of His divine presence. Oh, how precious, how glorious is this grace! Yet this gift of His presence is not the same as His presence in the divine Sacrament where His Sacred Body and Soul and Divinity in the most real sense dwell with us, and remain with us in our miserable tabernacles until the species is consumed. Nevertheless, in the gift of the presence of God this eternal Truth remains in us by essence, by power, and by grace, and to be conscious of this is an exceptional favor.

St. Jane Frances de Chantal (1572–1641)

AUGUST 13

Memorial of St. Hippolytus of Rome

St. Hippolytus of Rome (c. 170–235) was an early theologian whose intellectual pride led him into schism. Though reckoned as the first antipope, Hippolytus was reconciled to the Church before dying a martyr's death and has ever since been held as a saint. In his *Commentary on the Book of Proverbs*, St. Hippolytus interprets Wisdom's banquet as a prefiguration of the Eucharistic feast. Here, Wisdom personified—Christ—promises a share of His riches to him who hungers and thirsts for justice.

She has mingled her wine and set forth her table. She has sent forth her servants to call from the highest places in the town, "Whoever is simple, let him turn in here!" To him who is without sense she says, "Come, eat of my bread and drink of the wine I have mixed for you." (Prov 9:2–5)

"She [Wisdom] has mingled her wine" (Prov 9:2) in the bowl, which means that that the Savior, uniting His Godhead as pure wine with the flesh in the Virgin, was born both God and man, without confusion of the one in the other. "And she has set forth her table" (Prov 9:2), which signifies the promised knowledge of the Holy Trinity, as well as His venerable and undefiled body and blood, which are daily administered and sacrificially offered at the spiritual divine table as a memorial of that first and ever-memorable table of the spiritual divine supper. It further says: "She has sent forth her servants" (Prov 9:3), which is to say that Wisdom, Christ, has done so, summoning them with lofty proclamation. "Whoever is simple, let him turn to me" (Prov 9:4), Wisdom says, clearly alluding to the holy apostles, who traversed the whole world, and called the nations to the knowledge of Him in truth, with their lofty and divine preaching. And again, "to those who desire understanding" (Prov 9:4), which is to say, those who have not yet received the power of the Holy Spirit, "come eat of my bread, and drink of the wine that I have mixed for you" (Prov 9:5). And by this, it is meant that He gave His divine flesh and venerable blood to us to eat and to drink for the remission of sins.

St. Hippolytus of Rome (c. 170–235)

AUGUST 14

St. Maximus the Confessor (580–662) was one of the foremost opponents of Monothelitism, the erroneous teaching that Christ had one will only. By affirming that Christ possessed a divine and a human will, Maximus safeguarded the two complete natures of Christ, for which he suffered grievous bodily harm. In his *Mystagogy*, St. Maximus illuminates aspects of the liturgy using Byzantine terminology foreign to the West. Here, the word "symbol" (symbolon) refers to the Creed, while the "Trisagion" may be understood as parallel to the "Sanctus." Like so many Church Fathers, Maximus views the liturgy as the union of heaven and earth, allowing for the divinization of man.

Because of the sacred reading of the Holy Gospel, there is an end to the earthly mindset as of the visible world. Through the closing of the doors, there is a transition and transference from this corruptible world to the invisible world, seen only in the mind. For, as the doors are shut, the senses are purified of sinful idolatry. And by entering the Holy Mysteries, there is a more perfect and new mystical teaching about God's economy for us. Through the divine greeting of each and all, there is like-mindedness, agreement, and an identity of love. Through the profession of faith in the *Symbolon*, there is thanksgiving for the wonderful means of salvation brought to us. Through the *Trisagion*, there is union and equal honor with the angels in the symphonic fervor that never ceases in the holy doxology of God. Through prayer, by which we are made worthy to call God "Father," there is the truest adoption in the grace of the Holy Spirit. Through the "One Holy," there is the grace and indwelling that makes us one with God himself. Through the holy reception of the spotless and life-giving Mysteries, there is communion and identity by participation, which is permitted through likeness with God.

St. Maximus the Confessor (580–662)
[Memorial, August 13]

AUGUST 15

The Solemnity of the Assumption of the Blessed Virgin Mary

On the Solemnity of the Assumption of the Blessed Virgin Mary, the Church commemorates Mary's bodily assumption into heaven. In the West, it is believed that Mary experienced death, conforming her to the death of her Son. In the East, it is held that Mary simply fell asleep, escaping death entirely. In either case, both profess that Mary was bodily assumed into heaven at the end of her earthly life, and this truth was declared a dogma of the Catholic faith in 1950 by Ven. Pope Pius XII. In the following passage, St. Peter Eymard (1811–1868) recalls Mary's Eucharistic faith and piously writes of her death.

From Communion to Communion, the Blessed Virgin reached at last the one that was to be the seal of her life. Her raptures of love exhausted her strength, and swooning from the vehemence of her desires, the day came on which she could no longer go to her oratory, nor approach the Communion table to receive the Living Bread which formed her strength and her only nourishment . . . Jesus Christ Himself, attended by the whole celestial court, descended to Mary's humble little apartment and administered communion with tenderness and love, worthy of such a Son, and such a Mother. And Mary, having seen again the face of her most dear Son, having pressed Him once again to her heart, her soul burst from the immaculate envelope which had retained it for seventy-two years in this land of exile, and soared up to the heavens, carried on the wings of the seraphim. "Many die in love, Mary died of love!" She went to continue in heaven communion with her Son, no longer veiled, but unveiled, glorious, and triumphant.

St. Peter Julian Eymard (1811–1868)

AUGUST 16

In his *Second Tract on the Book of Exodus*, St. Gaudentius of Brescia (d.

410) offers an allegorical interpretation of the Passover meal. He sees the prohibition against boiling the lamb, "You shall not eat lamb . . . boiled in water" (Exod 12:9), as a moral command against unworthy reception of the Eucharist. He further understands the instruction to consume the entire lamb, "You shall eat the head with the feet" (Exod 12:9), as a command to receive the whole of Jesus' teachings, without exception. St. Gaudentius thereby emphasizes the Christian duty to receive the fullness of the faith, preserving it in its entirety.

> You should not reject this sacrament saying, "How can this man give his flesh to eat?" [John 6:52] Nor within the vessel of a sinful heart should you boil this Sacrament, thinking that it is common and earthly; rather, you should believe what the fire of the Divine Spirit has accomplished. For, what you receive is the body of the Heavenly Bread and the blood of that Sacred Vine.

> Accordingly, when Christ extended the consecrated bread and wine to His disciples, He said, "This is my body; this is my blood" [Matt 26:26, 28]. Let us believe Him whom we have believed. Truth knows nothing of a lie. When He spoke to the shocked and grumbling crowds about eating His body and drinking His blood, they said, "This is a hard saying. Who can listen to it?" [John 6:60] That by heavenly fire He might remove such thoughts—which I warned were to be avoided—He added: "It is the Spirit that gives life; for the flesh profits nothing. The words I have spoken to you are spirit and life" [John 6:64]. So, we are at once bidden to consume in the mysteries the "head and feet" together [Exod 12:9]—the head of His divinity and the feet of His humanity; that we may believe everything as it has been handed on, not breaking a bone of His utterly reliable word: "This is my body. This is my blood" [Matt 26:26, 28].

St. Gaudentius of Brescia (d. 410)

AUGUST 17

Memorial of St. Jeanne Delanoue

St. Jeanne Delanoue (1666–1736) was a French religious and the foundress of the Congregation of the Sisters of St. Anne of Providence. In the following exhortation, transcribed by her religious sister, St. Jeanne identifies the motivation and meaning behind each of Christ's mysteries: his infinite love. The Incarnation, Passion, and Crucifixion each express the self-emptying love of the Son, and the grace of each is communicated to man in the Holy Eucharist. With such proofs of His love, St. Jeanne reasons that man is bound to return love for love, holding nothing back.

> See then, it was His love that led Him to be born as man. For us men and women, and for our salvation, He descended from heaven. He was happy, but for our sake became miserable. He was free, but became captive and made Himself obedient unto death—even death on a cross. And after having given everything, He gave His last drop of blood so that we could not doubt that He has given all for us, reserving nothing for Himself. How often He gives Himself in Holy Communion, which is the Sacrament of His love, and the *love of loves*, as the saints call it! Yes, He gives Himself entirely. Do you not know that He gives His body, blood, soul, and divinity; His pains and death; His merits and graces? And since His person is inseparable from the other two adorable persons, He then gives us His Father and the Holy Spirit. This is what is called love! . . . And, after all this, is it not right that He asks us to love Him? Is He not justified in wanting all or nothing?

St. Jeanne Delanoue (1666–1736)

AUGUST 18

St. Ezequiél Moreno y Díaz (1848–1906) was a member of the Order of Augustinian Recollects in Spain who was appointed to the episcopal see of Pinara and Pasto, Colombia. In the following episcopal letter, St. Ezequiél speaks of the love and wisdom that inspired the institution of the Eucharist. In this sacrament, all loves are contained—the love of a father, brother, spouse, and friend—and each is communicated in its purest form. For God is the source and perfection of all loves.

Jesus Christ our Savior, seeing that the hour was near to depart from the world . . . took unleavened bread in His hands, looked to heaven, and manifested that omnipotent voice, which had said, "*Let there be*" [Gen 1:3] and it was made, pronounced these solemn words: "*Take and eat, this is my body: take and drink, this is my blood*" [Matt 26:26, 28]. Thus, He gave Himself entirely to His Apostles in the Eucharist. This is how Jesus Christ instituted the eternal memorial of His love for men, the august Sacrament of the Altar, where He remains with us until the end of time—not only to keep us company so that we can visit Him, talk with Him, adore Him, but also to sacrifice Himself in an unbloody manner upon our altars, renewing the bloody sacrifice of the cross. And to mysteriously feed our souls with His own flesh, and thereby unite Himself to us in an intimate and ineffable way. We call this Sacrament of the Eucharist the "*Mystery of Faith*," but we can also call it the "*Mystery of Love.*"

Yes, the Mystery of Love is the Holy Eucharist, which is ardent love, strong love, faithful love, the love of a friend, the love of a brother, the love of a father, the love of a husband. It is a generous love that gives all, because Jesus Christ has given everything to us in the Eucharist: His most holy body, His precious blood, His blessed soul, and His divinity with its infinite perfections. Could Jesus Christ have given us more than He has given in this Sacrament? No . . . Omnipotent as He is, He cannot give more. Wise as He is, He does not know how to give us more. Though rich with inexhaustible treasures, He does not have anything of greater value to give than that which He has already given to us.

St. Ezequiél Moreno y Díaz (1848–1906)
[Memorial, August 19]

AUGUST 19

Memorial of St. John Eudes

St. John Eudes (1601–1680) founded the Society of Jesus and Mary and ardently spread devotion to the Sacred Heart of Jesus. His kindness toward sinners is expressed in his work, *The Good Confessor*, which offers practical advice for confessors. Here, he instructs priests to meditate on Christ's mysteries as he greets each penitent, recalling that the Eucharist, the Passion, and the death of Christ all flow from God's infinite love. St. John thus counsels priests to apply the fruits of these mysteries in the celebration of the sacrament of reconciliation.

> With the [next penitent], look at the inconceivable love with which the Son of God became Incarnate in order to redeem this person, and enter into that love in order to help save this person; in union with this same love. This meditation may be applied to all of Christ's Mysteries. For, our Lord performed all the Mysteries of Life with this same ineffable love: His Passion, the Institution of the Most Holy Sacrament, His Death, His Resurrection, and His Ascension. Enter into this love, then, in order to apply the fruits of these Mysteries to the souls of those who confess; in union with this same love.

St. John Eudes (1601–1680)

AUGUST 20

Memorial of St. Bernard of Clairvaux, Doctor of the Church

For the spiritual depth of his writings, St. Bernard of Clairvaux (1090–1153) is often considered the last of the Western Fathers—

despite his living into the second millennium. St. Bernard's works are marked by a lofty spirit of contemplation, reflective of his life as a Cistercian abbot. In the following letter, he refutes those who believed that Christ was merely a moral example and was not Himself the cause of man's salvation. St. Bernard rejects this Pelagian view, which focused exclusively on man's own will, and instead holds the primacy of God's action, poignantly displayed in Holy Communion.

Whichever of these two opinions he holds, his ill-will toward the Sacrament of our Salvation is evident. And in attributing the whole of our salvation to devotion, and nothing of it to regeneration, it is also evident that, as far as he can, he would empty of meaning the dispensation of this deep mystery; for, he places the glory of our redemption and the great work of salvation not in the virtue of the cross, not in the blood paid as its price, but in our advances in a holy life. But *God forbid that I should glory save in the Cross of our Lord Jesus Christ* (Gal 6:14). I wish to follow with all my strength the lowly Jesus. I wish Him who loved me and gave Himself for me to embrace me with the arms of His love, which suffered in my stead. Yet, I must also feed on the Paschal Lamb; for, unless I eat His flesh and drink His blood I have no life in me. It is one thing to follow Jesus, another to hold Him, another to feed on Him. To follow Him is a life-giving purpose; to hold and embrace Him a solemn joy; to feed on Him a blissful life. *For His flesh is meat indeed, and His blood is drink indeed. The bread of God is He who came down from Heaven and gives life to the world* (cf. Jn 6:56, 33). What foundation is there for joy, what constancy of purpose, without life? Surely, no more than for an illustration without concrete basis. Similarly, neither the examples of humility, nor the proofs of charity, are anything without the Sacrament of our Redemption.

St. Bernard of Clairvaux, Doctor of the Church (1090–1153)

AUGUST 21

Memorial of Pope St. Pius X

Motivated by his extraordinary piety and love of the faith, Pope St. Pius X (1835–1914) fearlessly opposed theological modernism and sought to renew all things in Christ. His devotion to the Blessed Sacrament led him to lower the age of First Communion from twelve to seven and to exhort the laity to frequent, even daily, reception of Communion. Because clerics and laity alike feared such liberality, the pope promulgated *Sacra Tridentina*, settling the requirements for reception of the Eucharist. The following excerpt contains the first five recommendations, which encourage Catholics to daily partake of the Eucharist.

1. Frequent, even daily, Communion is open to all the faithful who are in the state of grace, and who approach the Sacred Table with right intentions.

2. This condition of mind implies that the Blessed Sacrament should be received not from habit, or vanity, or any worldly motives, but from a desire to please God, to be united to Him in the bonds of charity, and to provide against the various trials and tribulations to which flesh is heir.

3. Though it is desirable that those who frequently receive the Blessed Sacrament should be free from deliberate venial sins, still the absence of this perfection should not prevent anyone from receiving Holy Communion daily, since the graces of the Eucharist supply the best means of acquiring perfection.

4. Though the Sacrament of the Altar produces its effects *ex opere operato*, better dispositions gain more abundant fruit; hence previous preparation and subsequent thanks to the Almighty, according to the faculties, condition, and duties of each one are most desirable.

5. That more abundant graces be obtained, the advice of a prudent confessor ought to be sought and followed; but it is his duty to refuse Communion only to those who are not in the state of grace, or who have not right intentions in approaching the Altar.

Pope St. Pius X (1835–1914)

AUGUST 22

In the following passage, St. Caesarius of Arles (c. 468–542) outlines the principles of sacramental theology, focusing on the doctrine of transubstantiation. Many of the teachings defined at the Council of Trent (1545–63) are notably present in Caesarius' account, written a thousand years earlier. Teaching that Christ is the High Priest invisibly operative at Holy Mass, Caesarius places the person of Christ at the center of all sacramental actions, safeguarding the liturgy from human frailty and sin.

By the secret power of His word, the invisible priest converts visible creation into the substance of His body and blood. For, He says, "Take and eat, this is my body" [Matt 26:26]. The sanctification is then repeated, "Take and drink: this is my blood" [Matt 26:28]. Recall that at the prompting of God's command, the heights of heaven, the depths of the seas, and the vast lands came into being from nothing. By equal power in the spiritual sacraments, the power of the Word commands, and the effect of the reality complies. When the priest dispenses this body, there is as much in one little piece as there is in the whole. When the Church of the faithful partakes, it is clear that the whole is in each as the fullness is in all things.

St. Caesarius of Arles (c. 468–542)
[Memorial, August 27]

AUGUST 23

St. Poemen (c. 340–450) was a Desert Father whose deeds manifest the deepest humility, temperance, and forbearance. In the following saying, Poemen illustrates man's need of the Eucharist, referencing the ancient belief that wild stags would seek out serpents, trample, and consume them. Just as these animals would need refreshment from the bitterness withstood from serpents, so too do monks need refreshment from the trials of spiritual battle. The Eucharist is this one refreshment in life, lending grace, life, and renewal of spirit.

> Abba Poemen used to say, "This is what is written, 'As the hart cries out for flowing streams, even so my soul cries unto You, O Lord.' For the harts in the desert swallow many serpents, and when the poison of these makes them hot within, they cry out to come to the flowing streams. But as soon as they have drunk, the interior burning from the serpents is cooled. And thus it is with the monks who are in the desert. For they are burnt up by the envy of evil devils and wait for Saturday and Sunday so that they may come to the fountain of water, that is to say, to the Body and Blood of Christ. Thus, they sweeten and purify themselves from the gall of the Evil One."

> *St. Poemen, Desert Father (c. 340–450)*
> *[Memorial, August 27]*

AUGUST 24

Memorial of St. Ouen of Rouen

St. Ouen of Rouen (c. 609–686) faithfully served the Frankish court before founding a monastery at Rabais. After his elevation to the episcopacy at Rouen, he helped convert the remaining areas of paganism in his jurisdiction. In the following passage, St. Ouen contrasts the superstitious practices of the barbarians with the sacraments of the true God. He thus shows the Eucharist and the Anointing of the Sick to be the sure means of obtaining grace. Though his teachings would appear elementary, they are not without significance for the modern age.

Moreover, when someone is overcome by an illness, he should not turn to incantations, nor divination, nor sorcerers, nor fortune-tellers, nor even springs or trees, nor demonic amulets. Rather, he who is sick should solely trust in the mercy of God and the Eucharistic Body and Blood of Christ, and thus receive with faith and devotion. And he should faithfully ask for the blessed oil from the Church, by which his body would be anointed in the name of Christ. According to the Apostle, the prayer of faith will then save the infirm, and the Lord will raise him; not only in body, but in health of soul. This will be fulfilled as the Lord promised in the Gospel: "All that you ask in prayer, believing, you will receive" [Matt 21:22].

St. Ouen of Rouen (c. 609–686)

AUGUST 25

The Order of Discalced Carmelites celebrates an annual feast memorializing the transverberation of St. Teresa of Ávila (1515–1582), their foundress. Her personal accounts of mystical experiences are not without reference to the Eucharist, which she treasured above all such gifts. Here, St. Teresa records a moment of profound union with Christ upon receiving the Eucharist, illustrative of the love Christ has for each soul.

In the second year of my being prioress at the monastery of the Incarnation, on the Octave of St. Martin, when I was going to Communion, Fr. John of the Cross—it was he who was giving me the most Holy Sacrament—divided the Host between me and another sister. I thought he did so, not because there was any shortage of hosts, but because he wished to mortify me as I had said how much I delighted in hosts of a large size. Yet,

I was not ignorant that the size of the host does not matter; for, I knew that our Lord is whole and entire in the smallest particle. His Majesty said to me: "Have no fear, my daughter; for no one will be able to separate you from me," giving me to understand that the size of the host mattered not.

Then, appearing to me as on other occasions in an imaginary vision, most interiorly, He held out His right hand and said: "Behold this nail! it is the pledge of your being my bride from this day forth. Until now, you had not merited it, but from now on, you shall not only regard my honor as of one who is Your Creator, King, and God, but as your own, my veritable bride. My honor is yours, and yours is mine." This grace had such an effect on me that I could not contain myself. I became as one foolish and said to our Lord: "Either ennoble my vileness or cease to bestow such mercies on me; for I do not think that nature can bear them." I thus remained the whole day as one utterly beside herself. Afterwards, I became conscious of great progress, and also of greater shame and distress to see that I did nothing in return for graces so great.

St. Teresa of Jesus, Virgin and Doctor (1515–1582)
[Carmelite Feast of the Transverberation of St. Teresa, August 26]

AUGUST 26

Bl. Dominic Barberi (1792–1849) was an Italian priest dedicated to reconverting England to its Catholic roots. Patterned after the prophet Jeremiah, Dominic's *Lamentation of England* expresses anguish over the Church's legal exile from the Anglican country. Like the prophets before him, Dominic enumerates the sufferings of the faithful and pleads for renewal. His cry remains a testament to the precious gift of the sacraments, a gift tragically denied many.

O Eternal Father, at least listen to the voice of Your only be-gotten Son. Behold His wounds that He suffered for us, and the blood He shed for us. By those wounds and that blood, we beseech You to have mercy upon us. Take from our hands, O Lord, those chains that oppress us. Take from our shoulders that yoke of iron that has been imposed upon us. Oh, may the gates of Your mercy once more open to us: yes, vouch-safe to admit us again into Your house, and to Your table, that we may partake of Your Heavenly Eucharistic bread. Ah, my God, do you not see how we are waxed faint through want of this divine food? Do you not see what we suffer in order to procure the least morsel of it? We must, as it were, put our life in danger to obtain it.

. . . And we, poor and miserable, deprived of our inheritance, driven from our home, deprived of our churches and of our Sacraments, are left as orphans to bewail our woes. Yes, O Lord, we are orphans, deprived of our mother the Catholic Church, from whose bosom we have been violently torn. We are deprived of Your presence, from which we have separated ourselves.

Bl. Dominic Barberi (1792–1849)
[Memorial, August 27]

AUGUST 27

Memorial of St. Monica

In his autobiography, St. Augustine extols the Christian virtues of his mother, St. Monica (331–387), while offering a candid portrait of her struggles and failings. Here, St. Augustine references the pagan tra-dition of excessive feasting and drinking at the graves of relatives—a practice some Christians mimicked at the tombs of the martyrs. St. Ambrose of Milan forbade such practices for their intemperance and irreligion and redirected their devotion. St. Monica thus learned to fittingly honor the martyrs through the devout prayers of the Eucharistic liturgy, the very template for the martyrs' sacrifice.

So, when my mother learned that the outstanding preacher and holy bishop had forbidden these things, even to those who acted soberly lest there be an occasion for drunkards, she willingly abstained from this practice. She also abstained because these ancestral feasts were so similar to pagan superstitions. She learned to bring to the memorials of the martyrs a heart full of purgatorial vows, instead of a basket full of fruits of the earth, so that she might give to the needy as best she could, and rightly celebrate the communion of the Lord's body where the martyrs were sacrificed and crowned in imitation of the Lord's Passion. Yet it seems to me, O Lord God—it is in your sight that my heart says this—that my mother would not have so easily refrained from the custom of her country had she been forbidden by anyone except Ambrose, whom she loved because of my salvation.

St. Augustine of Hippo, Bishop and Doctor (354–430)

AUGUST 28

Memorial of St. Augustine of Hippo, Bishop and Doctor

Born in northern Africa, St. Augustine (354–430) studied rhetoric in Carthage, where his success earned him an invitation to Milan, the city where the emperor resided. There, Augustine met his match in St. Ambrose and under his influence was baptized into the Church. Augustine eventually returned to Africa and was ordained the Bishop of Hippo. Over five million of his words still survive and his *Confessions* remains his most popular work. In this excerpt below, Augustine speaks of the transforming power of the Eucharist: whereas earthly foods are integrated into the one who eats, the Eucharist integrates the one who eats into Itself, the body of Christ.

And being admonished to return within myself, I entered into my inmost being with you as my guide. I was able to do so because you became my helper. I entered, and with the eye of my soul, so to speak, I saw above the same eye of my soul, above my mind, the Unchanging Light. It was not common light, obvious to everyone, nor was it simply a greater version of the same kind. This is not that kind of light, but another, something far different from all those. Nor was it above my mind as oil is above water nor as heaven is above earth. Rather, this was superior because it made me, and I was inferior because I was made by it. Whoever knows truth knows that light; and whoever knows it knows eternity. Love knows it. O Eternal Truth, and True Love, and Loving Eternity! You are my God. For you I sigh day and night.

When I first recognized you, you lifted me up to see that there was something that I might see, and that I was not yet one who sees. And you broke through the weakness of my vision, powerfully radiating into me, and I trembled with love and fear; and I discovered that I was far from you in a region of dissimilitude as if I heard your voice from on high: "I am food for the strong. Grow and you will consume me. Nor will you change me into you as food for your flesh, but you will be changed into me." I learned that you corrected man for his iniquity, and you made my soul dissolve like a spider's web. I asked, "Is truth nothing, because it is not diffused or through finite or infinite physical spaces?" You cried to me from far away, "I am who I am" [see Exod 3:14], and I heard as one hears in the heart. There was, in fact, no reason why I should doubt. I would more easily doubt that I was living than that there is no truth.

St. Augustine of Hippo, Bishop and Doctor (354–430)

AUGUST 29

Before his conversion to Christianity, St. Moses the Ethiopian (c. 330–405) was part of a murderous group of thieves that terrorized the Nile. After taking refuge with the desert monks near Alexandria, he was converted by their example. Included in the ancient compilation of the Desert Fathers' sayings is the story of Moses' transformation from self-reliance to humble reliance on the Holy Spirit and the sacraments. In this way, Moses learned to daily receive the Eucharist as his source of strength and protection.

At the beginning, Abba Moses was ignorant of the rule of the ascetic life. Being healthy of body, he overworked himself, thinking he would be able to prevail against devils solely by the multitude of his works, and thereby vanquish them. Consequently, the devils perceived his designs, and attacked him with greater severity, warring against him both openly and in secret. Abba Isidore, wishing to teach him the truth, and lead him into humility, said to him, "Without the power of the Spirit, which our Lord gave us in Baptism to fulfill His commandments, and which He confirms in us each day by receiving His Body and Blood, our passions cannot be purified, nor can we vanquish devils, nor perform works of spiritual excellence." Learning these truths, Abba Moses was humbled in his thoughts, and partook of the Holy Mysteries. Thereafter, the devils were conquered, reduced their war against him, and Abba Moses lived in rest, knowledge, and peace. Many monks have imagined that strenuous labor alone would heal their passions and gain them health of soul; therefore, they were abandoned by grace, and fell from the truth. For just as a man sick in body cannot be healed without a physician and medicines, no matter how much he may watch and fast, so he who is sick in soul cannot he healed of his passions, nor receive a perfect cure, without partaking of His Body and Blood, the power hidden in His commandments, and the humility like that of His.

St. Moses the Ethiopian, Desert Father (c. 330–405)
[Memorial, August 28]

AUGUST 30

Jean Pierre de Caussade (1675–1751) was a French Jesuit priest and the author of the spiritual classic, *Abandonment to Divine Providence*. His writings emphasize the freedom born of surrendering oneself to the providence of God. In the following letter, de Caussade provides instructions for receiving Holy Communion, emphasizing the transformative power of the sacrament. Instead of relying on one's own strength to prepare for Communion, he recommends submitting to God's infinite capacity to sanctify man. In this way, he ensures that the communicant walks in the path of humility and is well disposed to receive the gift of grace.

Do you not know that the best preparation for Holy Communion is that which is operated in the soul by God Himself? Approach then with confidence, with complete abandonment to the state of poverty and deprivation in which it has pleased God to place you. Remain in it as though sacrificed, annihilated, and unseen like Jesus Christ in His Sacrament, because He is there in a kind of annihilation. Unite yours to His. Where there is nothing left that is created, or human, there is God. The more destitute of all things, and divested of self you become, the more will you be possessed by God. Make for yourself a spiritual treasure of this very poverty by a continual adherence to the will of God. From the time you begin this practice, you will become richer than any of those who possess the greatest gifts of joy and consolation. You will possess the riches of the holy will of God without fear of self-complacency, since this holy will is bitter to nature and humiliating to pride. Sweet and salutary bitterness, which serves as an antidote to the poison of self-love and the sting of the serpent of pride!

Jean Pierre de Caussade (1675–1751)

AUGUST 31

In his famous work *Dialogue with Trypho*, St. Justin Martyr (c. 100–165) records his debate with one of the leading rabbis of the day concerning salvation. St. Justin argues that Christianity is the completion of God's plan for the Hebrew people and here quotes the prophet Malachi as evidence. While temple sacrifices were halted in AD 70, St. Justin notes that the Eucharist fulfills the prophecy of Malachi regarding a perpetual sacrifice that extends to Gentilic lands.

> The offering of finest wheat, I say O gentlemen, which was passed down to be offered for those who had been cleansed from leprosy, was a type of the bread of the Eucharist. Jesus Christ our Lord passed this down to be done in remembrance of His Passion that He suffered on behalf of those souls of men, cleansed from all evil. He wanted us to give thanks for the creation of the world and all it contains; as well as His liberating us from the evil which we have done and for having destroyed the powers and authorities with a perfect destruction with the passion that was in His will. Therefore, God speaks about those sacrifices which were at one time offered by you all, as I said, through Malachi, one of the twelve prophets.

> "My will is not among you, says the Lord, and I will not accept the sacrifices from your hands. Therefore, from the rising of the sun to its setting my name is glorified among the Gentiles, and in every place incense and a pure offering is offered to my name because my name is great among the nations, says the Lord, but you defile it" [Mal 1:10–12].

Now, he speaks beforehand about the sacrifices offered by us Gentiles in every place—that is the bread of the Eucharist and similarly the cup of the Eucharist—when he says that we "glorify his name, but you defile it."

St. Justin Martyr (c. 100–165)

SEPTEMBER

SEPTEMBER 1

St. Jean-Louis Bonnard (1824–1852) was a French missionary to Vietnam during the height of Minh Mang's persecution of the Church. After ministering to several parishes in Tonkin for little more than a year, St. Jean-Louis was arrested and sentenced to death. In one of his last letters, he poignantly describes receiving Holy Communion while in prison, explaining how his dire circumstances renewed his appreciation for this heavenly gift.

> Yesterday, I had the blessing of receiving Holy Communion after confessing my sins. It has been a long time since I have felt so much joy in possessing the King of Angels. Truly, one has to be in prison, with the chain and clasp around one's neck, to be able to understand the sweetness of receiving one's God. Oh! then we are happy to suffer something for Him who has loved us so much. The two young men held captive with me also had the blessing of receiving communion. Oh! how happy I would be if I could once again receive Our Lord in His Sacrament of Love!
>
> *St. Jean-Louis Bonnard, Martyr (1824–1852)*

SEPTEMBER 2

Macarius of Magnesia (4th century) was a bishop whose *Apocriticus* records his debate with a pagan philosopher on the merits of the New Testament. In this excerpt, Macarius explains that those who are born anew by baptism require spiritual nourishment, just as newborn babies require sustenance for life. This supernatural food corresponds with the bread of Wisdom promised in Proverbs 9:5, which is why Macarius reverts to feminine designations: "her [Wisdom's] own flesh." This divine flesh feeds the children of men, allowing them to grow in grace and stature as children of God.

> *Unless you eat my flesh and drink my blood, you have no life in you. (John 6:53)*

Tell me, from where is one nourished who has come to birth? Is it not by the blood of her that bears him, and the flesh, as has been demonstrated? This is by the clever discovery of persuasive words, and yet it is by the same rule of truth. For if, indeed, Christ gave power to as many as received Him to become children of God, bringing them to birth by some mystical word, and then wrapping them in divine swaddling clothes that cannot be described, tell me, on what will these children of God live and be nourished when newly born? Will it not be by tasting the mystical flesh and drinking the mystical blood of her that bore them? And it is none other than the Wisdom of God that is constituted their mother, for she prepared her own table for her own children, and mingled her own wine for her own offspring (cf. Prov 9:2) . . .

It is indeed she who nourishes her offspring with her own flesh and blood, who makes them comrades and renders them disciples of the heavenly kingdom, and enrolls them in the assembly of the angels on high, bringing them into their pure council chamber. By filling them with immortality and all blessedness, she makes them like unto the Father, granting them eternal life.

Macarius of Magnesia (4th century)

SEPTEMBER 3

Memorial of Pope St. Gregory the Great, Doctor of the Church

Pope St. Gregory the Great (540–604) was one of the greatest popes who helped unify the Church in Europe. After spending his youth working in civil government, he joined the Order of St. Benedict only to be appointed a papal emissary by Pope Pelagius II. Though Gregory lamented his public life and longed to return to the monastery, he was elected pope by popular acclamation. In his commentary on Job, St. Gregory explains that the Eucharist is not some static presence of Christ, but rather, the sacrament of His Passion. This sacrament must imprint itself on man, conforming him to Christ's death and Resurrection. And this transformation must express itself in word and deed.

> If the sacrament of the Lord's passion is to work its effect in us, we must imitate what we receive and proclaim to mankind what we revere. The cry of the Lord finds a hiding place in us if our lips fail to speak of this, though our hearts believe in it. So that his cry may not lie concealed in us it remains for us all, each in his own measure, to make known to those around us the mystery of our new life in Christ.

> *Pope St. Gregory the Great, Doctor of the Church (540–604)*

SEPTEMBER 4

In his great work, *On the Orthodox Faith*, St. John Damascene (c. 675–749) explains the manner in which Christ is a cause of division: those who accept Him are incorporated into His saving body, while those who reject Him are cast away. Reflecting on St. Paul's admonition, "Whoever eats the bread and drinks the cup of the Lord in an unworthy manner will be guilty of the body and blood of the Lord" (1 Cor 11:27), St. John observes that the Eucharist possesses this same twofold character. And this is because it is no mere figure, but the real and substantial presence of Christ.

> For those who worthily partake [of the Body and Blood] in faith, it leads to the forgiveness of sins and eternal life, and is a safeguard for the soul and body. But for those who unworthily partake without faith, it leads to punishment and judgment. This is the same as in the death of the Lord, which became life and incorruption in the enjoyment of eternal blessedness for those who believe, but punishment and eternal judgment for those who disobey and who put the Lord to death. The bread and the wine are not a figure of the body and blood of Christ—may it not be—but it is itself the visible body of the Lord, as the Lord Himself said, "this is my body," not a figure of the body, but "the body." It is not a figure of the blood, but "the blood." And before this, He told the Jews, "unless you eat the flesh of the Son of Man and drink his blood, you have no life within you. For my flesh is true food and my blood is true drink" [John 6:53, 55]. And again He said, "he who eats me will live" [John 6:57].

> *St. John Damascene, Doctor of the Church (c. 675–749)*

SEPTEMBER 5

Memorial of St. Teresa of Calcutta

St. Teresa of Calcutta (1910–1997) was a renowned religious and missionary who ministered to the poorest of the poor, bringing the light of Christ to the darkest corners of the world. Her heroic life of service catapulted her to international fame, a position she utilized to spread the Gospel and to advocate for life. Here, Mother Teresa speaks on the living reality of Jesus' love, poured out in the Holy Eucharist. For St. Teresa, the Eucharist is the enduring sign of God's love in the present moment and the motivation behind all apostolic works.

The Eucharist is beyond understanding—we must accept it in deep faith and love. Jesus deliberately left us the Eucharist, lest we forget all that He came to show and to do. In the Gospel there are those few little words to describe His Passion and death: He was crowned, scourged, spat upon—those few little words which by now we could have easily forgotten. The Gospels are very short in their explanation of the Passion. They avoid great description. He was "scourged," but it doesn't say that it was forty lashes or what they used to scourge Him, just words that we would have easily forgotten. Jesus understood our human nature. He understood that far from the eyes is far from the heart also. Just imagine what our lives would be without the Eucharist. What would be there to make us love Him? What would be there to make us give up everything? I don't think any one of us would be here without the Eucharist!

Today let us not read much, or meditate much even, but just allow Jesus to love you. We always want to say, "Jesus, I love you," but we don't allow Jesus to love us. Today say often, "Jesus I am here, love me."

Every human being has a longing for God. "My soul is thirsting for God." Christians can go even further—they not only long for God, but they have the treasure of His presence always with them. We not only have this, but the joy of getting even closer to Him by receiving Him in Holy Communion. Jesus was not satisfied with just feeding us with [the] Bread of Life but He made Himself the Hungry One in the distressing disguise of the poor. For us Missionaries of Charity, we cannot say that we love Jesus in the Eucharist but that we have no time for the poor. If you really love Jesus in the Eucharist, you will naturally want to put that love into action. We cannot separate these two things—the Eucharist and the poor.

St. Teresa of Calcutta (1910–1997)

SEPTEMBER 6

In his meditations on the Triduum, St. Andrew of Crete (c. 660–740) offers a contemplative vision of the Last Supper, filled with scriptural allusions. In it, he employs several terms idiosyncratic of Eastern theology, such as "Lover of Mankind," a favorite term for God. St. Andrew also describes the Eucharistic sacrifice as "rational worship," a Pauline phrase that indicates its grounding in the Logos, reason itself ("logiken latreian," Rom 12:1). The rational worship of the Divine Liturgy allows man to become incorporated into, and to participate in, the self-offering of the Logos Incarnate.

> O Lover of Mankind, You revealed the great mystery of Your Incarnation among intimate friends when You sat at supper and said: "Eat the living bread. By faith, drink the blood from the side of God who was sacrificed." The upper room was thus a heavenly tabernacle. There, Christ fulfilled the Passover in an unbloody supper; a service of rational worship [see Rom 12:1]. There was the table of fulfilled mysteries, a heavenly altar. Christ, the great and revered Passover, is eaten like bread and sacrificed like a lamb. He was offered up as a sacrifice on our behalf and we all devoutly partake of His body and mystically receive of His blood.

> . . . You, the heavenly bread, blessed the bread. You gave thanks to the Father, the Creator. Taking the cup, you gave it to your disciples crying out, "Take, eat. This is my body and the blood of incorruptible life." Pronouncing the "Amen," Christ, who is the truth and the vine, told the apostles, His branches: "From now on, I will not drink from this vine until I drink it anew in the glory of my Father; that is, with those who share in me."

> *St. Andrew of Crete (c. 660–740)*

SEPTEMBER 7

In the following letter, St. Basil the Great (329–379) offers practical advice on the reception of Holy Communion during times of persecution. Observing that some Christians feared to receive the Eucharist when a priest was not present, St. Basil defends the extraordinary practice of communicating by oneself. He encourages regular participation of Holy Communion, appealing to tradition, the example of the Desert Fathers, and necessity. That St. Basil had to address this question at all evidences the profound reverence early Christians had for the Eucharist.

It is a good and beneficial practice to commune daily and share in the holy body and blood of Christ, because He clearly says, "He who eats my flesh and drinks my blood has eternal life" [John 6:54]. Who doubts that continuously partaking of life is nothing less than the abundant life?

As for us, we commune four times each week: on the Lord's Day, Wednesday, Friday, and Saturday. We also do so on other days, if it is a memorial of any saint. Now, there is no need to show that in times of persecution it is acceptable for a person to receive communion from his own hand if there is no priest or minister present. This has been sanctioned by long-standing custom from the necessity of circumstances. All of the monks in the desert keep communion at home and receive from themselves when no priest is present. In Alexandria and Egypt, most every person, including the laity, has communion in his own house and partakes of it when he desires. For, once the priest has completed the sacrifice and distributed it, the one who then receives it as a whole should believe that he is properly partaking and receiving it from the priest. For even in the church, the priest distributes the part, and the recipient holds it with all authority and brings it to his mouth with his own hand. So it is the same with respect to whether someone receives one portion from a priest or many portions at once.

St. Basil the Great, Bishop and Doctor (329–379)

SEPTEMBER 8

Feast of the Nativity of the Blessed Virgin Mary

On the Feast of the Nativity of the Blessed Virgin Mary, the Church honors the birth of the Mother of God, that most blessed of all women, conceived without sin. In this excerpt from the *Dolorous Passion of Our Lord Jesus Christ*, Bl. Anne Catherine Emmerich (1774–1824) relates her vision of the Last Supper, highlighting Mary's priority in receiving Holy Communion. In Anne's account, Mary is mystically afforded pride of place in receiving the Eucharist, befitting her status as Mother of God.

Meanwhile, our Divine Lord became more and more tender and loving in His demeanor. He told His Apostles that He was about to give them all that He had, namely, His entire self, and looked as though perfectly transformed by love. I saw Him becoming transparent, until He resembled a luminous shadow. He broke the bread into several pieces, which He laid together on the paten and then took a corner of the first piece and dropped it into the chalice. At the moment when He was doing this, I seemed to see the Blessed Virgin receiving the Holy Sacrament in a spiritual manner, although she was not present in the supper-room. I do not know how it was done, but I thought I saw her enter without touching the ground, and come before our Lord to receive the Holy Eucharist; after which I saw her no more. Jesus had told her in the morning, at Bethany, that He would keep the Pasch with her spiritually, and named the hour at which she was to enter into prayer, in order to receive it in spirit.

Again he prayed and taught. His words came forth from His lips like fire and light, entering into each of the Apostles, with the exception of Judas. He took the paten with the pieces of bread—I do not know whether He had placed it on the chalice—and said: *"Take and eat; this my Body, which is given for you."* He stretched forth His right hand as if to bless, and as He did so, a brilliant light came from Him. His words were luminous. The Bread entered the mouths of the Apostles as a brilliant substance, and light seemed to penetrate and surround them all, Judas alone remaining dark.

Bl. Anne Catherine Emmerich (1774–1824)

SEPTEMBER 9

The following text is a fourth-century Byzantine poem that expresses the reality of Christ's presence in the Eucharist. The anonymous author highlights the intrinsic connection between the Blessed Sacrament and Christ's body on earth. For the Eucharist is the selfsame body that healed the sick, absolved sins, and was raised on the third day. The author thus encourages Christians to approach the Eucharist with faith and to profit from their intimate encounter with Christ.

Today, we have beheld our Lord Jesus Christ on the altar.
Today, we have grasped the coal of fire of which the Cherubim sang in a shadow.
Today, we have heard that great and sweetest voice crying out:
This is the body that burned off the thorns of sins and enlightens human souls.
This is the body the woman with a hemorrhage touched and was delivered from her suffering.
This is the body that the daughter of the Canaanite woman saw and was healed.
This is the body that the prostitute, by approaching with her

MYSTERY OF THE ALTAR

whole soul, wiped away the filth of her sins.

This is the body that Thomas touched and cried out "My
Lord and My God!"

This is the body that brought us so great and wondrous a
salvation.

Byzantine-Greek Poetry (4th Century)

SEPTEMBER 10

Memorial of St. John Francis Regis

St. John Francis Regis (1597–1640) was a Jesuit priest who ministered to victims of the plague, served the poor, and worked for the
reconversion of those who had abandoned the faith. In the following
letter to his siblings, St. John speaks of the gravity of sin and recommends the strongest means of overcoming faults: the sacraments
of Reconciliation and Holy Communion. Confession purifies the soul
from sin, sensitizing and strengthening it against temptations, while
Holy Communion soothes the soul, binding it to the Risen Christ.

Sin, I tell you again, is what changes us from children of God
to children of the devil. Just think a little of what sort of a father a sinner has when he offends God mortally, thus leaving
God for the devil. Yes, mortal sin makes us heirs of eternal
fire and the pains of the damned! *Oh, how I wish that everyone
could realize the seriousness of mortal sin!* Then, who could be
so unfortunate as to commit even one!

For this reason I exhort you to go frequently to Confession
and Holy Communion—perhaps, on the first Sunday of each
month. For, this is the most efficacious means of guarding
against sin and rising again should one have fallen.

St. John Francis Regis (1597–1640)

SEPTEMBER 11

St. Thomas Aquinas (1225–1274) composed the Eucharistic hymn *Verbum supernum prodiens*, which recounts the salvific mission of Christ and His gift of the Eucharist, for the Feast of Corpus Christi. Emphasizing paradoxes of the faith, Thomas recalls that Christ was both the savior and sacrifice who willingly gave His blood to those who sought it. The final two verses form the popular hymn, *O salutaris Hostia*, frequently recited at Exposition of the Blessed Sacrament. The following translation foregoes a consistent rhyming scheme in order to present a more literal rendering of the text.

> The Celestial Word proceeding forth,
> yet departing not the Father's hand,
> going to fulfill His earthly work,
> has come at last to life's end.

> To death delivered by an Apostle,
> handed over to jealous men;
> having first freely given
> the Bread of Life to friends.

> Under twofold species,
> He gave His Flesh and Blood:
> Man's twofold nature
> now satisfied.

> While at birth, He became our Brother
> at supper, He became our Bread.
> In His death, He became our Ransom,
> so in heaven, He may be our Reward.

> O saving Victim!
> opening wide the gates of heaven!
> Hostile wars press upon us,
> Grant us strength, and give aid.

To the Lord, who is One in Three
be everlasting glory!
May He grant us life without end,
in the House of the Father in heaven.

St. *Thomas Aquinas, Doctor of the Church (1225–1274)*

SEPTEMBER 12

In his famous work *On the Unity of the Catholic Church*, St. Cyprian (c. 210–258) explains how the liturgy manifests the unity of the Church. Echoing Christ's words in the Sermon on the Mount, St. Cyprian warns that Christians cannot offer the Eucharistic sacrifice while divisions exist among them. Not only does this serve as a moral command for individual Christians, but Cyprian shows how it applies to schismatic groups. Those outside the Church, he explains, cannot please God in their offerings and must be gathered into the unity of Christ's body.

When He gave the law of prayer, He added: "And when you stand to pray, if you have anything against your brother, forgive, so that your Father who is in heaven may forgive your sins" [Matt 5:23]. He calls back from the altar the one who comes to the sacrifice in strife and bids him to first reconcile with his brother, and then return to offer his gift to God in peace. For, God was not pleased with Cain's offerings; for he could not be at peace with God who, through envious discord, was not at peace with his brother. What sacrifices do those rivals of priests think that they celebrate? What peace, then, do the enemies of the brethren promise themselves? Do they think that Christ is with them when they are gathered together, who are gathered outside of the Church?

St. *Cyprian of Carthage (c. 210–258)*

SEPTEMBER 13

Memorial of St. John Chrysostom, Bishop and Doctor

Known as the "Doctor of the Eucharist," St. John Chrysostom (349–407) expressed the Real Presence and power of Jesus Christ in the Blessed Sacrament as clearly as any Church Father. Born in Antioch, St. John became Patriarch of Constantinople in 397, and there remained until his exile and death in 407. The following reading comes from his treatise *On the Priesthood*, wherein he describes the majesty of the Divine Liturgy. Shaking his readers from any complacency, St. John recalls that the Holy Sacrifice of the Mass grants man vision of the heavenly liturgy and draws him into its celestial feast.

When you see the Lord sacrificed and lying there, and the priest standing and praying over the sacrifice with all those who have become stained with that precious blood, do you think you are still among men and standing on earth? Are you not rather transported immediately into heaven? Once you cast aside every carnal thought of your soul, do you not see the things in heaven with a transparent soul and pure mind? O what a marvel! O the love of God for humanity! He who sits on high with the Father is at that hour in the hands of all, and gives Himself to those who desire to embrace and enfold Him. Now, accomplish this all through the eyes of faith!

St. John Chrysostom, Bishop and Doctor (349–407)

SEPTEMBER 14

The Feast of the Exaltation of the Holy Cross

On the Feast of the Exaltation of the Holy Cross, the Church celebrates the recovery of the true cross of Christ, upon which the salvation of the world was won. In the following passage, St. John Chrysostom (349–407) provides a sober reflection on the scene of the crucifixion, recalling the soldier's unwitting fulfillment of Scripture: "neither shall you break a bone of it" (Exod 12:46). This Old Testament prophecy points to the piercing of Christ's side (Zech 12:10), from which streams of blood and water gushed forth, indicating the Sacraments of Baptism and the Eucharist.

> "Because it was the Preparation, that the bodies should not remain upon the cross, they besought Pilate that their legs might be broken" [John 19:31]. Do you see how powerful is the truth? By means of the very objects of their zeal, prophecy is fulfilled. For, by means of those things, this plain prophecy—unconnected with them—is accomplished. The soldiers came to break the legs of others, but not those of Christ. Yet, to satisfy the Jews, they pierced His side with a spear, insulting the dead body. O abominable and accursed purpose! But, beloved, do not be confounded nor despondent, because the things these men did with a wicked will fought on the side of truth. For, the prophecy had stated, "They shall look upon Him whom they have pierced," (Zech 12:10). And what is more, this deed became a demonstration of the faith to those who should later disbelieve, such as Thomas, and those like him. With this also, an ineffable mystery was accomplished; for, "there came forth blood and water" [John 19:34]. These founts did not come forth by chance nor without purpose; rather, by means of the two together the Church consists. And the baptized know it, being regenerated by water and nourished by the Blood and Flesh. Hence, the Mysteries have their beginning; so that when you approach that awesome cup, you may approach as drinking from the very side.

> St. John Chrysostom, Bishop and Doctor (349–407)

SEPTEMBER 15

Memorial of St. Catherine of Genoa

St. Catherine of Genoa (1447–1510) was the author of the famous

Treatise on Purgatory, which treats the sufferings and consolations of those souls awaiting the Beatific Vision. Her own life was transformed by a mystical experience during the Sacrament of Penance, which shattered her acedia and opened her to a life of extraordinary grace. Here, St. Catherine describes how the pains of those in Purgatory are as the soul's desire for the Bread of Life. A close reading reveals the explicitly Eucharistic meaning of her teaching.

Let us suppose that there existed in the world but one loaf of bread to satisfy the hunger of every creature, and that the mere sight of it could do this. In such a case, a healthy man with a natural desire for food would grow more and more hungry—so long as he was kept from falling sick or dying—and his craving would unwaveringly continue. He would know that this bread, and nothing but this bread, could satisfy him. And not being able to reach it, he would remain in intolerable pain. The nearer he got to the bread without seeing it, the more ardently he would crave it and wholly direct himself towards it; it being the only thing that could afford relief.

If he were assured that he could never see the bread, he would have within him a perfect hell and become like the damned who are cut off from all hope of ever seeing God their Savior, who is the true Bread. The souls in purgatory, on the other hand, hope to see this Bread, and satiate themselves to the full therewith; whence they hunger and suffer pain as great as will be their capacity of enjoying that Bread, which is Jesus Christ the true God, our Savior and our love.

St. Catherine of Genoa (1447–1510)

SEPTEMBER 16

Born in Italy during the Counter-Reformation, St. Robert Bellarmine (1542–1621) gained renown as a leading apologist against the errors of Protestant Reformers. For his efforts, Bellarmine was made a cardinal of the Church, and his writings received special approbation by the pope. In his work, *The Art of Dying Well*, he explains that Christians ought to be filled with virtues in order to fittingly receive the Body of Christ. Furthermore, he teaches that frequent and worthy reception of the Eucharist is the measure by which man may judge himself.

> Lastly, this Holy Sacrament is not only the food of the traveler and the medicine of the sick, but it is also a wise and loving physician. Therefore, it is to be received with great joy and reverence, and the house of our soul ought to be adorned with all kind of virtues; especially, faith, hope, charity, devotion, and the fruits of good works, such as prayer, fasting, and almsgiving. The sweet Guest of our soul requires these ornaments, though He stands not in need of our goods.

> Remember that the Physician who visits us is our King and our God, whose purity is infinite, and therefore, He requires a most pure dwelling. Listen to St. John Chrysostom in his sermon to the people of Antioch: "How pure ought he be that offers such a sacrifice! Ought not the hand that divides this flesh be purer than the rays of the sun? Ought not the tongue be filled with a spiritual fire?" Whoever, then, desires to live and die well, let him enter into the chamber of his heart and shut the door. Alone before God who searches the heart, let him carefully consider how often, and in what manner, he has received the body of the Lord. If he finds that, by the grace of God, he has frequently and worthily communicated—and thereby has been well-nourished and gradually cured of his spiritual maladies, daily advancing in virtue and good works— then let him exult with trembling and serve the Lord in fear; not so much with a servile fear, but with a filial and chaste fear.

St. Robert Bellarmine, Bishop and Doctor (1542–1621)
[Memorial, September 17]

SEPTEMBER 17

Memorial of St. Hildegard von Bingen, Doctor of the Church

St. Hildegard von Bingen (1098–1179) possessed a wealth of gifts as a visionary, author, and composer. Her famous work, *Scivias*, canvasses the whole of salvation history, describing mystical visions of God's approach to man. In the following passage, the Eucharist is hailed as a summary of Christ's salvific actions, from His Nativity to the Ascension. Christians are, therefore, invited to enter into the grace of each mystery as they offer themselves to the Father through the Son, present in the Most Blessed Sacrament.

As if in a mirror, you can see [in the Eucharist] the Nativity, Passion, and Burial of the Savior signified, as well as the Resurrection and Ascension of the Only-Begotten Son of God, seen in the various stages that the Son of God lived and performed them when on earth. For if you consider the true meaning of the mystery of the Virgin Birth, the patient suffering of the cross, and the burial in the sepulcher, as well as the Resurrection from the dead, and Ascension into heaven, they clearly illuminate the reason He came down to earth; which was for the good of man. This same purest light shines in the Sacraments, as the Only-Begotten of God lived each state when He dwelt in the world by the will of God, for the redemption of mankind. How is this?

Because, the various states and sufferings of my Son, for love of man, remain clearly before my eyes: And the Nativity, Passion, Burial, Resurrection, and Ascension of My Only-Begotten slayed death itself for man. Therefore, they shine before me in heaven, never to be forgotten, but dawn before me in brightness, even until the consummation of the ages.

St. Hildegard von Bingen, Doctor of the Church (1098–1179)

SEPTEMBER 18

In the following sermon, St. Caesarius of Arles (c. 468–542) identifies the Liturgy of the Eucharist as the heart of the Mass. While the Liturgy of the Word is not unimportant, Caesarius notes that Christ is present in a singular and substantial way in the Eucharist. He therefore cautions his hearers not to leave Mass before this central act is complete.

> Brothers, I ask that you accept our humble suggestion with patience and a willing spirit. If you are in diligent attendance, you know that the Mass is not complete when the sacred readings are recited in church, but when the gifts are offered and the body and blood of the Lord is consecrated. For the readings—whether those of the prophets, the apostles, or the gospels—you can read in your own homes, or hear others read them. But you cannot witness the consecration of the body and blood of Christ anywhere else than in the house of God. Therefore, whoever wants to celebrate Mass with a pure heart, and thereby profit in soul, ought to remain in church until the Lord's Prayer is said and the benediction is given, prostrating oneself with a penitent heart.

> *St. Caesarius of Arles (c. 468–542)*

SEPTEMBER 19

Memorial of St. Émilie de Rodat

St. Émilie de Rodat (1787–1852) struggled to find her vocation before founding the Religious Congregation of the Holy Family of Villefranche, which served the poor and disenfranchised. After her death, St. Émilie's diary was discovered, which revealed the mystical life she had kept secret. In the following letter, St. Émilie instructs her sisters on how best to receive the sacraments, warning against indifference born of routine.

The only thing we should aspire to in our holy state of life is intimate union with God. . . . One way to do this is to approach the Sacraments with a great spirit of faith, appreciating these precious gifts of divine mercy with all our powers. Our holy state gives us the advantage of going frequently to draw from these fountains of grace and mercy, where we are washed and abundantly nourished. Ever approach them with respectful fear and the most animated love: we should not grow accustomed to the blessings of God. We should frequently reflect on this when we receive holy absolution. And after having received it, let us remember it with lively thanksgiving. We should do the same for Holy Communion so that the very idea and remembrance of making it recollects and animates us. And above all, it should dispose us to make those small sacrifices demanded by Him who gives Himself to us with such great love.

St. Émilie de Rodat (1787–1852)

SEPTEMBER 20

St. Cyril of Alexandria (378–444) was a leading voice of orthodoxy during the Christological controversies of the fifth century. In his *Commentary on the Gospel of Luke*, Cyril affirms that Christ's human flesh was the source of life and healing for sinners precisely because it was hypostatically united to the Word of God. This same flesh is present in the Blessed Sacrament, which effects the same miracles of grace today. On this basis, Cyril argues that Christ still desires to touch and heal each person in the Holy Eucharist, the "Mystical Blessing."

He entered into Peter's house, since the poor woman was confined to bed, consumed with a burning fever. Although as God He could say, "Away with this illness, arise"; this He did not do. He wanted to show that His own flesh was powerful, so He touched her hand, and Scripture says, "immediately, the fever left her" [cf. Luke 4:39]. But let us also take Jesus in. For whenever He enters into us, we will possess Him in mind and heart, and He will snuff out the fever of disordered passions. He will raise us up and make us strong, so we may spiritually serve Him, fulfilling those things that are pleasing to Him.

Consider again the benefit of touching His holy flesh, because it expels all manner of illness. It repels a host of demons and the devil's power. He heals many people in a split second. Although He could work such wonders by a word or nod, He places His hands on those with a fever in order to impart an important lesson. It was necessary, absolutely necessary, for us to learn that His holy flesh, which He made His own, bore the effective working of the power of the Word, having embedded within it a power fitting for God. So then, let Him touch us, or rather, we touch Him with the Mystical Blessing that He may free us from fevers of the soul, as well as the wiles and assault of demons.

St. Cyril of Alexandria, Bishop and Doctor (378–444)

SEPTEMBER 21

St. Adomnán (624–704) was the abbot of Iona Abbey in Scotland and a missionary to Ireland. His travels yielded ecclesial developments and social reforms, notably securing the rights of women and children in war. He composed the definitive biography of his relative, St. Columba, detailing his life and miracles. In this passage, St. Adomnán recounts Columba's most famous miracle, which recounts God's power and providence at Holy Mass.

On a festival day, by some chance, no wine could be found for the mystic sacrifice. Hearing the ministers of the altar complaining of this want, he took the vessel and went to the fountain to bring the water for the ministry of the Holy Eucharist;

for at that time, he was serving as deacon. The holy man then blessed the element of water from the spring in faith, invoking the name of our Lord Jesus Christ who had changed water into wine at Cana in Galilee, and by whose operation in this miracle the inferior element of water was also changed into the more agreeable kind, wine, by the hands of this admirable man. The holy man then returned from the fountain, entered the church, and placed the vessel containing this liquid near the altar, saying to the ministers: "You have wine, which the Lord Jesus has sent to perform His Mysteries."

St. Adomnán of Iona (624–704)
[Memorial, September 23]

SEPTEMBER 22

Memorial of St. Thomas of Villanova

St. Thomas of Villanova (1488–1555) was a priest in the Order of Saint Augustine whose life of charity earned him the title "Father of the Poor." His sermons not only reveal mystical insights into Scripture, but his own mastery of the spiritual life. In the following excerpt, St. Thomas speaks on the divinizing effects of the Eucharist. Building upon the parable of the leaven and dough, he illustrates God's desire to unite all men together as participators in the divine nature.

You remember this parable of the Gospel where "the Kingdom of Heaven is like leaven which a woman took and hid in three measures of flour, till it was all leavened" [Matt 13:33]. An admirable parable! Divine Wisdom has also united in Christ three measures of flour: the body first, then the soul and spirit (two faculties of the same soul), and He made them ferment by the leaven of the Divinity. Then, He made a mysterious bread, which He gives in the Sacrament of Love to the entire human race until the whole mass of the elect is fermented, arriving at deification. As one who burns a coal, throwing it into the middle of the hearth in order to inflame all around it, in this same manner—since He is not able to deify all men by uniting them hypostatically—the Savior will deify men when they receive Communion. By Communion, It will become incorporated—so to speak—in them.

Nevertheless, we do not yet see the fruit of this mysterious fermentation: *though we are children of God, what we shall be one day* [see 1 John 3:2] has not been revealed. But when Christ our life appears, then will the divine fruits of this fermentation be manifest to all our eyes, because we will be like Him.

St. Thomas of Villanova (1488–1555)

SEPTEMBER 23

After the tragic loss of her husband and three children, Bl. Émilie Tavernier-Gamelin (1800–1851) dedicated herself to charitable works, founding the Sisters of Providence in Montreal to serve the poor. In the following passage from her diary, Bl. Émilie writes of the surpassing joy she found in spiritual communion. Her remarks offer a glimpse into her intimate conversations with the Lord and her freedom of spirit in Him.

I experienced great happiness and ardent desire communicating this morning, but I could only do so spiritually. Many blessings in prayer. It seemed to me that I was in heaven because of the ease and happiness I felt conversing with God. I felt an inebriation that I cannot better define. It is necessary to experience it in order to understand this state of the soul with God, which I have sometimes tasted in my communions. . . .

I spent the evening before the Blessed Sacrament; I enjoyed the happiness of religious life . . . I would, as it seemed to me, do anything to preserve the interior peace which I enjoyed at that moment. Never while in the world did I enjoy the peace and the delight of conversing with You, O my God. How much to be pitied are they who do not love You! How You do overwhelm with happiness those who labor for You. Yes, it is sweet to be attached to the service of such a Master.

Bl. Émilie Tavernier-Gamelin (1800–1851)
[Memorial, September 24, Canada]

SEPTEMBER 24

St. Vincent Strambi (1745–1824) was a Passionist bishop who composed a biographical account of St. Paul of the Cross, the founder of his order. In the following meditation, St. Vincent teaches that Christ instituted the sacraments as a means of accessing the life-giving fount of blood that poured forth from His wounded side. In this way, St. Vincent understands the sacraments to be directly connected to the Paschal Mystery, granting redemption to all those who worthily approach.

How great was the desire that Jesus had throughout His earthly life to shed His Blood for the redemption of the world. With the same ardor, He desires that all profit from it; that all souls share in it. Inviting us to the fountain of mercy, He says: *Drink of it, all of you* [Matt 26:28]. From His most holy wounds, as St. Bernard says, He opens four founts: the fount of mercy, the fount of peace, the fount of devotion, and the fount of love. All souls are called to quench their thirst therein: *If anyone thirsts, let Him come to me* [John 7:37]. And why did He institute the most Holy Sacraments, which are like channels of grace for His Precious Blood? Why does He continue to offer it to the Eternal Father in heaven, and desire that it be daily offered by His ministers upon the holy altar? Why has He awakened in the hearts of the faithful of our day devotions of this kind? Is it not because of the ardent yearning of His heart that all draw from the fountain of His most holy wounds, and by the means of His Blood acquire grace? And oh! The monstrous ingratitude of those who do not profit and neglect so efficacious a means of salvation!

St. Vincent Strambi (1745–1824)
[Memorial, September 25]

SEPTEMBER 25

In response to the theological confusion of the twentieth century, Pope St. Paul VI (1897–1978) issued the encyclical *Mysterium Fidei* to re-affirm the Church's ancient faith in the Eucharist. In this excerpt, he speaks of the universal priesthood of all faithful and their sacrificial role at the Mass. While maintaining the essential distinction between the ministerial priesthood and the laity, Pope Paul emphasizes the Christian privilege of offering oneself to the Father, together with Christ, at the Holy Sacrifice of the Mass. This teaching underscores the very nature of Christian living, which aims at union with the Father, through the Son, in the Holy Spirit.

But there is something else that we would like to add that is very helpful in shedding light on the mystery of the Church. We mean the fact that the whole Church plays the role of priest and victim along with Christ, offering the Sacrifice of the Mass and itself completely offered in it. The Fathers of the Church taught this wondrous doctrine. A few years ago our predecessor of happy memory, Pius XII, explained it. And only recently the Second Vatican Council reiterated it in its Constitution on the Church, in dealing with the people of God. To be sure, the distinction between the universal priesthood and the hierarchical priesthood is something essential and not just a matter of degree, and it has to be maintained in a proper way. Yet we cannot help being filled with an earnest desire to see this teaching explained over and over until it takes deep root in the hearts of the faithful. For it is a most effective means of fostering devotion to the Eucharist, of extolling the dignity of all the faithful, and of spurring them on to reach the heights of sanctity, which means the total and generous offering of one-self to the service of the Divine Majesty.

Pope St. Paul VI (1897–1978)
[Memorial, September 26]

SEPTEMBER 26

Memorial of Ss. Cosmas and Damian

On the Memorial of Ss. Cosmas and Damian (d. c. 287), the Church honors those third-century twin brothers, martyred for the faith under Emperor Diocletian. In the following sermon, St. Maximus of Turin (c. 380–c. 465) lauds all martyrs as deserving a place beneath the altar of God in heaven, citing Sacred Scripture, "I saw underneath the altar the souls of those slain for the word of God and the testimony they held" (Rev 6:9). Maximus' words underscore the intrinsic link between Christ's sacrifice upon the altar of God and that of the martyrs. In this way, the Eucharistic liturgy manifests the communion of Christ with His Church who are together offered to the Father.

The blessed martyrs are, therefore, in a great and most high place because of their faith. But look at the place that those who were so treated by men merited; for, they merited a place under the altar with God. For sacred Scripture says, "I saw underneath God's altar the souls of those slain for the word of God, and for the testimony they held. And they cried out with a loud voice . . ." [Rev 6:9–10]. He says that the souls of those slain were under the altar. What could be more awesome, more honorable than to rest under that altar on which the sacrifice for God is celebrated, on which the victims are offered, at which the Lord is a priest. As has been written, "You are a priest forever in the order of Melchizedek" [Ps 110:4]. Rightly, the martyrs gather under the altar since Christ is placed on the altar. And rightly, the souls of the just rest under the altar since the body of the Lord is offered upon the altar.

St. Maximus of Turin (c. 380–c. 465)

SEPTEMBER 27

Memorial of St. Vincent de Paul

After his ordination to the priesthood, St. Vincent de Paul (1581–1660) was taken captive by Barbary pirates and sold into slavery. After converting his Muslim captors, Vincent returned to Europe, resumed his priestly service, and established the Congregation of the Mission and the Daughters of Charity. In the following sermon, St. Vincent paints an arresting picture of the Mass and its fulfillment of the rituals of the Old Covenant. Whereas the temple of old was made of stone, Christ has made men living stones, filled with the Holy Spirit and sated with His Precious Blood.

It is no longer the angel of the Lord who proclaims God's will to men from the Mercy Seat. Rather, it is Jesus Christ Himself who, before returning to heaven whence He descended for our salvation, left us this August Testament in which is contained all that we must believe. For here, the victim offered is the Lamb of God, the consecrated bread is the Bread of Angels and of men, and the mysterious wine that we receive at Holy Mass is the Drink of the Saints in heaven. Indeed, the prayers that are said, and the hymns that are chanted, are those songs of joy that the blessed spirits proclaim, resounding in the realm of glory. Indeed, our bodily temples are the new heaven, which the Prophet had promised to men [see Jer 31:31; 1 Cor 6:19].

St. Vincent de Paul (1581–1660)

SEPTEMBER 28

St. Isaac Jogues (1607–1646) was a missionary priest to New France—present-day New York—who was captured and cruelly tortured by Mohawk tribesmen. Despite his extreme sufferings, St. Isaac returned to evangelize Canada and was there martyred. In this account of his first capture, he relates the difficult scene of a march, which had followed upon brutal physical torture. Crucially, St. Isaac reveals the motivation for his perseverance: he wills to make the sacraments present to the new colony. All of his sufferings are, therefore, meritoriously ordered toward the administration of the holy sacraments of the Church.

Those warriors, having made a sacrifice of our blood, pursued their course, and we ours. The tenth day after our capture, we came to a place where it was necessary to cease navigation [by water], and proceeded by land. That road, which was about four days long, was extremely painful for us. The guard placed over me was unable to carry all of his belongings, and so placed a part of it on my back, which was all torn. In three days' time, we ate only a few wild fruits, which we had gathered along the way. The heat of the summer sun was at its warmest, and our wounds greatly weakened us, causing us to lag behind the others. Seeing ourselves considerably separated from them, I told poor René at nightfall that he should escape. Indeed, we were able to do so; but, for myself, I would rather have suffered all sorts of torments than abandon to death those whom I could somewhat console; and upon whom I could confer the blood of my Savior through the Sacraments of His Church. This good young man, seeing that I wished to follow my little flock, would never leave me.

St. Isaac Jogues (1607–1646)
[Memorial, October 19; Canada, September 26]

SEPTEMBER 29

Feasts of Ss. Michael, Gabriel, and Raphael

St. Francis Borgia (1510–1572) belonged to the highest rank of nobility in Spain and served as the viceroy of Catalonia. After the death of his wife, St. Francis renounced all worldly titles in favor of the priesthood, eventually becoming the third superior general of the Jesuit order. In the following passage, St. Francis offers a template for making a prayer of thanksgiving after Communion. Echoing the Canticle of the Three Holy Youths, St. Francis instructs the angels and all of creation to praise God for the gift of the Eucharist. Though the angelic nature surpasses that of man, union with Christ in the Eucharist raises man above his original state, making him a partaker of the divine nature (see 2 Pet 1:4).

We should thank the Eternal Father for the benefit of creation, which He so often renews in the Blessed Sacrament. He created us like unto Himself by a wondrous act of goodness, imprinting His own image upon us. Since we had nearly effaced all traces of this image, He willed to re-establish it in us by the communion of the body of Jesus Christ. It is only right, then, to profess the most ardent gratitude for such unspeakable goodness, and to invite all creatures of heaven to thank Him in the following manner:

O all you works of the Lord, bless the Lord: praise and exalt Him above all forever. O all you angels of the Lord, bless the Lord: bless the Lord, you heavens. O all you waters above the heavens, bless the Lord: bless the Lord, all you powers of heaven. O you sun and moon, bless the Lord: bless the Lord, you stars of heaven. O you fire and heat, bless the Lord: bless the Lord, you winter and summer. . . . (cf. Dan 3:57–67).

Let us thus incite the works of the Lord to give Him thanks for us, in whom He has worked effects like those which all these creatures produced, by giving us the body of His only begotten Son. He has raised us to the condition of the angels, and earthly as we are, He has made us all heavenly. He has purified us by the saving waters of His grace and by the abundance of our tears. He has enlightened us with the rays of the Sun of Justice and has melted the ice of our hearts. He has warmed our coldness by the fire of His divine love, and in short, He has dissipated the darkness by the splendor of His light. We should in this manner apply verses of the Canticles to the particular graces each one of us has received from God.

St. Francis Borgia (1510–1572)
[Memorial, September 30]

SEPTEMBER 30

Memorial of St. Jerome, Doctor of the Church

St. Jerome (c. 347–420) was the foremost biblical scholar of his time who produced the Latin Vulgate and numerous scriptural commentaries. Drawn to the ascetic life, Jerome eventually chose to retire to a monastery in Bethlehem. In his treatment of the Book of Zephaniah, he contrasts the priests of the Old Covenant, to whom it was said, "her priests have polluted the sanctuary, they have acted unjustly against the law" (Zeph 3:4), with those of the New Covenant. Accordingly, he praises priests under the New Law for diligently applying themselves to the prayers of the Eucharist.

Priests who grant baptism and pray for the advent of the Lord at the Eucharist are not as unworthy, in our estimation, as those that the prophets expound upon and prophesy; for, these beseech the Lord and diligently perform their service lest they be accounted among those priests who violate the holy things of the Lord. For, true dignity is not having dignified titles, but dignified work, and a priest is accustomed to maintain this: "Whoever desires the office of bishop desires a good work" (1 Tim 3:1), which Paul writes. Desire the work, not the dignity. But if a man despises the work and has only the dignity in view, the tower of Siloam quickly collapses [see Luke 13:4], and the high cedars are struck by lightning [see Ps 29].

St. Jerome, Doctor of the Church (c. 347–420)

OCTOBER

OCTOBER 1

Memorial of St. Thérèse of Lisieux, Virgin and Doctor

St. Thérèse of Lisieux (1873–1897) was a French Carmelite nun, renowned for her "little way" of spiritual childhood. Here, St. Thérèse touches upon the heart of her spirituality as she explains that the Eucharist provides the necessary strength to aid her weakness. She further reflects on the tragic loss of her mother, recalling that the Eucharist gives her access to the entire communion of saints—including her mother—who are inextricably united to Christ. Together, these varied sentiments are vividly expressed in her recollection of her first Communion.

> How sweet was the first kiss of Jesus! It was indeed a kiss of love. I felt that I was loved, and I said: "I love You, and I give myself to You forever." Jesus asked nothing of me, and claimed no sacrifice. For a long time, He and little Thérèse had known and understood one another; that day our meeting was more than simple recognition, it was perfect union. We were no longer two. Thérèse had disappeared like a drop of water lost in the immensity of the ocean; Jesus alone remained—He was the Master, the King! Had not Thérèse asked Him to take away her liberty which frightened her? She felt herself so weak and frail, that she wished to be forever united to the Divine Strength.

And then my joy became so intense, so deep, that it could not be restrained; tears of happiness welled up and overflowed. My companions were astonished, and asked each other afterwards: "Why did she cry? Had she anything on her conscience? No, it is because neither her Mother, nor her dearly loved Carmelite sister, is here." No one understood that all the joy of Heaven had come down into one heart, and that this heart, exiled, weak, and mortal as it was, could not contain it without tears.

How could my Mother's absence grieve me on my First Communion Day? As Heaven itself dwelt in my soul in receiving a visit from Our Divine Lord, I received one from my dear Mother as well. Nor was I crying on account of Pauline's absence, for we were even more closely united than before. No, I repeat it—joy alone, a joy too deep for words, overflowed within me.

St. Thérèse of Lisieux, Virgin and Doctor (1873–1897)

OCTOBER 2

Bl. Raymond of Capua (c. 1330–1399) was a Dominican priest who zealously fought to reform his order by establishing houses of strict observance. As the spiritual director of St. Catherine of Siena, Bl. Raymond composed a firsthand account of her life, providing valuable insight into her life of sanctity. In the following excerpt, Bl. Raymond recounts a miraculous event that took place during the Holy Sacrifice of the Mass. Not only does the heavenly sign betoken St. Catherine's holiness, but it highlights the living reality that is the Eucharist.

I clothed myself in my priestly vestments and celebrated the Mass of the day. I consecrated one small Host for [St. Catherine], and when I had communicated, I turned to give her the ordinary absolution. Her countenance was angelic and beaming with light. So changed was she that I hesitated recognizing her, and asked interiorly: "Is the Lord truly your faithful and beloved Spouse?" and on turning again to the altar, I added mentally: "Come Lord to your spouse." At that same instant, before I touched the Sacred Host, it *moved* and came a short distance to the paten, which I had been holding in my hand. I was so occupied with the light beaming from Catherine's countenance, and the motion of the consecrated Host which I distinctly saw, that I do not perfectly remember whether it placed itself alone on the paten, or whether I laid it there. I dare not affirm it, but I think it deposited itself thereon. God is my witness that I tell the truth . . . I am positive that I beheld the Sacred Host, without the least exterior agency, move and advance toward me.

Bl. Raymond of Capua (c. 1330–1399)
[Memorial, October 5]

OCTOBER 3

Memorial of Bl. Columba Marmion

Bl. Columba Marmion (1858–1923) was a Benedictine abbot who composed several major works of spiritual theology. His emphasis on Sacred Scripture and the Fathers of the Church helped spark a contemporary return to the ancient sources of the faith. In the following passage, Marmion compares the sublime union between God and man in Holy Communion with the hypostatic union. Without confusing terms, Marmion suggests that the hypostatic union is the pattern that Christ intends to "replicate," however distantly, in man through Communion.

See what took place in the Incarnate Word. There was in Him a very intense human and natural activity. But the Word, to Whom the Humanity of Christ was indissolubly united, was the furnace where all His activity was nourished, and whence it radiated.

The desire of Christ in giving Himself to us is to produce something analogous within us. Without establishing a union as close as that of the Word with His Sacred Humanity, Christ, in giving Himself to us, wills to be in us, by His grace and the action of His Spirit, the principle of all our inner activity: *Et ego in eo;* He is in the soul, He abides in it, but He is not idle, He wills to work in it, and when the soul remains given up to Him, to His every will, then Christ's action becomes so powerful that this soul will infallibly be carried on to the highest perfection, according to God's designs. For Christ comes to the soul with His Divinity, His merits, His riches, to be its Light and Way, its Truth, Wisdom, Justice, and Redemption: *Qui factus est nobis sapientia a Deo, et justitia, et sanctificatio et redemptio,* in a word, to the the Life of the soul, to life Himself within the soul: *Vivo ego iam non ego; vivit vero in me Christus.* This is the dream of the soul: to make only one with the Beloved. Communion, in which the soul receives Christ as Food, brings about the realization of this dream, by transforming it little by little into Christ.

Bl. Columba Marmion (1858–1923)

OCTOBER 4

Memorial of St. Francis of Assisi

Born into a wealthy family, St. Francis (1181–1226) renounced the world and its comforts in order to seek those riches found only in Christ. A radical disciple of the gospel, St. Francis was uncompromising in his self-denial so as to be united with the Crucified Christ. In his writings, he shows the greatest respect for the Holy Eucharist and warns his brothers against any sign of dishonor. In the passage below, Francis praises God's condescension in the Blessed Sacrament, tacitly revealing it as the template for his own humility.

Man should be seized with fear, the earth should tremble, and the heavens rejoice exceedingly when Christ, the Son of the Living God, descends upon the altar in the hands of the priest. O admirable greatness and stupendous condescension! O humble sublimity!

O sublime humility! that the Lord of the universe, God, and the Son of God, so humbles Himself that for our salvation He hides Himself under the form of a morsel of bread. Consider, brothers, the humility of God! Pour your hearts out before Him (cf. Ps 61:9), and be humbled so that you may be exalted by Him (1 Pet 5:6). Do not, therefore, keep back anything of yourselves so that He may receive you entirely Who gives Himself entirely to you.

Here, St. Francis passionately counsels his brothers on the dignity due the Eucharist.

Wherefore, brothers, kissing your feet and with the charity of which I am capable, I call upon you all to show all reverence and all honor possible to the most holy Body and Blood of our Lord Jesus Christ, in whom the things that are in heaven and on earth are pacified and reconciled to Almighty God.

St. Francis of Assisi (1181–1226)

OCTOBER 5

Memorial of St. Maria Faustina Kowalska

St. Maria Faustina Kowalska (1905–1938) was a Polish religious and mystic who, in 1931, received the now-famous message of Divine Mercy. Though she served as a second-choir nun and died in obscurity, Faustina was ultimately successful in establishing the Feast of Divine Mercy through the agency of Pope St. John Paul II. Her devotional life was intensely Eucharistic, and in this passage, she honors the Blessed Sacrament as an expression of God's infinite mercy.

O Blessed Host, in whom is contained the testament of
  God's mercy for us, and especially for poor sinners.
O Blessed Host, in whom is contained the Body and Blood
  of the Lord Jesus as proof of infinite mercy for us, and
  especially for poor sinners.

O Blessed Host, in whom is contained life eternal and of infinite mercy, dispensed in abundance to us and especially to poor sinners.

O Blessed Host, in whom is contained the mercy of the Father, the Son and the Holy Spirit toward us, and especially toward poor sinners.

O Blessed Host, in whom is contained the infinite price of mercy which will compensate for all our debts, and especially those of poor sinners.

O Blessed Host, in whom is contained the fountain of living water which springs from infinite mercy for us, and especially for poor sinners.

O Blessed Host, in whom is contained the fire of purest love which blazes forth from the bosom of the Eternal Father, as from an abyss of infinite mercy for us, and especially for poor sinners.

O Blessed Host, in whom is contained the medicine for all our infirmities, flowing from infinite mercy, as from a fount, for us and especially for poor sinners.

O Blessed Host, in whom is contained the union between God and us through His infinite mercy for us, and especially for poor sinners.

O Blessed Host, in whom are contained all the sentiments of the most sweet Heart of Jesus toward us, and especially poor sinners.

St. Maria Faustina Kowalska (1905–1938)

OCTOBER 6

Memorial of St. Bruno of Cologne

Today, the Church honors that illustrious founder of the Carthusian Order, Bruno of Cologne (1030–1101). Though well positioned to become the bishop of Rheims, Bruno fled to Chartreuse with six of his companions, where he laid the foundations of the most austere order in the Church. The following passage, written by an anonymous Carthusian of Nuremburg, illustrates the exalted love born of such asceticism. Far from living as one in deprivation, this Carthusian monk gives witness to the hundredfold promise of Christ, eminently realized in the Blessed Sacrament.

In the desert, Moses struck the rock, and there came out refreshing water for the use and comfort of the people of Israel and their flocks, but when the soldier Longinus, with his sturdy hand, struck the Rock with the spear—that is to say—when he cleft the right side of Christ, there came out then and evermore a mysterious fountain of blood and water, from which our chaste Mother, the Holy Catholic Church, draws her saving Sacraments. Eve was called the mother of the living and was formed from the side of her husband, Adam. The Holy Church militant is called the mother of all who are living by faith, and she is formed from the side of Christ, her spouse.

O great, precious and loving Wound of my Savior—you are deeper than all others, and opened so wide that the faithful can enter in! O Wound from which flow unlimited and endless blessings. Wound of the side inflicted last, but most celebrated! Whoever drinks deeply from the holy and divine source of this wound, or even takes even a few drops, will forget all his ills, will be set free from the thirst for fleeting and vile pleasures, will be inflamed with the love of eternal and heavenly things, and filled with the unutterable sweetness of the Holy Spirit. Then will flow into his soul "a fountain of water springing up to eternal life" [John 4:14].

Carthusian of Nuremberg, Anonymous (c. 1180)

OCTOBER 7

Feast of Our Lady of the Rosary

Joseph Ratzinger (b. 1927) served as a theological advisor at the Second Vatican Council and later provided for its interpretation as head of the Congregation of the Doctrine of the Faith (1981–2005) and pope (2005–2013). During his pontificate, Pope Benedict XVI emphasized the centrality of the person of Christ and His saving presence in the Mass. In this excerpt from *Deus Caritas Est*, Pope Benedict offers a Trinitarian view of the Eucharist. By receiving Holy Communion, Christians are incorporated in Christ's body and thus partake in the Trinitarian exchange of love.

> Jesus gave this act of oblation an enduring presence through his institution of the Eucharist at the Last Supper. He anticipated his death and resurrection by giving his disciples, in the bread and wine, his very self, his body and blood as the new manna (cf. Jn 6:31–33). The ancient world had dimly perceived that man's real food—what truly nourishes him as man—is ultimately the Logos, eternal wisdom: this same Logos now truly becomes food for us—as love. The Eucharist draws us into Jesus' act of self-oblation. More than just statically receiving the incarnate Logos, we enter into the very dynamic of his self-giving. The imagery of marriage between God and Israel is now realized in a way previously inconceivable: it had meant standing in God's presence, but now it becomes union with God through sharing in Jesus' self-gift, sharing in his body and blood. The sacramental "mysticism," grounded in God's condescension towards us, operates at a radically different level and lifts us to far greater heights than anything that any human mystical elevation could ever accomplish.

Pope Benedict XVI (b. 1927)

OCTOBER 8

Though frequently misinterpreted by modern commentators, Pope
Pius XII (1876–1958) was praised by leading figures of his day for his
heroic efforts during World War II. Among such figures were Golda
Meir, the prime minister of Israel, and Israel Zolli, the chief rabbi of
Rome. After the war, Rabbi Zolli converted to the Catholic faith and
paid tribute to Pope Pius XII's personal assistance by adopting his
baptismal name, Eugenio. In this excerpt from *Haurietis Aquas*, Pope
Pius XII writes on the human love of Jesus Christ, which burned with
emotion during the institution of the Most Holy Eucharist.

But who can worthily depict those beatings of the divine
Heart, the signs of His infinite love, of those moments when
He granted men His greatest gifts: Himself in the Sacrament
of the Eucharist, His most holy Mother, and the office of the
priesthood shared with us?

Even before He ate the Last Supper with His disciples Christ
Our Lord, since He knew He was about to institute the sacrament of His body and blood by the shedding of which the
new covenant was to be consecrated, felt His heart roused by
strong emotions, which He revealed to the Apostles in these
words: "With desire have I desired to eat this Pasch with
you before I suffer." And these emotions were doubtless even
stronger when "taking bread, He gave thanks, and broke, and
gave to them, saying, 'This is My body which is given for you,
this do in commemoration of Me.' Likewise the chalice also,
after He had supped, saying, 'This chalice is the new testament in My blood, which shall be shed for you.'"

It can therefore be declared that the divine Eucharist, both
the sacrament which He gives to men and the sacrifice in
which He unceasingly offers Himself "from the rising of the
sun till the going down thereof," and likewise the priesthood,

are indeed gifts of the Sacred Heart of Jesus.

Ven. Pope Pius XII (1876–1958)
[Memorial, October 9]

OCTOBER 9

Memorial of St. John Henry Newman

St. John Henry Newman (1801–1890) was a prominent Anglican priest whose work in the Oxford Movement led to his conversion to the Catholic faith. Faced with harsh criticism from Anglican quarters, Newman publicly defended his embrace of Catholicism in the classic work, *Apologia pro vita sua*. In the following passage, Newman professes his belief in the doctrine of transubstantiation, emphasizing the need for humility before divinely revealed truths. He teaches that the mysteries of God, while not unintelligible, surpass the comprehension of man. Man must, therefore, exercise faith, placing trust in the authority of God's self-revelation to man.

People say that the doctrine of Transubstantiation is difficult to believe; I did not believe the doctrine till I was a Catholic. I had no difficulty in believing it as soon as I believed that the Catholic Roman Church was the oracle of God, and that she had declared this doctrine to be part of the original revelation. It is difficult, impossible to imagine, I grant—but how is it difficult to believe? Yet Macaulay thought it so difficult to believe, that he had need of a believer in it of talents as eminent as Sir Thomas More before he could bring himself to conceive that the Catholics of an enlightened age could resist "the overwhelming force of the argument against it." "Sir Thomas More," he says, "is one of the choice specimens of wisdom and virtue; and the doctrine of transubstantiation is a kind of proof charge. A faith which stands that test, will stand any test." But for myself, I cannot indeed prove it, I cannot tell *how* it is; but I say, "Why should it not be? What's to hinder it? What do I know of substance or matter? just as much as the greatest philosophers, and that is nothing at all;"—so much is this the case, that there is a rising school of philosophy now, which considers phenomena to constitute the whole of our knowledge in physics. The Catholic doctrine leaves phenomena alone. It does not say that the phenomena go; on the contrary, it says that they remain: nor does it say that the same phenomena are in several places at once. It deals with what no one on earth knows anything about, the material substances themselves. And, in like manner, of that majestic article of the Anglican as well as of the Catholic Creed— the doctrine of the Trinity in Unity. What do I know of the essence of the Divine Being? I know that my abstract idea of three is simply incompatible with my idea of one; but when I come to the question of concrete fact, I have no means of proving that there is not a sense in which one and three can equally be predicated of the Incommunicable God.

St. John Henry Newman (1801–1890)

OCTOBER 10

St. John of Ribera (1532–1611) helped promulgate the reforms enacted by the Council of Trent and founded a seminary for the orthodox formation of priests. In his commentary on the Lord's Prayer, St. John considers several interpretations of the petition, "give us this day our daily bread." In this excerpt, he identifies the Eucharist as this daily bread and encourages those properly disposed to receive daily. To those not in the state of grace, St. John counsels to seek reconciliation with God.

And as we say *Our Father*—for He is the Father of those who believe and have understanding—we ask for our daily bread, because Christ is our bread. Indeed, it is His most precious Body that we receive. We ask that this Bread be given to us each day so that we, who are in Christ, receive Him daily as heavenly food. Yet, if we commit mortal sin, we make ourselves unworthy to receive His Most Holy Body and are forbidden to receive the Bread from heaven. And if we cease receiving communion [altogether], we will be cut off from His Body. . . .

St. John clearly teaches that Christ is this bread: "I am the Bread of Life that came down from heaven. If anyone eats this Bread, he will live forever, and the Bread that I will give is my flesh for the life of the world" [John 6:51]. So we can say with certainty that this Bread is Christ. And when Christ said "those who eat this bread will live forever" [John 6:51], it is clear that an *eternal giving* is found in receiving Christ's Most Holy Body in Communion.

Nevertheless, one fears for him who is in mortal sin, excommunicated, or separated from the Body of Christ as he is far from a healthy state. The Lord warned such as those, saying, "unless you eat the flesh of the Son of man and drink His blood, you do not have life in you" [John 6:53]. Thus, we ask in prayer, *give us this day our daily bread* [Matt 6:11].

St. John of Ribera (1532–1611)

OCTOBER 11

Memorial of Pope St. John XXIII

The affable character and childlike spirit of Pope St. John XXIII (1881–1963) earned him the nickname, "il Papa Buono," the good pope. Completing the unfinished business of the First Vatican Council, he convened the Second Vatican Council, which reaffirmed the ancient teachings of the faith. In this excerpt from his encyclical, *Sacerdotii Nostri Primordia*, St. John explains the centrality of the sacraments and the need for priests and laity to offer themselves to God at Mass.

For, if you give careful consideration to all of the activity of a priest, what is the main point of his apostolate if not seeing to it that wherever the Church lives, a people who are joined by the bonds of faith, regenerated by holy Baptism and cleansed of their faults will be gathered together around the sacred altar? It is then that the priest, using the sacred power he has received, offers the divine Sacrifice in which Jesus Christ renews the unique immolation which He completed on Calvary for the redemption of mankind and for the glory of His heavenly Father. It is then that the Christians who have gathered together, acting through the ministry of the priest, present the divine Victim and offer themselves to the supreme and eternal God as a "sacrifice, living, holy, pleasing to God." [Rom 12:1] There it is that the people of God are taught the doctrines and precepts of faith and are nourished with the Body of Christ, and there it is that they find a means to gain supernatural life, to grow in it, and if need be to regain unity. And there besides, the Mystical Body of Christ, which is the Church, grows with spiritual increase throughout the world down to the end of time.

Pope St. John XXIII (1881–1963)

OCTOBER 12

In the following sermon, Caesarius of Arles (c. 468–542) warns of irreverence at Mass and exhorts his listeners to worship in spirit and truth. Distinguishing pious attendance from mere physical presence, he encourages Christians to plumb the depths of the liturgy, immersing themselves in the Mystery of Faith present before them. Scandalized by those who amuse themselves with distractions at Mass, St. Caesarius wonders if they are not guiltier than those who fail to attend.

Beloved brothers, I ask and exhort you with a fatherly devotion that whenever Masses are occurring on the Lord's Day, or on other major feasts, that no one leave the church until after the Divine Mysteries are finished. Although there are many in whose faith and devotion we rejoice, there are also many who leave the church immediately after the reading of the Divine Scriptures, because they do not think sufficiently about the salvation of their soul. There are also some who occupy themselves with pleasurable and worldly stories while the Scriptures are read. The result is that they do not hear them, nor allow others to do so. We would think such people would less guilty if they did not come to church, because there they are shown to offend God more, precisely in the place they could have merited forgiveness of their sins.

St. Caesarius of Arles (c. 468–542)

OCTOBER 13

St. Gerard Majella (1726–1755) was a religious brother of the Redemptorist Order, known for his childlike obedience and simplicity of soul. When falsely accused of immorality, he famously remained silent, believing that God Himself would clear his name. Here, St. Gerard writes to his superior, detailing his own prayers of Eucharistic devotion.

Acts when visiting the Blessed Sacrament:

O my Lord! I believe that You are present in the Most Blessed Sacrament. I adore You with my whole heart, and by this visit intend to adore You in all those places where You are present in the Blessed Sacrament. I offer You Your most Precious Blood for all poor sinners. At the same time, I wish to receive You spiritually wherever You are sacramentally present.

St. Gerard also explains his manner of preparation for Holy Communion. These simple instructions reveal the intensity with which he approached the Eucharist.

My thanksgiving after Holy Communion is to last from the time I communicate till noon; my preparation for the next day, from noon till evening.

... When rising and going to bed, I will say the usual community prayers of thanksgiving. In both the morning and evening, I will say the acts for Holy Communion. Lastly, I shall examine my conscience at noon and in the evening, and then make an act of contrition.

St. Gerard Majella (1726–1755)

OCTOBER 14

St. Jean de Brébeuf (1593–1649) was a Jesuit missionary to Quebec who suffered a most cruel martyrdom of cutting, burning, and lancing. Like many North American Martyrs, St. Jean demonstrated an astonishing degree of abandonment to Divine Providence and a willingness to endure the most inhuman tortures for the Gospel. In this passage from the *Jesuit Relations*, St. Jean describes the humble dwellings of the missionaries and confesses his contentment to be near the Blessed Sacrament.

Here, we certainly do not have the exterior solemnity that awakens and sustains devotion. Only what is essential to our religion is visible: the Holy Sacrament of the Altar. To perceive Its marvels, we must open the eyes of our faith without the aid of any sensible mark of its grandeur; no more than the Magi had in the stable. But it seems that God supplies for what we lack in the midst of these infidel peoples (and as a recompense of grace that He has given us for transporting it, so to speak, beyond so many seas, and for finding it a place in these poor cabins), and wishes to crown us with those same blessings that He bestows upon persecuted Catholics in the countries of heretics. These good people hardly ever see church or altar; yet, the little they see is worth double what they would see in full liberty. Do you not see what consolation it would be to prostrate ourselves at times before a cross in the midst of this barbarism? to turn our eyes toward and to enter, in the midst of our petty domestic duties, even into the room which the Son of God has been pleased to take in our little dwelling? Is it not paradise day and night for us, since we are not separated from this well-beloved of the nations, save by some bark or branch of a tree? *En ipse stat post parietem nostrum. Sub umbra illius quem desideraveram, sedi.* [Behold, He stands behind our wall. Beneath the shadow of him whom I desired, I sat (*cf.* Song 2).] See what we have within. If we go outside our cabin, heaven is open to us. And those great buildings that lift their heads to the clouds in large cities do not here obstruct our view. Thus, we can say our prayers in full liberty before the noble oratory that saint Francois Xavier loved better than any other.

St. Jean de Brébeuf (1593–1649)
[Memorial, October 19]

OCTOBER 15

Memorial of St. Teresa of Jesus, Virgin and Doctor

St. Teresa of Ávila (1515–1582) was a Carmelite nun whose life of radical conversion inspired a reform of the Carmelite Order, culminating with the establishment of the Order of the Discalced Carmelites. Her writings offer a systematic account of the mystical life, detailing the gifts given to those on the extraordinary path of grace. In this passage from her *Life*, Teresa explains that Christ's hiddenness in the Eucharist is actually a work of his mercy, which safeguards man from terror.

Once when I went to Communion, I called to mind the exceedingly great majesty of Him who I had seen, and considered that it was Him who is present in the most Holy Sacrament. Very often our Lord was pleased to show Himself to me in the Host—the very hair on my head stood, and I thought I should come to nothing. O my Lord—ah, if You did not throw a veil over Your greatness, who would dare, being so foul and miserable, to come in contact with Your great Majesty? Blessed may You be, O Lord. May the angels and all creation praise You, who order all things according to the measure of our weakness, so that, when we have the fruition of Your sovereign mercies, Your great power may not terrify us, so that we dare not, being a frail and miserable race, persevere in that fruition!

It might happen to us as it did to a laborer—I know it to be a certain fact—who found a treasure beyond his expectations, which was nevertheless not very great. When he realized his possession, he was seized with melancholy, which by degrees brought him to his grave through simple distress and anxiety of mind, because he did not know what to do with his treasure. If he had not found it all at once, and if others had given him portions of it by degrees, maintaining him thereby, he might have been happier than he had been in his poverty, and it would not have cost him his life.

O You Treasure of the poor! How marvelously You sustain souls, showing them not all at once, but by little and little, the abundance of Your riches! When I behold Your great Majesty hidden beneath that which is so slight as the Host is, I am filled with wonder, ever since that vision, at Your great wisdom; and I know not how it is that our Lord gives me the strength and courage necessary to draw near to him, were it not that He who has had such compassion on me, and still has, gives me strength, nor would it be possible for me to be silent, or refrain from making known marvels so great.

St. Teresa of Jesus, Virgin and Doctor (1515–1582)

OCTOBER 16

Memorial of St. Margaret Mary Alacoque

Though devotion to the Sacred Heart of Jesus was implicitly present since Apostolic times (see John 13:23), St. Margaret Mary Alacoque (1647–1690) helped spread its modern cult, emphasizing Christ's tender love for each person. In the following prayer of adoration, St. Margaret voices her desire to return "love for love" through her self-offering at Holy Mass. For the Eucharistic liturgy allows man to unite himself to the sacrifice of Christ, which is directed to the Father, in union with the Holy Spirit.

Act of Adoration of the Holy Sacrament

Jesus Christ, my Lord and my God, whom I believe is really and truly present in the Most Holy Sacrament of the altar: receive this most profound act of adoration as a token of my desire to worship You without ceasing, and in thanksgiving for the love Your Sacred Heart has for me. I cannot better repay your sentiments of love than by offering You all the acts of worship, of resignation, of patience, and of love that this same Heart made during Its mortal life, and that It still makes, and will eternally make, in heaven. This I offer in order to love You, praise and worship You through It as much as possible. I unite myself to this divine offering that You made to Your divine Father, and I consecrate to You all of my being, asking You to destroy the sin in me, and to not allow me to ever be separated from You.

St. Margaret Mary Alacoque (1647–1690)

OCTOBER 17

Memorial of St. Ignatius of Antioch

In his *Letter to the Ephesians*, St. Ignatius of Antioch (d. 107) illustrates the rich ecclesiology of the early Church, which is Eucharistic in nature. The modern tendency to separate institutional structure from personal faith was not a part of the Apostolic doctrine as received and handed down by St. Ignatius. Rather, he teaches that union with Christ is found through union with the bishop and the Eucharist confected at his hands. St. Ignatius thus warns that those outside the sanctuary of the Church are deprived of that blessed bread of God, which is Christ Himself.

> If in a brief time I gained such fellowship with your bishop—a kind that is not human but spiritual—how much more do I bless you who are so mingled with him as the Church is with Jesus Christ, and as Jesus Christ is with the Father, so that all may be united as one. Let no one deceive you: unless someone is within the sanctuary, he does not have the bread of God. If the prayer of one or two has such great power, how much more does the prayer of the bishop and the whole Church? He who does not come together in unity is proud and judges himself; for it is written, "God opposes the proud" [Prov 3:34]. So let us not oppose the bishop that we may be subject to God.
>
> *St. Ignatius of Antioch (d. 107)*

OCTOBER 18

Memorial of St. Peter of Alcántara

St. Peter of Alcántara (1499–1562) was a Franciscan priest, known for his extreme asceticism and mystical life of prayer. Details of his extraordinary mortifications are related in St. Teresa of Ávila's autobiography and surpass natural explanation. In his treatise on prayer, St. Peter speaks of the immense love that impelled Christ to institute the Blessed Sacrament. This gift is to be a memorial and pledge of His presence as well as a means of accessing grace.

> He that desires to understand anything of this noble Sacrament must know that no tongue is able to express that im-

mense love and ardent affection with which our Blessed Savior was inflamed towards His Holy Church, and all faithful souls, in instituting this stupendous mystery. For when the Bridegroom was about to depart from this mortal life and leave His Beloved Spouse, lest His departure should be any occasion of forgetting her Redeemer, He gave her this Sacrament wherein He Himself is present as a pledge and memorial of His perpetual love.

Then, seeing He was to be long absent, lest His spouse should remain solitary and alone, He, for His consolation would leave Himself for her companion in this Holy Sacrament.

When our Blessed Savior was about to suffer death for the redemption of His spouse, to enrich her with His most precious blood and purge her from sins, lest she should be defrauded of so great a treasure, He would give her a key in this sacrament, whereby she might enjoy these riches at her pleasure.

St. Peter of Alcántara (1499–1562)

OCTOBER 19

Memorial of St. Paul of the Cross

St. Paul of the Cross (1694–1775) founded the Congregation of the Passion to honor and extol that central mystery of faith, the Passion of Christ. Known for his piety and preaching, St. Paul was elected the superior of the order against his own wishes. In this extract from a letter, St. Paul describes the Eucharist as the means of attaining heaven. Notably, St. Paul remains ever aware of the living presence of Christ, hidden in the Holy Host.

Holy Communion is the most efficacious means of uniting the soul to God. The best preparation for the divine banquet is to keep ourselves well purified and to watch over our tongue, which is the first member that touches the sacred Host. On the day that we receive Holy Communion, we should endeavor to keep our hearts as living tabernacles of our Eucharistic Jesus, and then frequently visit Him with acts of adoration, love, and gratitude; this is what divine love will teach us. When a prince sends one of his ministers to a distant country, he provides him with all that is necessary for safely reaching his destination: the Lord, my God and my Father, has given me as my viaticum His only Son.

Elsewhere, St. Paul reflects on the Feast of Corpus Christi, prescribing a generous spirit of self-giving.

The Feast of the Blessed Sacrament is the feast of love. Oh, what great love! What immense charity! The moth is drawn to the light, and burns itself in it. May your soul likewise draw near to the divine light! May it be reduced to ashes in that sacred flame, particularly during this great and sweet octave of *Corpus Christi*. Ah! Eat, drink, run, sing, rejoice in honor of your Divine Spouse.

St. Paul of the Cross (1694–1775)

OCTOBER 20

In his famous work *On the Mysteries*, St. Ambrose (c. 340–397) distinguishes earthly food from the spiritual food found in the Blessed Sacrament. Referencing the Song of Songs, he invites all Christians to this feast of divine love wherein souls are nourished unto eternal life. St. Ambrose's words culminate in praise, borrowing the words of the Psalmist, "taste and see that the Lord is good" (Ps 34:8); for the Eucharist is the singular expression of God's self-giving love.

Understand, O faithful one, why He spoke of food and drink. Without doubt, just as He speaks of Himself as in prison, even so does He in us eat and drink [see Matt 25:36]. Wherefore, the Church, seeing such great grace, exhorts her sons and neighbors to run to the sacraments with these words: "Eat my friends, drink, and be inebriated, my brothers" [Song 5:1]. What we eat and drink, the Spirit expresses elsewhere through the prophet, "Taste and see that the Lord is good; blessed the man who hopes in him" [Ps 33:9]. Christ is in that sacrament, because it is the body of Christ. So, it is not food for the body, but spiritual food. The Apostle says about the type, "Our fathers ate spiritual food and drank spiritual drink" [1 Cor 10:3]. For the body of God is a spiritual body; Christ's body is the body of the Divine Spirit.

St. Ambrose of Milan, Bishop and Doctor (c. 340–397)

OCTOBER 21

Bl. Thomas Bullaker (1604–1642) was a Franciscan priest and martyr who suffered at the hands of his own government. Arrested by English authorities while saying the Mass, he was thus charged for treason and hanged. In the passage below, Bl. Thomas relates the events of his own trial, which debate his use of sacred vessels in the liturgy. Thomas argues his innocence by highlighting a fundamental moral principle: unjust laws do not bind as they fail to be true law. The Holy Mass was instituted by God and is required by Him (Matt 26:26). Consequently, no human law can abrogate its demand.

The chairman gravely said, as fine as [these vessels] are, they can serve for an idolatrous worship. I asked, what idolatrous worship, sir? Why, said he, is it not idolatry to worship bread for God? I replied, we worship not bread and wine for God in the tremendous Mysteries, but we worship Jesus Christ under the species of bread and wine as the Church of God has always done from the days of the Apostles. While this controversy was in agitation, one of the company looking me over and examining the vestments, uncovered the altar-stone, and seeing the crosses upon it, cried out that he had discovered the Number of the Beast: I could scarce keep from laughing at his ignorance. . . .

The clerk ordered me to hold up my hand, and after my indictment was read, asked if I was *guilty* or *not guilty*. I answered, if by *guilty* you mean a *criminal*, as if by taking Holy Orders I was guilty of any crime or fault, I am *not guilty*. But a priest I am, and that I will never deny. . . . They asked again if I were *guilty* or *not guilty* of any treason, or any other capital crime. I said, I confess I am a priest and that I was taken at Mass; nor will I ever deny my priesthood ever if I were to die a thousand deaths for it; but to say that I am *guilty* in being a priest, as if there were any *guilt* in the matter, whereas nothing can be more honorable, that I will never do. . . . Then the recorder said, *Mr. Bullaker*, you have here confessed over and over again that you are a priest; plead therefore to your indictment directly, *guilty* or *not guilty*. I answered as before, I am not guilty of any treason, but a priest I am. He said, your being a priest makes you guilty of treason by transgressing the laws of the land. I answered, laws were not to be observed which are repugnant to the Law of God.

Bl. *Thomas Bullaker (1604–1642)*
[Memorial, October 23]

OCTOBER 22

Memorial of Pope St. John Paul II

Pope St. John Paul II (1920–2005) reigned as supreme head of the Church from 1978 to 2005, the third-longest pontificate in history. His intellectual and artistic strengths were complemented by a heart of contemplation and adoration. In his great encyclical, *Ecclesia de Eucharistia*, St. John Paul II highlights the intrinsic connection between the Holy Sacrifice of the Mass and the cross of Calvary. In this way, he reiterates the sacrificial nature of the Mass against those who would reduce it to only a meal.

> The Mass makes present the sacrifice of the Cross; it does not add to that sacrifice nor does it multiply it. What is repeated is its *memorial* celebration, its "commemorative representation" which makes Christ's one, definitive redemptive sacrifice always present in time. The sacrificial nature of the Eucharistic mystery cannot therefore be understood as something separate, independent of the Cross or only indirectly referring to the sacrifice of Calvary.
>
> By virtue of its close relationship to the sacrifice of Golgotha, the Eucharist is a sacrifice in the strict sense, and not only in a general way, as if it were simply a matter of Christ's offering himself to the faithful as their spiritual food. The gift of his love and obedience to the point of giving his life (*cf.* Jn 10:17–18) is in the first place a gift to his Father. Certainly it is a gift given for our sake, and indeed that of all humanity yet it is first and foremost a gift to the Father: "a sacrifice that the Father accepted, giving, in return for this total self-giving by his Son, who 'became obedient unto death' (Phil 2:8), his own paternal gift, that is to say the grant of new immortal life in the resurrection."

> *Pope St. John Paul II (1920–2005)*

OCTOBER 23

In his classic defense of the Trinitarian dogma, *On the Trinity*, St. Hilary of Poitiers (c. 310–367) discusses the consubstantial union of divine persons as it relates to the union between God and man. In this way, he touches upon the essence of salvation: man is not saved through a mere union of wills; rather, he becomes a participator in the divine nature by grace. This union, forged in the waters of Baptism, is perfected by the reception of Holy Communion.

Christ Himself testifies how it is possible for us to be in Him through the sacrament in which His flesh and blood are communicated: "This world will not see me now but you will see me. Because I live, you too will live. For I am in my Father and you are in me and I in you" [John 14:20]. If He only wanted a unity of will understood, why did He reveal a kind of gradation and perfect order of a unity, unless it were that, since He was in the Father through the nature of divinity, and we, on the one hand, are in Him through His physical birth, He would have us believe that He is in us through the mystery of the sacraments? And thus a perfect unity through the mediator is taught, because He Himself would remain in the Father while we remain in Him. He would remain in us while remaining in the Father, and so we progress toward the unity of the Father, since in Him who dwells naturally in the Father by birth, we also dwell naturally, while He Himself abides naturally in us also.

St. Hilary of Poitiers, Bishop and Doctor (c. 310–367)

OCTOBER 24

As Bishop of Santiago, Cuba, St. Anthony Mary Claret (1807–1870) enacted widespread reforms, helping spark a renewal of faith. His prolific writings reveal the intimate life of prayer that inspired his zeal for the gospel. In the following sermon, St. Anthony speaks of God's gratuitous love for man, expressed in the sending forth of His only-begotten Son. St. Anthony's arresting words urge thanksgiving for the many proofs of God's love, particularly the gift of Himself in the Blessed Sacrament.

What more can be given us Christians? [The Father] gives us His Son, who is of His own substance; His Son who is begotten from all eternity in the splendor of His glory; His Son who is the sole object of His most tender joy. He allows this most adorable Son to be sacrificed and to die upon a cross for us. Yes, my God, with this extreme love, with this incomprehensible fire, you have loved men unto tearing from your heart, so to speak, the Consubstantial Word in order to give Him to ungrateful, perfidious, and sinful men, making Him a victim of them. O extreme charity of our God! What heart is so obstinate and unfeeling as to not be penetrated and burned by these flames? But divine love goes further. It is not enough to have given Him in the adorable mystery of the Incarnation by becoming man and dying for us upon a cross. This same God comes to us every day under the appearance of bread and wine in the august Sacrament of the Eucharist in order to unite Himself most intimately to our hearts: to attend to us, to sustain us, and to share His most tender delights.

St. Anthony Mary Claret (1807–1870)

OCTOBER 25

In his Tract on the Exodus, St. Gaudentius of Brescia (d. 410) describes the completion of the Old Covenant and its typological signs in the New. Inasmuch as the Passover lamb found its fulfillment in Christ, Gaudentius warns Christians against looking back to the shadow of the Mystery now fully present. Consequently, St. Gaudentius speaks of the Eucharist as the source of life, refreshment, and sanctification for all who worthily receive.

Let us learn to eat the Passover; not as the Jews who, after the advent of the Truth, unwisely still follow a shadow. Each of them continues to slaughter and eat a sheep in his own house on the fourteenth day of the first month; whereas, this sheep was a shadow, standing in the place of Christ who came. The true Lamb of God is the Lord Jesus who takes away the sin of the world, and He said, "unless you eat my flesh and drink my blood, you will not have life within you" [John 6:53]. The Jews do this in vain in a bodily sense, but unless they do this with us in a spiritual sense, they have no life in them. "For the law is spiritual" [Rom 7:14], as the apostle says, "and Christ our Passover is sacrificed" [1 Cor 5:7].

Not one, but many lambs, were slaughtered in the shadow of that Passover of the law. Each was slaughtered at home, for one lamb could not be sufficient for all as it was a figure, not the reality of the Lord's Passion. For a figure is not the truth, but an imitation of the truth: man was made in the image of God, and yet he is not God, even if he is called a god by reason of being in God's image.

Then, in this reality that we are in, one died for all, and this same one is sacrificed in the mystery of bread and wine in each house of the Church, which refreshes, is believed in, imparts life, is consecrated, and sanctifies the consecrators. This is the flesh of the Lamb, and this is his blood. The Bread that descended from heaven said: "The Bread that I will give is my flesh for the life of the world" [John 6:51].

St. Gaudentius of Brescia (d. 410)

OCTOBER 26

In the final book of *The Imitation of Christ*, Thomas á Kempis (1380–1471) observes the great asymmetry between God and man and expresses his astonishment that God should invite man to Holy Communion. Struggling to prepare himself for so great a gift, Thomas recalls the holy dwelling places of God in the Old Testament—the ark and the temple—and confesses his own unworthiness to approach so great a King. His words are a perennial reminder of the intimacy and wonder of the New Covenant.

"Come unto Me all you that labor and are heavy laden, and I will refresh you" [Matt 11:28]. O sweet and amiable words spoken in the ears of a sinner, that You my Lord God, should invite the poor and destitute to commune with Your most holy Body. But who am I Lord, to presume to come unto You? Behold: the very heaven of heavens cannot contain You, and yet You say, "come unto me, all of you?" What is the meaning of so reverend an honor and so gracious an invitation? How do I dare to come, who are conscious of nothing good on which to rely? How can I welcome You into my house, when I have so often offended your kindly countenance? The angels and archangels stand in awe of You, the saints and the just fear you, and yet you say "come unto me, all of you?" Unless You Yourself had not said it, who could have believed it to be true? And unless You Yourself had not commanded it, who would dare draw near?

Behold, the just man Noah labored for a hundred years in building the Ark: how can I prepare myself in one hour to fittingly receive the Creator of the world? Moses, your great servant and friend, made an ark of incorruptible wood and covered it with the purest gold in order to place the tablets of the law therein. And should I, a corrupt creature, lightly receive You, the Maker of the law, and the Giver of life? Solomon, the wisest king of Israel, spent seven years building a magnificent temple to the praise of Your name, celebrating an eight-day feast of its dedication with a thousand peace-offerings and solemnly set the ark of the covenant within it to the sound of trumpets and shouting. And I, unhappy and poorest of men, how shall I bring You into my house?

Thomas á Kempis (1380–1471)

OCTOBER 27

Nicholas of Cusa (1401–1464) was a fifteenth-century bishop and scholar who composed works on astronomy, mathematics, and the vision of God, demonstrating the Church's holistic view of knowledge. In the following excerpt from *On the Peace of Faith*, he answers the Hussite objection that transubstantiation is too difficult to understand. Borrowing the voice of St. Paul, Nicholas emphasizes that transubstantiation is not something the senses may perceive, but something the intellect itself grasps by faith. Because transubstantiation deals with substance, which has no extension in space, this in turns explains how many hosts may be transformed into the one Body of Christ.

> Paul: [It can] very easily [be grasped] by faith. For this [truth] is attainable by the mind alone, which alone views a substance with respect to *the fact that it is*, though not with respect to *what it is*; for substance precedes every accident. And so, since substance is neither a quality nor a quantity and since [in the Eucharist] only the substance is transformed, so that there is no longer the substance of the bread but rather there is the substance of flesh, this transformation is only immaterial, because it is very far removed from whatever is attainable by the senses. Therefore, as a result of this transformation, the quantity of flesh is not increased, nor is [the flesh] multiplied in number. For this reason there is only one substance of flesh into which the substance of the bread is transformed, even though bread is offered up on different places and even though there is more than one piece of bread that is used in the sacrifice.

Nicholas of Cusa (1401–1464)

OCTOBER 28

Guitmund of Aversa (d. 1090) was a French Benedictine whose treatise, *The Truth of the Body and Blood of Christ in the Eucharist*, refuted the false teachings of Berengarius of Tours, who believed the Eucharist to be a mere symbol. Guitmund laid the philosophical groundwork for the doctrine of transubstantiation, which distinguished the essence of the Eucharist—the Body of Christ—from its accidents, or its appearance, as bread. Here, Guitmund searches for this distinction in his account of the Mystery of Faith. Adding a spiritual note, he observes how man is redeemed by the same mode in which he first sinned—through eating.

> He did not spurn to be beaten with rods by unbelievers, wear a crown of thorns, suffer death on the cross with nails and a lance—in short, suffer all these irreligious indignities. It was written of Him: "He was crushed for our crimes" (Isa 53:5). Is it, then, unworthy of Him, for the salvation of believers, to be eaten with religious devotion? If He endured what was so unworthy for us, how could what is less undignified be wrong?

> It was necessary that the Lord Jesus Christ, suspended on a tree, did conquer by that tree of the cross the death that had come by a tree. So too, it is necessary that Christ be eaten. This is because the old man did not eat merely a shadow of the fruit, but experienced death by truly eating the fruit of the ancient tree; so the new man truly avoids death and receives life by eating not a shadow, but Him who hung on the tree of obedience, the cross itself.

> The bread and wine of the Lord's table, not sensibly but intellectually, not by destruction but by assumption, not through the door of the flesh contrary to the Scriptures, but according to the Scriptures, are changed into the whole body and blood of Christ ... We believe that nothing is contained in the whole which is not in each separate part.

> *Guitmund of Aversa (d. 1090)*

OCTOBER 29

Bl. Jacobus da Varagine (1230–1298) was a Dominican priest and bishop who compiled *The Golden Legend*, a monumental collection of the lives of saints. In this excerpt, Bl. Jacobus recounts a story from Peter the Venerable concerning votive Masses for the dead. This brief narrative highlights the power and necessity of offering the Holy Sacrifice of the Mass for the faithfully departed.

> And Peter, the abbot of Cluny, said that there was a priest who said the Mass of requiem for all Christian souls every day. For this, he was accused before the bishop and suspended from his office. And on a day of great solemnity, as the bishop went through the cemetery, all the dead arose against him, saying: "This bishop gives us no Mass, and yet takes away our priest. Now, he shall certainly die if he does not amend." And the bishop then approached the priest and gladly sang the Mass himself for the faithfully departed. So it is evident that the prayers of the living are profitable to those that have departed.
>
> *Bl. Jacobus da Varagine (1230–1298)*

OCTOBER 30

Ven. Mary of Ágreda (1602–1665) was a Spanish mystic whose visions of the Blessed Virgin Mary were transcribed in her extensive work, *The Mystical City of God*. Her book was censured before it gained approval and has since gained great popularity as a devotional work. In the following excerpt, the Blessed Virgin Mary speaks of the power of the Eucharist to overcome evil and warns against lukewarm reception. Christ's operations in the soul require a docile and loving spirit, open to His transformative actions. In this way, Mary was unparalleled in her receptivity to grace.

> For the overthrow of hell, and the terror of demons, all the holy Sacraments of the Church are most powerful means, but

above all, the Holy Sacrament of the Eucharist. This was one of the hidden purposes of the Lord, my Son, in the institution of the sovereign Mystery and of the other Sacraments. If, in present times, men do not feel these powerful effects, it is because much of the veneration and estimation in receiving them has been lost through the frequency of reception. But do not doubt that souls who frequent them with devotion and piety are formidable to the demons, and that they exercise great power and dominion over them in the same way as you have seen and described it of me. The explanation is this: in pure souls, this divine fire finds itself, as it were, in its own element. In me, it was active to the limit of possibility in a mere creature, and therefore, I inspired such terror in the demons.

Ven. Mary of Ágreda (1602–1665)

OCTOBER 31

Memorial of St. Alphonsus Rodriguez

Widowed at the age of thirty-one, St. Alphonsus Rodriguez (1532–1617) entered the Jesuit order and became known for his extraordinary spirit of devotion. Writing for the feast day of St. Ignatius of Loyola, St. Alphonsus here compares the work God accomplished through Moses with the wonders He worked through St. Ignatius. The juxtaposition of these figures highlights the exalted status of the Eucharist as God among us. As God was present to the Israelites in the desert, He remains substantially among us in the Blessed Sacrament.

Again did Moses speak with God, whereupon Our Master sent him as captain of His people against Pharaoh. With the help of God, Moses worked wonders, overcoming Pharaoh and releasing his own people from captivity. He outwitted Pharaoh and all his people, and they were lost in the Red Sea. Freedom was thus restored to the people of God so that they rejoiced in festivity, giving thanks and praise to God for having delivered them from their enemies. The same, in his own way, did God accomplish with our Father Ignatius. For, God took him out of the world to make him the captain and defender of His own people, so great a number of whom were in slavery that Ignatius might free them from the bondage of the heretics and Satan, who held many prisoners in his power. And Ignatius, through the favor of God, by his teaching and holy life, delivered them from this bondage. And when they were free, they sang the praises of God who had delivered them from the captivity of Satan.

And just as God gave to His people who had been freed the manna from heaven, and sustained them by it, so too God divinely refreshed those with manna from Heaven who had been freed by our Father from the power of the heretics. And this manna is God Himself. This manna is that most exalted kind of food, the Blessed Sacrament of the altar, with which He will feed us till He leads us to the land of promise, which is Eternal Glory.

St. Alphonsus Rodriguez (1532–1617)

NOVEMBER

NOVEMBER I

Solemnity of All Saints

On the Solemnity of All Saints, the Church celebrates all those saints in heaven who, by the grace and mercy of God, share in the fulfillment of their faith and hope. In the passage below, St. John Chrysostom (349–407) explains how the Divine Liturgy unites men on earth to the unending worship in heaven. Marveling that the hymn of the angels was given to men in the Sanctus, St. John describes the universal worship of all creation, human and angelic, gathered around the heavenly throne.

> Do you recognize the sound? Is it ours or that of the Seraphim? It is in fact ours *and* the Seraphim's sound. This is because Christ destroyed the dividing wall of partition when he made peace between the things in heaven and on earth, making them both one. At first, this hymn was known only in heaven, but the Master deemed it right to descend to the earth and bring this melody down to us. Therefore, when this great high priest stands at the holy table, offering rational worship [see Rom 12:1], and lifting up the bloodless sacrifice, he is not simply calling on us for this praise: when he spoke to the Cherubim, and reminded the Seraphim, he commanded everyone to send up this most awesome sound. And thereby, our understanding is drawn away from earth and into heaven

by the memory of this united chorus, each crying out. You sing with the Seraphim. You stand with the Seraphim. Stretch your wings and fly with them around the royal throne.

St. John Chrysostom, Bishop and Doctor (349–407)

NOVEMBER 2

Commemoration of All the Faithful Departed

On the Commemoration of All the Faithfully Departed, commonly known as All Souls Day, the Church prays for the repose of those who have died in grace. Because souls in Purgatory can no longer merit, they depend on the prayers of the Church on earth to speed their purification. Bl. John of La Verna (1259–1322) here speaks of the inestimable value of the Holy Sacrifice of the Mass for those souls of the Church Suffering. This story, recorded in the *Fioretti*, is a powerful corrective to the modern forgetfulness of the faithful departed.

Brother John was once saying Mass for the souls of the deceased, the day after All Saints Day as the Church has ordained. He offered the most High Sacrament (which the souls of the departed desire above all other blessings for its saving power) with such effectual charity and merciful compassion that he seemed as though melted with the sweetness of pity and brotherly love. Thus, he devoutly elevated the Body of Christ in that Mass and offered it to God the Father, praying that for the love of His beloved Son, Jesus Christ who hung upon the cross for the redemption of souls, He would be pleased to set free from Purgatory the souls of the dead He had created and redeemed. Immediately, he saw a multitude of souls coming forth from Purgatory, like countless sparks of fire from a blazing furnace. And he beheld them rising into heaven through the merits of the Passion of Christ, who is offered every day for the living and dead in that most sacred Host, which is worthy to be adored in *saecula saeculorum*.

Bl. John of La Verna (1259–1322)

NOVEMBER 3

In the Divine Liturgy of St. James, the most ancient Eastern liturgy still in use, the priest intones the following prayer between the words of institution ("this is my body") and the epiclesis. The epiclesis is the invocation of the Holy Spirit, which the Church in the East views as the central act of consecration. Here, the texts begins with "remember," corresponding with the "anamnesis" of the Latin rite. The priest thus recalls the saving work of Christ and pleads for mercy in view of the Holy Sacrifice at hand.

The priest: We sinners remember His life-giving Passion, His saving cross, His death, and Resurrection on the third day from the dead, His ascent into heaven and His sitting at the right hand of his God and Father, and His glorious and fearful second coming, when He will render to each one his due in accord with his works. Master, we offer You this awesome and unbloody sacrifice that You may deal with us not according to our sins, nor reward us according to our iniquities. Please deal with us according to Your gentle and ineffable love for mankind, because by overcoming and wiping away the written ordinance against us by Your mercies, You graciously granted us your heavenly and eternal gifts which eye has not seen, nor ear heard. The things You have prepared for those who love You have not even entered into the human heart. Do not reject Your people on my account, nor on account of my sins, O Lord, Lover of Mankind.

Divine Liturgy of St. James

NOVEMBER 4

Memorial of St. Charles Borromeo

St. Charles Borromeo (1538–1584) was an Italian cardinal who organized the final session of the Council of Trent, assisted in the publication of the Catechism of Trent, established seminaries, and rebuilt the collapsing Diocese of Milan. His lofty achievements flowed from his zeal for the gospel and his determination to follow the will of God. In this passage, St. Charles recalls the heart of the Christian message: God so loved man that He gave His only-begotten Son who was handed over for the salvation of man. This extravagant proof of His love is not sealed in the past, but ever remains present in the Sacrament of the Altar.

O what ingratitude! What more can the Lord God do for us? For my own part, I cannot say. His great Majesty descends from heaven to earth for us poor sinners, and for many years bestows the divine presence upon this valley of tears, covering His most splendid and illustrious light with the darkness of our mortal vestment. He innocently and righteously suffers injury upon injury, torments, afflictions, and even death. He, the Son of God made man, dies upon the wood of the cross. Yet, He does not remain satisfied and content with all this; rather, burning ever more with love, He leaves us His Spirit, His Soul, and His Body for our food, and for our nourishment, to sustain us, to invigorate us, to console us, and to give us joy. And He does this not only for a time, but for the whole of our lives, because this great benefit will remain until the end of the world: *"Behold, I am with you always, even to the consummation of the world"* [Matt 28:20].

St. Charles Borromeo (1538–1584)

NOVEMBER 5

After years of defending the faith, Tertullian (c. 160–220) fell into the Montanist sect, succumbing to his tendency toward extremes. Though not a saint, Tertullian is a voice of great historical importance as he helped develop Western theology. In his tract against heretics, Tertullian lists the central tenets of Christian faith, stressing that all must adhere to them. In this way, it is clear that the dogmas of the Church are not a matter of personal opinion, but God's revelation to man. By Tertullian's own reckoning, the Eucharist is an essential matter of the faith, which binds the conscience of all Christians.

> [The Church of Rome] recognizes only one God, the Lord, who is Creator of all, and Christ Jesus, the Son of God the Creator, born of the Virgin Mary, and the resurrection of the flesh. It mingles the law and the prophets with the gospels and the letters of the apostles. From this it drinks the faith, signs with water, clothes with the Holy Spirit, feeds with the Eucharist, encourages martyrdom, and thus receives no one against these principles.
>
> *Tertullian of Carthage (c. 160–220)*

NOVEMBER 6

St. Athanasius of Alexandria (c. 296–373), the famed defender of Christ's divinity, here reflects on the typological mysteries of the Old Covenant and their completion in the New Covenant. Athanasius masterfully describes the Passover meal and Jesus' transcendent fulfillment of it. What the Hebrews commemorated with symbols and figures, Christ now celebrates in truth.

> [The Word of God] said to His disciples, "With desire I have desired to eat this Passover with you" [Luke 22:15]. Now this is a wonderful account, for a man might have seen them at that time girded as for a procession or a dance; going out with staffs, sandals, and unleavened bread. These things, which had previously taken place, were typological. But now the Truth has drawn near to us, "the image of the invisible God" (Col 1:15), our Lord Je-

sus Christ, the true Light, who instead of a staff, is our scepter; instead of unleavened bread, is the bread that came down from heaven; and who, instead of sandals, has furnished us with the preparation of the Gospel. In brief, by all these has guided us to His Father. And if enemies afflict us and persecute us, He again, instead of Moses, will encourage us with better words, saying, 'Be of good cheer; I have overcome the evil one' (cf. Jn 16:33). And if after we have passed over the Red Sea, heat should again oppress us, or bitterness of the waters befall us, even then the Lord will appear to us, imparting to us of His sweetness, and His life-giving fountain, saying, "If any man thirst, let him come to me, and drink" [John 7:37]. Why then do we wander about, and why do we delay, and not come with all eagerness and diligence to the feast, trusting that it is Jesus who calls us? Who is all things for us, and was laden in ten thousand ways for our salvation; who hungered and thirsted for us, though He gives us food and drink in His saving gifts.

St. Athanasius of Alexandria, Bishop and Doctor
(c. 296–373)

NOVEMBER 7

Though often misattributed to St. Ignatius of Loyola, the *Anima Christi* first appeared during the pontificate of Pope John XXII (1249–1334), to whom it is traditionally attributed. The stanzas of this medieval prayer appear almost unchanged from its earliest days; however, minor variations do appear. Some additions are purely ornamental, so that "Soul of Christ" became "O Most Holy Soul," and "Body of Christ" became "O Most Sacred Body," and so forth. Other variations offer entirely new invocations: "Sweat of Christ's Wonder-Working Face, heal me," "Death of Christ, give me life," "Love of Christ, purify me." This profoundly Eucharistic text may well have been promulgated during Holy Week, namely, for Holy Thursday devotions. Its traditional form is here presented in both Latin and English.

Anima Christi, sanctifica me.	Soul of Christ, sanctify me.
Corpus Christi, salva me.	Body of Christ, save me.
Sanguis Christi, inebria me.	Blood of Christ, inebriate me.
Aqua lateris Christi, lava me.	Water from the side of Christ, wash me.
Passio Christi, conforta me.	Passion of Christ, strengthen me.
O bone Jesu, exaudi me.	O good Jesus, hear me.
Intra tua vulnera absconde me.	Within Thy wounds, hide me.
Ne permittas me separari a Te.	Permit me not to be separated from Thee.
Ab hoste maligno defende me.	From the malignant enemy, defend
In hora mortis mea voca me;	me.
Et iube me venire ad Te.	At the hour of my death, call me;
Ut cum sanctis tuis laudem Te	And bid me come to Thee,
In saecula saeculorum. Amen.	That with Thy saints I may praise Thee.
	Forever and ever. Amen.

Pope John XXII (1249–1334)

NOVEMBER 8

Memorial of St. Elizabeth of the Trinity

St. Elizabeth of the Trinity (1880–1906) was a French Carmelite whose spirituality of surrender echoes that of St. Thérèse of Lisieux. Her writings overflow with mystical insights born of contemplative prayer, frequently highlighting the indwelling of the Trinity. Here, St. Elizabeth meditates on the nature of love and its tendency toward union. Because love is directed toward union, St. Elizabeth observes that Holy Communion is the consummate expression of God's nature as love.

It seems to me that nothing better expresses the love in God's Heart than the Eucharist: it is union, consummation, He in us, we in Him, and isn't that Heaven on earth? Heaven in faith while awaiting the face-to-face vision we so desire. Then "we will be satisfied when His glory appears" [Ps 16:15], when we see Him in His light. Don't you find that the thought of this meeting refreshes the soul, this talk with Him whom it loves solely? Then everything disappears and it seems that one is already entering into the mystery of God! . . .

This whole mystery is so much "ours," as you said to me in your letter. Oh! pray, won't you, that I may live fully my bridal dowry. That I may be wholly available, wholly vigilant in faith, so that Master can bear me wherever He wishes.

St. Elizabeth of the Trinity (1880–1906)

NOVEMBER 9

In his landmark treatise, *On the Trinity*, St. Augustine (354–430) identifies Christ as the High Priest who offers Himself as a sacrifice for men. Exploring the Trinitarian dimensions of this offering, Augustine explains how all might be united to Christ's self-gift in the Eucharist and thus be drawn into the Trinitarian exchange of love. In this way, man has communion with God the Father through his union with God the Son in the Eucharist.

Who is so just and holy a priest as the only Son of God who had no need to offer a sacrifice to purge sins; neither original sin nor those added by life? And what could so fittingly be taken by men to be offered for them as human flesh? And what is so pure for the worldly vice of mortals as flesh born in and from the virgin womb without any contagion of fleshly concupiscence? And what can be so gratefully offered and received as the flesh of our sacrifice, made the body of our priest? There are four things to be considered in every sacrifice: to whom it is offered, by whom it is offered, what is offered, and for whom it is offered. It is the same for the one true Mediator who reconciles us to God by the sacrifice of peace. He remains one with Him to whom it is offered, making one in Himself those for whom it is offered. He is one and same who offered it and was what was offered.

St. Augustine of Hippo, Bishop and Doctor (354–430)

NOVEMBER 10

Memorial of Pope St. Leo the Great, Doctor of the Church

Pope St. Leo the Great (c. 400–461) was a judicious leader who helped settle the fifth-century Christological debates at the Council of Chalcedon. In his famous *Tome*, he synthesized the traditional teachings on Christ's two natures, affirming their hypostatic union. Here, St. Leo movingly writes on the Passion of Christ and its intrinsic relationship to the Mass. For at each celebration of the Eucharist, the same Victim is made present upon the altar as was on Calvary. Holy Mass is, therefore, a true manifestation of that one sacrifice upon the cross.

How marvelous the power of the cross; how great beyond all telling the glory of the passion: here is the judgment-seat of the Lord, the condemnation of the world, the supremacy of Christ crucified . . . The different sacrifices of animals are no more: the one offering of your body and blood is the fulfillment of all the different sacrificial offerings, for you are the true Lamb of God: you take away the sins of the world. In yourself you bring to perfection all mysteries, so that, as there is one sacrifice in place of all other sacrificial offerings, there is also one kingdom gathered from all peoples.

Pope St. Leo the Great, Doctor of the Church (c. 400–461)

NOVEMBER II

In the following sermon on St. Matthew's Gospel, St. Peter Chrysologus (c. 380–450) speaks on the woman with the flow of blood, healed by the touch of Christ's garment. St. Peter relates this story to contemporary Christians who reach out to Christ at Holy Communion. Affirming that the Lord's healing ministry continues today, St. Peter counsels communicants to benefit from their encounter with the Christ, approaching Him with the same living faith.

Scripture says that the woman suffering from a hemorrhage "approached from behind" [Matt 9:20]. But from where? "She touched the edge of His clothes" [Matt 9:20]. She approached from behind, but where? There was nothing behind Him. There, He found her face turned away. In Christ, there was a body with many parts, but simple deity. There was a whole eye that saw her begging behind Him. "She approached from behind and touched the edge of his clothes" [Matt 9:20]. O what did that woman see dwelling in the inner heart of Christ? She saw total power dwelling on the edges of Christ's divinity. O how that woman taught the greatness of Christ's body which dwells even in the edges of Christ Himself! Let Christians who touch the body of Christ today hear what medicine they can take from His own body when that woman grasped complete health from only the edges of Christ. We should weep that this woman obtained medicine for her wound, while in our case, the medicine itself turns back into a wound. So it is that the Apostle admonishes and deplores those who touch the body of Christ in an unworthy manner. For whoever touches the body of Christ unworthily receives judgment for himself [see 1 Cor 11:27]. In her case, boldness overtakes sickness; in our case faith should receive wholeness.

St. Peter Chrysologus, Bishop and Doctor (c. 380–450)

NOVEMBER 12

St. Thomas Aquinas (1225–1274) composed the Eucharistic hymn *Adoro te devote* for his own private use; however, it has become one of the most well-known verses of the Church. Thomas' words offer a rich meditation on faith, contrasting the bodily senses with the surpassing light of faith. Lacking the natural power to glimpse the essence of God, Thomas emphasizes the need for supernatural faith.

Devoutly I adore You, hidden Deity,
truly veiled beneath these signs.
Wholly do I submit my heart to You
as You surpass my understanding.

Sight, touch, and taste are deceived;
yet, upon hearing Your Word, I believe,
and hold to all that the Son of God has revealed.
For nothing is surer than this word of truth.

On the cross, Your Divinity alone was concealed:
Here, Your Humanity likewise lies hidden.
But believing and confessing both,
I beg for what the penitent thief sought.

Your wounds, I do not see, as St. Thomas;
yet, still do I confess You as my God.
Make me to believe ever more in You,
to hope in You, and to love You.

O Memorial of the death of the Lord!
Living bread, which gives life to man!
Grant that my mind may on Your life live,
and that I may ever taste Your sweetness.

Faithful Pelican, Lord Jesus,
Cleanse my impurities with Your Blood,

of which one drop can save and restore
the entire world from its offenses.

Jesus, upon whom I gaze, now veiled,
grant unto me what I desire:
reveal to me the sight of Your face,
that I might be blessed to behold Your glory.

St. Thomas Aquinas, Doctor of the Church (1225–1274)

NOVEMBER 13

Memorial of Pope St. Nicholas I

Pope St. Nicholas I (c. 800–867) was named pontiff during a period of cultural instability, moral decline, and collapsing government.
Exercising strong papal supremacy, St. Nicholas fought to renovate
Christendom and to renew its moral frame. In the following letter to
the emperor, Nicholas explains how ordinary objects are consecrated
to God's purpose, making them holy. Applying this truth to the bread
and wine at Mass, he professes the unchanging faith of the Church:
in the Eucharistic liturgy, ordinary bread and wine are consecrated to
God such that they become the body and blood of Christ.

The holy altar on which we perform votive sacrifices to Almighty God is a natural and common stone, differing in no
way from other tablets adorning our pavements and walls.
But, God having cooperated at its consecration on receiving
the benediction, it became the holy table that it is. Similarly,
the bread which is offered on it is common bread, but when it
has been sacramentally consecrated, it becomes and is called
in truth the Body of Christ. So the wine before benediction
is a small thing too, but after sanctification of the Spirit, it is
made the Blood of Christ.

Pope St. Nicholas I (c. 800–867)

NOVEMBER 14

Hincmar (806–882), the ninth-century archbishop of Rheims, was at the center of the major theological debates of the day; namely, on the question of predestination and free will. In his letter on the clergy, Hincmar laments reports of immorality and warns against unworthy reception of the Eucharist. Comparing sacrilegious communions to Judas' betrayal, Hincmar emphasizes the need for purity of heart when receiving the Eucharist.

As for this man, you have the example of Judas in the Scriptures themselves. For this man hands the Son of Man over— not indeed to the Jewish leaders—but to sinners who are their very members who presume to profane the inestimable Body of the Lord. Woe to him who unworthily approaches the table of the Lord and does not fear to participate in the Mysteries of Christ with a duplicitous mind, a covetous heart, or some other stain of sin. Woe, I say, to that priest, woe to that deacon, woe to that subdeacon, woe to that cleric!

Woe to that man of whom Jesus spoke when He was about to consecrate the gifts of sacrifice upon the holy altar. For He did not hesitate to lament of Judas to those disciples gathered at supper, saying: *Behold, the hand of him who betrays me is with me on the table* [Luke 22:22]. And woe to that person of whom St. Paul said, *Whoever eats and drinks the cup of the Lord without discerning the body eats and drinks judgment upon himself* [1 Cor 11:29]. For, to approach the table of the Lord in this thoughtless manner, without reverence or fear for one's sins, one feasts rather upon his own trespass when partaking at that plenteous table.

Hincmar (806–882)

NOVEMBER 15

Memorial of St. Albert the Great, Bishop and Doctor

In his Commentary on the Gospel of Luke, St. Albert the Great (c. 1200–1280) meditates on the multiplication of loaves, offering a symbolic interpretation for each of the fives loaves given to the crowds (Luke 9:13). Demonstrating his vast knowledge of the Scriptures, St. Albert grounds each of his symbolic interpretations on scriptural references to bread. Among these five, St. Albert identifies the "daily bread" of the Lord's Prayer as the Eucharist (Matt 6:11).

> [Next is] the moral interpretation of this passage. One may so discover the bread of compunction and tears, the spare bread, the daily bread, the bread of life, and the bread of fattening. The bread of compunction and tears is the bread of penitence: "*You have fed them with the bread of tears*" [Ps 80:5]. The spare bread is the bread of satisfaction and justice: "*The Lord will give you spare bread and short water*" [Isa 30:20]. The daily bread is the Eucharist Bread of the traveler: "*Give us this day our daily bread*" [Matt 6:11]. The bread of life is the bread of grace: "*She [Wisdom] shall feed him with the bread of life*" etc. [Sir 15:3], and "*We will eat our own bread, and wear our own clothes*" [Isa 4:1]. The bread of fattening is the bread of devotion and spiritual consolation: "*Asher's bread shall be fat, and shall yield dainties to kings*" [Gen 49:20]. All these five loaves are commended to the Apostolic men to give to the crowds.
>
> St. Albert the Great, Bishop and Doctor (c. 1200–1280)

NOVEMBER 16

Memorial of St. Gertrude the Great

St. Gertrude the Great (1256–1302) was a Benedictine mystic who helped spread devotion to the Sacred Heart of Jesus centuries before the visions of St. Margaret Mary Alacoque. St. Gertrude's writings reveal an extraordinary life of grace, reminiscent of the greatest mystics. In the following passage, St. Gertrude describes her reception of the Eucharist, which occasions the gift of transverberation. Her narrative highlights the profound intimacy and union found in Holy Communion.

[At Sunday Mass,] when in your infinite mercy and liberality you permitted me to approach the Communion of Your adorable Body and Blood, You infused a desire within me that broke forth in these words: "Lord, I am not worthy to receive the least of Your gifts; but I beg You, by the merits and prayers of all here present, to pierce my heart with the arrow of Your love." I soon perceived that my words had reached Your Divine Heart—both because of an interior outpouring of grace and because of a miraculous vision upon the crucifix. After I had received the Sacrament of Life and returned to pray, I seemed to see a ray of light, like an arrow, coming forth from the wound of the right side of the crucifix, which waxed and waned, kindling my cold affections. . . . [The following Wednesday, after the Mass of the Annunciation] You suddenly came before me, and imprinted a wound upon my heart, saying: "May the full tide of your affections flow from this wound, so that all your pleasure, your hope, your joy, your grief, your fear, and every passion be sustained by My love!"

St. Gertrude the Great (1256–1302)

NOVEMBER 17

In his book on the sacraments, *On the Mysteries*, St. Cyril of Jerusalem (c. 313–386) offers a detailed portrait of the liturgy, noting its essential features. Naming the "kiss of peace," the "sursum corda," and the "Sanctus," St. Cyril's description bespeaks the unchanged nature of the Eucharistic Liturgy. While ornamental features of the Mass may change over time, its essential constitution remains inalterable. When

treating the miracle of transubstantiation, he reverently urges communicants to discern the presence of Christ's body, hidden to the senses.

> Then the deacon cries aloud, "Receive one another, and let us
> kiss one another." . . . After this the priest cries aloud, "Lift
> up your hearts." . . . Then you answer, "We lift them up to
> the Lord." . . . Then the priest says, "Let us give thanks to the
> Lord." . . . Then you say, "It is right and just." . . . We mention
> also the Seraphim who Isaiah saw by the Holy Spirit encir-
> cling the throne of God . . . who cried *Holy, Holy, Holy, Lord
> God of Sabaoth* (Isa 6:3). For this reason, we recite this confes-
> sion of God, delivered down to us from the Seraphim, that we
> may join the hymns with the hosts of the world above.

> Then, having sanctified ourselves by these spiritual hymns,
> we call upon the merciful God to send forth His Holy Spir-
> it upon the gifts lying before Him; that He may make the
> bread the body of Christ, and the wine the blood of Christ;
> for whatsoever the Holy Spirit has touched is sanctified and
> changed. Then, after the spiritual sacrifice is perfected, the
> unbloody service upon that Sacrifice of Propitiation, we en-
> treat God for the common peace of the Church, for the tran-
> quility of the world; for kings, soldiers, and allies; for the sick,
> the afflicted, and in a word, all those who stand in need of
> succor, we supplicate and offer this Sacrifice. . . .

> After this, you hear the sacred melody of a chanter inviting
> you to the communion of the Holy Mysteries, saying, "*O taste
> and see that the Lord is good*" (Ps 34:8). Trust not the discern-
> ment to your bodily taste; no, but to unwavering faith. For
> when we taste, we are bidden to taste not bread and wine, but
> the Sign of the body and blood of Christ.

> *St. Cyril of Jerusalem, Bishop and Doctor (c. 313–386)*

NOVEMBER 18

Memorial of St. Rose Philippine Duchesne

Twelve years before St. Rose Philippine Duchesne (1769–1852) journeyed to the New World, she wrote to St. Madeleine Sophie Barat of her travels there in spirit. In the following letter, she describes her all-night vigil before the Eucharist in which she prayerfully applied the merits of Christ to the Americas. St. Rose would later found the first convent of the Society of the Sacred Heart in the New World, a work built upon her years of prayer and sacrifice. In this way, she witnesses to the primacy of God's action in prayer for missionaries and evangelists.

> All night I was in the New World, but I travelled in good company. First, I reverently gathered up all the Precious Blood from Gethsemane, the Praetorium, and Calvary. I then took possession of our Lord in the Blessed Eucharist, and bearing my treasure, I went forth to scatter it abroad, but without any fear that it would be exhausted. St. Francis Xavier helped me to make this priceless seed bear fruit and prayed before God's throne that new lands might be opened to the light of truth. St. Francis Regis steered our course, with other saints jealous for God's glory. All went well, and no sorrow, not even holy sorrow, could find a corner in my heart, because it seemed to me that a new application was about to be made of the merits of Jesus Christ. The twelve hours of the night passed rapidly and without weariness, though on my knees. And yet, the previous evening I could not hold out for one hour.
>
> *St. Rose Philippine Duchesne (1769–1852)*

NOVEMBER 19

Memorial of St. Mechtilde of Hackeborn

St. Mechtilde of Hackeborn (1240–1298) was the younger sister, and religious daughter, of St. Gertrude the Great. Her life and extraordinary revelations were recorded by the nuns of the Helfta abbey, an early center of devotion to the Sacred Heart of Jesus. In the following excerpt from her revelations, Jesus speaks to St. Mechtilde on the proper disposition for Holy Communion and the transformative effects of its reception.

Offer your heart to God at the Mass, and before beginning your prayer, purify and detach it from all earthly thoughts, preparing it to receive the inflow of divine love that inundates and fills the hearts of those who assist. I, too, deliver Myself entirely into the power of your soul, bringing all that I possess. In this way, you can dispose of Me as you will.

. . . The more often a soul communicates, the purer it becomes; just as we become cleaner by washing often. The more often a soul communicates, the more I operate in it; and the more it works with Me, its actions become more holy. The more often a soul communicates, the more profoundly does it dwell in Me. And the more it penetrates into the abyss of My divinity, the more the soul is dilated and capable of containing the divinity, even as water wears a cavity to fill by falling on a certain spot of stone at length.

. . . When you are preparing for Holy Communion and feel only dryness of heart, without desire or love for prayer, nor any of the love you ought to have, cry out with all your strength to the Lord: "Draw us, and we will run after You to the odor of Your ointments" (Song 1:4). And in saying this word, "Draw us," think how strong and powerful was the love which drew the almighty and eternal God down to the ignominious death of the cross. Filled with an ardent desire for Him who said, "When I shall be lifted up from the earth I will draw all things unto Myself" (John 12:32), beg of Him that He would draw your heart and all the powers of your soul so strongly to Himself that He will cause you to run with love and desire.

St. Mechtilde of Hackeborn (1240–1298)

NOVEMBER 20

St. Gregory of Nyssa (c. 335–395) here observes how perfumes tend to diffuse themselves, imparting their sweet scents to others. Applying this idea to the Eucharist, St. Gregory explains how Christ desires to communicate Himself to man in the Blessed Sacrament. Having contracted the foulness of sin, man may cleanse and perfume himself with the odor of sanctity found in this sacrament. Rightly then do Christians relish the sweetness of grace found therein.

> Whatever is received in nature goes on to transform the receiver. For example, the mouth of one who receives some sweet smelling aroma becomes fragrant. And again, for the one who consumes garlic, or something more pungent, his mouth becomes foul smelling. So, all filth of sin is foul smelling, and the opposite is true of Christ's virtue; it is sweet smelling. And a loving union naturally effects a mingling with the beloved. Whatever we proclaim through love is the very thing we become, either the fragrance of Christ or a foul smell. For, the one who loves goodness is himself good—as the goodness of it transforms the receiver into itself. For this reason, He who lives forever places Himself before us as food so that once we receive Him in them, we may become precisely what He is. For He says, "my flesh is truly food, and my blood truly drink" [John 6:55]. So, the one who loves this flesh is not a friend of his own flesh. And the one who arranged His blood for this purpose will cleanse our bodily blood. The flesh of the Word, and the blood in that flesh, does not have one kind of grace only. Rather, He becomes sweet to those who taste, and desirable to those who desire, and beloved to those who love.

St. Gregory of Nyssa (c. 335–395)

NOVEMBER 21

At the end of the liturgical year, the Church celebrates the Feast of Christ the King, honoring Christ's everlasting reign over all creation. As the Blessed in heaven everlastingly share in the hidden manna (Rev 2:17), those on earth may participate in this feast at Mass. Here, St. Caesarius of Arles (c. 468–542) awakens his listeners to this profound reality, exhorting them to prepare for the wedding feast of the Lamb. Notably, the wedding garment Christ requires of man is not one of luxurious cloth, but one of purity and virtue.

> We are invited to the wedding where, if we act well, we will be a spouse. Let us think on what kind of wedding this is, and what kind of spouse, or what kind of banquet, we are invited to. We are invited to the table where human food is not found, but the bread of angels is placed. And so let us carefully observe, lest inwardly in the soul we are found to be wrapped in the old rags of vices, when we ought to be adorned with the pearls of good works. And when purity renders those who are good in the eyes of God radiant, the opposite renders those who are evil in luxurious dress shabby.
>
> *St. Caesarius of Arles (c. 468–542)*

NOVEMBER 22

Memorial of the Martyrs of England, Scotland, and Wales

Bl. John Thulis (1568–1616) was an English priest, martyred for the Catholic faith under King James I. The following poem, written during his imprisonment, expresses the unusual mixture of suffering and joy that belongs to a martyr. These words reveal Bl. John's foretaste and participation in the resurrected life of Christ, even in the midst of grave persecution. Though keenly aware of his peril, Bl. John expresses his satisfaction at having celebrated the sacraments and looks forward to their fulfillment in the life to come.

As for myself, I am not afraid
To suffer constantly,
For why due debt must needs be paid
Unto sweet God on high.
Saint Paul, he being firm of faith,
Hoping with saints to sing,
Most patiently did suffer death.
Lord send us happy rising!

I have said Mass and Matins both,
And true instructions taught,
Confirmed by the Holy Ghost,
And mighty power wrought:
The Holy Communion also
With manna ever living;
The Holy Sacraments I taught:
Lord send us happy rising!

And then why should I be afraid
To suffer constantly,
Since in this cause so many saints
Did suffer patiently,
And left examples for us all,
That we with them may sing.
God grant we may for mercy call,
And have a happy rising.

Bl. John Thulis, Martyr (1568–1616)

NOVEMBER 23

Memorial of St. Gregory of Agrigentum

In his commentary on Ecclesiastes, St. Gregory of Agrigentum (c. 559–638) contemplates the voice of Wisdom who exclaims, "Come, eat my bread and drink my wine which I have mixed" (Prov 9:5).

Rightly, Gregory perceives that no ordinary table is indicated for this promised feast, but the holy altar of the Lord. For the fruit of Wisdom is not merely the bread and wine that sates, but the body and blood of Christ that satisfies with divine grace.

> If anyone wishes to interpret "eating" and "drinking" in a more mystical sense so as to express the loftiest meaning intended by the Teacher, he could not unreasonably say that the mystical table is indicated, which manifests "the one who came down from heaven and gives life to the world" [John 6:33]. The Lord Himself spoke about this when He said, "Take, eat, this is my body" [Matt 26:26]. And He spoke of the mystical cup by saying, "Drink from it, all of you. This is my blood which is poured out for you for the forgiveness of sins" [Matt 26:27–28]. Surely then, in discussing physical and corporeal substances and other things, the wise Teacher, inspired by the grace breathed down from above, understands it to mean the spiritual and supernatural enjoyment we know to come about specially and preeminently by the hand of God. Is this not what was said in the book of Proverbs by that Wisdom, which is substantial and divinely ruling: "Come, eat my bread and drink my wine which I have mixed" [Prov 9:5].

> *St. Gregory of Agrigentum (c. 559–638)*

NOVEMBER 24

Memorial of St. Théophane Vénard, Martyr

St. Théophane Vénard (1829–1861) was a French missionary to Vietnam, sentenced to death for his witness to the faith. His spirit of self-surrender inspired St. Thérèse of Lisieux, who believed him an exemplar of the "little way." The following letter was written during St. Théophane's missionary travels at sea and expresses his sincere hunger for the Bread of Life.

The sea, I confess, wearies me to death. It is certainly fine to see great waves rolling one over another, but I should prefer seeing it from *terra firma*. We had the unspeakable consolation of daily Mass for the first month and a half; but afterwards our altar-breads became spoiled. How I have longed for the possibility of paying a visit to the Blessed Sacrament, or of assisting once more at some Catholic ceremony! When the body is deprived of food, it languished and dies; and it is the same with the soul, without the Bread which sustains its life.

In the final letter addressed to his father, St. Théophane writes of the extraordinary grace of receiving Holy Communion in prison. Echoing the words of St. Thomas the Apostle, St. Théophane wonders at the Eucharistic Lord before him.

Father Tinh will tell you of his visit, when I gave him some tea in the midst of all the crowd. He brought me, on the other hand, the Bread of the traveler—"*Mi Jesus, Deus meus*," in my cage! Think of that!

St. Théophane Vénard, Martyr (1829–1861)

NOVEMBER 25

Pope St. Clement (d. 99) reigned as the fourth pope of the Church (AD 88–99), following upon Ss. Peter, Linus, and Anacletus. In the following passages from his *Letter to the Corinthians*, Clement speaks of the Eucharistic sacrifice celebrated among Christians. This first passage contains the unusual expression, "let us fix our gaze upon the blood of Christ," making possible reference to the elevation of the chalice. For this atoning Blood is referenced in connection with the Father, to Whom the chalice is raised at mass.

Beloved, we are not only commanding you with an admonition, but also reminding ourselves. We are in the same arena, and the same contest is set for us. So, let us leave the empty and futile ways of thought, and come to the renowned and pious rule of our tradition. Let us observe what is beautiful, pleasing, and acceptable in the sight of Him who made us. Let us fix our gaze on the blood of Christ, and know how precious it is to his Father. Because, having shed it for our salvation, He brought the grace of repentance to the whole world.

This second passage speaks of the hierarchical structure of the Church and the roles dedicated to each. Together, these ancient words offer insight into the office of the priest and his distinct ministry in the early Church.

We ought to do in an orderly fashion everything the Master commanded us to fulfill in the properly established times. He commanded that the offerings and liturgical services be fulfilled, not in empty or disorderly ways, but at predetermined seasons and hours. But where and by whom he wants it to be fulfilled he himself determined by his sovereign will . . . To the high priest belong particular liturgical services; the priests have their own place, and Levites have their own ministries too. The layman is given orders appropriate for the laity. Let each of you, brothers, please God in his own proper place with a good conscience by not transgressing the determined rule of ministry in dignity.

Pope St. Clement of Rome (d. 99)
[Memorial, November 23]

NOVEMBER 26

St. Sechnall (c. 372–457) was appointed the first Bishop of Dun-shaughlin by his uncle, St. Patrick, who laid the foundations of the Church in Ireland. He is credited with the earliest known Eucharistic hymn, "*Sancti venite*," which praises Christ for His redeeming sacrifice. In this hymn, St. Sechnall summons all souls to the sacred banquet, drawing upon a variety of scriptural images.

Come, You Holy Ones! Receive the Body of Christ,
and the Holy Drink, the Blood of Redemption.

Saved by the Body and Blood of Christ,
refreshed, we sing praises to God.

By this Sacrament of His Body and Blood,
all are drawn back from Hell's chasm.

Giver of Salvation, Christ the Son of God,
saved the world by His cross and Precious Blood.

The Lord was immolated for all mankind:
He, Himself, both Priest and Victim.

These Divine Mysteries were foreshadowed
by the precepts of the sacrificial law.

Giver of light and Savior of all:
Christ bestows grace on His holy saints.

Go forth, all you with pure hearts of faith:
seize the safeguard of salvation.

Protector of the saints, and Master of all:
Lord, we have faith in your gift of eternal life

Celestial bread for the hungry,
and living water for the thirsty.

Christ the Lord, the Alpha and Omega,
soon comes to judge all men.

St. Sechnall (c. 372–457)
[Memorial, November 27]

NOVEMBER 27

Memorial of St. Leonard of Port Maurice

St. Leonard of Port Maurice (1676–1751) was a Franciscan priest who helped spread devotion to the Stations of the Cross, constructing hundreds of stations throughout Italy. In his lengthy treatise on the Eucharist, St. Leonard proposes various prayers to be said during Mass. Here, St. Leonard recalls the intimacy of Christ's presence in the Eucharist and asks Christ to capture his senses, transforming them in His service.

Prayer Before Holy Communion: Awake, slumbering soul, to bless your God for all His mercies! Remember that He became incarnate for you. Remember that Jesus who was born in the manger of Bethlehem, who conquered death, and who is enthroned at the right hand of His Father, is now really and truly present in the Most Holy Sacrament of the Eucharist. O thrice holy belief! O greatest of all consolations! Here, God is really present under the appearances of bread and wine! He, the Almighty One, is ready to take up His abode in my heart and to become entirely mine!

Act of Oblation: Jesus, my loving God, You have given Yourself entirely to me, and gratitude requires that I should give myself wholly to You. You have sanctified me by coming to dwell in my heart, and henceforward I will, with Your divine assistance, be entirely consecrated to You. My eyes, which You have opened to the true light, shall be Yours. My ears, which have heard Your gentle invitation, shall be Yours; and this tongue, which has been sanctified by Your adorable Body and Blood, shall be Yours for evermore. Oh, may all my senses be devoted to Your greater honor and glory; may they never rebel against Your holy law; may my memory teem with grateful recollections of Your goodness; may this will, which You have sanctified, postpone everything to the love of You. To You I offer my body and my soul—all my senses, and all my faculties—my entire being. O celestial fire! Consume in me all that is base and impure. O Omnipotent love! Teach me to love You with fidelity, now and for evermore. Amen.

St. Leonard of Port Maurice (1676–1751)

NOVEMBER 28

Memorial of St. Catherine Labouré

St. Catherine Labouré (1806–1876) belonged to the Daughters of Charity of St. Vincent de Paul and was witness to the apparitions of the Blessed Virgin Mary at Rue de Bac, Paris. There, the Miraculous Medal was revealed to her, which she anonymously propagated through her spiritual director. In the following excerpts from her writings, St. Catherine recounts her visions of Christ in the Eucharist, offering a personal witness to the truth of the Real Presence. The latter vision is wed to a prophecy of the overthrow of the French monarchy, headed by King Charles X.

I was also favored with another grace, which was to see our Lord in the Blessed Sacrament during all my time in the seminary, except when I doubted or feared I might be the victim of self-deception.

. . . During Mass on the feast of the Most Holy Trinity, Our Lord appeared to me in the Blessed Sacrament in the form of a king with a cross on His Breast. At the Gospel it seemed to me that the cross slipped under the feet of our Lord, and that all His kingly jewels fell to the ground. Then I was filled with the gloomiest thoughts about our earthly king being dethroned and despoiled of his royal garments, and from that came thoughts that I cannot explain about the ruin that would result. Nevertheless, I could not resist speaking of it to my confessor who calmed me as much as possible by turning me from these thoughts.

St. Catherine Labouré (1806–1876)

NOVEMBER 29

St. Chromatius (d. 406), bishop of Aquileia, was an early theologian who encouraged the scholastic pursuits of his fellow bishops. In his treatise on the Gospel of St. Matthew, St. Chromatius offers a Eucharistic vision of the Lord's Prayer and its petition, "give us this day our daily bread." Referencing the Bread of Life discourse and St. Paul's admonitions concerning Holy Communion, St. Chromatius emphasizes that this petition is directed toward reception of the Eucharist. He thus teaches that Christians must remain within the Mystical Body by fitting conduct and worthy reception of the Eucharist.

> "Give us today our daily bread" [Matt 6:11] . . . We are commanded in a spiritual sense to seek daily bread, that is, that heavenly and spiritual bread we daily receive to heal the soul, and as hope of eternal salvation. The Lord says in the Gospel, "The bread from heaven is my flesh, which I will give for the life of the world" [John 6:50, 52]. And we are urged to ask for this bread daily, that is, that we may be worthy to receive the bread of the body of the Lord while His mercy is present. For the Apostle says: "Let a man test himself and thus let him eat from the bread of the Lord and drink the cup" [1 Cor 11:28], and again, "whoever eats the bread of the Lord unworthily and drinks the cup will be guilty of the body and blood of the Lord" [1 Cor 11:29]. For this reason, we ought always to strive to pray worthily that we may be counted fit to receive this heavenly bread and not be separated from the body of the Lord by some lurking sin.
>
> St. Chromatius of Aquileia (d. 406)
> [Memorial, December 2]

NOVEMBER 30

St. Edmund Campion (1540–1581) is among the most venerated English Martyrs. In his youth, he took the Anglican Oath of Supremacy and was well positioned to marry into the royal family. Moved by grace to reconcile with the Catholic Church, St. Edmund was eventually ordained a Jesuit priest in Prague. When he returned to England to administer the sacraments, he was imprisoned in the Tower of London, racked, hanged, and beheaded. In this excerpt from *Ten Reasons*, Campion lays out a scriptural argument for Christ's Real Presence in the Eucharist.

Suppose, for example, we ask our adversaries why they have devised that novel and sectarian opinion that banishes Christ from the Mystic Supper. If they name the Gospel, we meet them promptly. On our side are the words: *This is my body, this is my blood (Mt 26:26)*. This language seemed so forcible to Luther himself that for all his strong desire to turn Zwinglian, thinking it would make things most awkward for the Pope, he was nevertheless caught and fast-bound by this most open context and consented to it (*Luther, epistol. ad Argent*). Luther thus confessed Christ truly present in the Most Holy Sacrament no less unwillingly than the demons of old who cried aloud at the sight of Jesus' miracles that He was the Christ, the Son of God.

Well then, the written text gives us the advantage: the dispute now turns on the sense of what is written. Let us examine the words in context, *my body which is given for you, my blood which shall be shed for many (Mt 26:28)*. Still the explanation on Calvin's side is most hard, on ours easy and quite plain.

What further? Compare the Scriptures [our adversaries] say, one with the other. By all means. The Gospels agree, Paul concurs. The words, the clauses, the whole sentence reverently repeat living bread, signal miracle, heavenly food, flesh, body, blood. There is nothing enigmatic, nothing shrouded in a mist of words.

St. Edmund Campion (1540–1581)
[Memorial, December 1]

DECEMBER

DECEMBER I

Memorial of Bl. Charles de Foucauld

Bl. Charles de Foucauld (1858–1916) was a French solider whose early life was marked by agnosticism and dissipation. A profound conversion experience in the sacrament of Reconciliation led him back to the Church and eventually to the eremitic life. In time, he was ordained to the priesthood and founded a religious institute dedicated to adoration of the Blessed Sacrament. Despite local threats of violence, Bl. Charles faithfully remained in his hermitage, and on December 1st 1916, he was martyred by a man associated with the Senussi. In the following letter, Bl. Charles reveals his Eucharistic faith and expresses profound thanksgiving for so great a gift.

May 1903.

Today is thirty years since I made my first communion; that I received the good God for the first time. . . . This is now the first time that I celebrate the Holy Mass on this date. . . . What graces I have received for thirty years! How good God has been! How many times since have I received Jesus on these unworthy lips! And see! Now I hold Him with my miserable hands! Him. He places Himself into my hands! And I serve in a chapel where, day and night, I delight in the holy tabernacle that I have, so to speak, all to myself. Look! Each morning I consecrate the Holy Eucharist so that I may offer benediction with It each evening. Here at last, and above all, I have finally received permission to found! What graces!

Bl. *Charles de Foucauld (1858–1916)*

DECEMBER 2

Memorial of Bl. Jan van Ruysbroeck

Bl. Jan van Ruysbroeck (1293–1381) was a Flemish mystic whose spiritual works freely treat the contemplative life, emphasizing union with God. His writings are not without controversy as they variously blur the line between the Creator and created; nevertheless, they represent the mature fruit of the Medieval Flemish school. In the following passage, Ruysbroeck speaks of the divinizing effects of the Eucharist and man's participation in the sonship of Christ.

Now, Christ desires that we remember Him so often as we consecrate, offer, and receive His Body. Consider now how we remember Him. We shall acknowledge and behold how Christ inclines Himself towards us with loving affection, with great desire, with yearning delight, and with a warm and tender outpouring of Himself into our bodily nature. For He gives us what He has in common with our manhood; that is, His Flesh, His Blood, and His bodily nature. We shall also acknowledge and behold that precious body, martyred, pierced, and wounded for our sake, out of His love and His faithfulness towards us. Herewith we are adorned and nourished in the lower part of our manhood. In this most high gift of the Sacrament, He also gives us His spirit, full of glory, rich gifts of virtue, and unspeakable marvels of charity and nobleness. And we are thereby nourished, adorned, and enlightened in the unity of our spirit, and in the higher powers, through the indwelling of Christ with all His riches. Moreover, in the Sacrament of the Altar, He gives us His most high personality in incomprehensible splendor. And through this, we are lifted up to, and united with, the Father. And the Father receives His adopted sons together with His natural Son, and we thus enter into our inheritance of the Godhead in eternal blessedness.

Bl. Jan van Ruysbroeck (1293–1381)

DECEMBER 3

Memorial of St. Francis Xavier

St. Francis Xavier (1506–1552) was one of the seven founding members of the Society of Jesus whose extensive travels merited him the title, Patron of Missionaries. He journeyed to India and Japan in service of the Gospel, but died within sight of his desired destination, the Chinese mainland. St. Francis here offers brief prayers to be said during the elevation of the Eucharist, recalling the expiatory value of this sublime sacrifice. By offering such prayers, one may more fully participate in the liturgy as the soul is stirred to devotion.

Every morning when he leaves his home, the Christians's first steps should be to the church, and there let him be present at the Holy Sacrifice of the Mass. While Mass is being said, he may say within himself, or with his lips if he prefers, these prayers, or others like them . . .

When the most holy Body of the Lord is elevated and shown to the people, let him say: *I adore Thee, O Lord Jesus Christ, and I bless Thee for having ransomed the world and me by the holy Cross. Amen.*

When the sacred chalice of the precious Blood of our Lord is elevated, let him say: *I adore Thee, O most sacred Blood of Jesus my Lord, shed upon the Cross to save sinners and me. Amen.*

St. Francis Xavier (1506–1552)

DECEMBER 4

Memorial of St. John Damascene,
Doctor of the Church

In his catechetical work, *On the Orthodox Faith*, St. John Damascene (c. 675–749) contemplates the Real Presence of Jesus in the Eucharist, linking the prophecies of Isaiah with the Bread of Life Discourse in John's Gospel. Damascene stirs the faith of his hearers that they might approach the Eucharist with all due reverence, free from any stain of unbelief. Rising still higher, he connects the vision of Isaiah—"one of the seraphim flew to me, and in his hand was a burning coal" (Isa 6:6)—to the Eucharist, emphasizing its purifying effects. These celestial images express the heavenly character of this sacrament, inspiring love in those with the light of faith.

> He had said to the Jews: "Unless you eat the flesh of the Son of Man and drink His blood, you have no life in you. For my flesh is food indeed, and my blood is drink indeed" [John 6:53], and again, "he that eats me, shall live forever" [John 6:51]. Therefore, let us approach with all reverence, a pure conscience, and a strong faith, and it will be so to us as we believe, doubting nothing. Let us honor that body with all purity, both in soul and body: for it is twofold. Let us come to Him with burning desire, and with hands in the form of a cross, let us receive the body of the Crucified. Let us apply our eyes, lips, and foreheads, and receive the divine coal so that the fire of longing in us, with the added heat of the coal, may utterly burn away our sins, and enlighten our hearts, and that we may be inflamed and deified by sharing in the divine fire. Isaiah saw the coal. A piece of coal is not a plain piece of wood, but is joined to fire. So too, the bread of communion is not plain bread but is united to divinity.
>
> *St. John Damascene, Doctor of the Church (c. 675–749)*

DECEMBER 5

St. Eligius (588–650) served on the French court before his appointment to the episcopal see of Noyon-Tournai. He utilized his political power to help establish monasteries, evangelize pagan territories, and secure financial help for the poor. In the following homily, St. Eligius addresses the impassibility of Christ's glorified body as it is present in the Holy Eucharist. Underscoring fundamental truths of sacramental theology, he explains that the Eucharistic species is truly the glorified Body of Christ and is thus immune to corruption. Although the Mass constitutes a true sacrifice, the risen body of Christ remains ever impassible.

Beloved brothers, you must know and firmly believe in truth that as Christ assumed flesh in the womb of the Virgin, and His true body was slain for our salvation, even so is the bread that He gave to His disciples, and that which is daily consecrated by priests in the Church, the true Body of Christ. There are not two bodies that are assumed—one of flesh and one of bread—but one body only. So that while He is broken and consumed, Christ is sacrificed and eaten; yet, ever remains one and entirely intact.

Certainly our Redeemer gave us this Sacrament, being mindful of our frailty. And since He no longer dies—yet we sin daily—we have a true sacrifice for the expiation of our sins. Therefore, with holy fear, compunction of heart, and all reverence, we ought to approach the altar and table of the Body and Blood of the Lord in humility, professing with the Centurion, *"Lord, I am not worthy that you should enter under my roof"* [Matt 8:8].

St. Eligius (588–660)
[Memorial, December 1]

DECEMBER 6

In the following passage from *On the Trinity*, St. Hilary of Poitiers
(c. 310–367) teaches that the Father, Son, and Holy Spirit are one in
essence and likens this unity to the communion between God and man
in the Eucharist. Affirming that the Eucharist is the substantial presence of Christ's body and blood, Hilary explains that this sacrament
effects true communion with Christ vis-a-vis grace. While man is never conjoined to God in such a way as to blur the essential distinction
between the two, he nevertheless becomes a "partaker in the divine
nature" (2 Pet 1:4).

> But the Lord, because He did not want to leave anything un-
> certain for the conscience of the faithful, explained the man-
> ner in which His nature operates, saying: "that they may be
> one, as we are one. I in them and you in me that they may be
> perfected into one" [John 17:23]. I would like to ask those
> who insist on a unity of will between the Father and the Son
> whether Christ is in us today through the truth of nature (*per
> naturae veritatem*) or through an agreement of will (*per con-
> cordiam voluntatis*)? For if the Word was truly made flesh, and
> truly we take the Word made flesh in the Lord's food, how can
> He be judged not to dwell in us in a natural manner? He who
> assumed the nature of our flesh is now born a man with our
> nature inseparable from Himself. He also joined the nature
> of His flesh to the nature of eternity under the sacrament of
> His flesh communicated to us. Thus, we are all one because
> the Father is in Christ and Christ is in us. Whoever denies
> that the Father is in Christ by nature denies that he himself is
> in Christ by nature, or that Christ is in him. Because the Fa-
> ther is in Christ, and Christ in us, they make us one in them.
> Therefore, if Christ truly assumed the flesh of our body, and
> He who was born of Mary was truly a man, Christ, then we
> truly receive the flesh of Christ's body under the Mystery. By
> this, we will be one, because the Father is in Him, and He in

us. How can a unity of will be asserted when the natural property effected by the sacrament is a sacrament of perfect unity?

St. Hilary of Poitiers, Bishop and Doctor (c. 310–367)

DECEMBER 7

Memorial of St. Ambrose of Milan, Bishop and Doctor

St. Ambrose of Milan (c. 340–397) was a respected civil lawyer before his appointment to the episcopal see of Milan. His intellectual and moral integrity well equipped him to form St. Augustine, who in turn gave his life in service to the Church. The following selection compares the miraculous works of the Old Testament prophets with those of Jesus Himself. Though many readily accept miracles wrought by prophets, they object to the doctrine of transubstantiation. St. Ambrose explains that a greater power acts in the conversion of the Eucharistic species, for it is Christ Himself who acts in the sacraments, consecrating the bread and wine.

We observe that grace is of greater power than nature, yet we have only thus far considered the grace of a prophet's blessing. But if a human blessing was powerful enough to change nature, what do we say of the divine consecration itself, where the very words of the Lord and Savior act? For, the Sacrament that you receive, is consecrated by the word of Christ. But if the word of Elijah was powerful enough to bring down fire from heaven, will not the word of Christ be powerful enough to change the substance of the elements? You have read of the work of creation that "he spoke, and they were made; he commanded and they were created" (Ps 33:9). If the word of Christ could make out of nothing that which was not; can it not then change the things which are into that which they were not? For to give new natures to things is quite as wonderful as to change their natures.

St. Ambrose of Milan, Bishop and Doctor (c. 340–397)

DECEMBER 8

The Solemnity of the Immaculate Conception of the Blessed Virgin Mary

On the Solemnity of the Immaculate Conception of the Blessed Virgin Mary, the Church celebrates that singular woman, Mary, conceived without sin in view of the merits of her Son. Her conception fulfilled the prophetic types of the faithful Daughter of Zion, the untouchable Ark of the Covenant, and the victorious New Eve. Here, St. John Damascene (c. 675–749) reflects upon Christ's own miraculous conception, likening it to His appearance on the altar at Mass. As the Holy Spirit brought about the coming of Christ through Mary, so too does the Spirit work His coming under the appearances of bread and wine.

> The body born of the Holy Virgin is truly united to divinity. Not that the body descends from heaven, but that the bread and wine are transformed into the body and blood of God. You seek to know how this comes about: let it be enough to hear that it happens through the Holy Spirit, just as the Lord took on flesh that subsisted in Him, taking it from the Holy Mother of God through the Holy Spirit. We know nothing further, except that the word of God is true and that it is effective and all-powerful [see Heb 4:12]; yet the manner itself is inscrutable.

> It may be well said that just as bread and wine through eating and drinking are naturally changed into the body and blood of the one who eats and drinks—and do not become a different body than the former—so also the bread presented and the wine with the water are supernaturally transformed into the body and blood of Christ through the descent [*epiclesis*] and visitation of the Holy Spirit; and these are not two, but one and the same.

> *St. John Damascene, Doctor of the Church (c. 675–749)*

DECEMBER 9

St. Bonaventure (1221–1274) worked to reconcile opposing factions within the Franciscan Order, earning him the title of "the second founder" of the Franciscans. Here, he reflects on the veiled nature of the sacramental system and argues God's wisdom in its institution. For, if Christ were to visibly appear to man, Bonaventure explains that man could not merit by faith. Furthermore, he notes the natural barrier that would be posed if human flesh were to visibly appear in the Eucharist. In everything, St. Bonaventure emphasizes the virtue of faith, which rises above all human understanding.

> You should note that it was fitting for Christ to be given to us under a veil. For, what strength would your faith have if Christ were to visibly appear to you in His own proper form? You certainly would adore Him immediately. Or how would your physical eyes be able to bear such glory? Who would be so foolish to say that he could eat and drink the natural flesh and blood of a man in its own proper form? Let every doubt pass away, because as divinity once lay hidden in the Virgin's womb, and the Son of God appeared visibly in the world under the veil of human flesh, so His glorified humanity, united to divinity, lies hidden under the form of bread and wine so that He can communicate Himself to us mortals.

> *St. Bonaventure, Bishop and Doctor (1221–1274)*

DECEMBER 10

St. Peter Chrysologus (c. 380–450) here looks to the Second Coming of Christ, highlighting the Eucharist as the foretaste of that heavenly banquet to come. Inspiring the virtue of hope in those who hear, he notes that God, who so freely gives Himself in Holy Communion, will not fail to grant the reward of faith in heaven. Finally, St. Peter teaches that the kingdom of God is contained in the Eucharist itself, subsuming all earthly delights.

Did he not willingly promise to His disciples: "You are those who have persevered with me, and you will eat and drink at my table in my kingdom" [Luke 22:28–30]? O Christian, what will He be able to deny you in the future who gave Himself to you now to be eaten? And what has He not done to prepare a place for you in an eternal mansion who has prepared such a great food for the journey [*viaticum*] of life?

"You will eat at my table in my kingdom" [Luke 22:30]. You have heard of God's banquet—do not be anxious about the quality of the banquet. Whoever merits to come to the table of the King will eat of whatever the dominion and power of the kingdom possesses. Thus, whoever comes to the Creator's banquet will have in his delights whatever is contained in the creature.

St. Peter Chrysologus, Bishop and Doctor (c. 380–450)

DECEMBER 11

The Armenian Liturgy has its roots in the directives of St. Gregory the Illuminator (c. 257–331), the father of Armenian Christianity. The following prayer is taken from the "prothesis," which corresponds with the Western "offertory." This ecstatic hymn of praise speaks directly to Holy Mother Church, affirming the Real Presence of Christ within her sanctuaries. Recalling the propitiatory nature of the Eucharistic sacrifice, the prayer urges Christians to rejoice in their reconciliation with God.

Rejoice greatly, O Zion, Daughter of Light, Holy Mother Church with your children: adorn and embellish thyself, O fair spouse and heavenly sanctuary. For the anointed God, being of being, is ever sacrificed in you, unconsumed in reconciliation of the Father, and distributes His own body and blood in expiation for us, for the fulfillment of his dispensation.

May He grant forgiveness to the founder of this temple. The Holy Church confesses the pure Virgin Mary, Mother of God, from whom has been given us the bread of immortality and the cup of rejoicing. Give Him blessings in spiritual songs.

The Armenian Liturgy

DECEMBER 12

St. Gregory of Agrigentum (c. 559–638) was a Sicilian bishop whose only surviving work is his *Commentary on Ecclesiastes*. In the following passage, Gregory treats Wisdom's invitation to bread and wine, employing both a literal and allegorical interpretation. Relating the Old Testament to the New, Gregory explains that Wisdom's food and drink is the body and blood of Christ. Like so many Church Fathers, St. Gregory weaves a tapestry of Scripture in praise of the Holy Eucharist.

Then the wise Teacher says, *"Come, eat your bread in gladness and drink your wine with a good heart, because God is pleased with your works. At each moment, let your garments be white and oil for your head not be lacking"* [Eccl 9:7].

The message of ascents lifts us to a loftier and more mystical understanding, leading us to consider a heavenly and mystical bread, that is, "the One who came down from heaven and gives life to the world" [John 6:33]. In fact, it leads us to drink the supernatural wine with a good heart, which is to say, the wine that gushed forth from the side of the True Vine at the moment of his life-giving Passion. The Gospel of our salvation speaks about this as it says: "Taking bread, Jesus blessed it and said to his holy disciples and apostles, 'Take, eat. This is my body that is broken for you for the forgiveness of sins.' Similarly, he took the cup and said, 'Drink of it, all of you. This is my blood of the new covenant, which is poured out for you for the forgiveness of sins'" [Matt 26:26–28]. Those who eat such bread and drink the mystical wine are made good and cry out in joy, "You have put gladness in our heart" [Ps 4:7].

Now, I think that the substantial Wisdom of God foreshadowed such bread and wine in the Book of Proverbs, saying, "Come, eat my bread and drink my wine that I have mixed" [Prov 9:5]. The Word thus hints at a mystical participation. For those worthily partaking each time, clothed with the garments of the works of light, they will be found to be white as light, as the Lord says in the Gospels: "So let your light shine before men that they may see your good works and glorify your Father in heaven" [Matt 5:16].

St. Gregory of Agrigentum (c. 559–638)

DECEMBER 13

Memorial of St. Lucy, Virgin and Martyr

In the following excerpt from *Ecclesia de Eucharistia*, Pope St. John Paul II (1920–2005) treats the eschatological dimensions of the Eucharist. Gazing toward the life of the world to come, St. John Paul II explains that the Eucharist contains the fullness of eternal life within itself. In this way, each Holy Communion draws the soul closer to its goal, granting the communicant a foretaste of the resurrected life in Christ.

The acclamation of the assembly following the consecration appropriately ends by expressing the eschatological thrust which marks the celebration of the Eucharist (cf. 1 Cor 11:26): *"until you come in glory."* The Eucharist is a straining towards the goal, a foretaste of the fullness of joy promised by Christ (cf. Jn 15:11); it is in some way the anticipation of heaven, the "pledge of future glory." In the Eucharist, everything speaks of confident waiting "in joyful hope for the coming of our Savior,

Jesus Christ." Those who feed on Christ in the Eucharist need not wait until the hereafter to receive eternal life: *they already possess it on earth*, as the first-fruits of a future fullness which will embrace man in his totality. For in the Eucharist we also receive the pledge of our bodily resurrection at the end of the world: "He who eats my flesh and drinks my blood has eternal life, and I will raise him up at the last day" [John 6:54]. This pledge of the future resurrection comes from the fact that the flesh of the Son of Man, given as food, is his body in its glorious state after the resurrection. With the Eucharist we digest, as it were, the "secret" of the resurrection. For this reason Saint Ignatius of Antioch rightly defined the Eucharistic Bread as "a medicine of immortality, an antidote to death."

Pope St. John Paul II (1920–2005)

DECEMBER 14

Memorial of St. John of the Cross, Doctor of the Church

Inspired by St. Teresa of Ávila's reform of the Carmelite Order, St. John of the Cross (1542–1591) abandoned his plans to join the Carthusians and established the Order of Discalced Carmelites for men. His writings treat the soul's radical purification from all created goods in its ascent toward God in contemplation. In this excerpt from *Dark Night of the Soul*, St. John criticizes those who seek sensible consolation in the Eucharist, emphasizing instead the exercise of faith.

> When these persons communicate, they strive with all their might to find some sensible sweetness in the act, instead of worshipping in humility and praising God within themselves. So much are they inclined this way that when they derive no sensible sweetness from Communion, they think they have accomplished nothing; so meanly do they think of God. Nor do they understand that the least of the blessings of the Most

Holy Sacrament is that which touches the senses. Rather, the invisible grace it confers is far greater. For, God frequently withholds such sensible favors from men so that they may fix the eyes of faith upon Himself. But these persons will [seek to] feel and taste God, as if He were palpable and accessible to them, not only in Communion, but in all their other acts of devotion. All this is a great imperfection and directly at variance with the requirements of God, which demand the purest faith.

St. John of the Cross, Doctor of the Church (1542–1591)

DECEMBER 15

In his catechetical work, *On the Mysteries*, St. Ambrose (c. 340–397) instructs catechumens on the sacraments of the Church, here offering an argument for the doctrine of transubstantiation. Ambrose rhetorically asks: if Christ was born in a miraculous way, what objection can be made against His miraculous appearance upon the altar? The same body that was conceived in a supernatural way is similarly manifest in the Blessed Sacrament. Ambrose thus exhorts catechumens to contemplate these truths, allowing them to pass from the mind and to the heart.

But why do we use arguments? Let us seek the truth of this mystery through the example of the Incarnation. Was it purely according to nature that the Lord Jesus was born of Mary? In the normal order, a woman gives birth by union with a man, but in the Virgin's case, she gave birth in a manner beyond the course of nature. And the body that we bring about through consecration comes from the Virgin. Why, then, do you seek a natural explanation here in the case of Christ's body, when the Lord Jesus Himself was born of the Virgin in a manner beyond nature? In fact, the true flesh of Christ, which was crucified and buried, is the same flesh that is truly in the sacrament. The Lord Himself declares, "This is my body" [Matt 26:26]. Before the blessing of these heavenly words, one type of thing was named; after the consecration, a body is signified. He Himself says it is His blood. Before the consecration, it is called one thing; after the consecration, it is declared as blood. And you respond, "Amen," which is to say, "it is true."

St. Ambrose of Milan, Bishop and Doctor (c. 340–397)

DECEMBER 16

Fr. Augustine of the Blessed Sacrament (Hermann Cohen) (1821– 1871) was a Jewish pianist and a student of Franz Liszt. His miraculous conversion to Christianity was closely tied to the Eucharistic rites of the Church. While present at Benediction of the Blessed Sacrament and Holy Mass, the God of Israel was revealed to him. Resigning his musical career, Cohen was baptized, entered the Carmelite order, and was ordained a priest. His cause for canonization is currently open.

At the moment of Benediction, I sensed for the first time a most lively but indefinable emotion. The following Friday, I felt the same sensation more powerfully and felt a considerable weight, which having descended upon my entire body, forced me lean forward, and even bow towards the ground, in spite of myself. . . .

There, I attended the mass where the ceremonies captivated my attention as always. And, little by little, the prayers of the Holy Sacrifice, the chants, and the presence (invisible, though sensed by me) of a more-than-human power began to agitate and trouble me, making me tremble. In a word, *divine grace was pleased to pour upon me with all its force.* At the moment of elevation, I suddenly felt a flood of tears burst forth from my eyes without ceasing; flowing with exceeding abundance down my burning cheeks. O blessed moment! O most memorable moment for the salvation of my soul.

Augustine of the Blessed Sacrament (1821–1871)

DECEMBER 17

In his *Commentary on Matthew*, St. Jerome (c. 347–420) provides an allegorical reading of the multiplication of the loaves, highlighting its Eucharistic overtones. Linking the angel's admonition to Elijah, "Get up and eat, for you will be walking a great distance" (1 Kgs 19:7), to Jesus' own words, "I will not send them away hungry lest they expire on the way" (Matt 15:32), Jerome emphasizes man's need of sustenance to make life's journey. By invoking the term, "heavenly bread," St. Jerome intimates the need for spiritual food in order to reach a supernatural end.

When His disciples had gathered, Jesus said to them, "I have compassion on the crowds, because they have been with me now three days, and have nothing to eat; and I am unwilling to send them away hungry, lest they faint on the way" [Matt 15:32]. He wanted to feed those whom He had cared for. First, He healed them of their weakness, and then He offered them food for the strong. . . . He says, "I have compassion on the crowd, because they have been with me now three days" [Matt 15:32]. He had compassion because they believed in the number of three days: the Father, the Son, and the Holy Spirit. "They have nothing to eat" [Matt 15:32]. The crowds are ever hungry and lacking food, unless they are fed by the Lord. "I am unwilling to send them away hungry, lest they faint on the way" [Matt 15:32]. They were hungry after great weakness and patiently awaited the food to come. Jesus did not want to dismiss them in hunger, lest they expire on the way. So the crowd, which had hastened to their chosen destination without heavenly bread, was in danger. And this was just as before, when the angel said to Elijah, "Arise and eat, else the journey will be too great for you" [1 Kings 19:7].

St. Jerome, Doctor of the Church (c. 347–420)

DECEMBER 18

In his commentary on the Gospel of John, St. Gaudentius (d. 410) comments on Christ's words, "I am the true vine" (John 15:1). Noting the prophetic symbolism of wine in Genesis, ("He will wash his robe in wine and his garment in blood," Gen 49:11), St. Gaudentius here argues that this figure is fulfilled upon the cross of Calvary. In no uncertain terms, St. Gaudentius professes the ancient faith of the Church, affirming that the Eucharistic wine becomes the blood of Christ.

In this truth in which we live, one died for all and feeds all the individual churches by His immolation in the Mystery of the bread and wine. Having been believed, He gives life to them. Having been consecrated, He sanctifies those who are consecrating. This is the flesh of the lamb, and this, the blood. For the Bread who descends from heaven says, "the bread which I shall give for the life of the world is my flesh" [John 6:51].

He rightly expresses His blood under the form of wine when He says in the gospel, "I am the true vine" [John 15:1]. He declares that wine is His blood, since it is offered in the form of His Passion. The blessed patriarch Jacob prophesied concerning Christ: "He will wash his robe in wine and his garment in blood" [Gen 49:11]. Indeed, He was to cover the robe of our body, His garment, with His own blood. Thus, He is the Creator and Lord of nature who produced bread from the earth, and brought about His own body from bread, because He can and promises to do so. He who made wine from water also made His blood from wine.

St. Gaudentius of Brescia (d. 410)

DECEMBER 19

In the following homily, St. John Chrysostom (349–407) exhorts Christians to forgive one another so as to fittingly honor the Eucharistic Lord. Drawing upon Jesus' command, "first be reconciled to your brother, and the come and offer your gift" (Matt 5:24), St. John proposes a holistic view of the gospel, challenging men to integrated lives of faith. To those who honor Christ in the Eucharist while on earth, St. John promises the reward of faith in heaven.

Have you been greatly wronged and cannot bear to let go of your anger? What greater and more severe wrong will you do unto yourself? The things that your enemy has done, however great they may be, are not as bad as what you do to yourself, if you are not reconciled, but rather, trample the law of God. Has he insulted you? So, will you then insult God? Tell me. Not being reconciled to the one who has caused your pain is not so much a matter of the one who defends himself as it is of the one who insults God who established these laws. So, do not look to your fellow servant, nor at the greatness of his offenses; rather, as you are mindful of God, and your respect for him, think on this: the greater the violence of soul you suffer in being reconciled to the one who offended you, after being troubled by a thousand evils, that much more will you enjoy a reward from God who commanded these things. And as you receive Him here [in the Eucharist] with great honor, so He will also receive you there [in heaven] with much glory, rewarding your obedience infinitely greater. May it be that we all attain to the grace of our Lord Jesus Christ and His love for mankind. Along with Him, glory, honor, power, and adoration belong to the Father together with the Holy Spirit forever and ever. Amen.

St. John Chrysostom, Bishop and Doctor (349–407)

DECEMBER 20

In his landmark treatise, *Against Heresies*, St. Irenaeus of Lyons (c. 130–202) discusses the nature of religious sacrifice, offering insight into God's commands. Though God stands in need of nothing, He instructs offerings to be made so that man might freely return all of creation—including man himself—back to the Father. The faithful Christian offers to the Father not only creation but also His only-begotten Son, sacrificed for the salvation of the world. In this way, God's gratuitous love is diffused through creation, multiplying itself, so to speak.

> We offer to Him, not as if He needed it, but as giving thanks to His Sovereignty, and sanctifying creation. For as surely as God does not need the things that are ours, so surely do we need to offer something to God as Solomon said, "He that is kind to the poor lends to God" [Prov 19:17]. For God, who stands in need of nothing, receives our good works in order that He may grant us a return of the good things that belong to Him; as our Lord says, "Come you blessed of My Father, receive the Kingdom prepared for you. For I was hungry, and you gave me to eat. I was thirsty and you gave me to drink. I was a stranger, and you took me in; naked and you clothed me, sick and you visited me; in prison and you came to me" [Matt 25:34–36]. Just as He does not need these things, yet He wills them to be done by us, for our own sake, that we may not be unfruitful. Therefore, the Word Himself gives the people the command to make oblations, though He needs them not, that they may learn to serve God. Accordingly, He wants us also to frequently offer gifts on the altar often without ceasing. And the altar is in heaven—for it is there that our prayers and offerings are directed—and the temple, as John says in the Apocalypse, "and the temple of God was opened" [Rev 21:19], and the Tabernacle, for he says "Behold, the tabernacle of God in which he dwells with man" [Rev 21:8].

St. Irenaeus of Lyons (c. 130–202)

DECEMBER 21

St. Peter Canisius (1521–1597) zealously worked to re-catechize Germany, which had been divided in belief by Martin Luther. Preferring charity to divisive polemics, St. Peter's gentle approach to evangelization earned him the respect of both Catholics and Protestants. In response to Luther's catechism, St. Peter published his own summary of Catholic teachings. In the following excerpt, St. Peter enumerates scriptural teachings on Christ's Real Presence in the Eucharist, citing the Psalms, Gospels, and St. Paul.

> Together with the whole Church, and against all [those who dissent], we hold certain that beneath the species of bread and wine is the true flesh of Jesus Christ, and His true Blood, present in the Eucharist, which is from the ministry of the priest, by virtue of the power of our Lord JESUS CHRIST, with whom nothing is impossible. *He spoke, and they were made. He commanded, and they were created* [Ps 33:9].

> On the night before He was to suffer, He spoke to them at supper, instructing them first with the bread, and then with the wine. Taking each in His hands, He spoke over them. And desirous to make the truth certain to all, He said most plainly: *This is my body, which is given up for you.* He said: *This is my blood, which is poured out for many* [see Matt 26:26, 28].

> Prior to the Institution, He had said: *My flesh is true food, and my blood is true drink.* He had also said: *Therefore, I am the bread of life that came down from heaven. If you eat this bread, you will live forever. And the bread that I will give is my flesh for the life of the world* [see John 6:51].

> Neither is uncertain to the Evangelists, nor is it unclear in the testimony of St. Paul, whereupon we have further evidence of this faith, which no one can doubt: Christ is in the Eucharist,

whole and entire, according to His Divine and Human natures, and will remain with us until the consummation of the ages.

St. Peter Canisius, Doctor of the Church (1521–1597)

DECEMBER 22

St. Fulgentius (467–532) was an ardent disciple of St. Augustine who here describes the sacramental nature of Christ's presence in the Eucharist. Quoting St. Augustine at length, Fulgentius teaches that the sacraments are veiled so that the senses perceive one thing, while faith perceives another. Together, they mutually profess that the Eucharist is the very body of Christ, born of the Virgin Mary, and crucified upon the cross of Calvary. Nevertheless, the presence of Christ remains sacramentally hidden, just as Christians—who are the body of Christ—do not betray any visible sign of their identity.

What you see is bread and a cup; for, that is what your eyes tell you. But your faith demands instruction: the bread is the body of Christ and the cup is the Blood of Christ. It was said earlier that a strong faith suffices; however, faith desires illumination. For the prophet says, "Unless you believe, you will not understand" [Isa 7:9]. So, you might say to me, "You have taught us to believe. Now, explain that we may understand." Such a thought can arise in someone's mind. We know that our Lord Jesus Christ took flesh from the Virgin Mary, and that He nursed as an infant, was fed, grew up, suffered persecution from the Jews, was hung on a tree, died on a tree, was buried, rose on the third day, and on the day of His choosing, willed to ascended into heaven to that place from where He will come again to judge the living and the dead. There He sits at the right of the Father. . . . How is the bread His Body, and how are the contents of the cup His Blood? Brothers, these are called sacraments because one thing appears in them, and another is understood. That which is visible has a physical appearance, yet it is understood to have spiritual fruit. So, if you wish to understand the Body of Christ, hear the apostle speaking to believers: "You are the body of Christ and His members."

St. Fulgentius of Ruspe (467–532)

DECEMBER 23

In the following passage from *On the Trinity*, St. Augustine (354–430) contemplates the finite nature of man's knowledge and the humility that ought to accompany such limits. While many seek to understand the mystery of Christ's presence upon the altar, St. Augustine cautions that human frailty can scarcely grasp the appearance and workings of angels. For this reason, Christians must become as children who accept a higher authority than their own, taking care not to claim understanding in matters beyond their capacity.

Who among men knows how the angels made those clouds and flames, which they used to signify the message they were proclaiming—even if we supposed the Lord or the Holy Spirit was manifest in these physical forms? It is as with infants who do not know what is placed on the altar and consumed when the celebration of devotion is finished, or from what it is made, or from where it is taken for devotion. If they never learn from their experience, or that of another, and never see that species except when it is offered and given among the celebrations of the sacraments; if it is told them with the weightiest authority that it is His body and blood, they will believe only that the Lord has absolutely appeared to the eyes of mortals in that species, and that liquid truly flowed from His pierced side. But, it is certainly a useful caution to myself to remember what my powers are, and admonish my brothers to also remember what theirs are, lest human infirmity pass beyond what is safe.

St. Augustine of Hippo, Bishop and Doctor (354–430)

DECEMBER 24

The Vigil of the Nativity of the Lord

On the Eve of the Nativity of the Lord, St. John Chrysostom (349–407) exhorts Christians to follow the example of the Magi as they honored the birth of the Christ. If Persian kings crossed the desert to adore the Christ Child, Chrysostom wonders how Christians could fail to reverence Jesus upon the altar. Relating the manger to the sacred table, St. John encourages his flock to immerse themselves in the Mystery of Love, born in a stable at Bethlehem and present upon the altar.

> I greet and love this day of Christ's birth. I place its love front and center that I may make you sharers in this love. For this reason, I beg and entreat you all to attend with all diligence and readiness; for each should flee his own house to see our Master lying in a manger, wrapped in swaddling clothes; that awesome and incredible spectacle. What defense or excuse can we make when He has come down from heaven for our sake, yet we do not leave our own house for Him? The Magi, those barbarians and foreigners, ran from Persia to see Him lying in a crib, but you, O Christian, do not even remain for a short time so as to enjoy this blessed sight. For when we approach with faith, we too will certainly see Him lying in the manger; for this table fulfills the purpose and plan of the manger.

> St. John Chrysostom, Bishop and Doctor (349–407)

DECEMBER 25

The Solemnity of the Nativity of the Lord

On this joyful day, the Church honors the newborn Lord, the King of Kings, born in a stable at Bethlehem. In the following meditation, St. Peter Julian Eymard (1811–1868) describes the Nativity of the Lord as the beginnings of the Eucharist. For the Bread of Life was laid in a manger to give life to the world. Connecting the Incarnation to the

Passion, St. Peter explains how both express Christ's self-giving love, and that both are embraced by the Eucharist. As Mary treasured the Christ Child in her arms, so must Christians honor the Eucharistic Lord on Christmas Day.

> Ah, yes! The Eucharist began at Bethlehem and in the arms of Mary. It was she who brought to humanity the Bread for which it was famishing, and which alone can nourish it. It was she that took care of that Bread for us. Divine Lamb, she nourished the Lamb whose life-giving Flesh we feed upon. She nourished Him with her virginal milk, she nourished Him for the sacrifice, for she already foreknew His destiny. Yes, she knew, and soon she will know still better, that her Lamb is only for immolation.
>
> She accepted God's will and, bearing Him in her own arms, she prepares for us the Victim of Calvary and of our altars. On the day of sacrifice, she will herself conduct her Divine Lamb to Jerusalem, to deliver Him up to Divine Justice for the world's salvation. Ah, Bethlehem already foretells Calvary!—Truly, Mary had heard her Son's first word: "Father, sacrifice and oblation Thou would not. Behold I come!"—and she united in His offering and anticipated immolation.
>
> St. Peter Julian Eymard (1811–1868)

DECEMBER 26

Memorial of St. Stephen, Deacon and Martyr

The day after the Nativity of the Lord, the Church celebrates that preeminent Christian martyr, St. Stephen. In his *Letter to the Romans*, St. Ignatius of Antioch (c. 35–107) underscores the sacrificial love common to both the Eucharist and Christian martyrs. As Christ offers Himself in the Eucharistic liturgy, even so do Christians unite their self-offering to His. This reciprocal self-giving is realized in its supreme form in martyrdom, wherein one gives his life to Christ. Here, St. Ignatius prays that his own offering will make him "the pure bread of God," united to the Eucharistic Lord.

I write and impress upon all the churches that I willingly die for God, if in fact you do not prevent me. I appeal to you not to be inopportune, even with a noble purpose. Permit me to be food for the beasts; through them I will reach God. I am the wheat of God and I compete through the beasts' teeth to be found the pure bread of Christ. Rather flatter the beasts to become my tomb and to leave nothing of my body that by dying I may not be a burden to you. Then, I will be truly a disciple of Jesus Christ when the world will not even see my body. Beg Christ in my behalf that I may be found a sacrifice to God through these instruments. . . .

While I am alive, I write to you, but I desire death. My desire for this world has been crucified and there is no fire in me burning for material things. Rather, there is a water that lives and speaks within me, saying, "Come to the Father." I have no desire for corruptible food or for the pleasures of this life. I want the bread of God that is the flesh of Jesus Christ, of David's seed, and I want his blood as my drink that is love incorruptible.

St. Ignatius of Antioch (c. 35–107)

DECEMBER 27

Before his elevation to the papacy, St. Dionysius (d. 268) was forced to confront one of the major theological questions of the day: were the baptisms performed by heretics valid? In this letter, he writes of a man who desired to be re-baptized because of his doubts over the legitimacy of the sacrament. St. Dionysius affirms the validity of the sacrament and encourages him to receive the Eucharist. Whereas sacramental Reconciliation is necessary for anyone conscious of grave sin, St. Dionysius here judges that the man in question is in good standing and may be spiritually healed by the Eucharist.

> For truly, brother, I have need of advice and greatly desire your judgment, lest I should be mistaken in these matters. One of the faithful who comes to the church, and who has been esteemed as a believer for some time, came to me in tears bewailing his lot. For he had been a part of the assembly before my own ordination and (if I am not mistaken) that of Heraclas' episcopacy, and he was concerned in those then baptized, and heard the interrogatories and their answers. Throwing himself at my feet, he began to confess and to protest that this baptism, by which he had been initiated among heretics, was not of this kind, nor had anything in common with ours, because it was full of blasphemy and impiety. He said that his soul was pierced with bitter sorrow, and that he did not dare to even life up his eyes to God as he had been initiated by those wicked words and things. Thus, he sought that by this purest laver, he might be endowed with adoption and grace. I, indeed, have not dared to do this, and told him instead that the long course of communion had been sufficient for this. For I should not dare to renew afresh, after all, one who had heard the thanksgiving, and who had answered with others *Amen;* who had stood at the holy table, and had stretched forth his hands to receive the blessed food, and had received it, and for a very long time had been a partaker of the body and blood of our Lord Jesus Christ. Therefore, I bade him to be of good courage, and approach the sacred elements with a firm faith and a good conscience, and to partake in them.

Pope St. Dionysius (d. 268)
[Memorial, December 26]

DECEMBER 28

Before the liturgical reforms of the Council of Trent, the Medieval period saw the rise of many sequences and poetic texts integrated into the liturgy. The responsorial chant O *magnum mysterium*, composed for Christmas matins, remains a popular meditation on the mystery of the Incarnation as it relates to the Eucharist. This hymn is here paired with another devotional text, *Ave verum Corpus*, intended for recitation at the elevation of the Sacred Host. Both texts are Eucharistic in nature and express the solemn grandeur of Christ's self-emptying love.

O magnum mysterium	O great mystery
et admirabile sacramentum,	and wondrous sacrament,
ut animalia viderent Domi-	that animals should behold the
num natum	newborn Lord
iacentem in praesepio.	lying in a manger!
Beata Virgo, cujus viscera	O Blessed Virgin, whose womb
meruerunt portare	was found worthy to bear
Dominum Iesum Christum.	the Lord Jesus Christ.
Alleluia!	Alleluia!

Responsorial Chant for Christmas
Pope Innocent VI (c. 1282–1362)

Ave verum corpus, natum	Hail true Body, born
de Maria Virgine,	of the Virgin Mary
vere passum, immolatum	truly suffered, immolated
in cruce pro homine	on the cross for mankind,
cuius latus perforatum	from whose side was pierced
fluxit aqua et sanguine	and blood and water flowed
esto nobis praegustatum	Be for us heaven's foretaste
in mortis examine.	in the trial of death.

O Iesu dulcis, O Iesu pie,	O most sweet Jesus! O most
O Iesu, fili Mariae	gentle Jesus!
	O Jesus, son of Mary,

Miserere mei.	Have mercy on me.
Amen.	Amen.

DECEMBER 29

Adam of Perseigne (1145–1221) was a Cistercian abbot, known for his holiness, wisdom, and eloquence of speech. In this excerpt from his Christmas homily, Adam relates the mystery of Christ's birth with the advent of the Eucharist. For the sacrament upon the altar is none other than the newborn Lord, placed in a manger at Bethlehem. Here, Adam emphasizes that the mystery of the manger bespeaks the nourishing gift of the Eucharist, the Bread of Life.

> Why is God placed in a manger, except to be food for souls, which is placed upon the altar? The manger surely represents the altar, for in His consecrated Body, He lovingly feeds His flock. All this reveals God's love for us. It is to nourish us and to inflame our love. These contemplations inspire holy fear, move our piety, enlighten us with knowledge, increase our fortitude, illuminate the intellect, inflame us with wisdom, and prepare for us the crown. For, without any doubt, the Omnipotent Word abases Himself. He makes Himself a child for children, and humbles Himself for us [upon the altar].
>
> *Adam of Perseigne (1145–1221)*

DECEMBER 30

Marie-Eustelle Harpain (1814–1842), affectionately called the "Angel of the Eucharist," was a French laywoman whose life was marked by an intense devotion to the Blessed Sacrament. Moved by her extraordinary virtue, Harpain's own bishop initiated work on her biography. In the following extracts from her letters, she describes a life wholly centered on the Eucharist. Here, Harpain expresses the sublime exchange that takes place between Christ and the soul as the soul begins to subsist wholly upon God.

Ah, brother of Jesus, child of Mary, consume yourself at the Eucharistic flame; have no soul, no heart, spirit, intention, love, life, breath, taste, but only for the Eucharist: in a word, let your entire being be ever flowing in one perpetual sacred stream towards this Jesus so unknown, so lovingly hidden in the prison of the Tabernacle. Let Him be ever our joy, our peace, our aim. Insofar as it depends on yourself, frequently approach the Holy Table to taste the sweetness of this delicious honey. . . .

It is at that source of all good that you must often go and draw. Oh, if the people of the world but knew what exquisite pleasures are tasted at that sacred banquet, I do not doubt that they would renounce all their false joys to come and take long inebriating draughts at the fountainhead of everlasting truth. As for you who have already tasted of this ineffable joy, be diligent to increase it by receiving communion as frequently as possible. Place all your delight in this divine aliment. Let Jesus in the Eucharist be *all in all* to you [see 1 Cor 15:28].

Marie-Eustelle Harpain (1814–1842)

DECEMBER 31

On the Vigil of the Solemnity of Mary, Mother of God, the Church looks to that singular woman who brought forth the Savior of the world. In this passage from the *Didache* (c. 100), the early Church speaks on the importance of breaking the bread within the body of the

Church. All transgressions must be confessed, and all divisions must give way to reconciliation. In this way, a pure sacrifice may be offered to the Lord in the great thanksgiving known as the Eucharist.

> On the Lord's Day, once you have gathered, break the bread and celebrate the Eucharist, after having confessed your transgressions that your sacrifice may be pure. Let no one who has a quarrel with his friend join you, until they reconcile, that your sacrifice may not be defiled. This is what was spoken by the Lord, "In every place and time offer to me a pure sacrifice because I am a great king, says the Lord, and my name is marvelous among the Gentiles" [Mal 1:11].
>
> *The Didache (c. 100)*

AUTHOR AND SOURCE INDEX

The authors and sources of the daily readings are listed by the most commonly known names. Modern authors who have a true family name (e.g. Alphonsus Liguori) are listed by their last name. Ancient and medieval authors, who often did not have last names, are listed by their only name or the one best known to modern readers. Italicized entries are documents.

Ave Verum Corpus (Eucharistic Hymn), Dec 28

Barat, Madeleine Sophie (1779–1865), May 22

Barberi, Dominic (1792–1849), Aug 26

Basil the Great (330–379), July 5, Sep 7

Beatus (d. 798), Feb 19

Bede, The Venerable (673–725), May 24

Bellarmine, Robert (1542–1621), Sep 16

Benedict XVI (b. 1927) (*see* Ratzinger, Joseph)

Berchmans, John (1599–1621), Aug 10

Bernadette Soubirous (*see* Soubirous)

Bernard of Clairvaux (1090–1153), Aug 20

Bernardine of Siena (1380–1444), May 20

Bernardino Realino (*see* Realino)

Berneux, Siméon-François (1814–1866), Mar 7

Bonaventure (1221–1274), Feb 16, Apr 15, Jul 15, Dec 9

Bonnard, Jean-Louis (1824–1852), Sept 1

Borgia, Francis (1510–1572), Sep 29

Borromeo, Charles (1538–1584), Nov 4

Bosco, John (1815–1888), Jan 31, May 6

Brébeuf, Jean de (1593–1649), Oct 14

Bridget of Sweden (1303–1373), Jul 23

Bullaker, Thomas (1604–1642), Oct 21

Byzantine-Greek Eucharistic Poetry (4th century), May 11, Aug 3, Sep 9

Cabasilas, Nicholas (1322–1392), Feb 13, Jun 19

Caesarius of Arles (c. 468–542), Feb 8, Apr 19, Jun 24, Jul 25, Aug 22, Sep 18, Oct 12, Nov 21

Cafasso, Joseph (1811–1860), Jun 23

Cajetan, Thomas (1480–1547), Aug 7

Camilla Battista de Varano (*see* Varano)

Campion, Edmund (1540–1581), Nov 30

Canisius, Peter (1521–1597), Dec 21

Carthusian of Nuremburg (1480), Oct 6

Cassian, John (360–435), Jul 21

Cassiodorus (c. 490–583), Mar 28, Jul 13

Catherine of Bologna (1413–1463), Mar 9

Catherine of Genoa (1447–1510), Sep 15

Catherine of Siena (1347–1380), Apr 29

Jun 8

Escrivá, Josemaría (1902–1975), Jun 26

Eudes, John (1601–1680), Aug 19

Eugène de Mazenod (*see* Mazenod)

Eymard, Peter Julian (1811–1868),
Mar 19, Aug 2, Aug 15, Dec 25

Ezequiél Moreno y Díaz (*see* Moreno)

Faber, Peter (1506–1546), Jul 28

Faustina (*see* Kowalska)

Ferrer, Vincent (1350–1419) Apr 5

Fisher, John (1469–1535), Jun 21

Foucauld, Charles (1858–1916), Dec 1

Francis of Assisi (1181–1226), Oct 4

Francis de Sales (1567–1622), Jan 24

Francis Borgia (*see* Borgia)

Francis Liberman (*see* Libermann)

Francis Xavier (*see* Xavier)

Francisco Marto (*see* Marto)

Fulbert of Chartres (c. 960–1029), Apr 10

Fulgentius of Ruspe (467–532), Jan 3, Dec 22

Fulton J. Sheen (*see* Sheen)

Galgani, Gemma (1878–1903), Apr 11

Gaudentius of Brescia (unknown–410), Mar 13, Jun 14, Aug 16, Oct 25, Dec 18

Gelasius of Cyzicus (5th century), Feb 11

Gemma Galgani (*see* Galgani)

Gerard Majella (*see* Majella)

Germanus of Constantinople (634–733), May 12, Jul 17

Gertrude the Great (1256–1302), Nov 16

Giuliani, Veronica (1660–1727), Jul 9

Gregory of Agrigentum (c. 559–638), Jul 20, Nov 23, Dec 12

Gregory of Narek (c. 951–1010), Feb 27

Gregory of Nazianzus (329–390), Jan 2

Gregory of Nyssa (c. 335–395), Jan 10, Feb 24, Apr 14, Jun 17, Jul 24, Nov 20

Gregory the Great (540–604), Feb 14, Jun 29, Jul 11, Sep 3

Gregory VII (Pope) (1015–1085), May 25

Grignion de Montfort, Louis-Marie (1673–1716), Apr 28

Guitmond of Aversa (c. 1025–1094), October 28

Harpain, Marie-Eustelle (1814–1842), Dec 30

Hart, William (1558–1583), Mar 15

Henry Suso (*see* Suso)

Hilary of Poitiers (c. 310–367), Jan 13, Apr 18, Jul 18, Oct 23, Dec 6

Hildegard von Bingen (1098–1179), Sep 17

Hilton, Walter (c. 1340–1396), Jan

John Thulis (see Thulis)

Joseph Cafasso (see Cafasso)

Josefa Menendez (see Menendez)

Josemaría Escrivá (see Escrivá, Josemaría)

Julian of Norwich (c. 1342–1416), Jul 8

Julian of Toledo (642–690), Mar 8

Juliana of Liège (c. 1192–1258), Apr 6

Junípero Serra (see Serra)

Justin Martyr (c. 100– c. 165), Jan 9, Mar 2, Jun 1, Aug 31

Justin de Jacobis (1800–1860), Jul 29

Kowalska, Faustina (1905–1938), Mar 25, Oct 5

Labouré, Catherine (1806–1876), Nov 28

Lanfranc (1005–1089), May 28

Leo the Great (400–461), Nov 10

Leo XIII (1810–1903), Mar 27

Leonard of Port Maurice (1676–1751), Nov 27

Libermann, Francis (1802–1852), Feb 2

Liguori, Alphonsus (1696–1787), Aug 1

Liturgy of St. James, May 3, Jul 10, Nov 3

Liturgy of St. Mark, Feb 23

Liturgy of the Armenian Church (see Armenian Liturgy)

Lorenzo Scupoli (see Scupoli)

Louis of Grenada (1504–1588), Jan 19

Louis-Marie Grignion de Montfort (see Grignion)

Louis and Zélie Martin (see Martin)

Louise de Marillac (1591–1660), May 9

Lúcia of Fatima (1907–2005), May 13

Luis de León (1527–1591), Jun 15

Macarius of Magnesia (4th century), Sept 2

Madeleine Sophie Barat (see Barat)

Magnum Mysterium (Eucharistic Hymn), Dec 28

Majella, Gerard (1726–1755), Oct 13

Mallinckrodt, Pauline von (1817–1881), Apr 25

Margaret of Cortona (1247–1297), Feb 22

Margaret Mary Alacoque (1647–1690), Oct 16

Marie of the Incarnation (1599–1672), Apr 27

Marie-Thérèse of the Heart of Jesus (1809–1863), Apr 13, May 8

Marie-Eustelle Harpain (see Harpain)

Marmion, Columba (1858–1923), Oct 3

Martin of León (1130–1203), Jan 16

Martin, Thérèse (1873–1897), Oct 1

Martin, Louis and Zélie (1823–1894;

ENDNOTES

January 1
Andrew of Crete, *Canon on Pentecost*. Translated by Howell.
John Chrysostom, *Homily 6: On Blessed Philogonius*. Translated by Howell.

January 2
Gregory of Nazianzus, *Funeral Oration for His Sister Gorgonia*. Translated by Howell. Adapted from the public domain.

January 3
Fulgentius of Ruspe, *Epistle 12*. Translated by Howell.
The memorial feast for Fulgentius of Ruspe is January 1 on the Church's universal calendar, but January 3 for the Augustinian Order, of which Fulgentius was a member.

January 4
Elizabeth Ann Seton, *Memoir, Letters and Journal of Elizabeth Seton*, vol. 2, ed. Robert Seton (NY: P. O'Shea, 1869), 142–143. Edited by Crownwood.

January 5
Charles of Sezze, *Camino Interno Dell'anima: sposa dell'humanato Verbo Christo Giesu* (Rome: Nella Stamparia di Francesco Moneta's, 1664), 161. Translated by Crownwood.

January 6
John Chrysostom, *Homily 6: On Blessed Philogonius*. Translated by Howell.

January 7
Angela of Foligno, *The Book of Divine Consolation of the Blessed Angela Foligno*, trans. Mary G. Steegmann (London: Chatto & Windus,

1909), 152. Edited by Crownwood.

January 8
Didache, 9. Translated by Howell. Translations of the *Didache* are adapted from Kenneth Howell, *Clement of Rome & the Didache: A New Translation and Theological Commentary*, Early Christian Fathers Series 2 (Zanesville, OH: CHResources, 2012).

January 9
Justin Martyr, *First Apology*, 67. Translated by Howell.

January 10
Gregory of Nyssa, "Catechetical Oration" in *Nicene and Ante-Nicene Fathers*, Second Series, vol. V, ed. Philip Schaff and Henry Wace (NY: Charles Scribner's Sons, 1904), 504–505. Edited for this book, consulting the Latin text.

January 11
Paulinus II of Aquileia, *Against Felix of Urgel*, 3:2, 10. Translated by Crownwood.

January 12
Aelred of Rievaulx, *Sermon: On the Birth of the Lord*. Translated by Crownwood.

January 13
Hilary of Poitiers, *On the Trinity*, bk. 8, 13–17. Translated by Howell.

January 14
Ignatius of Antioch, *Letter to the Smyrnaeans*, 8:1–2. Translated by Howell. Translations of Ignatius of Antioch are adapted from Kenneth J. Howell, *Ignatius of Antioch & Polycarp of Smyrna: A New Translation and Theological Commentary*, Early Christian Fathers Series 1 (Zanesville, OH: CHResources, 2009).

January 15
Walter Hilton, *The Scale of Perfection* (Westminster: Art and Book Company, 1908), 50–51. Edited by Crownwood.

January 16
Martin of León, *Exposition on the Book of the Apocalypse*. Translated by Crownwood.

January 17
Athanasius of Alexandria, "Life of St. Anthony," in Philip Schaff, ed., *Nicene and Post-Nicene Fathers, Second Series*, vol. IV, (New York: Christian Literature Publishing Co., 1902), 218. Edited by Crownwood.

January 18
Cyprian of Carthage, *Epistle 69*, 4. Translated by Howell.

January 19
Louis of Granada, *The Sinner's Guide* (Philadelphia: Henry McGrath, 1845), 48. Edited by Crownwood.

January 20
Thomas á Kempis, *Imitation of Christ*, bk. 4, ch. 8. Translated by Crownwood. Adapted from the public domain.

January 21
Augustine, *Tracts on the Gospel of John*, 11, 4. Translated by Howell.

January 22
Ildefonsus of Toledo, *On Baptism*, 136. Translated by Crownwood.

January 23
Henry Suso, *A Little Book of Eternal Wisdom* (London: Burns, Oates & Washbourne, 1910), ch. 23. Edited by Crownwood.

January 24
Francis de Sales, *Introduction to the Devout Life* (London: Longmans, Green, and Co., 1891), 82–83. Edited by Crownwood.

January 25
Apollo, "Saying," in Hieronymus Palladius, *The Book of Paradise*, vol. 1, trans. Ernest A. Wallis Budge (London: 1904), 536. Edited by Crownwood.

January 26
Irenaeus of Lyons, *Against Heresies*, 5:2, 2. Translated by Howell.

January 27
Angela of Merici, *St. Angela Merici and the Ursulines* (London: Burns & Oates, 1880), 304–305. Edited by Crownwood.

January 28
Thomas Aquinas, *The Summa Theologiae, Part III*, trans. Fathers of the English Dominican Province (London: R. & T. Washbourne, Ltd., 1914), q. 75, a. 4. Edited by Crownwood.

January 29
John Damascene, *On the Orthodox Faith*, bk. 4, 13. Translated by Howell.

January 30
William of St. Thierry, *Meditative Prayers*, 6. Translated by Crownwood.

January 31
John Bosco, *Life of Dominic Savio* (London: Salesian Press, 1914), ch. 13. Edited by Crownwood.

February 1
John Paul II, Encyclical Letter on the Eucharist in Its Relationship to the Church *Ecclesia de Eucharistia*, April 17, 2003, §§1, 3.

February 2
Prosper Goepfert, *The Life of the Venerable Francis Mary Paul Libermann* (Dublin: M.H. Gill & Son, 1880), 52, 121. Edited by Crownwood.

February 3
Rabanus Maurus, *On the Formation of Clerics*, bk. 1, 31. Translated by Crownwood.

February 4
Isidore of Pelusium, *Letter 123: To Count Dorotea*. Translated by Howell.

February 5
Catherine Ricci, *Le letter Spirituali e Familiari di S. Caterina de' Ricci*, ed. Cesare Guasti (Prato: Ranieri Guasti, 1861), 85. Translated by Crownwood.

February 6
Joseph Broeckaert, *Life of the Blessed Charles Spinola of the Society of Jesus* (NY: P.J. Kenedy, Excelsior Catholic Publishing House, 1899), 172, 175. Edited by Crownwood.

February 7
Pius IX, Encyclical On Priests and the Care of Souls *Amantissimi Redemptoris*, 1858, §§1, 3.

February 8
Caesarius of Arles, *Sermon 73*. Translated by Howell.

February 9
Anne Catherine Emmerich, *The Dolorous Passion of Our Lord Jesus Christ* (London: Burns & Lambert, 1862), 83. Edited by Crownwood.

February 10
Johannes Tauler, "First Sermon for Corpus Christi," in *The Sermons*

and *Conferences of John Tauler of the Order of Preachers*, trans. Walter Elliott (Washington, DC: Apostolic Mission House, 1910), 371. Edited by Crownwood.

February 11
Gelasius of Cyzicus, *History of the Church*, 2:31, 6. Translated by Howell.

February 12
Celtic Missal: The Liturgy and Diverse Services from the Lorrha ("Stowe") Missal, trans. Maelrúain Kristopher Dowling (Akron, OH: Ascension Western Rite Orthodox Church, 1997), 73. Available online: https://www.faithandworship.com/pdf/stowe%20missal.pdf

February 13
Nicholas Cabasilas, *Explanation of the Divine Liturgy*, no. 27. Translated by Howell.

February 14
Gregory the Great, *Homily 14*, 1. Translated by Howell.

February 15
Claude de la Colombiére, *Lettres spirituelles du r.p. Claude de la Colombiére*, vol. 2 (Lyons: Chez les Freres Bruyset, 1725), 6–7. Translated by Crownwood.

February 16
Bonaventure, *On the Most Holy Body of Christ*. Translated by Howell.

February 17
Fulton Sheen, *Letter to a Friend* (April 9, 1948), printed with permission of Mike Fulton, president of the Archbishop Fulton John Sheen Spiritual Center.

February 18
Augustine, *Tracts on the Gospel of John*, 11:4–5. Translated by Howell.
Adapted from the public domain.

February 19
Beatus, *Letter to Elipandum*, bk. 1, 75. Translated by Crownwood.

February 20
Lúcia of Fátima, *Fátima in Lúcia's own Words: Sister Lúcia's Memiors*,
16th edition, ed. Louis Kondor, trans. Dominican Nuns of the Perpetual Rosary (Fátima: Secretariado dos Pastorinhos, 2007), 156–157.

February 21
Peter Damian, *Dominus Vobiscum*, 8. Translated by Crownwood.

February 22
Giunta Reveignati, *Life and Revelations of St. Margaret of Cortona*,
trans. F. M'Donagh Mahoney (London: Burns and Oates, 1883), 171,
181. Edited by Crownwood.

February 23
"Liturgy of St. James" in *Ante-Nicene Fathers*, vol. 7, ed. Alexander
Roberts and James Donaldson (Buffalo, NY: The Christian Literature
Publishing Company, 1886), 554–555. Edited by Crownwood.

February 24
Gregory of Nyssa, *On the Song of Songs*, 10. Translated by Howell.

February 25
The Anaphora of Serapion. Translated by Howell.

February 26
John Chrysostom, *On the Priesthood*, bk. 3, 4. Translated by Howell.

February 27
Gregory of Narek, "Prayer 33," in *Liturgies Eastern and Western*, vol. 1, *Eastern Liturgies*, ed. F. E. Brightman (Oxford: Clarendon Press, 1896), 418. Edited by Crownwood.

February 28
Thomas Aquinas, *Lauda Sion*. Translated by Cronwood. Adapted from the public domain.

February 29 [*leap year*]
Clement of Alexandria, *Paedagogus*, 2, 2. Translated by Howell.

March 1
Lorenzo Scupoli, *The Spiritual Combat* (Manchester: R.W. Dean, 1801), 123. Edited by Crownwood.

March 2
Justin Martyr, *First Apology*, 65. Translated by Howell.

March 3
Jacopone da Todi, "Laude," in *Jacopone da Todi: Poet and Mystic*, ed. Evelyn Underhill, trans. Mrs. Theodore Beck (London: J.M. Dent & Sons, Ltd., 1919), 321, 323. Edited by Crownwood.

March 4
St. Paulinus of Nola, *Letter 32: To Sulpicius Severus*. Translated by Howell.

March 5
John Berger, *Life of Right Rev. John N. Neumann*, trans. Eugene Grimm (NY: Benziger Brothers, 1884), 153–154, 372. Edited by Crownwood.

March 6
Louis Sellier, *Vie de Sainte Colette* (Paris: Caron, 1855), 123. Translated by Crownwood.

March 7

Frédéric Pichon, *The Life of Monseigneur Berneux*, trans. Lady Herbert (London: Burns, Oates, and Company, 1872), 6. Edited by Crownwood.

March 8

Julian of Toledo, *Contrariorum sive contrapositorum*, bk. 2, 24. Translated by Crownwood.

March 9

Catherine of Bologna, *The Seven Spiritual Weapons*, in Peregrina Translations Series 25, trans. Hugh Feiss and Daniela Re (Toronto: Peregrina Publishing Co., 1998), ch. 8, pp. 3–5, https://monasticmatrix.osu.edu/cartularium/seven-spiritual-weapons.

March 10

John Ogilvie, "Account," in Charles Karslake, *An Authentic Account of the Imprisonment and Martyrdom in the High Street at Glasgow of Father John Ogilvie* (London: Burns and Oates, 1877), 23, 32. Edited by Crownwood.

March 11

Thomas á Kempis, *De Imitatione Christi*, bk. 4, 18 (London: Kegan Paul, Trench, Trubner & Co., 1892). Translated by Crownwood. Adapted from the public domain.

March 12

Symeon the New Theologian, *Ethical Discourse* 1, 3. Translated by Howell.

March 13

Gaudentius of Brescia, *Tract 2: On the Exodus*. Translated by Howell.

March 14

Didache, 10. Translated by Howell.

March 15

William Hart, "Letter to Matthew Hutton," in *Lives of the English Martyrs*, vol. 1, ed. Bede Camm (London: Longmans, Green and Co., 1914), 613–614. Edited by Crownwood.

March 16

John Chrysostom, *Homilies on the Letter to the Ephesians*, no. 3. Translated by Howell.

March 17

Columbanus, "Instruction 13, De Christo fonte vitae," in *Liturgy of the Hours*, vol. 4, trans. ICEL (New York: Catholic Book Publishing, 1975), 168–169.

March 18

St. Cyril of Jerusalem, *Mystagogy*, 4, in *Nicene and Post-Nicene Fathers*, vol. 7, ed. Philip Schaff (New York: The Christian Literature Company, 1894), 152. Edited by Crownwood.

March 19

Peter Eymard, *Month of Our Lady of the Blessed Sacrament*, trans. a Visitandine of Baltimore, MD (NY: The Sentinel Press, 1903), 86–88. Edited by Crownwood.

March 20

Josefa Menendez, The Way of Divine Love (Rockford, IL: Tan Books and Publishers, Inc., 1972), 244.

March 21

Augustine, *Letter 98: To Boniface*. Translated by Howell.

March 22

Ignatius of Antioch, *Letter to the Philadelphians*, 3, 4. Translated by Howell.

March 23

Thomas Aquinas, *Panis Angelicus*. Translated by Crownwood. Adapted from the public domain.

March 24

Oscar Romero, *The Violence of Love*, compiled and trans. James Brockman (Farmington, PA: Bruderhof Foundation, Inc.), 153. Reprinted from www.bruderhof.com. Copyright 2003 by the Bruderhof Foundation, Inc. Used with Permission. Available online: http://www.romerotrust.org.uk/sites/default/files/violenceoflove.pdf.

March 25

Faustina Kowalska, *Diary of Saint Maria Faustina Kowalska: Divine Mercy in My Soul*, 3rd ed. (Stockbridge, MA: Marian Press, 2005), par. 1114, 1233.

March 26

The Ancrene Riwle, ed. and trans. James Morten (London: J.B. Nichols and Sons, 1853), 269–271. Edited by Crownwood.

March 27

Leo XIII, Encyclical Letter on the Holy Eucharist *Mirae Caritatis*, May 28, 1902, §11.

March 28

Cassiodorus, *Commentary on the Psalter*, 78:23, 24. Translated by Howell.

March 29

Andrew of Crete, *Triduum of Holy Saturday*. Translated by Howell.

March 30

Irenaeus of Lyons, *Against Heresies*, bk. 4, ch. 18, 5. Translated by Howell.

March 31

Theodore of Mopsuestia, *Catechetical Homilies*, Woodbrooke Studies: Christian Documents, vol. VI, ed. and trans. A. Mingana (Cambridge: W. Heffer & Sons Limited, 1933), 102. Edited for this book.

April 1

Cyprian of Carthage, "Epistle 63," in J.H. Parker, *The Epistles of S. Cyprian with the Council of Carthage on the Baptism of Heretics* (Oxford: John Henry Parker, 1844), 183–184. Edited for this book, consulting the Latin text.

April 2

Richard Rolle, *The Prick of Conscience*, ed. Richard Morris (Berlin: A. Ascher & Co., 1863), 73. Edited by Crownwood.

April 3

John Damascene, "On the Orthodox Faith" in *Nicene and Post Nicene Fathers of the Christian Church*, Series 2, vol. 9, ed. Philip Schaff and Henry Wace (New York: Charles Scribner's Sons, 1908), 82. Edited for this book, consulting the Latin text.

April 4

Isidore of Seville, *Etymologies*, bk. 4, ch. 19, 36. Translated by Crownwood.

April 5

Vincent Ferrer, "Sermon," in *Sancti Vincentii Ferrarii: Opera: complectens sermons*, vol. 2, ed. Ioannis Thomae de Rocaberti (Valcencia: Iacobi de Cordazar & Artazù, 1694). Translated by Crownwood.

April 6

Juliana of Liège, "Letter to Bl. Eva of Liège," in George Ambrose Bradbury, *St. Juliana of Cornillon* (London: Thomas Richardson and Son, 1873), 86–87. Edited by Crownwood.

April 7
Jean-Baptiste de La Salle, *Explication de la method d'oraison* (Langres: Chez Laurent-Bournot, 1816). Translated by Crownwood.

April 8
Pope Innocent III, *De sacro altaris mysterio*, bk. 4, 3. Translated by Crownwood.

April 9
Meister Eckhart, "Sermon," in Odilia Funke, *Meister Eckehart*, PhD diss. (Washington, DC: Catholic University of America, 1916), 110–111. Edited by Crownwood.

April 10
Fulbert of Chartres, "Letter," in "The Month: A Catholic Magazine and Review," vol. 78 (London: Burns and Oates, 1893). Edited by Crownwood.

April 11
Gemma Galgani, "Letter" in *Lettres et Extases de Gemma Galgani* (Arras, Pas-de-Calais: Brunet, 1920), 105–106. Translated by Crownwood.

April 12
Adam of St. Victor, "Pentecost Sequence," in *The Liturgical Poetry of Adam of St. Victor*, trans. Digby S. Wrangham (London: Kegan Paul, Trench & Co., 1881), 86–87. Edited by Crownwood.

April 13
Marie-Thérèse of the Heart of Jesus, "Meditations on the Eucharist." Translated by Howell. Available in French online: https://www.adorationreparatrice.fr/ses-ecrits.

April 14
Gregory of Nyssa, *Catechetical Oration*, 37. Translated by Howell. Adapted from the public domain.

April 15
Bonaventure, *The Life of Our Lord and Saviour Jesus Christ* (Dublin: Richard Grace, 1840), 225. Edited by Crownwood.

April 16
Patricia A. McEachern, *A Holy Life: The Writings of St. Bernadette* (San Francisco: Ignatius Press, 2005), 48.

April 17
Irenaeus of Lyons, *Against Heresies*, bk. 5, ch. 2. Translated by Howell. Adapted from the public domain.

April 18
Hilary of Poitiers, *On the Trinity*, bk. 8, 13–14. Translated by Howell.

April 19
Caesarius of Arles, *Sermon 73*. Translated by Howell.

April 20
Augustine of Hippo, *Letter 98: To Boniface*. Translated by Howell. Adapted from the public domain.

April 21
St. Anselm, "Meditation," in *St. Anselm's Book of Meditations and Prayers*, trans. M. R. (London: Burns and Oates, 1872), 22–23. Edited by Crownwood.

April 22
Hugh of St. Victor, *On the Sacraments*, bk. 2, 8, in *On the Sacraments of the Christian Faith*, trans. Roy J. Defarrari (Cambridge, MA: The Medieval Academy of America, 1951), 309. Edited by Howell.

April 23
Peter Lombard, *Distinction*, 8:1, 2, in Elizabeth Frances Rogers, *Peter Lombard and the Sacramental System* (New York, 1917), 118. Edited

by Crownwood.

April 24

A. M. Clarke, *Life of Reverend Mother Mary of St. Euphrasia Pelletier* (London: Burns and Oates, 1895), 198. Edited by Crownwood.

April 25

Pauline Mallinckrodt, "Diary," in *Life of Mother Pauline von Mallinckrodt* (NY: Benziger Brothers, 1917), 107, 110. Edited by Crownwood.

April 26

Paschasius Radbertus, *On the Body and Blood of the Lord*. Translated by Howell.

April 27

Marie of the Incarnation, "Letter," in L'Abbè Richaudeau, *Lettres de la révérende mére Marie de l'Incarnation* (Paris: Librairie international catholique, Vvh. Casterman, 1876), 168–169. Translated by Crownwood.

April 28

Louis de Montfort, *A Treatise on the True Devotion to the Blessed Virgin Mary*, trans. Frederick William Faber (London: Burns and Lambert, 1863), 188–189. Edited by Crownwood.

April 29

Catherine of Siena, *The Dialogue of the Seraphic Virgin Catherine of Siena*, trans. Algar Thorold (London: Kegan Paul, Trench, Trubner & Co., Ltd., 1896), 234. Edited by Crownwood.

April 30

The Catechism of the Council of Trent: The Sacrament of the Eucharist, trans. J. Donovan (Dublin: W. Folds and Son, 1829), 249–250.

May 1

Francesco Palmero, *Opere a ben vivere de Santo Antonino, Arciescovo di Fi-*

renze (Florence: M. Cellini, 1858), 277–278. Translated by Crownwood.

May 2

Athanasius of Alexandria, "Letter 4" in *Nicene and Post-Nicene Fathers of the Christian Church*, Second Series, vol. 4, ed. Philip Schaff and Henry Wace (New York: The Christian Literature Company, 1892), 516–517. Edited by Crownwood.

May 3

"Liturgy of St. James." Translated by Howell.

May 4

Robert Southwell, "On the Blessed Sacrament of the Altar," in *The Complete Poems of Robert Southwell, S.J.*, ed. Alexander B. Grosart (London: Robson and Sons, 1872), 178–179. Edited by Crownwood.

May 5

Procopius of Gaza, *Commentary on Isaiah*. Translated by Howell.

May 6

John Bosco, *Life of St. Dominic Savio* (London: Salesian Press, 1914), ch. 19. Edited by Crownwood.

May 7

Daniel Parnaya, "Saying, 642," in *The Paradise of the Holy Fathers*, vol. 2., trans. Ernest A. Wallis Budge (London: Chatto & Windus, 1907), 819. Edited by Crownwood.

May 8

Marie-Thérèse of the Heart of Jesus, "Meditations on the Eucharist," trans. Howell. Available in French online: https://www.adorationreparatrice.fr/ses-ecrits.

May 9

Alice Lovat, *Life of the Venerable Louise de Marillac* (New York: Longmans, Green & Co., 1917), 143. Edited by Crownwood.

May 10

John of Ávila, *Letters of the Blessed John of Ávila*, trans. Benedictines of Stanbrook (London: Burns & Oates, 1904), 42–43. Edited by Crownwood.

May 11

Fourth-Century Byzantine-Greek Poetry. Translated by Howell.

May 12

Germanus of Constantinople, *Commentary on the Liturgy*. Adapted from the public domain.

May 13

Lúcia of Fátima, *Fátima in Lúcia's own Words: Sister Lúcia's Memiors*, 16th edition, ed. Louis Kondor, trans. Dominican Nuns of the Perpetual Rosary (Fátima: Secretariado dos Pastorinhos, 2007), 79.

May 14

Theodoret of Cyrrhus, *Commentary on the Letter of the Hebrews*. Translated by Howell.

Epiousios: Translated as "daily" in the Lord's Prayer. Literally, *supersubstantial,* i.e., above substance. Faced with this New Testament neologism, St. Jerome translated *"epiousios"* as both "daily" and "supersubstantial" in different Gospel renderings.

May 15

John Damascene, *On the Orthodox Faith*, bk. 4, ch. 13. Translated by Howell. Adapted from the public domain.

May 16

Council of Nicaea, "Canon 18," in *Nicene and Post-Nicene Fathers*, Second Series, vol. 14, ed. Philip Schaff and Henry Wace (New York, Charles Scribner's Sons, 1905), 38–39. Edited by Crownwood.

May 17

Augustine, "Letter 54: To Januarius" in *Nicene and Post-Nicene Fathers of the Christian Church: The Confessions and Letters of St. Augustine,* ed. Philip Schaff (NY: Christian Literature Publishing Co., 1886), ch. 3, p. 301. Edited by Crownwood.

May 18

Thomas Aquinas, "On the Feast of Corpus Christi," in *Liturgy of the Hours,* vol. 3, ICEL (New York: Catholic Book Publishing, 1975), 610–611.

Thomas Aquinas, *O sacrum convivium.* Translated by Crownwood. Adapted from the public domain.

May 19

John Baptist de Rossi, "Sermon," in E. Mougeot, *St. John Baptist De Rossi,* trans. Lady Herbert (NY: Benziger Brothers, 1906), 142–143. Edited by Crownwood.

May 20

Bernadine of Siena, *Sermons,* ed. Nazareno Orlandi, trans. Helen Josephine Robins (Siena: Tipografia Sociale, 1920), 74. Edited by Crownwood.

May 21

Eugène de Mazenod, "Instructions," in Robert Cooke, *Sketches of the Life of Eugène de Mazenod* (London: Burns & Oates, 1879), 101. Edited by Crownwood.

May 22

Madeleine Sophie Barat, "Journal," in *Life of the Venerable Madeleine Louise Sophie Barat* (Roehampton, England: Convent of the Sacred Heart, 1900), 114. Edited by Crownwood.

May 23

Mary Magdalene de Pazzi, "Letter to Cardinal Alessandro de Medici," in *The Life of St. Mary Magdalen De-Pazzi: Florentine Noble, Sacred*

Carmelite Virgin, vol. 1, ed. Placido Fabrini, trans. Antonio Isoleri (Philadelphia: Antonio Isoleri, 1900), 442. Edited by Crownwood.

May 24
Bede the Venerable, "Letter to Egbert," in *Venerabilis Baedae: Historia ecclesiastica gentis Anglorum, historia abbatum et epistola ad Ecberctum*, ed. Georgii. H. Hoberly (Oxford: Oxford University Press, 1881), 403. Translated by Crownwood.

May 25
Gregory VII, "Epistle 47," in PL vol. 148. Translated by Crownwood.

May 26
Philip Neri, "Maxims," in *The Maxims and Sayings of St. Philip Neri*, trans. Frederic William Faber (London: Thomas Richardson and Son, 1847). Edited by Crownwood.

May 27
Peter Chrysologus, *Sermon 95*. Translated by Howell.

May 28
Lanfranc, *On the Body and Blood of the Lord*. Translated by Crownwood.

May 29
Augustine, *On the Trinity*, bk. 3, 10. Translated by Howell. Adapted from the public domain.

May 30
Lord Ronald Gower, *Joan of Arc* (New York: Charles Scribner's Sons, 1893), 215–216, 269. Edited by Crownwood.

May 31
Camilla Battista Varani, *Le Opere Spirituali della Beata Battista Varani* (Camerino: Tipografia Savini, 1894), 51. Translated by Crownwood.

June 1

Justin Martyr, *First Apology*, 66. Translated by Howell.

June 2

Adam of St. Victor, *Paschal Sequence*. Translated by Howell.

June 3

Urban IV, "Transiturus," in George Ambrose Bradbury, *St. Juliana of Cornillon* (London: Thomas Richardson and Son, 1873), 202–203. Edited by Crownwood.

June 4

Mary of the Divine Heart, "Letter to Confessor," in Louis Chasle, *Sister Mary of the Divine Heart* (London: Burns and Oats, 1903). Edited by Crownwood.

June 5

Marcellin Joseph Champagnat, "Maxims," in *Vie de Joseph-Benoit-Marcellin Champagnat*, vol. 1 (Lyon: Perisse Frères, 1856), 125. Translated by Crownwood.

June 6

Norbert of Xantan, "Maxim," in Cornelius Kirkfleet, *History of Saint Norbert: Founder of the Norbertine Order* (St. Louis, MO: B. Herder, 1916), 21. Edited by Crownwood.

June 7

Anne of St. Bartholomew, *Autobiography of the Blessed Mother Anne of Saint Bartholomew*, trans. Carmelite of St. Louis (St. Louis, MO: H.S. Collins Printing Co., 1917), 109. Edited by Crownwood.

June 8

St. Ephraem, "Sermon No. 3," in *The Liturgy of the Hours*, vol. III, trans. the International Committee on English in the Liturgy (New York: Catholic Book Publishing, 1976), 1460–1462.

June 9
Adomnán of Iona, *Life of St. Columba*, (Dublin: William B. Kelly, 1875), 129–131. Edited by Crownwood.

June 10
John Chrysostom, *Homily 47*. Translated by Howell. Adapted from the public domain.

June 11
Thomas Aquinas, *Pange lingua*. Translated by Crownwood. Adapted from the public domain.

June 12
Pius IV, "Tridentine Creed," in Theodore Alois Buckley, *Canons and Decrees of the Council of Trent; Second Part* (London: George Routledge and Co., 1851). Edited by Crownwood.

June 13
Anthony of Padua, "Sermon: Third Sunday after Epiphany," in Raffaelem Maffaeum, *Divi Antonii de Padua, Minoritae, Sermons Dominicales Moralissimi* (Venice: Ioan. Antonium Bertanum, 1574). Translated by Crownwood.

June 14
Gaudentius of Brescia, *Tract 2 on Exodus*. Translated by Howell.

June 15
Luis de León, *De Los Nombres de Cristo* (Valencia: Benito Monfort, 1770), 259–261. Translated by Crownwood.

June 16
Jerome, *Matthew*, bk. 1, ch. 6, 11. Translated by Howell.

June 17
Gregory of Nyssa, *On the Song of Songs*, 10. Translated by Howell.

June 18
Elisabeth of Schönau, *On the Ways of God*. Adapted from the public domain.

June 19
Nicholas Cabasilas, *Life in Christ*, bk. 1, sec. 19, 20. Translated by Howell.

June 20
Paulinus of Nola, *Letter to Augustine*. Translated by Howell.
Paulinus of Nola, *Letter to Sulpicius Severus*. Translated by Howell.

June 21
John Fisher, "Commentary on Psalm 51," in *The English Works of John Fisher*, vol. 1, ed. John E. B. Mayor (London: N. Trubner & Co., 1876), 110–111. Edited by Crownwood.

June 22
Thomas More, *Dialogue of Comfort against Tribulation* (London: Sheed and Ward Ltd., 1951), ch. 27. Edited by Crownwood.

June 23
Joseph Cafasso, *Meditazioni per Esercizi Spirituali al Cerlo* (Torino: Tipografia Fratelli Canonica, 1892), 300–301. Translated by Crownwood.

June 24
Caesarius of Arles, *Sermon 33*. Translated by Howell.

June 25
Augustine, *On Baptism*, bk. 3, ch. 19. Translated by Howell. Adapted from the public domain.
Augustine, *Against the Donatists*, bk. 5, ch. 8. Translated by Howell. Adapted from the public domain.

June 26

Josemaría Escrivá, *Camino*, 2nd bilingual ed., ed. and trans. Andrew Byrne (Leominster, England: Gracewing, 2002), 194–196.

June 27

Cyril of Alexandria, *Commentary on Matthew*. Translated by Howell.

June 28

Irenaeus of Lyons, *Against Heresies*, bk. 4, ch. 17, 5. Translated by Howell.

June 29

Gregory the Great, *Homily on Ezekiel*, bk. 2, 10. Translated by Howell. Gregory the Great, *Morals on the Book of Job* (Oxford: J.H. Parker, 1844), 109–110. Edited by Crownwood.

June 30

Antonio Rosmini-Serbati, "Letter to Giulio Padulli, 1828," in *Letters (Chiefly on Religious Subjects) of Antonio Rosmini Serbati: Founder of the Institute of Charity* (London: R. & T. Washbourne, 1901), 762–763. Edited by Crownwood.

July 1

Junipero Serra, "Letter to Palou," in Abigail Hetzel Fitch, *Junípero Serra: The Man and His Work* (Chicago: A.C. McClurg & Co., 1914), 154. Edited by Crownwood.

July 2

Bernadino Realino, "Jubilation after Hóly Communion," in P. Ettore Venturi, *Storia della vita del Beato Bernadino Realino* (Roma: Tipografia A. Befani, 1895), 465–466. Translated by Crownwood.

July 3

John Chrysostom, *Homily 82, On Matthew*, 4. Translated by Howell.

July 4
Didymus the Blind, *On the Trinity*, bk. 2, ch. 14. Translated by Howell.

July 5
Basil the Great, *On Baptism*, bk. 2, 3. Translated by Howell.

July 6
John Damascene, *On the Orthodox Faith*. Translated by Howell.

July 7
Thomas á Kempis, *De Imitatione Christi* (London: Kegan Paul, Trench, Trubner & Co., 1892), bk. 1, 10. Translated by Crownwood. Adapted from the public domain.

July 8
Julian of Norwich, *Revelations of Divine Love*, trans. Grace Warrack (London: Methuen & Company, 1911), 29–30. Edited by Crownwood.

July 9
Veronica Guiliani, "Diary," in Filippo Maria Salvatori, *The Lives of S. Veronica Guiliani, Capuchin Nun: and of the Blessed Battista Varani* (London: R. Washbourne, 1874), 114–115. Edited by Crownwood.

July 10
"Liturgy of St. James." Translated by Howell.

July 11
Gregory the Great, *The Life and Miracles of St. Benedict*, ed. Edmund J. Luck (London: R. Washbourne, 1880), 63–64. Edited by Crownwood.

July 12
Thérèse of Lisieux, *The Story of a Soul*, trans. Thomas N. Taylor (London: Burns, Oates & Washbourne, 1912), 31, 35–36. Edited by Crownwood.

July 13
Cassiodorus, *Commentary on the Psalter*, 78. Translated by Howell.

July 14
Anne-Marie Javouhey, "Letter," in R. P. Delaplace, *La R.M. Javouhey: Fondratrice de la Congrégation de Saint-Joseph de Cluny* (Paris: Victor Lecoffre, 1886), 501–502. Translated by Crownwood.

July 15
Bonaventure, *Breviloquium*, 6, ch. 9, 3, in José de Vinck, *The Works of Bonaventure, II: The Breviloquium* (Patterson, N.J.: St. Anthony's Guild, 1963), 254.

July 16
Ambrose, *On the Mysteries*, ch. 8, 47–49. Translated by Howell.

July 17
Germanus of Constantinople, *Ecclesiastical History*. Translated by Howell.

July 18
Hilary of Poitiers, *On the Trinity*, bk. 10. Translated by Howell. Adapted from the public domain.

July 19
Augustine of Hippo, *Tracts on the Gospel of John*, 11, 5. Translated by Howell. Adapted from the public domain.

July 20
Gregory of Agrigentum, *Commentary on Ecclesiastes*, 9, 17. Translated by Howell.

July 21
John Cassian, "Conferences, 2, 21," in *Nicene and Post-Nicene Fathers of the Christian Church*, vol. 9, ed. Philip Schaff and Henry Wace (New York:

The Christian Literature Company, 1894), 531. Edited by Crownwood.

July 22
Pauline Jaricot, *L'Amor infini dans la divine Eucharistie* (Paris: Les libraires associés, 1823), 29–31. Translated by Crownwood.

July 23
Bridget of Sweden, *The Fifteen O's and other Prayers* (London: Griffith and Farran, 1869). Edited by Crownwood.

July 24
Gregory of Nyssa, *On Christian Perfection*. Translated by Howell.

July 25
Caesarius of Arles, *Sermon 188*. Translated by Howell.

July 26
Ambrose, *On the Mysteries*, ch. 9, 56–57. Translated by Howell. Adapted from the public domain.

July 27
Origen of Alexandria, *Commentary on Matthew 14:15*. Translated by Howell.

July 28
Peter Favre, "Memoriale," in Guiseppe Boero, *The Life of the Blessed Peter Favre of the Society of Jesus*, trans. Henry James Coleridge, Quarterly Series, vol. 8 (London: Burns and Oates, 1873), 265. Edited by Crownwood.

July 29
Justin de Jacobis, "Letter," in Mary Elizabeth Herbert, *Abyssinia and its Apostle* (London: Burns, Oates & Co., 1867), 98, 153. Edited by Crownwood.

July 30

Peter Chrysologus, "Sermon," 70, 71, in Edward B. Pusey, *The Doctrine of the Real Presence* (Oxford: John Henry Parker, 1855), 686–687. Edited by Crownwood.

July 31

Ignatius of Loyola, "Letter," in *Letters and Instructions of St. Ignatius of Loyola*, vol. 1, ed. A. Goodier, trans. D.F. O'Leary (St. Louis, MO: B. Herder, 1914), 98–99. Edited by Crownwood.

August 1

Alphonsus de Liguori, *The Passion and Death of Jesus Christ*, ed. Eugene Grimm (New York: Benziger Brothers, 1887), 53–54, 61–62. Edited by Crownwood.

August 2

Peter Eymard, *Month of Our Lady of the Blessed Sacrament*, ed. Visitandine of Baltimore (New York: Sentinel Press, 1903), 132–133. Edited by Crownwood.

August 3

Fourth-Century Byzantine-Greek Poetry. Translated by Howell.

August 4

John Vianney, *Considérations sur la Nécessité de Connaître Jesus-Christ* (Lyon: Impremerie et Librairie Ecclésiastiques de Guyot Frères, 1851). Translated by Crownwood.

August 5

Didymus the Blind, *On the Trinity*. Translated by Howell.

August 6

Anastasius of Sinai, *Guide for the Way*. Translated by Howell.

August 7

Cajetan "Letter to His Niece, July 10, 1522," in *The Life of St. Cajetan*, trans. Lady Herbert (London: Thomas Richardson and Son, 1888), 68–69. Edited by Crownwood.

August 8

Ugolino Brunforte, *The Little Flowers of St. Francis of Assisi*, trans. T. W. Arnold (London: Chatto and Windus, 1908), 155–156. Edited by Crownwood.

August 9

Edith Stein (Teresa Benedicta of the Cross), *The Hidden Life: Hagiographic Essays, Meditations, Spiritual Texts*, in *Collected Works of Edith Stein, Sister Teresa Benedicta of the Cross, Discalced Carmelite 1891–1942*, vol. 4, ed. L. Gelber and Michael Linssen, trans. Waltraut Stein (Washington, DC: ICS Publications, 2014), 137.

August 10

John Berchmans, "Personal Devotions," in Francis Goldie, *The Life of Blessed John Berchmans* (London: Burns and Oates, 1873), 212–213. Edited by Crownwood.

August 11

Thomas of Celano, *The Life of Saint Claire*, ed. and trans. Paschal Robinson (Philadelphia: The Dolphin Press, 1910), 36–37, 104. Edited by Crownwood.

August 12

Jane Frances de Chantal, "Letter," in *Selected Letters of Saint Jane Frances de Chantal*, trans. Sisters of the Visitation, Harrow-on-the-Hill (London: R. & T. Washbourne, 1918), 137, 232. Edited by Crownwood.

August 13

Hippolytus, "Commentary on Proverbs 9," in *Ante-Nicene Fathers*, vol. 5, ed. Alexander Roberts and James Donaldson (New York: Charles

Scriber's Sons, 1903), 175–176. Edited by Crownwood.

August 14
Maximus the Confessor, *Mystagogy*, 24:27–47. Translated by Howell.

August 15
Peter Eymard, *Month of Our Lady of the Blessed Sacrament*, trans. Visitine of Baltimore (New York: Sentinel Press, 1903), 292–293. Edited by Crownwood.

August 16
Gaudentius of Brescia, *Tract 2 on the Exodus*. Translated by Howell. Adapted from the public domain.

August 17
Jeanne Delanoue, *Extraits ou Fragments des Discours our Entretiens de la Soeur Jeanne Delanoue* (Angers: Imprimerie-Librarie Germain et G. Grassin, 1889), 141–142. Translated by Crownwood.

August 18
Ezequiel Moreno y Diaz, "Episcopal Letter," in Santiago Matute, *Los Padres Candelarios en Colombia: O Apuntes para la historia*, vol. 2 (Bogota: Tipografia de los talleres Salesianos, 1897), 479–480. Translated by Crownwood.

August 19
John Eudes, *Le bon confesseur* (Lyon: Chez Benoist Vignieu, 1689), 129. Translated by Crownwood.

August 20
Bernard of Clairvaux, "Letter," in *Life and Works of Saint Bernard*, vol. II, ed. John Mabillon and Samuel J. Eales, trans. Samuel J. Eales (London: John Hoges, 1889), 590–591. Edited by Crownwood.

August 21
Pius X, "Sacra Tridentina, Decree on Frequent and Daily Reception of Holy Communion," in *The Irish Ecclesiastical Record* (Dublin: Browne & Nolan, 1906), 451–452.

August 22
Caesarius of Arles, *Sermon 7*. Translated by Howell.

August 23
Poemen, "Saying, 44," in *The Paradise of the Holy Fathers*, vol. 2, trans. Ernest A. Wallis Budge (London: Chatto & Windus, 1907), 165. Edited by Crownwood.

August 24
Ouen of Rouen, *Life of St. Eligius*. Translated by Crownwood.

August 25
Teresa of Ávila, *The Life of St. Teresa of Jesus of the Order of Our Lady of Carmel*, 3rd ed., trans. David Lewis (London: Thomas Baker, 1904), 360–361. Edited by Crownwood.

August 26
Dominic Barberi, *Lamentation of England* (Leicester: A. Cockshaw, 1831), 2, 8. Edited by Crownwood.

August 27
Augustine, *Confessions*, 6, 2. Translated by Howell.

August 28
Augustine, *Confessions*, 7, 10. Translated by Howell. Adapted from the public domain.

August 29
Moses the Ethiopian, "Saying, 617," in *The Paradise of the Holy Fathers*, vol. 2, trans. Ernest A. Wallis Budge (London: Chatto & Windus,

1907), 290. Edited by Crownwood.

August 30
Jean Pierre de Caussade, "Letter 18," in *Abandonment to Divine Providence*, 3rd ed., ed. J. Ramière, trans. E.J. Strickland (Exeter: Catholic Records Press, 1921), 260. Edited by Crownwood.

August 31
Justin Martyr, *Dialogue with Trypho*, ch. 41, 1–3. Translated by Howell.

September 1
Jean-Louis Bonnard, "Letter," in Etienne Vindry, *Vie du vén Jean-Louis Bonnard* (Paris: Delhomme et Briguet, 1891), 381–382. Translated by Crownwood.

September 2
Macarius of Magnesia, *Apocriticus*, in T.W. Crafer, trans., *The Apocriticus of Macarius Magnes* (London: SPCK, 1919), 81–82. Edited for this book, consulting the Greek text.

September 3
Gregory the Great, "Moralia on Job," in *The Liturgy of the Hours*, vol. II, trans. International Committee on English in the Liturgy (New York: Catholic Book Publishing, 1976), 257–259.

September 4
John Damascene, *On the Orthodox Faith*. Translated by Howell.

September 5
Teresa of Calcutta, *Where There Is Love, There Is God: A Path to Closer Union with God and Greater Love for Others*, ed. Brian Kolodiejchuk, (New York: Doubleday, 2010), 53–4.

September 6
Andrew of Crete, *Triduum of Holy Saturday*. Translated by Howell.

September 7
Basil the Great, *Letter 93*. Translated by Howell.

September 8
Anne Catherine Emmerich, *Dolorous Passion of Our Lord Jesus Christ* (London: Burns & Lambert, 1862), 83. Edited by Crownwood.

September 9
Fourth-Century Byzantine-Greek Poetry. Translated by Howell.

September 10
John Francis Regis, "Letter," in Robert Holland, *Life of Saint John Francis Regis of the Society of Jesus* (Chicago, Loyola University Press, 1922), 46. Edited by Crownwood.

September 11
Thomas Aquinas, *Verbum Supernum Prodiens*. Translated by Crownwood. Adapted from the public domain.

September 12
Cyprian of Carthage, "On the Unity of the Catholic Church," par. 13, in *The Ante-Nicene Fathers*, ed. Alexander Roberts, James Donaldson, Cleveland A. Coxe (New York: C. Scribner's Sons, 1919), 425. Edited for this book, consulting the Latin text.

September 13
John Chrysostom, *On the Priesthood*, bk. 3, ch. 4. Translated by Howell. Adapted from the public domain.

September 14
John Chrysostom, "Homily 85: On the Gospel of John," in *Nicene and Post-Nicene Fathers*, First Series, vol. 14, ed. Philip Schaff (Buffalo: Christian Literature Publishing Co., 1889), 319. Edited by Crownwood.

September 15
Catherine of Genoa, *Treatise on Purgatory*, 4ᵗʰ ed. (London: Burns and Oates, 1858), 17–19. Edited by Crownwood.

September 16
Robert Bellarmine, *The Art of Dying Well*, trans. John Dalton (London: Richardson & Son, 1847), ch. 12. Edited by Crownwood.

September 17
Hildegard of Bingen, *Scivias*, 2, 6. Translated by Crownwood.

September 18
Caesarius of Arles, *Sermon 73*. Translated by Howell.

September 19
Émilie de Rodat, *Lettres de la Vénérable Mére Émilie de Rodat*, ed. Henri Marty (Paris: Société Générale de Librairie Catholique, 1888), 141–142. Translated by Crownwood.

September 20
Cyril of Alexandria, *Commentary on Luke*, 4. Translated by Howell.

September 21
Adomnán of Iona, *Life of St. Columba* (Dublin: William B. Kelly, 1875), 129–130. Edited by Crownwood.

September 22
Thomas of Villanova, "Sermon," in *Oeuvres de Saint Thomas de Villeneuve: religieux Augustin et archeveque de valence*, trans. from Latin by V. Ferrier (Paris: Lethielleux, 1886), 273–274. Translated by Crownwood.

September 23
Emilie Tavernier-Gamelin, "Diary," in *Vie de Mére Gamelin* (Montréal: Eusébe Senécal & CIE, 1900), 281–282. Translated by Crownwood.

September 24
Vincenzo Maria Strambi, *Il Mese di Giugno Consecrato al Prezio-
sissimo Sangue del Nostro Amabilissimo Redentore*, 5th ed. (Naples:
Tipografia dello Stabilimento dell'Industriale, 1840), 40–41. Translated by Crownwood.

September 25
Paul VI, Encyclical Letter on the Holy Eucharist *Mysterium Fidei*,
September 3, 1965, §31.

September 26
Maximus of Turin, *Sermon 78*. Translated by Howell.

September 27
Vincent de Paul, "Sermon," in M. Jeanmaire, *Sermons de Saint Vincent
de Paul de ses Cooerateurs et Successeurs Immédiats Pour les Missions
des Campagnes*, vol i. (Paris: PH Baldeveck, 1859), 491. Translated by
Crownwood.

September 28
Isaac Jogues, "Relation," in *The Jesuit Relations and Allied Documents:
Travels and Explorations*, vol. 31, ed. Reuben Gold Thwaites (Cleve-
land: The Burrows Brothers Company, 1898). Edited by Crownwood.
"Poor René" is St. René Goupil, Martyr.

September 29
Francis Borgia "Thanksgiving after Communion," in *Spiritual Works
of St. Francis Borgia*, (London: Thomas Richardson and Sons, 1875),
83–85. Edited by Crownwood.

September 30
Jerome, *Commentary on Zephaniah*. Translated by Howell.

October 1
Thérèse of Lisieux, *The Story of a Soul*, trans. Thomas N. Taylor (Lon-

don: Burns, Oates & Washbourne, 1912), ch. 4. Edited by Crownwood.

October 2
Raymond of Capua, *Life of St. Catherine of Siena*, trans. Ladies of the Sacred Heart (Philadelphia: Peter F. Cunningham, 1860), 232–233. Edited by Crownwood.

October 3
Columba Marmion, *Christ the Life of the Soul: Spiritual Conferences*, 2nd ed., trans. a nun of Tynburn Convent (St. Louis, MO: B. Herder Book, 1925), 265.

October 4
Francis of Assisi, "Letter to Friars," in *The Writings of St. Francis of Assisi*, trans. Paschal Robinson (Philadelphia: Dolphin Press, 1906), 112, 114–115. Edited by Crownwood.

October 5
Faustina Kowalska, *Diary of Saint Maria Faustina Kowalska: Divine Mercy in My Soul*, 3rd ed. (Stockbridge, MA: Marian Press, 2005), par. 356.

October 6
Anonymous Carthusian of Nuremberg (c. 1480), "The Heart of Jesus," in *Ancient Devotions to the Sacred Heart of Jesus by Carthusian Monks of the XIV-XVII Centuries*," 4th ed., rev. Sebastian MacCabe (London: Burns, Oates, and Washbourne, Ltd., 1953), 20–21. Edited by Crownwood.

October 7
Benedict XVI, Encyclical Letter on Christian Love *Deus Caritas Est*, December 25, 2005, §13.

October 8
Pius XII, Encyclical Letter on Devotion to the Sacred Heart *Haurietis Aquas*, May 15, 1956, §§69–71.

October 9
John Henry Newman, *Apologia pro Vita Sua* (London: Longmans, Green, Reader, and Dyer, 1875), 239–240.

October 10
John of Ribera, *Declaration del Credo y Simbolo de los Apostoles* (Madrid: Luis Sanchez, 1591). Translated by Crownwood.

October 11
John XXIII, Encyclical Letter on St. John Vianney *Sacerdotii Nostri Primordia*, August 1, 1959, §53.

October 12
Caesarius of Arles, *Sermon 73*. Translated by Howell.

October 13
Gerard Majella, "Rule of Life," in *Life of Blessed Gerard Majella*, 2nd ed., trans. Charles Dilgskron (New York: Redemptorist Fathers, 1886), 319, 322. Edited by Crownwood.

October 14
Jean de Brébeuf, "Relation," in *The Jesuit Relations and Allied Documents: Travels and Explorations of the Jesuit Missionaries in New France*, vol. 10, ed. Reuben Gold Thwaites (Cleveland: The Burrows Brothers Company, 1897), 105, 107. Edited by Crownwood.

October 15
Teresa of Avila, *The Life of St. Teresa of Jesus of the Order of Our Lady of Carmel*, 3rd ed., trans. David Lewis (London: Thomas Baker, 1904), 363–364. Edited by Crownwood.

October 16
Marguerite-Marie Alacoque, *Vie et Oeuvres de la Bienheureuse Marguerite-Marie Alacoque*, vol. 2 (Paray-le-Monial: Monastère de la Visitation, 1867). Translated by Crownwood.

October 17

Ignatius of Antioch, *Letter to the Ephesians*, 5. Translated by Howell.

October 18

Peter of Alcantara, *A Golden Treatise of Mental Prayer*, trans. Giles Willoughby (Philadelphia, M. Fithian, 1844), 118–119. Edited by Crownwood.

October 19

Paul of the Cross, "Letters," in *Flowers of the Passion: Thoughts of St. Paul of the Cross*, ed. Louis Thérèse de Jésus-Agonisant, trans. Ella A. Mulligan (NY: Bengizer Brothers, 1893), 57–58. Edited by Crownwood.

October 20

Ambrose, *On the Mysteries*, 9, 57–58. Translated by Howell.

October 21

Thomas Bullaker, "Personal Account," in Richard Challoner, *Memoirs of Missionary Priests, as Well Secular as Regular, and of Other Catholics*, vol. 2 (Holborn: F. Needham, 1742), 232–235. Edited by Crownwood.

October 22

John Paul II, Encyclical Letter on the Eucharist in Its Relationship to the Church *Ecclesia de Eucharistia*, April 17, 2003, §§12–13.

October 23

Hilary of Poitiers, *On the Trinity*, bk. 8, 15. Translated by Howell. Adapted from the public domain.

October 24

Anthony Mary Claret, *Sermones de Mision escritos unos y escogidos otros por el Misionero Apostólico Antonio María Claret y Clará*, vol. 3 (Barcelona: Librería Religiosa, 1858), 260–261. Translated by Crownwood.

October 25
Gaudentius of Brescia, *Tract 2 on the Exodus*. Translated by Howell. Adapted from the public domain.

October 26
Thomas á Kempis, *De Imitatione Christi* (London: Kegan Paul, Trench, Trubner & Co., 1892). Translated by Crownwood. Adapted from the public domain.

October 27
Jasper Hopkins, *Nicholas of Cusa's De Pace Fidei and Cribratio Alkorani: Translation and Analysis*, 2nd ed. (Minneapolis, MN: The Arthur J. Banning Press, 1994), bk. 18, par. 65–66, pp. 667–668, https://jasper-hopkins.info/DePace12-2000.pdf.

October 28
Guitmund of Aversa, *On the Truth of the Body and Blood of Christ in the Eucharist*. Translated by Howell and adapted from the public domain.

October 29
Jacobus da Varagine, *The Golden Legend* (London: J.M. Dent and Co., 1900), 116–117. Edited by Crownwood.

October 30
Mary of Ágreda, *The Mystical City of God*, vol. 4, trans. Fiscar Marison (George J. Blatter) (Mount Vernon, OH: Louis W. Bernicken, 1902), par. 502. Edited by Crownwood.

October 31
Alphonsus Rodriguez, "Sermon on St. Ignatius de Loyola," in Francis Goldie, *The Life of St. Alonso Rodriguez* (London: Burns and Oates, 1889), 419. Edited by Crownwood.

November 1
John Chrysostom, *Homilies on Isaiah*, 6:1. Translated by Howell.

November 2
Ugolino Brunforte, *The Little Flowers of St. Francis of Assisi*, trans. T.W. Arnold (London: Chatto and Windus, 1908), 147–148. Edited by Crownwood.

November 3
"Liturgy of St. James." Translated by Howell.

November 4
Charles Borromeo, "Sermon," in *Sermoni Familiari di S. Carlo Borromeo*, ed. D. Gaetano Volpi (Padua: Giuseppe Comino, 1720), 110. Translated by Crownwood.

November 5
Tertullian of Carthage, *On the Prescription against Heretics*. Translated by Howell.

November 6
Athanasius, "Letter," in *Nicene and Post-Nicene Fathers of the Christian Church*, vol. 4, 2nd ed., ed. and trans. Philip Schaff and Henry Wace (New York: The Christian Literature Company, 1892), 542–543. Edited by Crownwood.

November 7
John XXII, "Anima Christi," in *The Month*, vol. 125 (London: Longmans, Green, and Co., 1915), 493, 504.

November 8
Elizabeth of the Trinity, *The Complete Works: Letters from Carmel, I Have Found God*, vol. 2, trans. Anne Englund Nash (Washington, DC: ICS Publications, 2014), 105.

November 9
Augustine, *On the Trinity*, bk. 4, ch. 14. Translated by Howell. Adapted from the public domain.

November 10
Leo the Great, "Sermon 8: On the Lord's Passion," in *The Liturgy of the Hours*, vol II., trans. the International Committee on English in the Liturgy (New York: Catholic Book Publishing, 1976), 358–360.

November 11
Peter Chrysologus, *Sermon 34*. Translated by Howell.

November 12
Thomas Aquinas, *Adoro te devote*. Translated by Crownwood. Adapted from the public domain.

November 13
Nicholas I, "Letter to Emperor Michael," in Edmund Saulsbury Ffoulkes, *Primitive Consecration of the Eucharistic Oblation* (London: Hayes, 1885). Edited by Crownwood.

November 14
Hincmar of Rheims, *Epistola XVI: au clericos Palatti*. Translated by Crownwood.

November 15
Albert the Great, "Commentary on Luke," in *Alberti Magni, Ratisbonesis Episcopi, Ordinis Praedicatorum, Opera Omnia*, vol. 22, ed. Auguste Borgnet (Paris: Apud Ludovicum Vivès, 1894). Translated by Crownwood.

November 16
Gertrude the Great, "Narrative," in *The Life of Revelations of Saint Gertrude* (London: Burns & Oates, Ltd., 1870), 82–83. Edited by Crownwood.

November 17
Cyril of Jerusalem, "The Catechetical Lectures of S. Cyril, Archbishop of Jerusalem," in *A Library of Fathers of the Holy Catholic Church* (Oxford: John Henry Parker, 1838), lec. 23. Edited by Crownwood.

November 18

Rose Phillipine Duchesne, "Letter to St. Madeleine Sophie Barat," in *Life of the Venerable Madeleine Louise Sophie Barat* (Roehampton, England: Convent of the Sacred Heart, 1922), 90–91.

November 19

Mechtilde of Hackenborn, *The Love of the Sacred Heart* (London: Burns, Oates, & Washbourne, 1922), 154–155. Edited by Crownwood.

November 20

Gregory of Nyssa, *Homily 8 on Ecclesiastes*. Translated by Howell.

November 21

Caesarius of Arles, *Sermon 188*. Translated by Howell.

November 22

John Thulis, "Song," in John Hungerford Pollen, *Acts of the English Martyrs* (London: Burns and Oates Ltd., 1891), 204–205. Edited by Crownwood.

November 23

Gregory of Agrigentum, *Commentary on Ecclesiastes*, ch. 2, 12, 67. Translated by Howell.

November 24

Théophane Vénard, "Letters," in James. A. Walsh, ed., *A Modern Martyr, Théophane Vénard* (Maryknoll, NY: Catholic Foreign Mission Society of America, 1913), 87–88, 189. Edited by Crownwood.

November 25

Clement of Rome, *Letter to the Corinthians*, 7, 40–41. Translated by Howell. Translations of the *Clement of Rome* are adapted from Kenneth Howell, *Clement of Rome & the Didache: A New Translation and Theological Commentary*, Early Christian Fathers Series, 2 (Zanesville, OH: CHResources, 2012).

November 26
Sechnall, *Sancti venite*. Translated by Crownwood.

November 27
Leonard of Port Maruice, *The Hidden Treasure: Or the Immense Excellence of the Holy Sacrifice of the Mass* (Dublin: James Duffy, 1861), 117, 131. Edited by Crownwood.
The term *seminary* here refers to the place of the novitiate for religious sisters. It may also be noted that her "doubts" refers to the veracity of the mystical experiences themselves, not to any article of the faith.

November 28
Catherine Labouré, "First Apparitions," in Edmond Crapez, *Venerable Sister Catherine Labouré* (London: Burns, Oates & Washbourne, 1920), 26–27. Edited by Crownwood.

November 29
Chromatius of Aquileia, *Tract on the Gospel of Matthew*, 14. Translated by Howell.

November 30
Edmund Campion, *Ten Reasons*, trans. J. R. (London: Manresa Press, 1914), 98–99. Edited by Crownwood.

December 1
Charles de Foucauld, "Letter," in René Bazin, *Charles de Foucauld: Explorateur du Maroc ermite au Sahara* (Paris: Plon-Nourrit, 1921), 223–224. Translated by Crownwood.

December 2
John of Ruysbroeck, *The Adornment of the Spiritual Marriage*, ed. Evelyn Underhill, trans. C.A. Wynschenk (London: J.M. Dent & Sons, 1916), 112–113. Edited by Crownwood.

December 3

Francis Xavier, "Daily Exercises," in Henry James Coleridge, *The Life and Letters of St. Francis Xavier*, vol. 1 (London: Burns and Oates, 1872), 312–313. Edited by Crownwood.

December 4

John Damascene, *On the Orthodox Faith*, 4, 13. Translated by Howell. Adapted from the public domain.

December 5

Eligius, *Homily*. Translated by Crownwood.

December 6

Hilary of Poitiers, *On the Trinity*, bk. 8, 13–17. Translated by Howell.

December 7

Ambrose, *On the Mysteries*, trans. T. Thompson, ed. J. H. Sprawley (London: Society for Promoting Christian Knowledge, 1919), par. 52. Edited by Crownwood.

December 8

John Damascene, *On the Orthodox Faith*, bk. 4, 13. Translated by Howell. Adapted from the public domain.

December 9

Bonaventure, *Tract on Preparation for Mass*. Translated by Howell.

December 10

Peter Chrysologus, *Sermon 95*. Translated by Howell.

December 11

Armenian Liturgy, "The Hymn of the Church," in *Liturgies Eastern and Western, vol 1, Eastern Liturgies*, ed. F. E. Brightman (Oxford: Clarendon Press, 1896), 420–421. Edited by Crownwood.

December 12
Gregory of Agrigentum, *Qoheleth*, ch. 8, 6. Translated by Howell.

December 13
John Paul II, *Ecclesia de Eucharistia*, §18.

December 14
John of the Cross, "The Dark Night of the Soul," in *The Complete Works of Saint John of the Cross*, vol. 1, ed. Oblate Fathers of Saint Charles, trans. David Lewis (London: Longman, Roberts & Green, 1864), 341–342. Edited by Crownwood.

December 15
Ambrose, *On the Mysteries*, ch. 9, no. 53, 54. Translated by Howell. Adapted from the Public Domain.

December 16
Augustine of the Blessed Sacrament, "Letter," in Jean-Baptiste Gergerès, *Conversion d'Hermann Cohen, père Augustin-Marie, du Très-Saint-Sacrement* (Paris: A. Bray, 1862), 31–33. Translated by Crownwood.

December 17
Jerome, *Commentary on Matthew*, bk. 2, ch. 15. Translated by Howell.

December 18
Gaudentius of Brescia, *Tract No. 2*. Translated by Howell.

December 19
John Chrysostom, *Homily 6*. Translated by Howell.

December 20
Irenaeus of Lyons, *Against Heresies*, bk. 4, ch. 18, 6. Translated by Howell. Adapted from the public domain.

December 21

Peter Canisius, *Summa doctrinae Christianae*, vol. 2 (Augburg: Carolum Kollmann, 1833). Translated by Crownwood.

December 22

Fulgentius of Ruspe, *Epistle 12*. Translated by Howell.

December 23

Augustine of Hippo, *On the Trinity*, bk. 3, 21. Translated by Howell. Adapted from the public domain.

December 24

John Chrysostom, *Homily* 6. Translated by Howell.

December 25

Peter Eymard, *Month of Our Lady of the Blessed Sacrament*, 6th ed., trans. Visitandine of Baltimore (New York City: Sentinel Press, 1903), 80–81. Edited by Crownwood.

December 26

Ignatius of Antioch, *Letter to the Romans*, 4, 7. Translated by Howell.

December 27

Dionysius, "Epistle to Sixtus," in *The Ante-Nicene Fathers: Translations of the Writings of the Fathers Down to A.D. 325*, vol. 6, ed. Alexander Roberts and James Donaldson (New York: Charles Scribner's Sons, 1899), 103. Edited by Crownwood.

December 28

O magnum mysterium. Translated by Crownwood. Adapted from the public domain.
Ave verum Corpus. Translated by Crownwood. Adapted from the public domain.

December 29
Adam of Perseigne, *Epistle*. Translated by Crownwood.

December 30
Marie-Eustelle Harpain, "Letters," in *The Life of Marie-Eustelle Harpain* (London: Burns, Oates, Co., 1868), 59–60. Edited by Crownwood.

December 31
Didache, 14. Translated by Howell.

ACKNOWLEDGEMENTS

The authors would like to thank the team at Emmaus Road Publishing for their belief in this project and for the hard work that went into its production. We remain grateful to Matthew Levering for his encouragement to bring this work to publication and to Monsignor Stuart W. Swetland for his unwavering support of this pursuit. Special thanks to Molly Henley, Prisca Tiassè-Yoder, Fernando Moreu, Robin Chin, and Teresa LaVoy for their consultation and assistance.